Object Modeling and User Interface Design

The Addison-Wesley Object Technology Series

Grady Booch, Ivar Jacobson, and James Rumbaugh, Series Editors

For more information check out the series web site [http://www.awl.com/cseng/otseries/].

Armour/Miller, *Advanced Use Case Modeling: Software Systems*

Binder, *Testing Object-Oriented Systems: Models, Patterns, and Tools*

Blakley, *CORBA Security: An Introduction to Safe Computing with Objects*

Booch, *Object Solutions: Managing the Object-Oriented Project*

Booch, *Object-Oriented Analysis and Design with Applications, Second Edition*

Booch/Rumbaugh/Jacobson, *The Unified Modeling Language User Guide*

Box/Brown/Ewald/Sells, *Effective COM: 50 Ways to Improve Your COM and MTS-based Applications*

Carlson, *Modeling XML Applications with UML: A Model-Driven Approach for e-Application Development*

Cockburn, *Surviving Object-Oriented Projects: A Manager's Guide*

Collins, *Designing Object-Oriented User Interfaces*

Conallen, *Building Web Applications with UML*

D'Souza/Wills, *Objects, Components, and Frameworks with UML: The Catalysis Approach*

Douglass, *Doing Hard Time: Developing Real-Time Systems with UML, Objects, Frameworks, and Patterns*

Douglass, *Real-Time UML, Second Edition: Developing Efficient Objects for Embedded Systems*

Fowler, *Analysis Patterns: Reusable Object Models*

Fowler/Beck/Brant/Opdyke/Roberts, *Refactoring: Improving the Design of Existing Code*

Fowler/Scott, *UML Distilled, Second Edition: A Brief Guide to the Standard Object Modeling Language*

Gomaa, *Designing Concurrent, Distributed, and Real-Time Applications with UML*

Gorton, *Enterprise Transaction Processing Systems: Putting the CORBA OTS, Encina++ and Orbix OTM to Work*

Graham, *Object-Oriented Methods, Third Edition: Principles and Practice*

Heinckiens, *Building Scalable Database Applications: Object-Oriented Design, Architectures, and Implementations*

Hofmeister/Nord/Dilip, *Applied Software Architecture*

Jacobson/Booch/Rumbaugh, *The Unified Software Development Process*

Jacobson/Christerson/Jonsson/Overgaard, *Object-Oriented Software Engineering: A Use Case Driven Approach*

Jacobson/Ericsson/Jacobson, *The Object Advantage: Business Process Reengineering with Object Technology*

Jacobson/Griss/Jonsson, *Software Reuse: Architecture, Process and Organization for Business Success*

Jordan, *C++ Object Databases: Programming with the ODMG Standard*

Kruchten, *The Rational Unified Process, An Introduction, Second Edition*

Lau, *The Art of Objects: Object-Oriented Design and Architecture*

Leffingwell/Widrig, *Managing Software Requirements: A Unified Approach*

Marshall, *Enterprise Modeling with UML: Designing Successful Software through Business Analysis*

McGregor/Sykes, *A Practical Guide to Testing Object-Oriented Software*

Mowbray/Ruh, *Inside CORBA: Distributed Object Standards and Applications*

Oestereich, *Developing Software with UML: Object-Oriented Analysis and Design in Practice*

Page-Jones, *Fundamentals of Object-Oriented Design in UML*

Pohl, *Object-Oriented Programming Using C++, Second Edition*

Pooley/Stevens, *Using UML: Software Engineering with Objects and Components*

Quatrani, *Visual Modeling with Rational Rose 2000 and UML*

Rector/Sells, *ATL Internals*

Reed, *Developing Applications with Visual Basic and UML*

Rosenberg/Scott, *Use Case Driven Object Modeling with UML: A Practical Approach*

Royce, *Software Project Management: A Unified Framework*

Ruh/Herron/Klinker, *IIOP Complete: Understanding CORBA and Middleware Interoperability*

Rumbaugh/Jacobson/Booch, *The Unified Modeling Language Reference Manual*

Schneider/Winters, *Applying Use Cases, Second Edition: A Practical Guide*

Shan/Earle, *Enterprise Computing with Objects: From Client/Server Environments to the Internet*

Warmer/Kleppe, *The Object Constraint Language: Precise Modeling with UML*

White, *Software Configuration Management Strategies and Rational ClearCase®: A Practical Introduction*

The Component Software Series

Clemens Szyperski, Series Editor

For more information check out the series web site [http://www.awl.com/cseng/csseries/].

Allen, *Realizing eBusiness with Components*

Cheesman/Daniels, *UML Components: A Simple Process for*

Object Modeling and User Interface Design

Edited by

Mark van Harmelen

ADDISON-WESLEY

Boston • San Francisco • New York • Toronto • Montreal
London • Munich • Paris • Madrid
Capetown • Sydney • Tokyo • Singapore • Mexico City

Many of the designations used by manufacturers and sellers to distinguish their products are claimed as trademarks. Where those designations appear in this book, and Addison-Wesley was aware of a trademark claim, the designations have been printed with initial capital letters or in all capitals.

Figure 9.6 in this book was adapted from Constantine and Lockwood's Figure 2.2 in *Software for Use: A Practical Guide to the Models and Methods of Usage-Centered Design*, page 34. Copyright © 1999 ACM Press, a division of the Association for Computing Machinery, Inc. Reprinted by permission of Addison-Wesley.

The authors and publisher have taken care in the preparation of this book, but make no expressed or implied warranty of any kind and assume no responsibility for errors or omissions. No liability is assumed for incidental or consequential damages in connection with or arising out of the use of the information or programs contained herein.

The publisher offers discounts on this book when ordered in quantity for special sales. For more information, please contact:

Pearson Education Corporate Sales Division
One Lake Street
Upper Saddle River, NJ 07458
(800) 382-3419
corpsales@pearsontechgroup.com

Visit AW on the Web: www.awl.com/cseng/

Library of Congress Cataloging-in-Publication Data

Object modeling and user interface design / [edited by] Mark van Harmelen.
    p.   cm. — (Addison-Wesley object technology series)
   Includes bibliographical references.
   ISBN 0-201-65789-9
    1. Object-oriented methods (Computer science)   2. User interfaces (Computer systems)   I. van Harmelen, Mark.   II. Series.

QA76.9.O35 O24 2000
005.4'28—dc21
                                                                                     00-048110

Copyright © 2001 by Addison-Wesley

All rights reserved. No part of this publication may be reproduced, stored in a retrieval system, or transmitted, in any form, or by any means, electronic, mechanical, photocopying, recording, or otherwise, without the prior consent of the publisher. Printed in the United States of America. Published simultaneously in Canada.

ISBN 0-201-65789-9

Text printed on recycled paper

1 2 3 4 5 6 7 8 9 10—EB—0504030201

First printing, March 2001

Brief Contents

Preface .... *xv*

PART I *Participatory Design* — *1*

    1 Accelerated Business Concept Modeling: Combining User Interface Design with Object Modeling *Simon McGinnes and Johnny Amos* — *3*

PART II *Scenario- and Task-Based Design* — *37*

    2 Scenarios, Objects, and Points of View in User Interface Design *Mary Beth Rosson and John M. Carroll* — *39*

    3 Designing with Idiom *Mark van Harmelen* — *71*

    4 Entity, Task, and Presenter Classification in User Interface Architecture: An Approach to Organizing HCI Practice *John M. Artim* — *115*

PART III *Use Case Based Design* — *159*

    5 User Interface Design in the Rational Unified Process *Philippe Kruchten, Stefan Ahlqvist, and Stefan Bylund* — *161*

    6 Wisdom—Whitewater Interactive System Development with Object Models *Nuno Jardim Nunes and João Falcão e Cunha* — *197*

    7 Structure and Style in Use Cases for User Interface Design *Larry L. Constantine and Lucy A. D. Lockwood* — *245*

PART IV *User-Centered Design* — *281*

    8 A User-Centered Approach to Object-Oriented User Interface Design *Jan Gulliksen, Bengt Göransson, and Magnus Lif* — *283*

    9 Toward Unified Models in User-Centered and Object-Oriented Design *William Hudson* — *313*

PART V *Summary* 363

    10 Interactive System Design Using Oo&hci Methods
        Mark van Harmelen *365*

About the Authors *429*

Index *437*

Contents

Preface .... *xv*

PART I *Participatory Design* — 1

1 Accelerated Business Concept Modeling:
  Combining User Interface Design with Object Modeling
  Simon McGinnes and Johnny Amos — 3
  1.1 Introduction — 3
      1.1.1 Mental Models, Business Concepts, and Object Models — 4
      1.1.2 Barriers and Enablers — 7
  1.2 Framework — 8
      1.2.1 Dynamic System Development Method (DSDM) — 8
      1.2.2 Facilitated Workshops — 11
  1.3 Accelerated Business Concept Modeling — 13
      1.3.1 Philosophy — 13
      1.3.2 Integrating User Interface Design and Modeling — 14
      1.3.3 Reducing Design Choice — 17
  1.4 Experience in Commercial Organizations — 20
      1.4.1 Introduction — 20
      1.4.2 Experiment — 22
      1.4.3 Qualitative Results — 23
      1.4.4 Quantitative Results — 25
      1.4.5 Combining the Results — 27
      1.4.6 Possible Further Research — 29
  1.5 Conclusion — 33
  1.6 References — 35

PART II Scenario- and Task-Based Design — 37

2 Scenarios, Objects, and Points of View in User Interface Design   *Mary Beth Rosson and John M. Carroll* — 39
- 2.1 Introduction — 39
  - 2.1.1 Designing with Objects — 40
  - 2.1.2 Responsibility-Driven Design — 41
- 2.2 Task-Object Interactions in Scenario-Based Design — 42
  - 2.2.1 An Example: The Virtual Science Fair — 45
  - 2.2.2 Developing Basic User Interaction Scenarios for the Virtual Science Fair — 45
  - 2.2.3 Elaborating Virtual Science Fair Scenarios with an Object Perspective — 49
  - 2.2.4 Trade-offs Suggested by Objects and Their POVs — 52
  - 2.2.5 User Interactions in the Virtual Science Fair Scenarios — 55
  - 2.2.6 Trade-offs in Object-Oriented User Interaction — 59
- 2.3 Discussion — 61
  - 2.3.1 Model-First Design — 61
  - 2.3.2 Refining the Object Metaphor — 62
  - 2.3.3 Tools for Scenario-Based Design — 64
- 2.4 Conclusion — 66
- 2.5 References — 66

3 Designing with Idiom   *Mark van Harmelen* — 71
- 3.1 Introduction — 71
- 3.2 Idiom — 73
- 3.3 Designing and Specifying User Interfaces with Idiom — 77
- 3.4 Early Work with Users and the Domain — 78
  - 3.4.1 Scenario Generation — 79
  - 3.4.2 Coarse-Grained Task Modeling — 80
  - 3.4.3 Interaction Exploration Using Sequence Diagrams — 82
  - 3.4.4 Describing Tasks and Identifying Referents — 84
  - 3.4.5 The Domain Model — 86
  - 3.4.6 Visualization Using Sketches — 87
- 3.5 Formulating Abstract Descriptions of the Interactive System — 89
  - 3.5.1 The Core Model — 89
  - 3.5.2 Finer-Grained Task Models — 92
  - 3.5.3 The View Model — 92

3.6	Concrete User Interface Design	102
	3.6.1 Interaction Sequences	103
	3.6.2 Prototypes	104
3.7	Generation of Use Cases	107
3.8	Conclusions	108
	3.8.1 How Does Idiom Perform?	108
	3.8.2 Idiom as an Accommodating Framework	111
3.9	Acknowledgments	111
3.10	References	112

4 Entity, Task, and Presenter Classification in User Interface Architecture: An Approach to Organizing HCI Practice *John M. Artim*   115

4.1	Introduction	116
4.2	CHI97 Workshop Framework	117
4.3	Organizing Descriptions	118
4.4	Architecture	120
	4.4.1 System Architecture	120
	4.4.2 User Interface Architecture	121
4.5	An ETP-Based User Interface Architecture	122
4.6	Key Processes in Practice	123
	4.6.1 User Task Modeling: Requirements	124
	4.6.2 Extracting a Domain Concept Description: Analysis	132
	4.6.3 User Interface Design	144
	4.6.4 Implications for Usability Testing	152
	4.6.5 System Design and Implementation	152
4.7	ETP Summary	155
	4.7.1 ETP and Ontological Drift	155
4.8	Conclusion	156
4.9	Acknowledgments	156
4.10	References	156

PART III *Use Case Based Design*   159

5 User Interface Design in the Rational Unified Process
Philippe Kruchten, Stefan Ahlqvist, and Stefan Bylund   161

5.1	The Rational Unified Process	161
5.2	The Structure of the Rational Unified Process	162
	5.2.1 Workers	163
	5.2.2 Activity	163

	5.2.3 Steps	163
	5.2.4 Artifacts	163
	5.2.5 Workflow	164
	5.2.6 Additional Process Elements	164
	5.2.7 Guidelines	165
5.3	User Interface Design in the Rational Unified Process	165
	5.3.1 Use Cases	166
	5.3.2 Analysis Model and Boundary Classes	167
	5.3.3 Workflow	167
5.4	Worker: The User Interface Designer	168
5.5	Artifact: The Use Case Storyboard	169
	5.5.1 Properties	169
	5.5.2 Timing	170
	5.5.3 Responsibility	171
5.6	Activity: User Interface Modeling	171
5.7	Artifact: The User Interface Prototype	176
	5.7.1 Purpose	176
	5.7.2 Timing	176
	5.7.3 Responsibility	177
5.8	Activity: User Interface Prototyping	177
5.9	Guidelines: Use Case Storyboard	185
	5.9.1 Describing the Flow of Events-Storyboard	186
	5.9.2 Desired Guidance	187
	5.9.3 Average Attribute Values and Volumes of Objects	189
	5.9.4 Average Action Usage	189
	5.9.5 Summary of the Flow of Events-Storyboard	190
	5.9.6 Creating Boundary Class Diagrams	191
	5.9.7 Creating Boundary Object Interaction Diagrams	191
	5.9.8 Complementing the Diagrams of a Use Case Storyboard	193
	5.9.9 Capturing Usability Requirements on the Use Case Storyboard	193
	5.9.10 Referring to the User Interface Prototype the Use Case Storyboard	195
5.10	Conclusion	196
5.11	References	196

6	**Wisdom—Whitewater Interactive System Development with Object Models** *Nuno Jardim Nunes and João Falcão e Cunha*	197
	6.1 Introduction	197
	6.1.1 The Working Context: SSDs and Lightweight Techniques	201
	6.1.2 Chapter Structure	202
	6.2 Wisdom: Process, Architecture, and Notation	203
	6.2.1 The Wisdom Process	203
	6.2.2 The Wisdom Architecture	208
	6.2.3 The Wisdom Notation	217
	6.3 The Wisdom Method	223
	6.3.1 Requirements Workflow	226
	6.3.2 Analysis Workflow	229
	6.3.3 Design Workflow	233
	6.4 Wisdom and the CHI97 Metamodel	238
	6.5 Conclusion	239
	6.6 Acknowledgments	240
	6.7 References	240
7	**Structure and Style in Use Cases for User Interface Design** *Larry L. Constantine and Lucy A. D. Lockwood*	245
	7.1 Introduction	245
	7.1.1 Use Cases Undefined	246
	7.1.2 Concrete and Essential Use Cases	248
	7.1.3 Notation	249
	7.2 Usage-Centered Design	250
	7.2.1 A Usage-Centered Process	250
	7.2.2 Task Modeling, Scenarios, and Use Cases	253
	7.2.3 Use Case Decomposition	255
	7.3 Use Case Narrative Style and User Interface Design	256
	7.3.1 Language and Structure in Models	256
	7.3.2 Common Narrative Styles	256
	7.3.3 Task Goals and User Intentions	263
	7.4 Structured Essential Use Cases	264
	7.4.1 Identity and Purpose	265
	7.4.2 Relationships	266
	7.4.3 Process	267
	7.5 Elements of Style in Structured Essential Narratives	268
	7.5.1 Objects	268
	7.5.2 Included Use Cases	269
	7.5.3 Conditional Interaction	269

		7.5.4 Partial Ordering	*269*
		7.5.5 Extensions	*270*
	7.6	Use Case Maps	*272*
		7.6.1 Representing Use Cases	*273*
		7.6.2 Representing Relationships	*273*
	7.7	Business Rules	*275*
	7.8	Recommendations	*277*
	7.9	References	*277*

PART IV *User-Centered Design* *281*

8 A User-Centered Approach to Object-Oriented User Interface Design
Jan Gulliksen, Bengt Göransson, and Magnus Lif — *283*

	8.1	Introduction	*283*
		8.1.1 Usability and User-Centered Design	*283*
		8.1.2 Design Methods and Tools	*285*
		8.1.3 Learning Object-Oriented Design	*287*
		8.1.4 Prototyping and Iterative Design	*289*
	8.2	System Development Processes	*289*
		8.2.1 ISO 13407: Human-Centered Design Processes for Interactive Systems	*290*
		8.2.2 The Rational Unified Process	*291*
		8.2.3 The Dynamic Systems Development Method	*294*
	8.3	Design in Context	*298*
		8.3.1 The Usability Designer	*298*
		8.3.2 User Interface Modeling	*301*
	8.4	Experiences in Promoting User-Centered Design at the Swedish National Tax Board	*304*
		8.4.1 Methods of Enhancing the User Interface Design Process	*305*
		8.4.2 Introducing User-Centered Design	*306*
		8.4.3 Obstacles to the Development Work	*308*
	8.5	Discussion	*310*
	8.6	References	*311*

9 Toward Unified Models in User-Centered and Object-Oriented Design *William Hudson* — *313*

9.1	Introduction	*313*
	9.1.1 Why Bring User-Centered Design to UML?	*313*
	9.1.2 Why Not Another New Method?	*315*
	9.1.3 How Can UML Be Made User-Centered?	*316*

9.2	Survey of User-Centered Techniques and Methods	317
	9.2.1 Description of the Survey	317
	9.2.2 The User-Centered Top Ten	321
	9.2.3 User-Centered Techniques	322
	9.2.4 User-Centered Methods	324
9.3	The Informal UML Method	331
	9.3.1 Perspectives	332
	9.3.2 Confusion over Use Cases	334
	9.3.3 No Separation of User and Domain Models	336
	9.3.4 No Deliberate User Interface Design	337
	9.3.5 Lack of Contextual Information	338
	9.3.6 No Usability Evaluation	339
9.4	A Unified Approach to Use Cases and Scenarios	339
	9.4.1 Goal-Based Use Cases	339
	9.4.2 Scenarios versus Use Cases	342
	9.4.3 Context of Use	343
	9.4.4 Essential Use Cases	344
	9.4.5 Use Cases as Requirements	344
9.5	A User-Centered UML Method	346
	9.5.1 Incorporating the User-Centered Top Ten	346
	9.5.2 Modifying UML for User-Centered Design	347
	9.5.3 Applying UML Notation to User-Centered Design	349
9.6	Comparisons with Other Use Case-Driven Methods	353
	9.6.1 Rational Unified Process	353
	9.6.2 Usage-Centered Design	355
9.7	Conclusions	356
	9.7.1 The Benefits	356
	9.7.2 The Challenges	357
	9.7.3 The Future	358
9.8	References	359

PART V *Summary* — 363

10 Interactive System Design Using Oo&hci Methods
Mark van Harmelen — 365

10.1	Introduction	365
	10.1.1 Problems in Object-Oriented Practice	367
	10.1.2 Oo&hci Methods	368

	10.2	An HCI View of the Design of Interactive Systems	*369*
		10.2.1 Cognitive Engineering	*370*
		10.2.2 User-Centered Design and Human-Centered Design	*375*
		10.2.3 Model-Based User Interface Design	*377*
		10.2.4 System Visualization and Design Using Scenarios	*384*
		10.2.5 Describing Concrete User Interface Designs	*385*
		10.2.6 The Process of Interactive System Design	*386*
		10.2.7 Ensuring Design Quality	*387*
		10.2.8 HCI Summary	*394*
	10.3	Creating an Integrated Oo&hci Approach	*394*
		10.3.1 The Foundations of an Integrated Approach	*394*
		10.3.2 Characteristics of an Oo&hci Approach	*397*
		10.3.3 Activities in the Oo&hci Process	*398*
		10.3.4 Activities and Examples	*400*
		10.3.5 An Oo&hci Domain Model	*407*
	10.4	Adopting an Oo&hci Approach	*416*
	10.5	Conclusion	*420*
	10.6	Acknowledgments	*422*
	10.7	References	*422*

About the Authors *429*

Index *437*

Preface

P.1 Introduction

Our basic premise is true: Many of the interactive systems that surround us either fail to work well for their users, do not do their job, or are simply unpleasant and frustrating to use. These problems are a result of inadequate methods for software development, particularly with respect to the design of system scope, contents, functionality, and interactivity.[1] By contrast, usable systems allow their users to achieve their goals with effectiveness, efficiency, and satisfaction within a particular context of use.[2] Highly usable systems have many positive benefits, especially productivity enhancements and user job satisfaction.[3]

While the design of usable interactive systems often remains a difficult endeavor, the human-computer interaction (HCI) field has made considerable progress in the creation of interactive system design methods that significantly contribute to increased end-system usability. These methods address the scope, content, functionality, and user interface of an interactive system according to a user-centered view that includes the users' understanding of the system and the users' envisioned behavior while using the system. Because object models are relatively central in the HCI field, appropriate HCI methods and method components can be integrated with object-oriented software engineering practice to create interactive system design methods that are specifically concerned with the design of usable

---

[1] Design is the activity of formulating an engineering solution to a problem in light of requirements, other pertinent design information, and technical and economic constraints. The interactive system design discussed here is different from the technical implementation design referred to as object-oriented design (OOD). Interactive system design is discussed later in this preface, but, for now, this is mostly an activity that establishes both the high-level system design and the design of the user interface as perceived, used, and experienced by its future users.

[2] Based on the International Standards Organisations definition: "Usability is the extent to which a product can be used by specified users to achieve specified goals with effectiveness, efficiency, and satisfaction in use" [ISO 1998]. Here efficiency refers to efficiency of interaction when used by users, rather than internal program efficiency. It is important to note that the ISO definition includes issues of system scope, contents, functionality, and impact on user work and leisure activities, as well as the more traditional notion of usability, namely, ease and efficiency in interactively invoking system functionality.

[3] See, for example, [Landauer 1995] for a readable and wide-ranging discussion of usability and its consequences.

An Example of Usability Failure

To focus on the need for augmented methods that integrate the consideration of user issues, it is informative to consider a real-life example that fails on usability issues. The example is provided by a receptionist who is a regular user of a computerized booking system in a relatively expensive London restaurant. The restaurant is divided into an upstairs and a downstairs section, each with different seating characteristics and menus. For the downstairs section of the restaurant, the computer-allocated dining time is as follows: For parties of ten or less a table will be occupied for up to 1¾ hours. For parties of eleven or more a table will be occupied for up to 2¼ hours. This automatic time allocation is on first sight a performance-enhancing feature; in principle it saves time and effort for telephone operators and the reception staff who take bookings from four locations dispersed throughout the restaurant. However, there is a problem that was not anticipated by the system's designers: The largest tables downstairs have thirteen seats. Consequently, parties larger than thirteen are split across tables. Here the computer accepts the split booking and allocates dining periods for the two tables based on the number of customers sitting at each particular table, not on the total party size. For two-table bookings at least one wrong time is allocated for parties of 14 to 21 diners, leading to overbooking on busy nights. The system reveals so little about a booking when it is made and when it is subsequently accessed that for the first four years of operation no one could work out why the downstairs restaurant was overbooked on, typically, Thursday, Friday, and Saturday.

My informant expressed some of the knock-on effects of failing system usability as: "This isn't good for the host of a large party—the host can end up buying two rounds of drinks while the party waits to be seated . . . The additional cost and a forty-five minute wait aren't what you'd expect when you're already paying an average cover of £60."* Of equal severity, the booking system also changes the nature of the receptionists' work. First, due to the imposed wait, the downstairs receptionists have to deal with customers that are sometimes irate, aggressive, or rude. Second, the receptionists have to take over and try to correct the work of the system, juggling tables and parties as best as they can to minimize waiting time. As yet, several months after identification of the problem, the suppliers of the system have not returned with a solution. The audience of this book could easily imagine how the given dining times are, with the best intent, "cannily" built into the booking system in several places, making the change hard to implement without rewriting the system completely.

This example has been characterized as an example of a failure in requirements gathering. However, the example is more significant. On deeper examination it contains salutary lessons for interactive system design methods. These lessons include the following: Usability issues are significant and wide-ranging and often affect more than the immediate system users. Interactive system design impacts work and is perforce concerned with the design of future work. Failing systems require user accommodation to compensate for their failures; this is seldom desirable.

---

* For anyone not familiar with the term, "cover" is the dining cost per person. £60 = US$90.

systems. Methods that integrate object-oriented and HCI practice (oo&hci methods) apply HCI design techniques early in the design life cycle, when the first visions of the scope, content, and functionality are formed and developed into analysis-level object models. Oo&hci methods offer improved interactive system design capability and increased end-system usability by basing system design on the users' world, goals, and tasks; by the use of design techniques that provide well-founded ways of systematically developing important parts of the interactive system design; and by the use of notations that are designed to convey the design information that is required for effective interactive system design. The output of oo&hci methods is an interactive system design that includes, as a bare minimum, a model of anticipated user behavior, an analysis-level object model, and the design of the appearance and interactivity of the user interface (the concrete user interface design). Oo&hci methods can serve as front-ends to any suitable object-oriented lifecycle or analysis and design method, replacing much of the analysis activity and all user interface design in the back-end method. At least one oo&hci method has been used as a front end to 4GL-based development processes.

Object Modeling and User Interface Design provides descriptions of nine such methods. Because all the methods use or are compatible with the Unified Modeling Language (UML), they integrate well with popular UML-based approaches to object- and component-based development. The final chapter provides details of relevant HCI theory and practice, a description of the methodological concerns relating to the integration of object modeling with user interface design, and a framework that describes oo&hci methods.

This book's groundbreaking contents are highly relevant to software engineers, user interface designers, and methodologists who work with either or both of object modeling and user interface design methods.

P.2 Oo&hci Methods

In more detail, the oo&hci methods in the book share many or most of the following characteristics:

- Interactive system design is an early, up-stream activity that determines the design of user work and/or leisure activities, the division of activities between users and the interactive system, the high-level design of system scope, contents and functionality, and the detailed design of the user interface. Design activities in these areas are often closely coupled; decisions in one area are likely to have an effect elsewhere. Described at a high level, interactive system design is an activity that is concerned with user activities, user understanding of the system, and the system's user interface.
- Interactive system design is predicated on information about users, their current activities, their needs, and the work and/or leisure context in which they will

use the proposed system. This information is gathered in interviews and by observation, and is used as the basis for the design of the interactive system and its anticipated use. User-developer contact is vital to gather information, to ground the design of the system in the world of the user according to user (and therefore, where applicable, business) need, and for the evaluation and improvement of the developing interactive system design.

- Abstract models are constructed to convey the designers' understanding of how the users will view and use the interactive system. User behavior is expressed in a task model or an augmented use case model. System content is expressed in an object model. Sketches, storyboards, prototypes, scenarios, and other concrete design artifacts, together with users' reactions to them, will probably be used to inform the design of the abstract models. User evaluation of the models (presented in a user-understandable form) and of very early model-based prototypes may lead to model redesign.
- The abstract models are used in the design of the concrete user interface of the system. This model-based design may be performed in a systematic series of steps, or, less desirably, in a single, unstructured step. User evaluation of prototypes of the developing design may lead to either redesign of the user interface, or redesign of the abstract models and the derived user interface.
- Successive prototypes are tested by users to provide information for iterative redesign. This is formative evaluation, where the results of the test help form the subsequent design, and where change as a result of evaluation is expected and welcomed as a way of ensuring system usability. An iterative design-prototype-test-evaluate cycle ensures that deeper problems with models and functionality and shallower problems with the operation of the user interface are detected and ironed out before any technical implementation activities are undertaken. Use of inexpensive and malleable prototypes can be used for much or all of this activity.
- Typically, the interactive system design process provides at least a model of envisioned system use, an analysis-level object model of the system that is composed of objects of interest and relevance to users during task execution, and a concrete user interface design. Some methods may deliver additional models, mostly to express information about system interactivity. These design artifacts enable the output of the interactive system design process to be used as input to any remaining object-oriented analysis (OOA) activities before being used in object-oriented design (OOD).

As discussed in Chapter 10, many of these are made possible because of significant commonalities and points of linkage between user interface design practice performed by

HCI designers[4] and object modeling based approaches to analysis-level descriptions of interactive systems.

P.3 Individual Contributions

The structure of this book reflects four of the major themes to methods which integrate object-oriented and HCI (oo&hci) approaches, namely, participatory design, scenario- and task-based design, use case based design, and user-centered design. Each method is described in a chapter in one of these thematic categories. Inevitably, several methods could have been placed in different categories, because these methods overlap categories. The last chapter is in a section on its own, and provides a discussion of the foundations and components of oo&hci methods.

Participatory design is an approach that brings users into the design cycle as active contributors to the developing system design, either for model formulation, or for the design of the concrete user interface. The premise that underlies participatory design approaches is that users have expert knowledge about their work domains, their existing work practices, and the kinds of systems that will support their daily activities. Generally, participatory design involves users as partners in design with developers, such that the users' domain expertise complements specific developer skills in the technical aspects of system design and construction.

Participatory design of the kind in which users themselves form models of the applications and application areas of interest is addressed in the chapter by Simon McGinnes and Johnny Amos, who are responsible for the theoretical background to and commercial practice with Accelerated Business Concept (ABC) modeling. ABC is an application design approach that is facilitated by the use of a modeling tool that helps users formulate models of application domains and interactive systems. These models are abstract models that are expressed in such a way as to allow their creation, communicative use, and modification by normal end users and domain experts in business domains. The associated tool helps in the composition, examination, and modification of models. The tool is subsequently used to automatically generate user interface prototypes for evaluation by users. ABC is designed to be able to be used within the broad design and development framework provided by the Dynamic System Development Method (DSDM). DSDM [Stapleton 1997] is a largely European development of a method framework that encourages participatory design within

---

[4] User interface design as practiced by HCI designers includes as its scope all the concerns of usability, from the abstract design of system scope, contents, and functionality, to the detailed design of the presentation and interactivity of the actual concrete user interface to the interactive system. This is in contrast to user interface design as practiced by software engineering professionals as an "add-on" activity that occurs after analysis as part of a subsequent implementation-centered OOD phase.

the DSDM approach to rapid application development. Some details of the DSDM approach are found in Chapters 1, 8, and 10.

Scenario- and task-based design methods constitute the second thematic section.

Scenario-based design is primarily concerned with how scenarios can contribute design information as a visualization of system use and context, and how scenarios can be used to determine the subsequent design of an interactive system. While scenarios are broadly defined elsewhere [Carroll 1995], the scenarios used here are simple textual descriptions of specific instances of system use. One advantage of scenarios written in the language of the users is that they can be created, understood, and modified by both users and designers, thereby allowing for participatory system visualization (with its own aspects of system design) and participatory evaluation and redesign of the vision.

Task-based design is fundamental to object-oriented and HCI design. It involves the use of task models to articulate existing and envisioned user behavior. The existing task model is used as the basis upon which to consider the design of future user activities, work, and interaction with the proposed system. These latter concerns are expressed in an envisioned task model, which supplies a model of how users are intended to interact with the future system, and thus provides the basis of the design of the system's functionality.

Mary Beth Rosson and Jack Carroll, two ex-IBM researchers and practitioners who are now academics, describe how scenarios can be used for object identification and application structuring, together with their subsequent use in detailed concrete user interface design. The authors point to the use of objects in the design process as a way of considering the allocation of additional functionality to the system, thanks to the tendency of designers to anthropomorphize the objects under consideration. The method includes the formation of descriptions of objects relative to the objects themselves (Point-of-View analysis). This not only provides a description of how objects form a structure and collaborate in an interactive system, but it also provides a vision of the system and its constituents that contributes to anthropomorphism and the consideration of variant functionality. Claims analysis is used to reason about the effects of particular design choices at both abstract and concrete design levels.

As a practitioner, consultant, and researcher, I tried an experimental modification to my own method, Idiom, to incorporate scenario-based design techniques and subsequent task-based design with the system specification techniques offered by an earlier version Idiom [van Harmelen 1994]. So far, the modified method is far more supportive of designers in their quest for a design solution than the earlier version of the method. Idiom now contains design activities and accompanying representations to enable designers to iteratively develop scenarios and a task model, identify referents (objects used by users), assemble the referents into a conceptual model of the system contents, identify task execution contexts, and develop a concrete user interface.

John Artim, a user interface design specialist and consultant with first IBM and then OOCL Inc., a large multinational shipping organization, and two start-up companies, provides a distillation of his and his colleagues' practice in the design and development of (often large) enterprise systems. The organization of HCI activities and their integration with other design and development activities is crucial to the success of any interactive system development, and becomes more difficult as the project's size increases. Entity objects, tasks, and presenters provide a framework for practitioners to organize and relate the products of their design activities, facilitating HCI design and its organization throughout the development life cycle. The adoption of UML for HCI design helps to integrate HCI design with other UML modeling activities.

Use case based design provides a way of specifying, through use case models, any of system requirements, user behavior, or system functionality, according to the purpose of the use case models. Use cases can be expressed in a wide variety of forms [Cockburn 1977a, 1977b]. One common style is to use a UML use case model together with some form of use case description for each use case in the model. The use case model depicts how, at a high or abstract level, users playing particular roles (described as actors) interact with the system to achieve some discernible result. The use case model can also depict relationships between use cases, such as inclusion of one use case by another. A use case description is often a finer-grained list of steps performed by an actor while using the envisioned system.

This kind of conventional use case model fails to provide sufficient user-derived and usability-related information in order to be able to reliably design usable interactive systems. Three methods extend and refine use case based practice for interactive system design.

Phillippe Kruchten, of Rational Software Canada, and Stefan Ahlqvist and Stephan Bylund, formerly of the same organization, present the user interface design activities in the Rational Unified Process (RUP). RUP [Kruchten 1998] is a well-known, commercially available development method [Rational 2000] that covers the entire product life cycle. The chapter provides an interesting illustration of how user interface design can be treated in a method for large developments and brings together topics that might not otherwise be discernible from the published material on RUP. Major components of user interface design within RUP reflect the general structure of RUP and consist of workers, activities undertaken by workers, artifacts used and produced in activities, and workflows that sequence and combine activities, including those of different workers. Here user interface designers, sometimes together with other kinds of workers, perform actor definition, application modeling, the construction of use case storyboards (textual descriptions of proposed use that augment use case models), and the construction and testing of user interface prototypes.

Nuno Nunes from the University of Madeira and João Falcão e Cunha from the University of Porto, both academics with extensive constancy experience, provide a description of Wisdom, which is an integrated lightweight UML-based interactive system design method developed by and used by the authors in small software engineering companies. This provides an interesting counterpoint to the RUP, which is primarily designed for projects that are larger than those that would be undertaken by these small resource-limited concerns. Wisdom uses a variety of object models that support interactive system design, together with an evolutionary design and prototyping process that contains elements of participatory design. In this, the authors make heavy use of the UML customization features.

Larry Constantine and Lucy Lockwood, user interface consultants and the originators of the usage-centered design [Constantine and Lockwood 1999], discuss further developments of their method in a chapter that can be read independently from their book. This is the chapter that contains the most information about the variety of use cases that have been used in object-modeling approaches to system design. The authors present a refinement of use case modeling, Essential Use Case modeling, which is part of their usage-centered design method. Essential use cases express user interaction and system behavior abstractly, without any details of implementation and implementation technology. Using an essential approach enables designers to concentrate on the functionality of the proposed system without being distracted by implementation details. The approach addresses one of the dominant issues in interactive system design: how to design interactive system contents and capability without committing to premature and often inappropriate detailed design that later and suboptimally constrains the formation of an appropriate design solution.

User-centered design approaches are discussed in the final theme-based section in the book. User-centered design, which is at the heart of the HCI side of oo&hci methods, is defined by Donald Norman [1986] as an approach that is based on user need as a formative determinant in the design of usable systems. Because Norman did not define the detailed constituents of such an approach, HCI theorists and practitioners have supplied a variety of interpretations. Frequently used components in user-centered design approaches include an early focus on, contact with, and involvement of users, including the early and continual testing of prototypes by users to ensure the quality of the developing design, an appropriate division of work between the users and the computer system, and a multidisciplinary and iterative-design process. Participatory design is a less frequently used component in the approach, but it is gaining in popularity. Accumulated experience in the HCI field is that all of the previous components[5] are important in the development of usable systems.

---

[5] This is not to say that these are the only determinants of successful interactive design. For example, the application of social science methods such as ethnography and ethnomethodology to extract design information from field studies of users and their environments is becoming more widespread within HCI practice. However, these methods are some way from being able to be *closely* integrated with mainstream software engineering approaches.

Jan Gulliksen, Bengt Göransson, and Magnus Lif from, respectively, the University of Uppsala Royal Institute of Technology, Enea Redina AB, and Icon MediaLab, describe the foundations of user-centered design and discuss various factors pertaining to user-centered methods and their use. Two methods discussed in previous chapters, RUP and DSDM, are examined in respect to their degree of user-centeredness, and the authors introduce the role of usability designer as a complement to RUP and DSDM. Magnus Lif's User Interface Modeling (UIM) method, an adjunct to use case based practice, is presented as an example of a user-centered design method. Finally, the description of the adoption of a customized user-centered method at the Swedish National Tax Board presents the authors' experience with and observations about one organization's development of a user-centered approach in the light of the organization's software development culture and needs.

William Hudson, a user interface design consultant, provides useful recommendations in adopting a user-centered approach to UML-based developments. Observing an informal UML-based design practice that is broadly adopted in industry, Hudson makes suggestions as to how to add to that practice using usability design techniques. In this the author's intent is to avoid the creation of another method, and to avoid the inevitable overhead in learning to use a new method. As a result of an Internet-based survey of effective usability-related practice adopted by usability practitioners, Hudson provides a ranking of 23 different user-centered techniques and tools and six user-centered design methods. Hudson then provides suggestions as to how the top ten most popular techniques may be integrated with the informal UML method, thereby creating a user-centered approach to interactive system design. The new approach is then compared to the usage-centered design and RUP approaches.

The summary contains a discussion of integrated oo&hci methods. While this is, in part, a vision of the developing field, it also provides a framework within which to view and relate the diversity of the individual contributions in this book. Topics only alluded to in this preface are expanded and related material is introduced. The chapter contains descriptions of background HCI material and information on the antecedents and the major constituents of an oo&hci approach.

P.4 Conclusion

The object-oriented and HCI methods discussed in this book can be grossly characterized as methods that diverge considerably in their approach, but generally contain the following features:

- The intervention of HCI design techniques in early analysis phases allows for the up-front use of user-derived design information at the point in the development life cycle where it has the best effect, that is, when the overall design of the

system is being formed. Notably, these techniques may involve participatory design techniques.
- A very strong emphasis on abstract model construction and a broad-ranging HCI perspective on interactive system design are the means to establish the scope, functionality, and concrete user interface for interactive systems. The methods treat interactive system design as an up-front and formative determinant on the design of user work, and the design of interactive system contents, functionality, and concrete user interface.
- The concrete user interface design and interactivity of the system is also designed up front, typically in a model-based design approach in which the previously designed abstract models are used in the design of the user interface. The actions of detailed concrete design can motivate changes in the abstract models. This is to be expected and welcomed as an early design activity because changes are introduced for reasons of usability before the models are reused for the remaining OOA and OOD activities.
- The application of quality checks to the developing interactive system design by the involvement of users in the evaluation of a range of prototypes throughout the design process. The evaluation must be performed formatively, that is, so that it contributes to the further design of the system. The process starts with the evaluation of prototypes that test and help establish the abstract design of the interactive system, and, over time, moves to evaluations of prototypes that contribute to the quality of the detailed concrete user interface design. Change as a result of formative evaluation is expected and welcomed.
- Iterative redesign based on formative evaluation to converge on viable and usable support of users in their task-based behavior, with an appropriate division of work and activities between users and the interactive system.

There is an important and general point to be made here: It is possible to integrate user interface design and object-oriented software engineering practice at a deep methodological level. The significance of this is of critical importance for software engineers; the integration brings the consideration of user concerns and system usability into the object modeling design and development cycle as an up-front and centrally important activity. Such consideration helps in more than just the formulation of a detailed concrete user interface; it also helps markedly in determining the scope, contents, and core functionality of the interactive system. Importantly, consideration of user concerns determines an appropriate division of work and activities between the users and the system, and determines the subsequent work and activities of both the users and those who come into contact with them.

The commonalities and linkage between object-oriented and HCI practice represents an opportunity for the software engineering community to integrate HCI design techniques with their own discipline of interactive system design. The evidence put forth in this book is that the adoption of an integrated approach leads to an overall increase in usability. Even the adoption of only some of the techniques advocated here, for example, simple and early prototype testing and evaluation, would lead to a reduction in usability flaws.

The editorial motivation for this book was primarily to make the object and component community aware of the possibilities for the integration of object modeling with the design of interactive systems as practiced in the HCI world. To ignore the overall potentialities of an integrated approach that draws on HCI expertise in interactive system design would, I feel, be a grossly negligent act. The consequences include continued exposure of software engineers to the real and considerable risk regarding lack of user acceptance. Worse still, neglect of the possibilities will certainly condemn our users to more decades of suboptimal and unusable systems. As software engineers and methodologists, the choice is ours to make.

P.5 Acknowledgments

John Artim, Tom Dayton, Barbara Hurwood, and Nuno Nunes commented on versions of this Preface. Any mistakes or errors remain my own responsibility.

P.6 Editorial Acknowledgements

As the editor of this volume, I would like to formally acknowledge the efforts of all the authors who appear in this book, as well as the efforts of those who submitted contributions that were not accepted.

This work could not have been produced without the kind help and support of several individuals: In Japan, Dr. Katsura Kawakami provided me with the freedom to consolidate my ideas about interactive system design in an object-oriented style at the beginning of the nineties. More recently, I could not have edited this book in the United Kingdom without broad and ongoing support and help from Sarah Fernley, Paul Hinds, and Tant Barlow. Later, in South Africa, Terry Dyssell, and Chris and Elana Verster helped by generously providing access to various facilities that I needed while I finalized and checked the contents of this volume. Various friends and relatives have been amazingly tolerant of my editing work during the past two years; thankfully my relationships with these individuals remain largely unchanged.

Two institutions have given me support during the editing of this book. The Department of Computer Science at the University of Manchester supplied me with library and other facilities; it has been particularly rewarding to continue my long association with this distinguished university, home of the first stored program computer (where, as in modern computers, machine code instructions and data were stored in the same loadable and modifiable memory). The Computer Science Department at the University of Cape Town kindly provided me with access to the university's library and Internet facilities during the last three months of the editing process.

Paul Becker and John Fuller took care of the book at Addison-Wesley. Kathy Glidden of Stratford Publishing Services provided immense help and skill in transforming the manuscript into final copy. It was a delightful privilege to have her work on this volume.

P.8 References

[Carroll 1995] J. M. Carroll, *Scenario-Based Design: Envisioning Work and Technology in System Development.* New York: Wiley and Sons, 1995.

[Cockburn 1997a] A. Cockburn. Goals and Use Cases. *JOOP,* 10 (6), SIGS Publications, 1997, 35–40.

[Cockburn 1997b] A. Cockburn. Using Goal-Based Use Cases. *JOOP,* 10 (7), SIGS Publications, 1997, 56–62.

[Constantine and Lockwood 1999] L. L. Constantine and L. A. D. Lockwood. *Software for Use: A Practical Guide to the Models and Methods of Usage-Centered Design.* Reading, MA: Addison-Wesley, 1999.

[Dix et al. 1993] A. Dix, F. Finlay, G. Abwood, and R. Beale. *Human-Computer Interaction.* Englewood Cliffs, NJ: Prentice Hall, 1993.

[Dumas and Redish 1993] J. S. Dumas and J. C. Redish. *A Practical Guide to Usability Testing.* Norwood, NJ: Ablex, 1993.

[ISO 1998] International Standardization Organization, ISO9241. *Ergonomic Requirements for Office Work with Visual Display Terminals (VDTs),* Part 11, Guidance on Usability, 1998.

[Kruchten 1998] P. Kruchten. *The Rational Unified Process.* Reading, MA: Addison-Wesley, 1998.

[Landauer 1995] T. K. Landauer. *The Trouble with Computers.* Cambridge, MA: MIT Press, 1995.

[Newman and Lamming 1995] W. M. Newman and M. G. Lamming. *Interactive System Design.* Reading, MA: Addison-Wesley, 1995.

[Norman 1986] D. A. Norman. Cognitive Engineering. In D. A. Norman and S. W. Draper, eds. *User Centered System Design.* Hillsdale, NJ: Lawrence Erlbaum Associates, 1996.

[Preece et al. 1994] J. Preece, Y. Rogers, H. Sharp, D. Benton, S. Holland, and T. Carey. *Human-Computer Interaction.* Reading, MA: Addison-Wesley, 1994.

[Rational 2000] Rational Unified Process 2000 Version 6, CD Manual. Rational Software Corporation, 2000.

[Stapleton 1997] J. Stapleton. *Dynamic Systems Development Method: The Method in Practice.* Reading, MA: Addison-Wesley, 1997.

[van Harmelen 1994] M. van Harmelen. Object Oriented Modelling and Specification for User Interface Design. In F. Paterno, ed. *Interactive Systems: Design, Specification and Verification.* Proceedings of First Eurographics ISDV Workshop, 1994.

[van Harmelen et al. 1997] M. van Harmelen, J. Artim, K. Butler, A. Henderson, D. Roberts, M. B. Rosson, J.-C. Tarby, and S. Wilson. Object-Oriented Models in User Interface Design: A CHI97 Workshop. *SIGCHI Bulletin,* October 1997.

PART I

Participatory Design

CHAPTER 1
Accelerated Business Concept Modeling
Combining User Interface Design with Object Modeling

Simon McGinnes

Johnny Amos

Abstract

Accelerated Business Concept (ABC) modeling is an application design and prototyping method that integrates business object modeling with prototyping and user interface design. It is based on the principle of *reduced design choice.* Intended to be simple to learn and use, it allows untrained business users to take a more active role in the design of their own systems. Integration of modeling with prototyping enables faster development and leads to higher-quality models based on a common view of the users' own business concepts.

ABC modeling is designed to be compatible with Dynamic Systems Development Method (DSDM), a rapid application development method built on user involvement and responsibility for system development.

This chapter briefly highlights some of the disadvantages of separating user interface design from business object modeling, and explains why a well-designed user interface must correspond closely with its user's mental models. Results from the application of the method in commercial organizations are given.

1.1 Introduction

Business modeling (object-oriented or otherwise) and user interface design deal with the same concepts—the business users' own business concepts (referents). Hence, they should be connected [Fischer et al. 1995]. In ABC modeling [McGinnes 1994], the object model is closely identified both with the user's mental model and with the application design. Modeling is made as simple as possible, and models are expressed in an easily understandable form: "The difficulties and unreliability of translating between user-centered work models and technology-centered software models undermines the value of both, and general solutions are needed to bridge between the two kinds of models" [van Harmelen et al. 1997].

The method is supported by a modeling/prototyping tool called *CORAS Concept*™. ABC modeling is compatible with DSDM, a non-proprietary rapid application development (RAD) approach [Stapleton 1997]. Models can be expressed using the graphical notation and as prototype user interface designs. The tool also enables simple process analysis to be carried out using the same accessible graphical representation.

The method is designed to be used in a workshop setting with (or by) business users, without the need for extensive prior training. ABC modeling limits the number of design options available so as to reduce the time and effort required to produce usable prototypes. Applications produced using CORAS Concept which can be used as first-cut designs or as applications in their own right.

1.1.1 Mental Models, Business Concepts, and Object Models

We argue that usable and maintainable business applications can and should be constructed from components that reflect the structure of the business itself [Partridge 1996]. The object-oriented approach embodies this thinking. But software objects and user interfaces are not always formulated in a way that recognizably reflects the structure of the business world.

1.1.1.1 Models Must Be Recognizable

Most people would agree that a well-designed software design matches its user's mental model and does not force the user to expend mental energy in translating between design and mental model. According to Johnson-Laird [1994], a mental model is a *recognizable analogue* of a corresponding real-world scenario, in the same way that an architectural scale model resembles the building that it represents.

But an object model is not a recognizable analogue of a business situation. Object models are based on an entirely different theory—that is, an earlier view of mental models as *conceptual schemata,* hierarchical categorization schemes [Bower et al. 1969], semantic networks [Collins and Loftus 1975], or conceptual graphs [Sowa 1984]. We argue that this rather inappropriate foundation makes object models hard for untrained end users to understand.

To illustrate, Figure 1.1 shows an object model for a simple financial system. This example is not particularly complicated; many business systems involve far more classes than are shown in Figure 1.1. As it stands, the model would clearly not be intuitively understandable by a business user as a description of a business area. The dilemma is that, after the designer has translated the business language into model form, quality procedures dictate that he or she must go back to the business user to verify that the translation is correct.

The *connectionist* view of brain function [Quinlan 1991] offers some support for Johnson-Laird's view of mental models. It postulates that mental processes come about through the action of the brain's neural networks. There is no obvious home in a neural network for mental concepts, crisp or otherwise. Similarly, proposed mental mechanisms based on theories of mental conceptual structures, such as *structure mapping* [Gentner 1983], are not easily accommodated.

The neural network model of the brain offers a simple and compelling chance of improving on object models as a vehicle for communication. We know that neural networks respond to stimuli purely on the basis of similarity. According to the connectionist view, our minds simply *associate* information, as words, sensory impressions, and ideas. To allow end users to understand models, we simply need to present them in a way that allows the brain's neural network to function most effectively, as follows:

1. Make the model a visually recognizable analogue of the relevant business situation.
2. Create meaning by ensuring that the way the chosen representation stimulates the most useful associations.

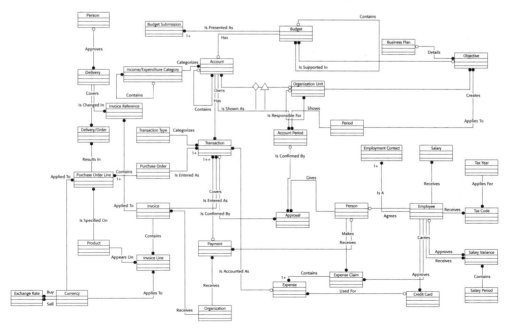

FIGURE 1.1 Sample object model of a financial system

1.1.1.2 Concepts Are Emergent

Things in the world have little or no existence for us until we are prompted to consider them actively [Flores et al. 1988]. Defining a concept precisely can be difficult or even impossible (for example, try defining "car"). People are far less clear about what they mean by something (or about what something is, exactly) than they might think.

Business concepts are *emergent* and may be arrived at only through a process of negotiation and discussion. They come into existence when business users are prompted to think and talk about them. It is unrealistic to believe that we can simply identify labels for pre-existing concepts and then incorporate these labels as classes and properties in an object model (and hence in an application). This is because:

1. The meaning of a concept is not found in its label. It is the sum total of the concept's associations to other concepts.
2. Attempting to identify pre-existing mental concepts does not afford business users a chance to participate, to understand, and to develop and verify ideas.

We need a means of capturing and representing ideas, as they evolve, in a way that is recognizable to the business user.

1.1.1.3 Conclusion

Object modeling relies on our ability to identify discrete, crisply defined concepts that can become classes in object models. Classes are, by definition, not fuzzy. The business user is presented with an object model that bears no visual resemblance to the business situation it describes, and the crisp concepts in the object model do not correspond to any mental structures that the user can call upon. Yet the user is expected to interpret and understand the object model, usually without training. For obvious reasons, this can require mental gymnastics and is often problematic for untrained end users [McGinnes 1992].

The result has historically been a message to business users that the outcome of the project is beyond their influence [de Brabander and Thiers 1984]. This is a bad thing, for the following reasons:

- At best, there is no enthusiasm for the project on the part of the business users. At worst, they are alienated and possibly even hostile to the project.
- There is no guarantee of quality in the models since the business users have accepted something they do not understand. This obviously affects the quality of the system.
- There is no ownership of the resulting system, and the very people who could be championing its use in the business lack confidence in it. Inevitably, they will

communicate their doubts to the rest of the organization, whether consciously or not.

In summary, conventional object modeling techniques, combined with the "quality process," lead to disenchanted business users and, paradoxically, to a lack of quality.

1.1.2 Barriers and Enablers

System development methods tend to get more complex over time. This tendency can be observed in the historical development of many well-known methods, such as Structured Systems and Design Method (SSADM) [Ashworth and Slater 1993], the Rational Unified Process, and UML (see Kruchten et al. in Chapter 5). Although the initial ideas for a methodology may be relatively simple, it is natural for method architects to want to complete and perfect their methods. This inevitably involves filling in gaps and catering for more special cases. Methods become richer, with more notations, techniques, and stages. There will always be calls for greater formality, completeness, and traceability, all of which push methods toward greater comprehensiveness. van Harmelen (Chapter 3) and Hudson (Chapter 9) give good overviews of the very wide range of activities that can constitute system design.

1.1.2.1 Is a More Complete Method a Better One?

One may question the assumptions underlying this process of development. Methods are not computer programs and are not executed by people in the same way that computers execute programs. People rarely follow a method as a stepwise sequence of activities. Tasks are infrequently carried out "by the book." Instead, people think ahead and around a problem.

For instance, it is difficult (and inadvisable) to avoid thinking about design when thinking about requirements, and vice versa. Software development, and especially user interface design, is an intuitive process in which the developer and business users grope toward an ideal (and usually unattainable) optimum system design. A software development method is therefore best thought of as a way of "explaining" design work rather than a way of describing it accurately or even of controlling it.

Complex and comprehensive methods are difficult for people to learn. It is very hard to start working with a method if you have to understand a lot of new ideas before you can begin to use it. Typically, people make many mistakes, and only exceptional individuals reach high levels of expertise. Most people muddle through. And once the team is up and running, it is hard to ensure that each team member performs his or her part of the method consistently and with sufficient accuracy. The more comprehensive the method, the harder it is to make the "machine" work.

This book asks how user interface design techniques can be used or integrated with object-oriented modeling techniques, but the world will not be served well if this goal is achieved by creating even larger, more complex methods that import techniques from both disciplines. It is easy to see how this could happen if object modeling techniques were grafted onto user interface design techniques, or vice versa.

1.1.2.2 Deliberate Simplicity

In short, complex methods are barriers to effective system development. To get started with a method, novices need simple, understandable techniques. For this reason, ABC modeling is deliberately simple, and we have avoided the temptation to make it a comprehensive method. Like many useful techniques, it addresses only a subset of the wider concerns in system design [Monk 1998].

ABC modeling is intended to be a small and easily learned method that can be applied by novice designers who are equipped with knowledge of their own businesses, but (initially, at least) who lack training or experience in system design.

We have also tried to make the method *self-correcting*. The business user or novice developer needs no prior experience to get started. But, as modeling and prototyping progress, we hope that he or she will learn through a feedback process encouraged by the modeling tool's checking and correction cycle.

Inexperienced developers can also learn through assistance from experts such as human-computer interaction (HCI) professionals and designers who understand good system design. ABC modeling facilitates mentoring because it is explicit, visual, and accessible. ABC models form a good basis for joint work. Knowledge is then built up through productive shared experience.

1.2 Framework

In this section, we discuss the Dynamic System Development Method and its relationship to ABC modeling. DSDM is one way of formalizing RAD, which retains the benefits of quick delivery while adding control and some formality to the development process. ABC modeling is a highly visual technique and lends itself to the production of dynamic and rapidly changing models and prototypes—a hallmark of the DSDM approach.

1.2.1 Dynamic System Development Method

DSDM is promoted as a nonproprietary method for RAD. In fact, it is less a method than a framework of concepts that can lead to rapid project delivery. DSDM may be used in a wide variety of projects, including systems development projects, process re-engineering exercises, business analysis studies and total quality management (TQM) initiatives. Its value derives from the fact that it is a careful amalgamation of techniques designed to promote quick, accurate, and correct development that is matched to business needs. DSDM is promoted by a not-for-profit consortium, which has set up training and certification programs [Stapleton 1997]. For an interesting treatment of DSDM, see Gulliksen, Göransson, and Lif (Chapter 8). OSDM is also discussed briefly in Chapter 10.

DSDM is fast becoming the de facto world standard for RAD. In the past, RAD has been seen as a relatively uncontrolled way of developing software. The DSDM Consortium was formed to address this issue by developing a RAD methodology that its members could use with confidence. It vigorously promotes DSDM as a way of quickly developing robust and fully tested systems.

Because DSDM is a framework, it does not dictate specific development techniques. Appropriate methods, such as UML and ABC modeling, can be used in DSDM projects and can provide as much rigor as desired.

The basis for DSDM is outlined in the following nine principles:

1. Active Business User Involvement Is Imperative

Business users must become an integral part of the project team and take ownership and responsibility for all products. Active user involvement reduces communication delays and allows immediate user feedback on design products. It addresses the issue of the business user's ownership not only by encouraging input at all stages of the project, but also by making the user share responsibility for the final product. The result is an intellectual and emotional investment by the business user that pays large dividends.

If software professionals wish to involve business users, they must communicate using language and conventions that users understand. Failure to do this means that user involvement amounts to little more than a public relations exercise.

2. DSDM Teams Must Be Empowered to Make Decisions

The project team (including both technical and business members) is given clear guidelines about its operating constraints and freedoms. This means that the team is not obliged continually to give feedback to a controlling panel or steering committee. The project management board expresses and gives its trust to the team. The team is more likely to take responsibility in the project and to respond to the trust placed in it by delivering quality products.

3. The Focus Is on Frequent Delivery of Products

The milestones of a project are products, not tasks. In DSDM, the project works to a fixed time scale to produce outputs whose purpose is clearly defined. How the products are created is up to the team, which is not burdened by an inflexible plan full of low-level tasks. The team can react quickly and creatively to anything that threatens timely delivery of the product.

Frequent product delivery (which in this context may mean every two weeks or so) provides the control that some managers may fear they are losing as a result of Principle 2. Moreover, it affords much more concrete evidence of progress than a statement of "hours used against plan," which can give little indication of quality or direction.

4. Fitness for Purpose Is the Essential Criterion for Acceptance of Products

This principle was originally worded as "Build the right product before you build it right." However, the implication that you don't have to "build it right" was felt to be unacceptable. This principle puts the focus heavily on the business problem or opportunity being addressed and helps to avoid "design for its own sake."

5. Iterative and Incremental Development Is Necessary to Converge on an Accurate Business Solution

In some projects, a new system or process is designed at an early stage, and thereafter effort is devoted to making the design work. But business needs often change during the life cycle of a project. In DSDM, prototyping technologies are used, and the design is allowed to evolve during the project. Everyone benefits from the feedback and increased understanding that is gained in the process.

CORAS Concept brings the idea of prototyping even further forward. Prototypes can be generated from even the earliest stages of a business model. The prototypes can be used to check the validity of the model and to provide a "sense" of the final product at the earliest possible stage.

6. All Changes during Development Are Reversible

Given an evolving product, it must be possible to recognize that a wrong path has been taken and to return to a safe point from which evolution may proceed in a different direction. This may give rise to the concern that large amounts of work will be discarded. However, if the other principles are applied, the amount of lost work need not be extensive. In particular, the focus on frequent delivery of products gives early feedback on design decisions.

Compare this to an IT project run along traditional lines, which delivers an inadequate product after months or even years of work. Many well-known projects have delivered the wrong product after wasting large amounts of time and money. A decade-long project and multi-million-pound system that was never completed at the London Stock Exchange leaps to mind—but this is by no means the only or the most recent example.

7. Requirements Are Baselined at a High Level

The important aspect of this principle is "high level." A fixed, detailed set of requirements can hamstring a project just as effectively as a prematurely fixed design. For example, effort goes into meeting performance criteria that are set before we know how we are going to satisfy business needs. A redesigned process may obviate the need for sub-second response time, but because nobody remembers the context in which the requirement was set, the effort and expense go into satisfying it anyway.

8. Testing Is Integrated throughout the Life Cycle

It is unwise to test products only at the end of a project, especially if you are working to fixed time scales. One cannot know in advance what testing might reveal. If testing is distributed throughout the project life cycle, unwelcome surprises and delays are easier to avoid.

9. A Collaborative and Cooperative Approach between Stakeholders Is Essential

Barriers between the parties involved in a project—consultants, business users, business managers, IT departments, suppliers, and contractors—must be torn down and relationships made to work. The most highly prized commodity in a DSDM project is often *time*. Bad communication, lack of coordination, conflicting agendas, and buck-passing are effective time wasters, especially with today's global orientation, in which it is increasingly likely that multiple vendors and multi-organizational customers will be involved.

It should be clear from these descriptions of the nine principles that DSDM is more than simply an iterative approach to software development. DSDM is highly effective in bringing together business users and technicians to ensure product quality.

1.2.2 Facilitated Workshops

Complementary to DSDM is a technique called *Joint Application Design* (JAD), which was developed by IBM Canada. In JAD, stakeholders collaborate to solve problems in *facilitated workshops* [Wood and Silver 1995]. DSDM encourages IT professionals and users to work together in project teams; JAD offers one structured way in which this can be achieved.

Since the development of JAD in the mid-1980s, the value of this workshop-based approach was quickly recognized, and the method has been applied throughout the IT industry to all aspects of development, including requirements gathering, system design, and strategic planning.

The facilitated workshop is a group approach to work. In a conventional project, the project manager delegates tasks to individuals. The tasks are designed such that the required outcome will be achieved, provided that everyone does his or her job. But in a project that uses facilitated workshops, the team members come together in a workshop setting to create the desired outcome.

Facilitated workshops provide an environment in which business users can drive the application development process and take responsibility for the results [Wood and Silver 1995]. Definitions of facilitated workshops are plentiful. For example, a short one is: a team-based approach to communication. A longer one that highlights all of the major components of facilitated workshop sessions is: "Using an interactive workshop environment, effective group dynamics and visual aids, facilitated workshops are designed to extract high quality information in a compressed time frame, to meet a predetermined set of deliverables" [Rogers 1994].

It is claimed that workshops cut communication time, enhance communication quality, and increase user confidence. Workshops provide more immediate validation and verification of designs, improved understanding of the business by users and IT personnel, and increased championing of the results by business users [de Brabander and Thiers 1984].

If a group is unstructured, chaos will inevitably arise. The main factor that prevents chaos in facilitated workshops is the presence of a *facilitator*. This individual is outside the group and has no direct influence on the content of the workshop products. However, the facilitator controls the group in that he or she "owns" both the process and the timetable. It is the facilitator's job to control group dynamics when appropriate—for instance, to ensure that the right individuals contribute at the right times. The facilitator knows how to manage conflict within the group.

Another important factor is the environment in which a facilitated workshop is conducted. Ideally, the group members are removed from their normal workplaces and from all of the distractions that exist therein. A large meeting room is used, with enough space for the facilitator to move both around and within the group, depending on where he or she wishes the focus of the group to be.

For the facilitator to exercise proper control, each person in the workshop must have one or more tightly defined roles. The roles include, but are not restricted to, *facilitator, scribe, business expert, specialist,* and *observer*. While the facilitator's role makes him or her responsible for control of the process and the group, it also excludes him or her from contributing to the product [Johnson and Johnson 1994].

1.3 Accelerated Business Concept Modeling

1.3.1 Philosophy

When designing the ABC modeling approach, we first asked two fundamental, linked questions:

1. Who must determine whether business applications and intermediate design products, such as requirements statements, are acceptable?
2. What means are used to determine whether business applications and intermediate design products such as requirements statements are acceptable?

In answer to the first question, we argue that it is the *business user* who must determine the acceptability of business applications. The customer is always right, especially in the world of custom software development. In answer to the second question, we assert that business users verify the acceptability of applications chiefly *by using them*, whether as part of formal acceptance testing or more informally in day-to-day use.

1.3.1.1 Questioning Current Practice

Our answers to the questions listed above lead us to challenge current practice. Software developers often ask business users to verify requirements specifications, object models, use case diagrams, and other intermediate design products. The logic behind asking business users to verify software designs rests on their ability to interpret the designs accurately. It is especially important that object models be verified as accurate representations of business concepts, which requires the end user's business knowledge. But end users can verify design deliverables only if they fully understand them and are aware of their implications.

It may be that users can understand user interface designs quite easily, but object and data models are abstract. Their abstract nature obliges users to think in an abstract way. We argue that business users generally *cannot* easily understand models or their implications, because they lack the relevant training in software development technologies and techniques and are often unused to thinking in the required ways.

Many people have recognized that business users need something more concrete to work with—hence all of the work in the last two decades on *prototyping* [Connell and Shafer 1995] and RAD [Stapleton 1997]. For example, business users may be presented with user interface designs and may be allowed to work with prototype software so that they can learn what they need to know about proposed designs. User interface designs (if realistic) and prototype systems are both *concrete,* not abstract, design products. The designer can observe the users' reactions to these products using various techniques, such as the *thinking-out-loud technique* [Cassell and Symon 1994]. But even a user interface is a rather opaque window through which to examine the concepts or assumptions inherent in a piece of software. The business user has to deduce—or mentally reconstruct—these concepts by seeing how they are reflected in the external representation presented by the software.

Consequently, many software developers believe that the most effective approach to software development is to combine user verification of *business models* with user verification of *user interfaces and prototypes*. This approach can be made even more effective if the user's involvement is extended to include a role in the *construction and design* of both models and prototypes.

1.3.1.2 Combining Modeling and Construction of Systems

Accordingly, we are interested in combining the two activities of modeling and user interface design. Merging these two apparently distinct activities into a single activity could help in the following ways:

- It might reduce the apparent pointlessness (from the business user's perspective) of creating and verifying business models such as object and data models.
- It could make user verification of models more effective, because the impact of model changes could be seen immediately in concrete changes in the software user interface.

Our CORAS Concept™ tool is designed to realize these advantages. Although many RAD tools exist, we are aware of none that explicitly attempt to present object models in a way that mirrors the business users' own mental models, and few that allow such a closely integrated use of models and user interface designs.

1.3.2 Integrating User Interface Design and Modeling

Our goal was to allow business users and inexperienced developers to create both models and user interface designs—quickly and easily—with a minimum of knowledge or training. Intervention by highly experienced IT specialists was to be kept to a minimum. These requirements could be met only by using a simplified modeling technique and suitable tools. The tools would support modeling and would allow seamless generation of prototype designs.

1.3.2.1 CORAS Concept™ Tool

To use the CORAS Concept™ tool, the developer or user does not need extensive prior knowledge of object modeling, programming, or prototyping. They *do* need to know about the relevant business areas, and they need a reasonable familiarity with Windows-style software. Using this tool, they can create and work with software prototypes that are fully working applications and can be used as such. CORAS Concept generates full applications complete with database and forms, together with those aspects of business logic that can be deduced from an object model (such as validation based on dependencies).

1.3.2.2 Model Construction

Models are constructed using CORAS Concept from business graphics (see Figure 1.2). The graphics can be chosen from any source, including a keyword-driven library of images incorporated into the CORAS Concept™ tool. The images are combined to represent business concepts associated with concept types. Abstract or meaningful backgrounds can be used to provide context. The business user can rapidly assemble an impressionistic but meaningful "collage" of information, much as one would create a presentation using graphics and text.

These models have meaning on more than one level. They can be interpreted in an impressionistic or intuitive manner in the same way that one might understand any multimedia presentation. But they can also be ascribed a formal meaning. Allowing the user to view a formal interpretation on demand helps ensure that everyone understands precisely what is being modeled.

1.3.2.3 Adding Meaning

We do not assume that well-defined mental concepts exist before or during modeling. Instead, the CORAS Concept™ tool allows the user to associate and re-associate concepts at will simply by dragging and dropping. This process helps to create meaning through a process of exploration.

The designer need not worry about design alternatives, such as having to choose whether a concept is best represented as a class, a property, or an association. Similarly,

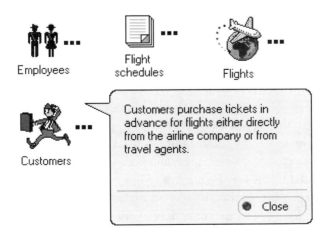

FIGURE 1.2 Use of business graphics

the designer does not have to consider when to use aggregation and when to use association, or even when to use inheritance. These design decisions are automated.

The business user is free to represent each business concept in any way that seems appropriate, especially at the earliest, most volatile stages of modeling. This is a deliberate attempt to reflect the way in which we mentally associate ideas—in a fluid and flexible way.

As in the mind, the meaning of a concept in an ABC model is the sum total of its connections to associated concepts. Operational definitions (Artim, Chapter 4) are, therefore, redundant, although short descriptions may be entered. As meaning is developed in the model, new concepts come to light and go through the same process of elaboration, as in POV analysis (Rosson and Carroll, Chapter 2).

The type of modeling described earlier would be impossible without the aid of a supporting tool. The CORAS Concept™ tool is designed to be used with data projectors, electronic whiteboards, and similar appliances and hence can easily be used in workshop settings or by individuals. Group methods such as brainstorming are well accommodated by both the tool and the method.

The tool is engineered to suit the rather loose way in which people think much of the time. It does not enforce a rigid "correct" modeling syntax, and users need not concern themselves with design alternatives. CORAS Concept models are presented in a way that is intended to be intuitively meaningful to untrained business users, although its models are equivalent to formally stated object models. Meaning is added to a model as it is refined. The tool can also depict the visual business model as a traditional "box-and-line" style class diagram, if required.

1.3.2.4 Automating Design

How does the tool automatically convert a model into a prototype user interface and database structure? It was our goal to make this process happen with as few transformations as possible, so that the business user would view the prototype simply as an alternative representation of the model itself (and, especially, vice versa). Therefore, similar graphics are used in the model and user interface, thereby aiding comprehension by creating a visual association between model elements and related application components. In addition, terminology is consistent, where possible, between the application and the model.

Behind the user interface is a complex object (database) structure. Typically, the business user does not see the object structure itself, because they interact with an application through the generated forms (see Figure 1.3). However, the object structure reflects the model. In the database objects, it is still easy to recognize the business concepts and data items defined in the model. The database may be used as a functional application in the absence of the generated user interface or as part of a different application if required.

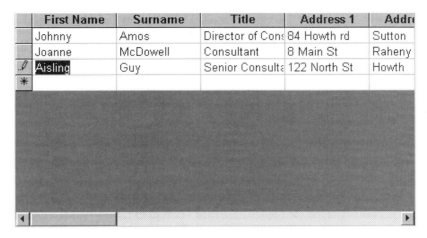

FIGURE 1.3 Generated user interface

1.3.3 Reducing Design Choice

1.3.3.1 "Good Enough" Design

The question most asked by experienced developers about ABC modeling is: "How is it possible to automate application design?" Professional software designers often find it implausible that usable and maintainable business software can be derived directly from business models without the need for programming or architectural design. The response to this question is based on the principle of *reduced design choice*. As we have already seen, the tool reduces the range of available design options and steers the software design (both database structure and user interface) toward a small range of well-thought-out solutions that can be produced directly from models with minimum intervention.

The use of a small range of solutions does not restrict CORAS Concept to any particular application domain. Just as spreadsheet software offers a reasonable solution to a broad range of financial system requirements, so the CORAS Concept™ tool offers a reasonable solution to the problem of business information system design.

There are many examples in software technology in which reduced design choice provides increased capability. The spreadsheet is one example. Another example is the relational database. As a one-size-fits-all solution, a relational database may not always be optimal. But, for most business information systems, using relational databases is usually a better idea than designing each system's data storage mechanism individually.

This thinking can be seen as an application of the *80/20 rule*; you can have 80% of the benefit with 20% of the effort. Or, stated another way, you can design 80% of systems with 20% of the skills. Obviously, the CORAS Concept application generator cannot cope with all business software requirements, and its output is often less than optimal, but it aims to produce a "good enough" design that will meet a large subset of business information system requirements. Generated applications can be used immediately or enhanced. Either way, they are created in a fraction of the time that would have been needed if more traditional systems development methods were used.

1.3.3.2 Stereotypical Design Solutions

To produce a one-size-fits-all design template, we took into account the fact that many business software systems conform to a stereotypical architecture and share certain characteristics:

- They are comprised of an object structure, a database, and a user interface for manipulating data.
- They provide access to data that is shared between many business users.
- The data they contain reflects people, organizations, documents, business transactions or activities, and other common business concepts.
- The chief function of these systems is record keeping.
- They are used primarily in an interactive manner.
- They may incorporate many different types of data, including both structured and unstructured information (that is, they may be complex from a data model perspective).
- The functionality they provide tends to be relatively simple and consists in large part of locating, adding, and modifying data in various forms.

Note that this commonality extends across platform boundaries. Business systems tend to be similar, at least in the ways listed earlier, regardless of whether they are implemented on client-server platforms, on stand-alone hardware, or with Internet-based technology.

1.3.3.3 Role of the Software Designer

What is the role of the software designer in systems of this type? Software designers must design the components of a system: its middleware, its data storage facilities, and its user interface. This is true regardless of design approach. A skilled designer will also help the business user to develop an appropriate way of working; it is only with this way of working that the software design makes sense.

Today, software designers have a wide range of design styles and technologies from which to choose (Artim, Chapter 4). Experienced and skilled designers can benefit from this wide choice, because they are able to select the most appropriate design strategies and create highly usable systems. Their knowledge and experience tell them what to do (and what not to do) in order to achieve the desired result.

However, much business software is produced by less experienced designers who can easily be overwhelmed by choice. The capabilities of RAD tools such as Visual Basic and Delphi, relational and object-oriented database management systems, middleware tools, and the variety of off-the-shelf packaged solutions all present the designer with a huge range of possible design solutions to any given problem. In facing this choice, it is easy to produce overly complex, poorly thought out, and ultimately unusable designs.

ABC modeling addresses each of the design tasks differently, but in each case the principle of reduced design choice is applied to help less experienced designers produce useful results. To create a database structure, an algorithm transforms the business model into an object-oriented or relational schema. To create the user interface, the tool applies rules that we have developed through our experience in designing client-server and Internet-based systems. This approach creates a usable, although not necessarily optimal, visual user interface that reflects the structure of the business model and hence the user's mental concepts (matching business concepts is, after all, a major aim in creating a prototype).

Also, a *standard way of working* is assumed, in which the business user is expected to record business events in the system as they occur, and associated information is recorded when it comes to hand. It is assumed that the system is a multi-user one in which the information is shared. In other words, we assume the system will be used in the way that most modern business database application systems are used. The generated application incorporates no functionality that makes decisions or takes actions without intervention; it is merely a record keeper.

In some respects, therefore, we avoid the need for comprehensive task analysis by assuming a standard task structure. To seasoned HCI practitioners, this may seem to be a draconian restriction, because it denies the uniqueness of each situation and goes against the idea that a system must be designed to suit each unique task.

But in fact a correct object model contains much information that is useful in task modeling. A user interface derived directly from a business model is therefore quite closely aligned to the business process itself. This way of producing systems does require, however, a measure of trust on the part of the designer. The designer must allow the tool to do its job and must not attempt to second-guess the tool by structuring the concepts in the model around some intended application architecture.

Generic functionality, such as the ability to search for data and to move between records, is built into the generated prototypes automatically. All possible navigation paths through the data are supported so that no particular way of using the system is favored. In real applications, it is often the case that many potential navigation paths are omitted because a particular way of using the system (that is, a particular task structure) is assumed. Explicitly leaving out possible but unneeded navigation paths (or other functionality) is one way of making a system more usable, because potentially distracting parts are omitted. This (omission of functionality) is one aspect of design that we do not attempt to automate.

It is possible, however, for the user to disable specific navigation paths or even whole functions (for security reasons, for example) once a suitable prototype has been developed.

In summary, the intention behind ABC modeling is to make it easier for untrained people to produce software by channeling them toward predefined but non-domain-specific design solutions. These pre-existing design rules may not produce the best possible choice in each situation but, overall, should offer a "good enough" design for prototyping to proceed in a wide range of circumstances. Even if a generated application is not usable as a finished product, it should provide a good basis for refinement and should take you further down the design path than you would otherwise be.

1.4 Experience in Commercial Organizations

1.4.1 Introduction

We have tested ABC modeling in many commercial and non-commercial projects for clients in several industries, including telecommunications, air travel, and retail distribution. The work done with a consortium of mobile telephone operators is described in Section 1.4.1.1 below. In this project, which was conducted as a commercial project, the aim was to map out an architectural design to act as a blueprint for the consortium's future systems. After initial sponsor interviews in which appropriate business users were identified, a series of workshops was set up that would cover all aspects of the consortium's business. The workshop schedule was structured according to the area of each business under consideration. First, a set of goals and objectives for the business area was agreed on. Next, a set of processes was identified that the relevant business users would carry out in support of the goals. Finally, for each of these processes, a workshop session was held in which the process was modeled in CORAS Concept using a projector.

1.4.1.1 Facilitated Workshops for a Telecommunications Consortium

In each workshop, the model was the focal point of activity. In sessions using ABC modeling, a scribe operated the modeling tool and carried out the instructions of the group with regard to how the application domain should be modeled.

There was a five-minute introductory session to describe the tool and its purpose, but according to the analyst who conducted the sessions, most learning about the modeling technique probably took place during the modeling itself. Because there were no concepts such as "entity" or "object" for the team to comprehend, the introduction needed only to be brief. The facilitator could have talked about "mental models" and "business concepts" but felt that this was not necessary and would have served only to mystify what was in essence a very simple process. He pointed out that the group was modeling with images and already knew that images represented things, people, and other familiar concepts.

In each session, the business users were asked to describe the relevant business process, perhaps by starting with a statement of the inputs and resources required for the process and the outputs derived from the process. Each sentence was considered as a source of candidate business concepts. At this stage there was no requirement to enforce rigor, and all candidate concepts were recorded using the tool.

Once the group had documented a fairly loose description of the process in this manner, the facilitator began to tease each concept out in greater detail, asking questions such as "What do we need to know about this thing?"; "How does this thing change during the process?"; "Where does this thing go when it is complete?"; and "How do we know when the process is finished?"

At all times, the business users conversed in their own terms about the business. They were not required to use technological language or to deduce object structures from their knowledge of the business process. They needed to know only their own business processes and concepts.

As might be expected at this finer level of detail, we found that some business concepts were poorly understood by the group. For instance, there was disagreement about the meanings of concepts as apparently simple as "customer." The very fact that disagreement existed about the precise meanings of some concepts often came as a great surprise to business users. The facilitator reported two specific advantages in using CORAS Concept in this situation. First, the tool would happily accept a degree of looseness in thinking, and so the facilitator could postpone the act of defining what a particular concept meant and pick his moment to return to it. Second, the group could delve into the tool's library of icons and images to choose one that best matched their concept. According to the facilitator, the subtleties conveyed by images provided a remarkably useful prompt to discussions that defined the meaning of a concept. The business users seemed to gain insight into their own business processes from these discussions.

1.4.1.2 Application Prototyping

A model defined in the CORAS Concept™ tool can be checked to determine whether it is able to generate a prototype application. The tool will highlight inconsistencies and identify incomplete structures. This leads the group naturally into thinking about resolving these issues.

The next step is to validate the model through the use of a generated prototype application. The group can "role-play" an instance of the process (essentially, a scenario) and determine:

- If the prototype application will support the process.
- How the process may be affected by the application.
- What the requirements might be for the user interface.

The role-playing sessions are normally repeated in order to test "non-standard" scenarios. In effect, the group is building the business model, rehearsing and re-designing the business process, and designing a suitable user interface, all in one step. While doing this, they are considering only those aspects of the system relevant to them. They learn first-hand about the practicalities of using the system and how it will help or hinder execution of their business process.

The method can be viewed as a form of model-first design (Rosson and Carroll, Chapter 2). However, ABC models are not simply task models; they extend to many aspects of the business.

1.4.2 Experiment

We have carried out an experiment to contrast ABC modeling with conventional object modeling. To this end, ten designers were asked to construct models using either ABC modeling or a conventional form of object modeling, as shown in Table 1.1. Of these, one used both techniques. The object modelers used classes and associations, but novice modelers were not asked to model methods or method invocation. Aggregation and inheritance could be used if desired, but the focus was placed on correctly identifying classes and relating them appropriately.

The object modeling method was intended to be a simplified form of object modeling, which minimized the number of modeling concepts that novices would need to grasp; because it concentrated on classes and associations, it was similar to entity-relationship modeling. In explaining the methods, we avoided the use of any technical terms such as "class," "key," or "inheritance."

The designers worked in ten different organizations and were well versed in the business areas under question. Most were novice designers with relatively little or no prior

TABLE 1.1 Models

Technique	Designer's Experience Level	Group		Number of Models
Conventional object modeling	Inexperienced/novice	1	No experience	2
		2	Some/little experience	3
	Experienced/expert	3	Very experienced	5
ABC modeling	Inexperienced/novice	4	No experience	3
		5	Some/little experience	2
	Experienced/expert	6	Very experienced	4

experience in system design. They were grouped as shown in Table 1.1. In Table 1.1, the groups with "some/little experience" had between one and five years experience in software, of which at least some time had been spent on system design related work. Within each experience level, model size was roughly consistent.

A total of 19 models were constructed, each with roughly five to ten versions reflecting its developmental stages. The models covered various aspects of business in the participating organizations. Every version of each model was analyzed to derive figures for productivity and model quality. The models were subjected to close scrutiny so that their quality could be assessed in a reasonably objective fashion.

To enable measurement, each model was taken through to completion and expert assistance was provided in the final stage so that a "correct" version could be produced. The "correct" version served as a benchmark against which earlier stages could be compared. It was produced after discussion with the relevant designer and represented an agreed final position.

Given the small sample size and the inability to replicate conditions or to exercise control over independent variables, quantitative methods would have been less appropriate and so the main focus of the experiment was on *qualitative* observation of the designers' and modeling group members' actions. This was achieved mainly through participant observation (for example, by the experienced analyst working with the consortium of mobile telephone operators mentioned earlier). Interviews and questionnaires were also used.

The results provided a rich source of insight into how and why designers worked the way they did when creating models and systems. By comparing the large volume of qualitative evidence with the more concise numerical results, a certain amount of triangulation (comparison of results gained by different means) was possible, which helped to form a view of the designers' mental states and intentions. In addition, a secondary study was performed, also for triangulation purposes. Some key observations, both qualitative and quantitative, are outlined in Sections 1.4.3 and 1.4.4.

1.4.3 Qualitative Results

1.4.3.1 Use of Prototypes by Less Experienced Developers

In the experiment we found that designers using ABC modeling fell into two camps:

1. Those who preferred to model first and then work with prototypes.
2. Those who preferred to model and work with prototypes at the same time.

This distinction tended to follow the designers' level of prior IT or systems development experience. Those with little or no prior IT experience generally preferred to combine modeling with prototyping. The small number who were more familiar with professional systems development methods preferred to do their modeling first and produced prototypes only once they had judged the model to be finished.

This meant that the first group made more use of the prototyping facilities than the second group. We cannot be certain why this was the case. Possibly it resulted from the first group not understanding the relationship between a model and a resulting piece of software. In the absence of this knowledge, less experienced designers needed to see the generated user interface to make the meaning of their object model concrete. Those who had previously seen the process through to conclusion already had some insight into the meaning of their object model. They did not need to view a generated user interface to appreciate the significance of the model.

1.4.3.2 Migration of Data between Prototypes

We found that most designers liked to try out prototype applications by using them to enter and modify data. This seemed to be the easiest way they could understand their object models and check whether or not they were correct.

When prototypes are coded by hand, it is easy enough for the developer to carry forward test data from one version to the next. But in our case, the prototypes were automatically generated and the object structure could change quite radically between versions.

Because modeling and prototyping are tightly integrated, a business user can easily make major structural changes to a prototype by modifying the business concept model only slightly. We found that designers were unhappy when they saw that the data they had keyed in was lost after each prototyping iteration. They did not regard the newly generated user interface as a "new" application, but as a modification of the previous version. Therefore, it was counter-intuitive to them that their test data was no longer available. Re-keying test data was seen as onerous, and it discouraged them from proceeding.

Consequently, we have invested some thought in designing a "data migrator" that will intelligently carry forward test data from one prototype to the next, even if major structural changes had been made. Although a completely universal data migrator is difficult to achieve, we noted that a designer will typically focus on one area of a model at a time. This means that, even if parts of a model have been modified significantly, most of the model will remain static over the course of several iterations. Hence, migrating at least some data from one prototype to the next is feasible and not as problematic as it may seem. The data migrator is still under development but is expected to make developing applications easier and quicker.

1.4.3.3 Design Clichés

A third practical issue concerns the role of experience. It is generally agreed that experienced designers tend to reproduce tried and tested design patterns or clichés that they have observed or formulated elsewhere. Their skill lies in seeing the potential for use of these patterns and successfully re-applying them. This is true both of modeling and of user interface design.

Obviously, novice designers without IT backgrounds cannot rely on this kind of prior experience. However, we wanted to find a way in which the knowledge of these less experienced designers could still be useful. At the most basic level, the ABC method forces designers to think not in terms of objects or classes but about people, organizations, documents, places, activities, and so on. These are inherently understandable concepts that a novice designer can relate to without training in system design. It so happens that in our method these elementary business concepts are also the building blocks of applications, and so the designer's existing knowledge about the application domain is useful for system design.

In addition, we tried to help designers by providing access to prefabricated model components that addressed certain standard business situations. For example, standard concepts included products, customers, and orders. At the micro level, prefabricated model components representing data items such as addresses, names, and so on were also provided. These pre-existing components illustrated how to model simply and effectively but, if suitable, could also be pasted directly into models and modified if necessary. Less experienced designers found it useful to observe how others had modeled different situations. With some practice, a designer could quickly construct complex models simply by combining and modifying pre-existing components.

1.4.4 Quantitative Results

We measured the *correctness* (percentage of model concepts defined as required), *completeness* (percentage of required model concepts present), and *complexity* (number of associations per concept) of each model version. We also measured the *productivity* (number of correct model concepts identified per unit design time) and the *error rate* (percentage of changes made to models that were errors) for each designer. In addition, we made a thorough analysis of the relative frequencies of different types of errors made by the designers. Using this information in conjunction with the qualitative observations, we attempted to assess both model quality and the designers' own effectiveness when using each technique.

Space restrictions preclude a full discussion of the quantitative results. However, some of the results of model analysis are plotted in Figure 1.4, which shows figures for productivity and model correctness. We measured correctness simply by comparing each model version with its final, agreed-upon state, which was judged to be acceptable as a reasonable and plausible object model by both designer and experimenter. The correctness of a model version was measured as the percentage of business concepts that it contained from

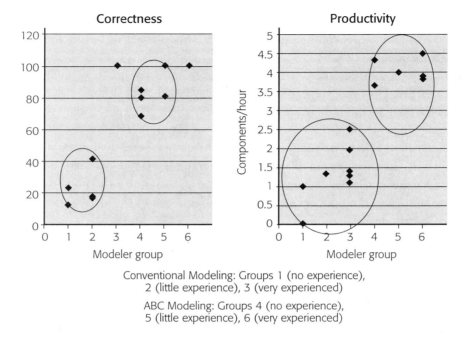

FIGURE 1.4 Model quality and designers' productivity

the final version of the model. For example, a model that referred to three out of the ten business concepts present in the completed version was deemed to be 30 percent correct.

Productivity was measured as the number of "correct" concepts (defined in the same way) captured in unit modeling time. Although not absolute measures, these figures for correctness and productivity provided a convenient and reasonably stable basis for comparing the evolution of models, at least in broadly qualitative ways. The data showed some clear trends.

1.4.4.1 Correctness

For both techniques, the average correctness was closely aligned with the designer's level of prior experience. In other words, the more experienced you are, the more likely you are to produce a model that an expert will judge reasonable and plausible.

The most expert of the designers (who had approximately 15 years of system design and modeling experience) produced models that were essentially 100 percent correct, regardless of which modeling technique was used. In fact, the quality of this designer's work was so high that it was effectively "off the scale." Our measure of quality was ideally suited to measuring the rather large and obvious errors made by novices, but it was far too coarse to register variations in the expert's performance.

Using conventional object modeling, inexperienced designers produced models that were predominantly incorrect (40 percent correct or less, with most worse than 25 percent). Inexperienced designers using ABC modeling produced models that were predominantly correct (65 percent correct or more, with most better than 80 percent).

1.4.4.2 Productivity

Designers using ABC modeling were generally more productive than those using conventional object modeling. Most designers who used conventional object modeling correctly identified concepts at a rate of less than 1.5 per hour. Most designers who used ABC correctly identified concepts at a rate of more than 3.5 per hour.

The most expert designer more than doubled his own productivity when using ABC modeling over conventional object modeling. In fact, almost all of the designers using ABC modeling achieved better productivity than was achieved by the expert designer using conventional modeling (and this included several novice designers with no prior IT experience).

Figures for the other measures of model quality (such as completeness and error rate) exhibited similar trends and so are not reproduced here.

1.4.5 Combining the Results

Observation of the designers in action revealed possible reasons for the observed variance in performance. In particular, it was apparent that the designers using the two techniques adopted different strategies.

Those using ABC modeling tended to adopt an iterative approach in which modeling was interspersed with pauses for interpretation and, for some, frequent generation and testing of the prototype user interface. These designers apparently gained useful insight into their models by virtue of being able to work with the resulting systems, and vice versa.

Designers using conventional object modeling, however, typically did not work in an iterative fashion (regardless of experience level) but simply continued to model until they judged their models to be complete. The least experienced of these designers clearly had little insight into the meanings or the implications of their models and consequently produced models that were in some cases almost incapable of interpretation and were of little use as the basis for prototypes. Perhaps surprisingly, this also applied to the designer in Group 2 (who had some system design experience).

A detailed analysis of modeling patterns confirmed a marked difference in design strategy. All inexperienced designers took time to produce finished models, and the accuracy of the changes they made to models fluctuated from one version to the next, but for those using ABC modeling the trend in accuracy was an improving one. Figure 1.5 illustrates this pattern for an inexperienced ABC designer.

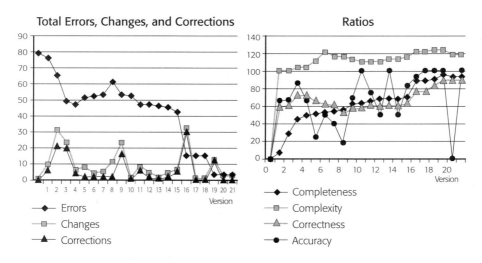

FIGURE 1.5 Typical pattern for an inexperienced designer using ABC modeling

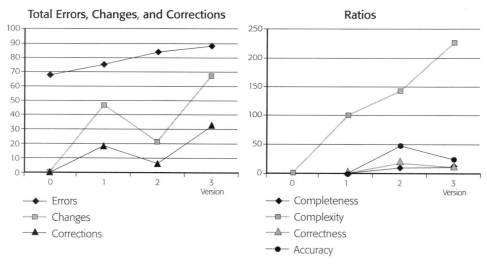

FIGURE 1.6 Typical pattern for an inexperienced designer using conventional object modeling

The typical pattern for an inexperienced designer using conventional object modeling is shown in Figure 1.6. In these models, the error count increases to a point at which the designer either gives up or wrongly judges the model to be complete. Complexity increases until it becomes significantly higher than it should be. Completeness and correctness fail to increase convincingly and may even decline. Accuracy is poor throughout.

According to these limited results, conventional object modeling may be harder than we might think. Even people who have worked in software development for some time turn out to be unable to perform it very successfully when their models are afforded close scrutiny.

1.4.6 Possible Further Research

1.4.6.1 Sampling Model States More Completely

The analysis attempted to measure the total number of changes made to models. However, only a finite number of versions were analyzed for each model. The versions selected for analysis were chosen to be representative of the models' states during modeling. Hence, the analysis is based on a sample of model states rather than the set of all states that each model passed through. It is therefore possible that some changes were missed when consecutive model versions were compared. For example, if a concept was renamed more than once after saving one version but before saving the next, the changes would be reported as a single change. A similar situation would occur if a concept had been deleted but then reinstated between two consecutive model versions.

Completeness, correctness, and error rate were unlikely to have been affected by the sampling of model concepts, because they tended to change slowly between model versions. However, the number of changes per concept may have been affected. To test the sensitivity of this value to the number of model versions, some models were analyzed using large numbers of versions (greater than 40). The results showed that the number of changes per concept was increased, but only by a few percentage points (less than 10 percent).

The best way to test whether a model is complete and lacking in errors is to measure the number of fault reports generated by the resulting application. As CORAS Concept comes to be used in more commercial applications, we will have a greater opportunity to measure its performance in this light, perhaps against published industry metrics.

1.4.6.2 Working with an Increased Sample Size

Only 19 models were fully analyzed as part of the primary study. Analysis of many more models could have provided more reliable evidence, but this was impractical because of the degree of effort involved in setting up the experiment and analyzing models afterward. Instead, the main defense against an unrepresentative sample was to use a secondary study for triangulation and to take care to use all available information when interpreting the results.

In the secondary study, conventional object models were produced by approximately 40 computer science students with introductory-level training in modeling. The results showed completeness figures of 26 to 64 percent, with an overall average of 43 percent.

This compared with an overall average of 35 percent (range 12 to 65 percent) in the main study for inexperienced designers using conventional object modeling.

One might expect the designers in the secondary study to have had some prior aptitude for modeling, both because of their training and because of the fact that they were computer science students. Therefore, the results of the secondary study provide some reassurance that the completeness figures are in the right "ball park." However, again the continuing use of CORAS Concept in commercial environments will afford more opportunity for study across a broad range of circumstances with different application domains and with modelers with different levels of experience.

1.4.6.3 Factoring out the Effects of Designers' Domain Knowledge

It is possible that some designers were hindered by a lack of domain knowledge. In most cases, the designers taking part in the study were already familiar with the relevant business area, having worked in it for months or years. However, Designer J (the most experienced designer) was unfamiliar with the digital mobile telephony industry and was new to the subject organization. In the absence of relevant knowledge about a business area, one can either try to gather information or attempt to model the business area anyway (which is perhaps less advisable). The expert designer chose to gather as much information as possible so that, when the modeling sessions took place, he was in a reasonable position to understand what was said by the group participants.

One model was produced using ABC modeling by the less experienced Designer I, who also was ignorant of the business area in question (investment banking, in this case). Her reaction was to start modeling. She attempted to gather information but did so by consulting general texts that gave only non-specific information. The result was an initial sharp increase in modeling errors, which were corrected only later when a reliable source of information became available (her contact at the investment bank).

We can conclude that bias may well have been introduced because of lack of domain knowledge for one model, but bias was probably not significant for any of the other models. Avoiding this kind of bias is hard because of the difficulty of measuring relevant prior experience levels, but tests with larger populations of modelers might allow skill levels to be matched more reliably.

1.4.6.4 Avoiding the Effects of Variation in Domain "Difficulty"

It would not make sense to compare modeling performance if some of the models in question were inherently more difficult than others. However, rating domain difficulty is not straightforward. It can be argued that most business models are of roughly equal difficulty because they tend to involve stereotypical situations. Business models typically refer to individuals or organizations that carry out business transactions such as ordering, checking, purchasing, and supplying. The kinds of information recorded about people, organizations, and business transactions tend to be quite predictable. Most of the models in this study involve scenarios of this type.

A further argument against the idea of inherent difficulty is that, at any given time, a designer is either creating a single concept (such as a class or an attribute) or relating one concept to another (creating an association between two classes, for example). Viewed in this way, all modeling can be reduced to a succession of similar actions, none of which is significantly easier or more difficult than any other. Provided that the modeling technique itself does not penalize one for having more concepts or more associations, there is no reason why one model should be significantly more difficult than any other of the same size.

However, this ignores the problem of conceptualizing "difficult" concepts. In this study, the models that were arguably more difficult involved non-concrete or conceptual entities in non-trivial ways. It may be less obvious how concepts like these ought to be represented. For example, modeling the structure of business policies or laws arguably requires a greater degree of abstract thought by the designer than, say, purchase order processing. Four models contained significant numbers of conceptual structures of this type. Of these, three were produced by the expert designer, and no discernible differences in performance were observed in comparison with more concrete models. Hence, we can conclude that no significant bias was introduced for these models.

One such model (homeopathic remedies), however, was produced using ABC modeling by an inexperienced designer. The designer experienced some difficulty in deciding how to represent the complex relationships between symptoms and treatments in this model. Significant bias probably was introduced because of the inherent difficulty of the model. Nevertheless, the numerical results do not suggest that the relative difficulty of the topic disadvantaged the designer in any significant way. The number of errors was low, and the productivity was high. This was a small model, which probably helped, because it allowed the model to remain relatively understandable and manageable.

Further experimentation with a wider variety of application domains will help to highlight the role played by variation in application domain complexity.

1.4.6.5 Factoring in Designers' Prior Training and Ability

Designer J had gained many years of experience in producing and reviewing conventional models, but had no experience at all in constructing ABC models. However, the skills were apparently transferable, and J quickly became proficient in the new technique. There is no evidence that Designer J's learning curve affected the quality of the models he produced. Any bias resulting from differences in the expert designer's ability between the two techniques was small.

However, the inexperienced designers' knowledge and skill levels varied considerably. To minimize the impact of this variation, designers were distributed between the two methods in an attempt to balance the mix of skills and knowledge. This seems to have been successful, but its effect is hard to quantify and could have been a source of significant bias.

Bias was probably also introduced when assistance was given to inexperienced designers using conventional object modeling, since they were helped more than those using ABC modeling. It was difficult not to give greater assistance to the inexperienced designers who were using conventional object modeling, because the absence of constraints allowed these designers so great a degree of freedom that they often produced meaningless results (for example, by drastically misusing the object modeling notation).

As modeling progressed, most designers using conventional object modeling remained unaware that their models were significantly incorrect and typically did not ask questions about their models or the modeling technique. In practice, this meant that the experimenters had to take the initiative by pointing out significant errors in the models (but not demonstrating how to fix them), thereby ensuring that the designers were able to get started and go on to generate measurable results.

There was some evidence that designers with intermediate levels of experience (for example, IT professionals with degree-level training and work experience in related areas such as programming or process modeling) found it hardest to come to grips with ABC modeling. They tried to apply design techniques they had learned elsewhere, but they did so inappropriately. In this situation, application of perhaps poorly understood design thinking from "traditional" software design techniques certainly had a negative impact. Further work is clearly needed to investigate how this group can be assisted, and especially how they can be discouraged from applying inappropriate methods.

1.4.6.6 Unbiased Correction of Models

Several of the models were corrected to provide a finished version for comparison. The method of correction is therefore a potential source of bias. Every attempt was made to correct models in a fair and reasonable way, by treating models in both techniques equally. However, whether or not this was successful cannot be proved.

The level of bias introduced in the correction process could be tested by soliciting the opinions of independent experts who are familiar with the relevant modeling techniques. However, there are as yet no independent experts familiar with ABC modeling, so this option would have been impractical in the present study.

An alternative route for further study would be to find a way to restate the models using a common notation, which would allow "blind," and therefore unbiased, correction. This common notation would obviously have to be one that resembled neither conventional object modeling nor ABC modeling. Prose is one possibility.

1.4.6.7 Investigating the Causes of Observed Performance Improvements

In organizational studies it is always possible that observed performance improvements are the results of novelty and observation, as in the classic "Hawthorne Effect" [Roethlisberger and Dickson 1939]. In this study it was certainly the case that Designer J (the most expert designer) became enthusiastic about ABC modeling to the point of wanting to use it to the exclusion of conventional object modeling. Possibly, therefore, the 147 percent productivity improvement observed when he used ABC modeling could have been due in part to this effect. However, this would suggest that the designer normally works at far below his maximum productivity, which seems unlikely.

In the case of inexpert designers, novelty and observation may well have had effects, but they were probably not sources of significant bias because all of the designers were doing something that was relatively new to them. Therefore, the effect, if any, could be expected to apply equally to all inexperienced designers.

1.4.6.8 Other Work

Longer-term experiments may help to investigate the use of ABC modeling in a more in-depth way. For example, use of the models could be studied directly by introducing them into "live" workshops in which the group has responsibility for modeling, with the facilitator observing. Some groups should be allowed to use prototype generation, and others should not; some groups should be told they are being observed, and others should not.

Finally, the experiment described in this chapter did not look in detail into the quality of the resulting prototype applications or user interfaces. Instead, it focused on the modeling process and on the end result of that process. However, the criteria used to judge the models that were produced during the process indicate the likely quality of user interface design. They reflect the extent to which the models are faithful to the end user's own business view, something that is an essential ingredient in any user interface design effort. Further experimentation in which the applications themselves are assessed would help determine the extent to which the improvements obtained in this experiment are reflected in the resulting application designs.

1.5 Conclusion

This chapter has shown how attention to the cognitive aspects of application design can lead to significant improvements in productivity and quality. Software design is often thought of as necessarily a complex activity that requires great expertise. Our experiment has shown that, in the right conditions, non-experts can design useful and usable software applications, of some complexity, more quickly than experts using conventional methods.

The key to empowering non-experts in this way is the principle of *reduced design choice*. Today's standard software design techniques aim to offer the designer maximum flexibility and choice. Choice is usually good, but the problem in software is that absolute flexibility comes at a price. The penalty is twofold. First, design languages must match the expressivity and flexibility of implementation languages (such as C++ and Visual Basic). It must be possible to state in a design anything that can be implemented. This makes design constructs necessarily verbose and complex, because they are general. Second, choice is confusing for the less experienced designer. Psychological research tells us that, to emulate experts, novices need predefined frameworks to guide their thinking, not a universe of possibilities from which to choose.

To make this argument more concrete, consider a situation in which a novice software designer must design a new software application for, say, an insurance company. The relevant business concepts might be insurance policy, broker, underwriter, claim, claimant, and so on. Conventional design methods provide a language for expressing designs but do not favor any particular design style or approach. Therefore our novice designer must first invent or choose an overall design approach; that is, *a way* of deciding which business concepts are represented as classes, windows, tables, and so on, and how these design components should be related to the underlying business concepts. If you can construct classes using any convention, which convention should you choose? If your user interface can take any form at all, what form should it take? These are questions that only expert designers are equipped to answer. But much software is not designed by experts.

We argue that this is too much choice for most software designers to be effective. Before operating systems became as sophisticated as they are today, software designers were free to formulate absolutely any structures they liked and to express them in assembly-language or machine-code programs. But this freedom led to complicated and error-prone programs. The ideas of the file and the directory structure, for example, and even the function and class, were introduced so that programmers would not have to keep inventing them in different forms.

Now we are seeing applications programmers, whose chief aim is to satisfy their users' requirements, having to make the same kinds of low-level architectural decisions about their software structures—database designs, object structures, and user interface designs. In our view, this is wrong. They should not have to make these decisions. There should be standard structures that work well for most situations and that applications programmers can work with. Nobody expects to have to design their own car from the ground up. Why do we expect to have to design every aspect of our own software?

In the late 1980s and early 1990s object orientation was heralded as the brave new way in which software would be constructed. Applications programming, as we knew it, would become a thing of the past. Programmers would construct whole new applications simply by plugging together existing business-level objects that already contained the desired functionality. For instance, if I needed a billing application that knows about customers, invoices, payments, and so on, I would simply have to source relevant objects and assemble them into an application. No programming would be needed.

Needless to say, this bold new vision has failed to materialize. Programmers still work at the lowest level: program code. Objects are now routinely used, but the idea of programmers or even of end users constructing whole applications from components they have selected, without programming, is as far away today as it was in the 1980s.

What went wrong? Obviously, there are many answers to this question and we hope that this book offers some. But in this chapter we argue that a prime cause has been an inappropriate focus on application or task-specific design, as opposed to generic design solutions. What makes one application usable is often what makes another usable, even if they are in widely differing application domains. Good design principles are universal. What changes from one application to the next are the *business concepts*. If we can stop focusing on what makes each specific application usable or well-structured, and start asking how we can encapsulate universal design principles, as CORAS Concept has begun to do, then we stand a chance of automating software design and perhaps even fulfilling the early vision of object orientation.

1.6 References

[Ashworth and Slater 1993] C. Ashworth and L. Slater. *An Introduction to SSADM Version 4.* Maidenhead, UK: McGraw-Hill, 1993.

[Bower et al. 1969] G. H. Bower, M. C. Clark, A. M. Lesgold, and D. Winzenz, Hierarchical Retrieval Schemes in Recall of Categorised Word Lists. *Journal of Verbal Learning and Verbal Behaviour,* 8, 1969, 232–243.

[Cassell and Symon 1994] C. Cassell and G. Symon. Qualitative Research in Work Contexts. In C. Cassell and G. Symon, eds. *Qualitative Methods in Organisation Research.* London: Sage Publications, 1994.

[Collins and Loftus 1975] A. M. Collins and E. F. Loftus. A Spreading Activation Theory of Semantic Processing. *Psychological Review,* 82, 1975, 407–428.

[Connell and Shafer 1995] J. L. Connell and L. Shafer. *Object-Oriented Rapid Prototyping.* Englewood Cliffs, NJ: Prentice Hall, 1995.

[de Brabander and Thiers 1984] B. de Brabander and G. Thiers. Successful Information System Development in Relation to Situational Factors Which Affect Effective Communication Between MIS Users and EDP Specialists. *Management Science,* 30 (2), 1984, 137–155.

[Fischer et al. 1995] G. Fischer, D. Redmiles, L. Williams, G. I. Puhr, A. Aoki, and K. Nakakoji. Beyond Object-Oriented Technology: Where Current Approaches Fall Short. *Human-Computer Interaction,* 10 (1), 1995, 79–119.

[Flores et al. 1988] F. Flores, M. Graves, B. Hartfield, and T. Winograd. Computer Systems and the Design of Organizational Interactions. *ACM Transactions on Office Information Systems,* 6 (2), 1988, 153–172.

[Gentner 1983] D. Gentner. Structure Mapping: A Theoretical Framework for Analogy. *Cognitive Science*, 7, 1983.

[Johnson and Johnson 1994] D. W. Johnson and F. P. Johnson. *Joining Together: Group Theory and Group Skills*. Boston, MA: Allyn and Bacon, 1994.

[Johnson-Laird 1994] P. N. Johnson-Laird. Mental Models and Probabilistic Thinking. *Cognition*, 50, 1994, 189–209.

[Martin 1993] J. Martin. *Extending Information Engineering with Rules and Objects*. White paper, Fairfax, VA: James Martin and Co., 1993.

[McGinnes 1992] S. McGinnes. How Objective Is Object-Oriented Analysis? *Advanced Information Systems Engineering, Proceedings of CAiSE 92*, Manchester, UK, and Berlin: Springer-Verlag, 1992.

[McGinnes 1994] S. McGinnes. CASE Support for Collaborative Modelling: Re-engineering Conceptual Modelling Techniques to Exploit the Potential of CASE Tools. *Software Engineering Journal*, July 1994, 183–189.

[Monk 1998] A. Monk. Lightweight Techniques to Encourage Innovative User Interface Design. In L. E. Wood, ed. *User Interface Design: Bridging the Gap from User Requirements to Design*. Boca Raton, FL: CRC Press, 1998, 1–14.

[Partridge 1996] C. Partridge. *Business Objects: Re-Engineering for Re-Use*. Oxford: Butterworth-Heinemann, 1996.

[Quinlan 1991] P. T. Quinlan. *Connectionism and Psychology: A Psychological Perspective on New Connectionist Research*. Hemel Hempstead, UK: Harvester Wheatsheaf, 1991.

[Roethlisberger and Dickson 1939] F. J. Roethlisberger and W. J. Dickson. *Management and the Worker*. Cambridge, MA: Harvard University Press, 1939.

[Rogers 1994] S. R. Rogers. *Workshop Facilitator Training*. Training Course Notes, London: Business Science and Logic Ltd., 1994.

[Rosson and Sherman 1990] M. B. Rosson and R. A. Sherman. The Cognitive Consequences of Object-Oriented Design. *Human-Computer Interaction*, 5, 1990, 345–379.

[Rumbaugh et al. 1991] J. Rumbaugh, M. Blaha, W. Premerlani, F. Eddy, and W. Lorensen. *Object-Oriented Modelling and Design*. Englewood Cliffs, NJ: Prentice Hall, 1991.

[Sowa 1984] J. F. Sowa. *Conceptual Structures: Information Processing in Mind and Machine*. Reading, MA: Addison-Wesley, 1984.

[Stapleton 1997] J. Stapleton. *Dynamic Systems Development Method*. Reading, MA: Addison-Wesley, 1997.

[van Harmelen et al. 1997] M. van Harmelen, J. Artim, K. Butler, A. Henderson, D. Roberts, M. B. Rosson, J. Tarby, and S. Wilson. Object Models in User Interface Design: CHI 97 Workshop Summary. *SIGCHI Bulletin*, October, 1997.

[Wirfs-Brock et al. 1990] R. Wirfs-Brock, B. Wilkerson, and L. Wiener. *Designing Object-Oriented Software*. Englewood Cliffs, NJ: Prentice Hall, 1990.

[Wood and Silver 1995] J. Wood and D. Silver. *Joint Application Development*. New York, NY: John Wiley and Sons, 1995.

PART II

Scenario- and Task-Based Design

CHAPTER 2
Scenarios, Objects, and Points of View in User Interface Design

Mary Beth Rosson
John M. Carroll

Abstract

We describe relationships between use-oriented and object-oriented analysis in the design of interactive systems. As part of scenario-based design, object-oriented analyses consisting of individual objects' points of view are generated. The object models encourage designers to view task entities metaphorically, which may suggest useful ways in which to elaborate the scenario. Claims analysis helps designers articulate and reason about the usability trade-offs associated with incorporating aspects of the object-oriented analysis into the user interaction scenario.

2.1 Introduction

Traditionally, software design is about procedures. The software designer specifies a flow of data and control and a series of computations that are applied successively. The entities of software in this approach are counters, loops, tests, and branches, arrays, symbols, integers, and real numbers. One of the key difficulties in this approach is learning to render real-world activities as computational procedures. In contrast, object-oriented design is about modeling and simulation. The software designer describes a set of objects—modular bundles of data and behavior—that can interact in specified ways. Indeed, many of the entities of object-oriented software are computational simulations of objects in the real-world domain: cards, decks, hands, players. Thus, instead of iterating through an array of symbols, the software deals a hand. Procedural software is a sequence of steps and conditions; object-oriented software is a model of the application domain [Cox 1986].

There is a significant shift underway in software development methods toward the object-oriented paradigm. Object-oriented design articulates object structures in terms of the interactions—often called collaborations—among the objects. Thus, objects are initially designed as sets of services provided to and received from other objects. Defining software objects in terms of their interfaces to other objects increases the modularity of the objects, thereby making them more reusable and extensible. We are particularly concerned with whether and how taking an object-oriented view of the problem can influence the usability of a system. For the purposes of this discussion, we take a broad view of usability: a *usable* system is one that users experience as useful, easy to learn, easy to use, and satisfying.

2.1.1 Designing with Objects

Rosson and Gold [1989] report the results of a verbal protocol study that illustrates how object-oriented designers approach the task of problem analysis. In their study, experienced programmers developed initial software designs for an online gourmet store. The problem requirements were presented through three sketchy task scenarios: finding the least expensive brand of low-sodium oyster sauce, adding French bread to a standard weekly shopping list, and removing a pound of Brie from the current shopping list. Six Smalltalk experts were asked to produce designs appropriate for implementation in an object-oriented language like Smalltalk or C++.

The six designers directly incorporated many items from the requirements scenarios into their solutions. For example, food items, orders, and shopping lists were included as focal software objects. These objects were not just identified and then modeled. They were actively recruited to the *process* of design reasoning. For example, one designer considered including pricing information in his standard shopping list object until he remembered that item prices frequently change. He concluded that price "belongs" with the item, not with the shopping list. Another designer used the shopping problem context to reason about recipes and concluded that the "shopping view" of a recipe is just the list of required ingredients.

Objects were often enhanced through this process. For example, some of the designers generalized the conventional notion of a shopping list into a preference object that was used to build task-specific shopping list instances. This abstraction was quite productive; it seemed to lead to other preference objects for brands, recipes, and diet. Sometimes the designers took an explicitly anthropomorphic view of the objects they were designing—they analyzed the entities of the shopping situation as communicating, intelligent agents. One designer analyzed the shopping cart as a container of products and explained that it must be able to add and delete these items. He then went on to make the cart even more active by suggesting that it should also be able to deliver itself.

Another designer suggested that the shopping process could be managed by a weekly meal plan. The plan would work with various recipes to determine quantities, and then with household inventory and dietary preferences to build a shopping list. This list, in turn, would work with brand preferences and current sales to produce an order. These metaphoric extensions were sources of both novel design ideas and constraints. Investigating questions like "What *should* a shopping list do?" can lead to a nontraditional understanding of a shopping cart but also to one that is intuitively consistent with real shopping carts and one that, consequently, might be more comprehensible to users and other designers.

2.1.2 Responsibility-Driven Design

A software object encapsulates data and operations on these data. For example, a shopping list might be implemented as an ordered list of shopping list items. Its operations might include adding and deleting list items, accessing items at a particular location, sorting them by name or date, and so on. Indeed, one could practice object-oriented design by specifying objects as data structures along with a set of operations. However, as observed by Wirfs-Brock and Wilkerson [1989], such an approach tends to undermine the modularity of objects. An object's operations will depend on its internal structure, which means that its interactions with other objects will also depend on the details of this structure.

Wirfs-Brock and Wilkerson describe an alternative design method that they term *responsibility-driven design*. In this approach, the designer is encouraged to defer design of the structural details of software objects. Initial design work focuses instead on the relationships among objects, on identifying the objects with which a given object interacts, and on the actions and information for which that object is responsible within those interactions. In the Rosson and Gold [1989] study, the design reasoning that led to the conclusion that item price belonged with the item and not with the shopping list is an example of responsibility-driven design. The items and the shopping list interact within the shopping system scenarios, and thus item price information is required for this interaction. Rosson and Gold's designers reasoned that the items themselves should be responsible for managing this information. The design conclusion was reached without any consideration of the internal structures of the shopping list or the items.

Some discussions of responsibility-driven design have suggested that objects and their responsibilities could be identified directly in requirements documentation by marking all nouns as candidate design objects and all verbs as candidate responsibilities (for example, see Wirfs-Brock et al. [1990], pp. 41 and 62). Wirfs-Brock et al. also suggest analysis of scenarios as a method for identifying responsibilities: "Imagine how the system will be invoked, and go through a variety of scenarios using as many system capabilities as possible. Look for places where something must occur as a result of input to the system. Has this need for action been accounted for? What new responsibilities are implied by this need?" [Wirfs-Brock et al., 1990, p. 62]. As illustrated by the Rosson and Gold study, these questions are often pursued by anthropomorphic reasoning—that is, by thinking of the objects of a software design as a team of intelligent agents working collaboratively.

2.2 Task-Object Interactions in Scenario-Based Design

Over the last decade, we have developed a general framework for scenario-based design (SBD) in which user interaction scenarios play an integrative role in requirements analysis, design, implementation, and evaluation [Carroll 1995, 1999, 2000; Carroll and Rosson 1992, 2000]. In scenario-based design, a *user interaction scenario* is a narrative describing one or more users who are interacting with a system in pursuit of one or more task goals. Importantly, the narrative description does more than list user actions and system responses; it also narrates the users' goals, expectations, and reactions to scenario events. A user interaction scenario describes an instance of the system in use that refers to specific persons, objects, and behaviors in the world, rather than to types of users or to users' roles. This specificity emphasizes that use of the system takes place in the real world; the specificity also gives scenarios a story-like quality that aids communication with end users and other stakeholders in the design project.

User interaction scenarios can be contrasted to *use cases* [Jacobson 1995; Jacobson et al. 1992]. Like scenarios, use cases describe users interacting with systems and aid communication between software designers and their customers. Unlike scenarios, however, use cases are developed as specifications of system functionality. Although project resources or schedules may ultimately constrain use case coverage, the intention is that every important contingency and outcome be illustrated. This tends to produce use cases that are mutually exclusive and that reflect a hierarchical decomposition of system functionality. In contrast, much of the relevance of user interaction scenarios comes from their rich, informal, and open-ended descriptions of real-world practice and experience. In other words, scenarios focus on situations most likely to impact usability. Use cases address functional goals and behavior, whereas user interaction scenarios emphasize the mental experience of the users as they pursue goals.

In scenario-based design, user interaction scenarios may be generated by designers but are typically based on real-life episodes that were captured and analyzed during requirements analysis. Scenarios are discussed and refined throughout system development as a means of representing and reasoning about users' needs and concerns. In this chapter, we discuss the potential interplay between user interaction scenarios and object-oriented analysis and design (see Figure 2.1).

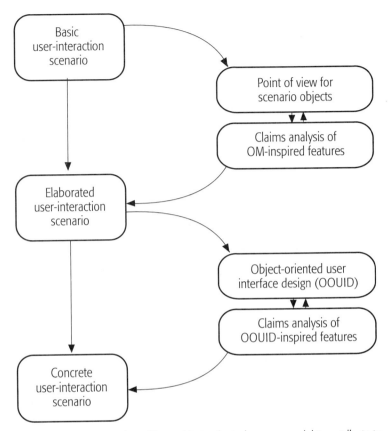

FIGURE 2.1 An overview of how object-oriented concerns might contribute to a scenario-based design process

Scenario-based requirements analysis (along with other development constraints such as technology options, marketing analysis, and so on) leads to a set of basic user interaction scenarios [Carroll and Rosson 2000]. These *basic user interaction scenarios* describe a user's (or users') experience, but only with respect to the basic functionality envisioned for a system, not to the concrete user interactions. In this sense, basic user interaction scenarios are the precursors of a *conceptual-core model,* as described by van Harmelen in Chapter 10.

Many factors contribute to the elaboration of basic user interaction scenarios; here we focus on task features that are inspired by considering problem entities as computational objects. A scenario-specific *object model* is developed for each basic scenario through object-oriented walkthroughs in which software objects are identified and analyzed for their roles in the scenario. This model is represented implicitly through *point-of-view scenarios* (POVs) that describe an object's responsibilities in the scenario, including its collaboration with other objects. In most cases, a POV represents a partial analysis of an object, because any one scenario will exercise only a portion of the object's ultimate functionality. Thus, an overall object model is developed in a distributed fashion across an entire set of scenarios. Importantly for user interaction design, the POV scenarios sometimes suggest new design features, or bits of functionality not yet envisioned for this particular usage situation. These ideas are analyzed using *claims analysis*, wherein positive and negative consequences for users are hypothesized and used as arguments for incorporating or rejecting a feature. The result is a synthesized model in which the initial user-centered scenarios have been extended by considering problem entities from a computational perspective. As the project evolves, the analyzed claims remain as design rationale [Moran and Carroll 1996].

As the design process continues, the basic scenarios are refined into *concrete user interaction scenarios*, which are narratives that include details about what representations users see on the display, how those representations are perceived and understood, how users interact with them, and what feedback is provided in the course of such interactions. Many of these elaborations are motivated by the guidelines and theories of human-computer interaction. However, in *object-oriented user interface design* (OOUID), designers also decide whether and how to emphasize the object-oriented characteristics raised by POV analysis in the concrete scenarios. These decisions are made by discussing their potential impact on the system's *conceptual model*, which is the set of constructs and relationships that designers intend users to learn and use. Claims analysis is again used to hypothesize and discuss these potential impacts.

Several points are worth noting about the analyses and scenario development in Figure 2.1. A variety of "upstream" design techniques can be used to elaborate basic user interaction scenarios (such as metaphor exploration, discovery of new requirements, and participatory design activities [Carroll and Rosson 2000]). Creating object-oriented perspectives on a problem space is just one method for envisioning and organizing system functionality. The same observation holds for development of concrete user interaction scenarios. Thinking about whether and how to convey aspects of an object-oriented model is just one technique for designing user interaction. Furthermore, although scenario-based design emphasizes the evolution from object model to an object-oriented user interface design, these two object-oriented influences may arise independently. For instance, software developers may use POV analysis to explore a software design space and/or to consider users' task requirements but may make no subsequent effort to express the resulting object model in the concrete user interface. A user interface design team may begin with a comprehensive list of system features and proceed to organize those features into an object-oriented conceptual model that will be conveyed through the user interface. Integrating object modeling and user interface design is the general topic of this book; using scenarios, object POVs, and claims analysis to do this integration is the topic of this chapter.

Finally, the activities and relations depicted in Figure 2.1 are just one portion of an overall scenario-based development framework [Carroll 1995, 2000; Carroll and Rosson 2000]. In the larger framework, user interaction scenarios are developed to analyze and synthesize system requirements, explore design ideas in an iterative and incremental fashion, serve as specifications for prototypes at varying levels of completeness, motivate and constrain evaluation activities, and provide design rationale for many development activities.

2.2.1 An Example: The Virtual Science Fair

The remainder of this chapter develops a hypothetical example—a virtual science fair as a vehicle for presenting and discussing the relationship between the design of user interactions and the underlying object model. The virtual science fair is intended to be a complement to traditional science fairs in which students (or groups of students) work on extended science projects and then present them at an event to be judged by experts (typically, individuals drawn from the community). As such, the virtual science fair extends both the concept of what might count as a project exhibit (for example, something elaborated with online content) and the process of carrying out and exhibiting the project (for example, students working together might collaborate online, interact online with a mentor, judge, or parent, and so on). We selected this example for several reasons: it provides a rich and open-ended problem domain but is still likely to be familiar to most readers; it emphasizes the creation, elaboration, and interaction with a variety of online entities, which allows us to examine a range of interactions between object models and usability; and it is one element of our larger community network research project [Carroll and Rosson 1999].

2.2.2 Developing Basic User Interaction Scenarios for the Virtual Science Fair

In scenario-based design, the design process begins by envisioning a set of user interaction scenarios. These scenarios should not be seen as a comprehensive specification of system functionality; rather, the intent is to embed enough functionality within a usage context so that a coherent vision of the user's experience is conveyed. At this early point in development, the user interaction in the scenario is abstract: users' goals and expectations about system functionality are envisioned, including how the system is (or is not) meeting users' needs, but not the interaction techniques used to pursue and evaluate task goals. In this we advocate a position similar to that expressed by Adele Goldberg, who argues for the primacy of application domain models in object-oriented system development [Goldberg 1990].

Table 2.1 summarizes a set of scenarios that lay out some of the functionality envisioned for the virtual science fair. At this very early phase, the design ideas appear as *thumbnail scenarios*, which are high-level descriptions of the users' goals and their actions in pursuit of those goals. Thumbnail scenarios such as these are useful upstream-design representations, because their relatively lightweight character makes them suitable for proposing and sharing the needs of a range of users and task settings. The brevity of these descriptions enables designers to propose and discuss a greater breadth of functionality, but the descriptions also demonstrate how even very brief usage descriptions can offer considerable insight into an emerging design vision.

Although the focus of this chapter is on the relation between object-oriented modeling and user interface design, we should emphasize that the thumbnail scenarios listed here are grounded in a number of requirements analysis and design activities. For example, we observed local science fairs in progress (see Figure 2.2); interviewed teachers and

TABLE 2.1 An Initial Set of Thumbnail Scenarios for the Virtual Science Fair

User Concern	Thumbnail Scenarios
Orienting	A friend from the Seniors' group has told Ms. Simpson about the virtual science fair, and she wonders how she can participate. On her first visit, she finds several projects already online, so she spends some time browsing them and leaving comments for the students.
Search	Jasper is doing a research project on Lyme disease. He visits the virtual science fair to see if he can find pointers to resources already discovered by other students working on science fair projects.
Opportunism	Craig is surfing the Web before starting to cram for his physics midterm. He happens across the virtual science fair, and while browsing notices that a small group (which includes his professor) is online in the physics room. He puts off studying a bit longer and joins the group discussion.
How-to	Marissa and Ben have just drafted their experimental plan for studying the effects of window coatings on heat transfer. They use the virtual science fair to share their plan with Mr. Ferris, their mentor.
How-to	Joelle and her college son Rob are both serving as judges in the virtual science fair. At separate times during judging day, they log in and review, make comments, and assign points to the exhibits. After all the judges have finished, they meet together to combine their scores and make the final decisions.
Reflection	During one visit to the virtual science fair, Susan signed Marissa and Ben's guestbook. When she received an e-mail a few weeks later, she realized that she would be receiving automatic updates about the students' progress on their project.

FIGURE 2.2 A student demonstrating his project to visitors at a high school science fair.

students about project goals and activities; collected and analyzed science fair artifacts; organized and observed student interactions with community mentors; and engaged teachers, students, and community members in open-ended participatory design sessions. We do not have the space to describe all of these activities in this chapter, but several other resources are available for interested readers [Carroll, 2000, Carroll and Rosson 2000, Carroll et al. 1998, Chin et al. 1997, Chin and Rosson 1998].

The listing in Table 2.1 also highlights a *scenario generation heuristic,* which is a general typology of user concerns that we use to encourage broad coverage of different usage situations [Carroll and Rosson 1992]. These categories were abstracted from some of our early work exploring the use of scenarios in the design of interactive learning systems [Carroll and Rosson 1990] and have subsequently been applied to the analysis and design of tasks in other domains (such as programming environments [Rosson and Carroll 1993]).

The first category, Orienting, connotes a user who knows little about an interactive system but wants to learn something about what it is and how he or she might use it. This concern focuses designers on first-time users (in some cases, this may be the first-time use of a subsystem, not of the entire system). The Search category contrasts to Orienting in that it assumes that the user has some beliefs about system functionality that are most often based on experiences with other systems and that the user is trying to find out how to pursue a particular goal. The third category, Opportunism, emphasizes a more casual usage context in which the user has no particular goal but is drawn in by something of "interest" that presents itself. The How-to category captures the most

TABLE 2.2 A Basic User Interaction Scenario

Marissa and Ben Share Their Experimental Plan with Mr. Ferris
After their last discussion with Mr. Ferris, Marissa and Ben have been refining the experimental plan for their science project. Marissa has been researching the independent variables (what window coatings to investigate and how many levels of each), while Ben has been working on the procedures (how to carry out the heat transfer, what to measure). Working mostly at home in the evenings for the last few days, they have updated their shared notebook to summarize their current plan. Last night they were working at the same time and talking about each others' updates. During their discussion they decided that they had gotten far enough that they needed more input from Mr. Ferris. Ben posted a project update; he and Marissa also sent some possible meeting times. The next day, they received a note confirming a meeting that following evening at 8 P.M. When they went to the virtual science fair, Mr. Ferris was already there and they could see that he had already provided some comments on their plan. They greeted him, and then all three talked about his comments, discussed the implications of each point, and refined the plan as they proceeded. At the end of the meeting, they agreed that this plan was sound enough to share.

common usage situation—a user who is familiar with the system and is carrying out a well-understood task. Scenarios from the How-to category are similar to those one might find as examples in a functional specification. The Reflection category directs design attention to features, errors, or other events that trigger users' problem solving and analysis of how the system works.

As design work continues, thumbnail scenarios are elaborated to incorporate more usage context, which provides more details about the users' concerns, such as what they hope to gain from their system interactions and what steps they will take to pursue their goals. However, these elaborations continue to focus on system functionality rather than on user-system interaction techniques. A basic user interaction scenario based on one of the thumbnails from Table 2.1 appears in Table 2.2; in this scenario, Marissa and Ben share their research plan with a community mentor. The remainder of this chapter will develop this particular scenario as an example. Its concern with project management and mentor interactions is fundamental to our overall vision of the virtual science fair, making it a canonical setting in which to consider impacts of an object-oriented perspective. At the same time, it is important to remember that the full analysis and design would depend on the reasoning associated with a *set* of scenarios.

Basic user interaction scenarios share some similarities with *essential use cases*, which are implementation- and technology-free descriptions of user intentions on the one hand, and system responsibilities on the other [Constantine 1995, Constantine and Lockwood 1999] (and see also Chapter 7 in this volume). Like essential use cases, basic scenarios emphasize users' goals by describing system support of these goals in a vague fashion.

One difference appears to be in scope: Use cases analyze a single goal or purpose (such as identifying oneself or downloading notes); this level of analysis is often referred to as the "unit task" in human-computer interaction [Card et al. 1983]. Individual use cases may then be composed into more complex episodes (such as getting class notes [Noble et al., 1999]). User interaction scenarios are less modular and often include multiple actors with interrelated goals. The actors interact with a system over an extended period of time, and there is no further decomposition into subtasks. Essential use cases are elaborated by modeling the relationships among cases, for example, by adding indications of contingent or synchronous subtasks. The elaboration of user interaction scenarios may imply these abstract relationships (for example, Table 2.2 indicates that Marissa and Ben are able to work concurrently on a shared document), but the emphasis is on enriching the *usage context* to envision more completely what requests are being made to the system, why they are being made, and how the system should respond to them.

2.2.3 Elaborating Virtual Science Fair Scenarios with an Object Perspective

At this point, we might simply continue to elaborate the virtual science fair scenarios by adding more details about system functionality and at the same time beginning to add concrete user interaction techniques [Carroll 1995]. However, this initial design phase is also an opportune time to consider the potential interplay between user-oriented and object-oriented views of the scenarios. In prior work, we have discussed the consequences of considering salient problem entities as computational objects and then taking individual objects' POVs as a sort of object-specific scenario "walkthrough" [Rosson 1999; Rosson and Carroll 1995a, 1995b]. The resulting POVs may suggest new system features that could enhance the users' experience.

The POV technique was motivated by the empirical study of Rosson and Gold [1989]; it also built on the Class Responsibility Collaborators (CRC) technique [Beck and Cunningham 1989]. CRC uses pencil and paper to record the responsibilities and collaborators analyzed for a class. The CRC technique explicitly encourages the tendency of designers to anthropomorphize or metaphorically extend their design objects and makes it a technique for exploring object interactions in scenario contexts.

Our adaptation of the CRC technique situates POV analysis within a usage context relevant to the problem domain [Carroll et al., 1994, Robertson et al., 1994]. A POV creates an object-specific version of a user-oriented scenario by narrating how it is "experienced" by a hypothetical software object. This analysis deliberately shifts designers from a real-world user-centric perspective to a metaphoric computational perspective. The use of a first-person viewpoint in POVs encourages designers to *anthropomorphize* objects and their behaviors as a heuristic for "thinking" about what the objects could or

TABLE 2.3 High-Level Scenario Objects with Brief POV Scenarios

Scenario Object	Point-of-View Scenarios
Virtual science fair	I gave Marissa and Ben the project. When the project told me that it had been updated, I helped it send out a notice. Later, I set up an online discussion. When the project was updated again, I helped it send out another notice.
Mr. Ferris	I gave Mr. Ferris's e-mail address to the notice. Later, I provided his mark to the comments. When the meeting began, I told it what color Mr. Ferris likes to use for his contributions to the discussion.
Marissa (or Ben)	I provided Marissa's icon to show where she was working. When she and Ben talked, I told the chat what color to use. Later, I told the calendar about Marissa's current commitments. A few days later, I gave her e-mail address to a notice. When the meeting began, I told the meeting what color to use for Marissa's input.
Science project	As Marissa and Ben worked, I provided access to my parts. When Ben told me about the update, I worked with the virtual science fair to send out a notice to Mr. Ferris. Later, I again allowed viewing and editing of some of my sections. When I was told to publish, I worked with the virtual science fair to send out a general interest notice.
Experimental plan	I accepted and displayed text describing the experiment. Marissa gave me text to put in my independent variables part, and Ben gave me text for procedures. Later, I accepted some comments from Mr. Ferris. I displayed the comments with his information. During the meeting, I took more input for my parts.
Shared notebook	I presented the project, first checking to see that Marissa and Ben were authors. As they worked, I checked to see if each part was available for editing or only for viewing and presented them appropriately. Later, I gave access to Mr. Ferris and worked again to coordinate viewing and editing.
Marissa-Ben chat	I was launched and given Marissa and Ben as participants. I got their colors and then kept track of who typed what by showing each participant's text with his or her nickname at the beginning and in the appropriate color.
Meeting times	I took a list of meeting days and times. I gave this information to the calendar.
Notice	I was created and given Mr. Ferris as a recipient and an update notice as my content. I got the e-mail from virtual science fair and created a note. Then I sent it to myself.
Comments	I was created by Mr. Ferris, and so I kept track of him and where he placed me. When the project wanted to display me, I told it where I should be. I displayed Mr. Ferris's mark until I was opened, and then I displayed my text.

should do to support the users in this particular scenario (see Table 2.3). Earlier, we described how Rosson and Gold [1989] observed expert object-oriented designers engaging in such reasoning to brainstorm initial design ideas; here we simply make this process more explicit and systematic.

Creating a POV scenario can help a software designer construct an initial analysis of the attributes and responsibilities of individual objects.[1] For example, how much management responsibility should be given to the virtual science fair? Is it simply a "traffic cop" whose role is to provide connections as needed between its components (users, e-mail, discussions, projects)? Are there any special jobs it should or could take on in this situation (for example, storing user profiles or managing the interface between the virtual science fair and other network systems)? Should individual projects know which user is viewing or editing which section, or should that be delegated to the shared notebook tool? Although many of these questions are relevant largely to software design, we are arguing that raising such questions *in the context of a user scenario* may lead designers to consider how different sorts of computational objects might influence what *users* will be able to do with the system.

Like CRC cards, POV analysis can bring to light "hidden objects." This technique helps designers find objects that other objects assume or interact with, when such objects are not obvious in the original description. On occasion, high-level objects may be discovered. The calendar is an example: although the basic scenario did not mention a calendar, the meeting time's POV made it clear that it was part of a more complex object that manages meeting times. More commonly, POV analysis will uncover objects needed in a support role. For example, the students browse Mr. Ferris's comments, but it is through the comment POV that we see how it will work with an attribute of Mr. Ferris's surrogate object (his "mark") to display itself appropriately.

To some extent, POV analysis can be seen as a first step toward developing the software that will implement the design being developed, because the designers end up with a rough object model that might ultimately be refined and built as a piece of software [Rosson 1999; Rosson and Carroll 1993, 1995a]. Here, though, our focus is on how object modeling might impact the ongoing development of the user interaction scenarios.

Each POV should be considered for its implications concerning users' interactions with the system. For example, the meeting time object's POV suggested a calendar object. If we now add a calendar to the object model, what might it add to users' task options? Should typical calendar functions (such as automatic scheduling and reminders) be added to the system vision? The POV for Mr. Ferris's comments suggests that a comment keeps track of who wrote it. Can we imagine ways that such information could enhance virtual science fair tasks? Generating POVs for key problem entities in the virtual science fair

---

[1] Note that we have finessed the issue of "which objects" in this analysis. The identification of candidate objects is clearly a key problem in object-oriented analysis and design but we do not have the space to discuss this here. Our general approach builds on the "underline the nouns" strategy suggested by Wirfs-Brock and others, but we bring in heuristics aimed at focusing first on the objects most important to the user's experience.

scenarios encourages designers to consider what a "helpful" science project (online discussion, mentor comment, and so on) "could" or "should" contribute to the user experience. Importantly, this reasoning takes place within a particular usage context, because it places implicit *use*-oriented constraints on the nature of the computation-oriented "innovations" that might be proposed.

Note that even though POV analysis has introduced some objects in charge of user interface services (the chat and the shared notebook, for example), the POV for these objects is still deliberately ambiguous with respect to concrete user interaction details. For now, the notebook simply says that it presents the project components "appropriately," thus leaving open how this will be implemented. This absence reflects the emphasis of this phase on basic functionality. Although interaction details could clearly be proposed at this point, our concern is that they would quickly become complex and would distract from this early analysis of *what* the system should do.

Our treatment of the virtual science fair end users in this analysis is also worth noting. The POV reasoning clearly shifts attention away from the real-world users. Instead, in this example we raise the possibility of "surrogate" users (Melissa, Ben, and Mr. Ferris in Table 2.3) who take responsibility for some of the end users' concerns as the activities take place. We do not mean to imply that the real users are of no interest at this point, because it is the real users' perspectives, after all, that the user interaction scenarios promote. However, the intent of POV analysis is to introduce a *computational* perspective into the user experience described by the scenario. Analyzing the possible role(s) of user surrogates through POV analysis is one way for designers to consider whether adding a computational "presence" for users has implications for system usability.

2.2.4 Trade-offs Suggested by Objects and Their POVs

POV analysis encourages designers to adopt object-oriented views of basic user interaction scenarios in order to explore whether this perspective suggests ways in which the system might better meet users' needs. However, the usability implications of scenario-based reasoning are often only implicit. Designers must be careful not to incorporate object model inspired features too readily into their design solutions (for example, if they are software engineers with an "object-oriented bias") or reject object model inspired features without consideration (for example, if they are user interface designers with an "anti-anthropomorphism bias"). In SBD, we use claims analysis to surface and document the usage implications of proposed design features. Claims analysis calls out features of a design that have usability consequences and makes these consequences explicit through trade-off analysis [Carroll and Rosson 1992]. Claims are similar to the Question-Option-Criteria (QOC) structures from design space analysis [MacLean et al. 1991], in which options correspond roughly to features and criteria correspond to the positive and negative consequences. A key difference is that claims analysis is motivated by specific usage situations, whereas QOC analysis begins with a general design question. Like QOC analysis, claims analysis forces designers to confront the trade-offs in design, because the designers always pit positive implications ("upsides," prefixed with "+" in Table 2.4) against negative implications ("downsides," prefixed with "–").

Table 2.4 lists claims for some of the design features that were inspired by POV analysis. Note that the intent of claims analysis is not to consider *every* design feature and its possible consequences but rather to identify features with significant usability implications. Claims analysis is an *intrinsic evaluation* method in that it analyzes the essential features of

TABLE 2.4 Examples of Usability Trade-offs to Consider in Light of POV Analysis

Scenario Feature	Possible Upsides (+) and Downsides (–) of Scenario Feature
Surrogate users for Mr. Ferris, Marissa, and Ben	+ Centralizes users' preferences for task-related activities. – Users (or their delegates) must create and maintain the information.
Project that manages plan and other parts	+ Emphasizes inherent structure of a science project. + Encourages flexible (for example, part-specific) viewing and handling. – May seem more complex or intimidating than a flat structure.
Project as a "sender" of an update notice	+ Simplifies frequent or well-known communication tasks. + Emphasizes the communication possibilities of online documents. – May conflict with users' current understanding of projects. – Decreases feeling of control over communication tasks. – Limits opportunities for exception-handling (for example, specialized notes).
Notebook as manager of project access	+ Emphasizes separation of a project's management from its content. + May promote attention to access and authorization concerns. – Merges content and presentation in the physical world.
Shared calendar for planning meetings	+ Simplifies task of collecting multiple related constraints. + May encourage opportunistic collaboration (for example, noticing free time). – Users (or their delegates) must input calendar data. – Users may not want to publicize all scheduling constraints.
Notice that sends itself	+ Minimizes network-related actions and knowledge required of user. – May result in suboptimal or even incorrect routing.
Comments that track position and author	+ Provides orienting and evaluative data about comments. + May suggest that comments can contribute in other task-relevant ways (for example, conveying seriousness or recency). – Adds to the complexity of the project viewing task. – Scales poorly to the case of many different commentators.

an artifact rather than observing the artifact in use [Scriven 1967]. As an analytic method, it depends greatly on the biases and expertise of the analyst. Thus, an expert in computer-supported cooperative work might analyze virtual science fair claims related to sharing and coordination, whereas a cognitive psychologist might instead raise issues relating to learning, metaphor, task planning, and so on. Like analytic methods in general, the validity of the claims is only as good as the evidence that can be adduced from them, either through logical argument or by references to prior art. Indeed, each upside or downside of a claim should be understood as a hypothesis that is useful for discussion but ultimately subject to empirical testing. Claims analysis has been used for reasoning about design trade-offs in general [Carroll 1995, 1996, 2000]. Here we focus on trade-offs that result from taking an object-oriented perspective on the functionality to be offered by a system.

Claims such as those in Table 2.4 are a usability-oriented counterpart to object model inspired design ideas. For example, deciding to include a project entity that is responsible for sending out status notices is a big step. A project entity such as this extends the naive model of science projects as containers of information (that is, as rendered on paper or other physical artifacts); it also simplifies user interaction by eliminating a portion of the updating task. But is this task simplification and conceptual extension worth the possible confusion or loss of control that comes along with it? Is a calendar tool that coordinates a group's schedule information worth the effort of inputting and maintaining the calendar data? Is the task structure provided by decomposing a project into parts worth the additional complexity it brings to the conceptual model? Will users be comfortable with comments that maintain some "intelligence" about who created them?

Claims analysis requires designers to consider *what-if scenarios,* which are variants of a scenario that highlights a different set of upsides or downsides than those that are apparent in the current design proposal. In claims analysis, each feature must be considered with respect not only to its reasons *for* inclusion but also to its reasons *against* inclusion. For example, the mentor scenario has an update notice that is automatically routed to Mr. Ferris. But what if Marissa and Ben happened to know that Mr. Ferris is now on a trip and using a relative's e-mail address for a few days? How would they ensure that the notice was delivered correctly? Raising a competing scenario such as this highlights the downside of making the notice responsible for sending itself.

In some cases, what-if scenarios may lead to significant revisions of a design. For instance, we may decide to remove the automated notice routing if we believe that recipient contact information will be unreliable, or we may introduce new scenarios (for example, we may develop a scenario in which Mr. Ferris sets up a forwarding address). Later in development, some of the questions raised in claims analysis might also be tested empirically, perhaps with an interactive prototype that implements one or more design scenarios. But even at this very early point in development, a scenario presents a sample usage context in which to "try out" a feature so as to better anticipate its possible impact on users. The claims are simply used to document the central trade-offs considered during these design deliberations.[2]

2.2.5 User Interactions in the Virtual Science Fair Scenarios

An implicit product of POV analysis is an object-oriented model of the emerging design. This is an instance-based model that includes candidate software objects, behaviors, and inter-object relationships (that is, as components or collaborators). Guided by claims analysis, design features suggested by the object model are incorporated into the user interaction scenarios with claims used to document any new usability concerns these additions may raise. As the design focus shifts to concrete user interaction techniques, the designers must now decide whether and how to convey object-oriented characteristics through the user interface.

In object-oriented user interface design (OOUID), designers deliberately explore techniques that emphasize the object-oriented character of the conceptual model. Of course, there will be many other contributing factors. User interface designers consider general or domain-specific guidelines, novel interaction technologies, constraints arising from existing systems or delivery platforms, and so on. Object-oriented user interface design is simply one more perspective to draw on in reasoning about the user interaction experience. What are the usability implications of conveying an object-oriented conceptual model? Will users' comprehension of such a model promote effective use? If the latter, how best can it be conveyed?

A traditional usability concern has been the mismatch between a user's ultimate understanding of a system (his or her *mental model*) and the actual conceptual model on which the system is based. Norman characterizes this mismatch as the "gulfs" of execution and evaluation [Norman 1986]. See also Chapter 10. Thus, the design of an effective conceptual model that will then be conveyed by the system is a key task for user interface designers. In earlier work, we have argued that object-oriented modeling may provide an important unifying function if it can simultaneously contribute to the design of the software and the conceptual model [Rosson and Alpert 1990]. However, simply producing an "object-oriented conceptual model" will not be sufficient; it is critical that user interface designers carefully consider *which* object-oriented characteristics of task objects or services will be most useful to users pursuing task goals. User interface elements can then be given affordances and interactive behaviors that suggest these capabilities and relationships.

---

[2] Clearly, many other trade-offs must be considered along with usability. For example, some design features will have implications for software complexity or maintainability. Such issues can be analyzed as nonfunctional requirements along with usability concerns [Mylopoulos et al. 1992].

Choosing to express object-oriented characteristics through the user interface is not an either-or decision. Using scenarios, designers can think about which portions of the object model will be beneficial if understood by the user, and which are more likely instead to complicate or confuse users' development of effective mental models. Designers must then consider how best to convey the beneficial characteristics while hiding the confusing ones. As with any user interface design effort, the ultimate goal is to guide users toward mental models that are consistent, flexible, and useful in achieving task goals. Learning the details of how a calendar object iterates through its meeting time parts is probably unnecessary for this purpose.

Table 2.5 presents a version of the mentor-interaction scenario elaborated to include concrete user interaction details. Some of these details simply offer a physical rendering of object behavior described earlier with more abstract terminology. For example, a smiley face is specified as Ben's identifying "mark." Other details have been added to suggest the active nature of scenario objects. For example, the fact that Marissa drags Ben's smiley face over to the chat tool to launch a session with him implies that these two objects know how to initiate a chat session. Similarly, dragging the notebook over to Mr. Ferris's icon to send him an update implies an intelligent interaction of these two objects, because the project can work out what Mr. Ferris needs to see. As with object modeling, on occasion object-oriented user interface design will suggest new responsibilities for existing objects. For example, in reasoning about how to launch the text chat, we extended Marissa's user-surrogate object to store information about her chat preferences. Finally, some design features inspired through the earlier object model will be hidden. For example, the user interface does not distinguish between the science project and the notebook the students use to interact with the projects. The conceptual distinction between the project data and its interactive view was not of sufficient benefit to warrant the additional complexity.

Also, as with object modeling, an object-oriented user interface design reasoning process may introduce new entities into the conceptual model. As a scenario is elaborated, there may be a need to support user actions that are not specified until interaction details are considered. For example, the basic user interaction scenario indicated that Marissa and Ben followed up on each other's work. But although POV analysis suggested that projects keep track of their own updates, it was our thinking about when and how the students would check on these updates that inspired a new user interface object (the message board) with the job of presenting this information. Use of this summary view is more lightweight than forcing the students to open and examine each project component. Similarly, working through the details of publishing a general update notice caused us to realize that an "interested parties" object could simplify the process of notifying the right users.

TABLE 2.5 A Concrete User Interaction Scenario

Marissa and Ben Share Their Experimental Plan with Mr. Ferris

After their last discussion with Mr. Ferris, Marissa and Ben have been refining the experimental plan for their science project. Marissa has been researching the independent variables (which window coatings to investigate and how many levels of each), while Ben has been working on the procedures (how to carry out the heat transfer, what to measure). Working mostly at home in the evenings for the last few days, they have updated their shared notebook to summarize their current plan. When Marissa logged into the project last night, she typed in her school user name and password as usual. The shared notebook appeared and was opened to the independent variables page, just as she had left it the day before. Over to the side, the message board showed which project pages she had changed in the last few days. She saw some messages with Ben's smiley face, so she saw that he too had been busy updating pages dealing with their procedures. She was glad to see that Ben was online (his icon in the project team list was animated). Mr. Ferris, however, was not online. She dragged Ben's smiley face over to the chat tool to start it up. As they typed messages, the chat reflected her preferences for chats. No names or icons were appended to each line, but it was easy to see who was who by looking at the two font colors. Marissa browsed Ben's pages (and vice versa) as they explained their updates. They decided that they were close to "going public" with their plan, but they wanted to get one last set of comments from Mr. Ferris. Ben collapsed the notebook and dragged it up to Mr. Ferris's icon; he then OK'd the confirmation message, which told him that an e-mail summarizing the updates was being sent to Mr. Ferris. Both he and Marissa opened the group calendar and selected some times over the next few evenings when they might meet.

The next day, Marissa and Ben received an e-mail message confirming a meeting the following night at 8 P.M. When Marissa logged in, she saw from their icons that Ben and Mr. Ferris were already there and that Mr. Ferris had already added comments to several pages. Ben launched a three-way video conference, because he knew that Mr. Ferris preferred this to the text chat (he wanted to see by their faces if they really understood his comments). They started at the beginning of the notebook and paged through the whole document, double-clicking to open each comment marked by Mr. Ferris's goofy Einstein icon to make sure they understood what he meant. Mr. Ferris left after a few minutes, and the two students made some finishing touches on their respective sections.

Finally, they decided to publish their plan. Marissa dragged the collapsed notebook icon to the crowd icon in their project team. She knew this would have an up-to-date list of virtual science fair members who had signed up as interested parties. As she dragged the notebook over the crowd icon, she and Ben saw from the feedback that the list had grown from eight to ten individuals. She released the icon and OK'd the message that would tell everyone that their project Web site had been updated.

As we mentioned earlier, considering whether and how to express an object model in a user interface is just one heuristic device to use in elaborating basic user interaction scenarios. The scenario in Table 2.5 reflects the impact of several more traditional usability concerns. For example, using the same images to identify online presence, updates in the activity log, and comments in the project text enhances the system's internal consistency by using a single visual representation for the same underlying concept (the user surrogate) in different settings. Marissa's ability to use her normal userid improves consistency and integration with other computer-based activities. The status information in the message board addresses awareness issues associated with computer-supported cooperative work [Dourish and Bellotti 1992].

The scenario in Table 2.5 is still missing many details. A calendar tool is now part of the user experience, but the interaction details for this particular tool have yet to be specified. As the virtual science fair project proceeds, such details may be added to this scenario, although many small details will not be decided until a physical prototype is constructed. It is not necessary to expand every scenario to specify the details of every subtask. With respect to the calendar, it may be more useful to feature it in a scenario requiring a more extended scheduling task, such as a situation in which several users are entering preferred (or blocked) times. Scenario-based design does not assume that any one scenario will provoke design thinking about all aspects of the problem space it touches; rather, we assume that elaboration of a **set** of scenarios (see Table 2.1) is needed to analyze and address different but overlapping aspects of the problem.

Earlier, we mentioned that object-oriented user interface design does not require designers to take an object-oriented view of the problem from the beginning of the project. Suppose, for instance, that the virtual science fair user interface designers are given a complete functional specification for describing the science projects to be supported, collaboration support, messaging, and so on. The designers might choose to recast this specification in terms of objects and actions by building an object-oriented conceptual model to which they would then apply an object-oriented user interface design process. Indeed, such a process might evoke some of the same reasoning that we discussed earlier in object modeling, perhaps by extending system functionality as well as pointing to effective user interaction techniques. The problem, of course, is that once basic functionality has been specified, there may be little opportunity to explore possible extensions or modifications. Furthermore, even if designers take an object-oriented perspective throughout, they will benefit from focusing separately on the object model and the object-oriented user interface design. The separation will lead them to emphasize "pure" functionality at the earliest phases of project development. This will allow them to consider object model inspired features at a time when significant design changes are still possible.

2.2.6 Trade-offs in Object-Oriented User Interaction

The addition of concrete interaction details to a scenario raises new sets of usage trade-offs that should also be made explicit as claims. Note that many of these trade-offs can be viewed as "descendents" of claims developed during POV analysis (see Table 2.4). For example, the animated smiley face was designed to suggest an intelligent surrogate-user object. Here, however, the claims emphasize the object-oriented perspective that the designers have applied to their concrete decisions about the representation and manipulation of model objects and actions. In this sense, the earlier claims can be seen as documenting interaction *possibilities*. The claims in Table 2.6 document how these possibilities will be communicated through actual elements of the user interface.

TABLE 2.6 Claims Associated with User Interface Design Features Inspired by Object-Oriented User Interface Design

UI Feature	Possible Upsides (+) and Downsides (−) of UI Feature
Smiley face used to identify all aspects of Ben's participation	+ Simplifies the user interface by limiting overall number of elements. + Emphasizes the uniqueness of individuals within the system. − Users may want their different roles to be visually distinct.
Animated smiley face	+ Emphasizes the active nature of the user-surrogate object. − May distract the user from more important task activities.
A message board that displays a synthesized log of project changes	+ Provides a single convenient site for evaluating update activity. − Creates a (spatial) distinction between a project and its updates. − Users may rely too much on the update notices (that is, on not reviewing the actual changes).
Dragging icons over chat tool to start a session (and dragging project icons to user surrogates to send updates)	+ Reinforces the direct manipulation of task-related objects. + Implies that these are intelligent objects cooperating in the task. − New users may not realize that the tools will know how to respond.
Close coupling of the project and notebook	+ Integrates project management and content development. − May imply that the project is just what is seen in the notebook.
Crowd icon representing interested parties list	+ Reinforces a larger "community" view of the activity. + Reminds the students of an audience waiting to interact with them. − A "waiting public" may be intimidating at times.
List size feedback appears when notebook is dragged to crowd icon	+ Helps users predict what will happen as the result of the operation. + Reinforces the active (communicating) nature of the crowd object. − The feedback may be distracting and interfere (for example, if user notices that the crowd size has changed).

Many trade-offs are introduced by taking an object-oriented perspective on user interaction. Electing to include user surrogates in the object model created the general possibility for user customization and preference-setting. But these opportunities could have been provided *without* emphasizing to users the active object metaphor implicit in the computational model (for example, by designing a preference dialog independent of other activity). The scenario in Table 2.5 instead conveys an object-oriented view. The unique visual representation reminds users that each of them has his or her own internal representation in the system. Using this visual element to mark all aspects of an individual's system "presence" conveys the broad contributions of this computational entity; animating the icon reinforces its active nature. But emphasizing such characteristics is not entirely positive, because animation used to convey an active entity may be distracting. Marissa's initiation of a chat session by dragging the smiley face to the chat tool reinforces a notion of cooperating objects, but Marissa may not be able to tell by looking at the two icons that they can interact in this way. Again, the user and situational details of the scenario help designers to reason through these trade-offs in refining the design.

Claims analysis is offered as an analytical evaluation technique, but it can also be used to guide subsequent *usability studies,* which are empirical tests of users' work with, and reactions to, the design ideas [Carroll 2000]. For example, the VSF design team might have low confidence in the relative weights of the upsides and downsides of the animated icon claim, and the team might decide to test the validity of their reasoning with representative users. Such a test can be carried out very early in system development if a concrete design artifact can be created. The artifact itself might be very rough (for example, a set of transparencies that display rough sketches of proposed displays supporting a task), or it might be more refined (for instance, an interactive prototype developed with rapid prototyping tools; see, for example, Chapter 1).

Table 2.6 also documents the reasoning behind the decision to merge the project and notebook objects. As in our earlier claims analysis of the POV-inspired ideas, we considered the implications of conveying this distinction by using what-if scenarios that highlighted various upsides and downsides of project-notebook collaboration. Ultimately, we decided that the downsides outweighed the upsides. Separating the presentation and manipulation of the project and the collaborative notebook would require more actions by Marissa and Ben. This separation also does not map well to the way students currently work with projects. However, once we made this decision, it was important to note the trade-offs that resulted. Thus, the students will now encounter a single "interactive project" object, but they may be less likely to predict other behaviors of the project (such as its sending of updates to the message board).

It is particularly important to analyze the trade-offs arising from new objects that emerge in object-oriented user interface design. For example, a message board was introduced to summarize project updates. But introducing this new object reinforces the conceptual distinction between the project and its update history. It is important to note this effect and to keep it in mind as scenario development continues. Similarly, the interested parties object that was introduced as an aid to project sharing has its own sets of upsides (such as emphasizing the community nature of the system or adding intelligence to the notification process) and downsides (for instance, the students may be intimidated or distracted by the constant reminder of this list or by changes in its composition).

2.3 Discussion

We have suggested that taking an object perspective during the design of interactive systems can guide elaboration of basic user interaction scenarios. Using the VSF as an example problem, we have shown how the metaphor of objects as active and responsible computational entities can guide designers in thinking about (a) new types of functionality that can enhance the users' experience and (b) whether or not to communicate an OM through elements of a user interface and how to do so. In the balance of this chapter, we speculate more broadly about the implications of this approach. We close with a brief summary of work on tools developed to support scenario-based design.

2.3.1 Model-First Design

SBD is an example of model-first design [Goldberg 1990]. System functionality is envisioned *prior* to the design and analysis of the appearance and detailed behavior of the user interface. This can be contrasted to approaches based on the rapid prototyping of user interaction. Constructing visual, interactive prototypes can help to evoke and evaluate conceptual models for a system, particularly if carried out early in development, in participation with end-users (see Chapters 1 and 10). However, such prototyping should be done with caution, because it can also promote attention to graphical representations, screen layout, and the details of user input and output events. We are concerned that an early emphasis on concrete user interaction may lead designers to 1) miss opportunities raised by more abstract computational models of the problem domain; 2) lead to premature commitments to specific visual representations or interaction techniques; or 3) produce attractive interactive prototypes that end users like but that cannot be implemented. If a design team first develops a "noninteractive" conceptual model, it can then be used to motivate selection of appropriate user interface techniques as well as guide software development.

The aim of first emphasizing a coherent object model highlights an important issue. How can designers ensure that the set of scenarios they select and elaborate will together comprise a complete and consistent task model? By nature, a scenario directs design attention to the *particulars* of the user experience described. Claims analysis yields a somewhat more abstract view (that is, it uses what-if reasoning to associate key features with a range of possible consequences). The concrete, informal, and open-ended character of a user interaction scenario is critical to its function as a source of reflection, but at the same time it is an obstacle to a more abstract and formal model that might, for instance, enable consistency checking [Carroll 1999].

This problem has no simple solution. Ultimately, a design team must decide whether the rich and usage-oriented perspective provided by user interaction scenarios is valuable enough to accept the cost of reduced formality. Of course, in many organizational contexts, scenarios will be recruited as just one of various design representations (see Chapter 9 for some survey results). Scenario-based design can easily be combined with other methods, with the caveat that other, perhaps more formal methods not be allowed to "muffle" the impact of scenario-based reasoning. POV analysis also helps designers to reason more systematically about scenarios. When designers analyze and merge the responsibilities of the same (or the same class of) object across different scenarios, they add coherence to the object model. In the virtual science fair example, analyzing different instances of the user-profile object within or across scenarios, or considering different activities in which a science project participates, helps to promote consistency and coherence across the design.

2.3.2 Refining the Object Metaphor

The characterization of a "good" object model is multifaceted. We emphasize responsibility assignment, because this is a good summary of what the expert designers in Rosson and Gold [1989] seemed to do, and it has become an accepted part of object-oriented analysis and design practice. However, giving objects the right responsibilities is just one feature of an effective design. In current work, we have begun to consider whether a more articulated view of the object-oriented perspective would provide additional power in understanding the interplay between OMs and user interface design.

Some of the attributes that we are now exploring include autonomy, encapsulation, delegation, collaboration, classification, inheritance, and polymorphism [Booch 1994, Coad et al. 1997]. The first four in this list—autonomy, encapsulation, delegation, and collaboration—are related to the general notion of object responsibilities. A responsible object takes actions when needed; it protects access to its internal parts and relies on those parts to implement requests for services, and it works with other objects as necessary to carry out complex tasks. The other three characteristics—classification, inheritance, and polymorphism—are related instead to the software abstractions used to implement object models. The concrete objects analyzed in scenarios are classified to create useful abstractions. The functionality of these abstractions is factored across an inheritance hierarchy of superclasses and specializations. A well-designed hierarchy includes polymorphic behavioral abstractions through which individual classes implement specialized versions of a generic behavior.

Given this more refined analysis of object modeling desiderata, we can consider how each characteristic might impact scenario-based design. Indeed, some of these concerns are already apparent in the virtual science fair example. For instance, the user-profile POV conveyed a sense of autonomy in that Ben's profile object took the initiative to "announce" its presence (see Table 2.3). The user interface elaboration emphasized this active nature by animating the icon, and by involving it in interactions with other task objects (see Table 2.6). The subparts of a project are encapsulated within the project itself. Although we did not examine scenarios involving concrete interactions with these subparts, we can assume that they will appear to be contained within the project itself.

Other design attributes suggest more extensive object-oriented reasoning: Ben, Marissa, and Mr. Ferris are all represented in the VSF through their user profiles, and the object model would represent these as instances of the same abstraction. POV analysis does not produce object abstractions (it is specifically object-based), but it is certainly reasonable to annotate these POVs to indicate that they share an abstraction. (Indeed, in Table 2.3 we focused on the Marissa object while implying that much of the POV also applies to Ben.) During object-oriented user interface design, such an abstraction could be demonstrated by giving all instances a similar look and feel. User icons might be required to have a minimal degree of visual similarity while still having some degree of personalization.

At the same time, we might conclude that Mr. Ferris's profile in fact instantiates a different abstraction (that is, assuming that the services provided by a mentor's profile differ from those of students' profiles). Such a decision is modeled naturally by inheritance, wherein mentor profiles and student profiles both specialize a generic virtual science fair participant profile. In this case, developing a corresponding user interface distinction would be a challenge, and the insight it provides into the object model is probably not worth the effort or added complexity.

The last feature in the list—polymorphism—appears in pervasive user interaction techniques such as selection feedback. An example from the virtual science fair scenarios is the differential feedback provided by Mr. Ferris's icon and the crowd icon when the notebook is dragged over them (see Table 2.6). The crowd is not an individual user profile but rather a list, and it reminds the students of this by displaying its size. Analysis of the underlying object represented by the two icons, and of what constitutes "helpful" behavior by these objects, points to an effective application of polymorphism in this scenario.

The analyses suggested in this section would extend the general process summarized in Section 2.2 and in Figure 2.1. They further articulate how designers might apply an object-oriented perspective to the design of user interaction scenarios [Collins 1995]. Thus, designers would consider not just how a "responsible" conceptual-level object should behave but also to what extent a design should reflect concepts like inheritance or polymorphism. However, encouraging designers to carry out these more detailed analyses would add significant effort to a scenario-based reasoning process that is already complex. It is by no means clear that the extra analytic power would be worth the added effort. We are currently exploring the usefulness of the more refined analysis in design education when first introducing designers to the potential interplay of software and user-oriented perspectives [Rosson 2000].

2.3.3 Tools for Scenario-Based Design

An important practical issue for scenario-based design is the management of a large and evolving set of qualitative analyses. Even the small example presented in this chapter requires considerable textual description and includes many relationships among scenarios, objects, POVs, and claims. On the one hand, we can simply leave with designers the responsibility for developing, maintaining, and evaluating a coherent set of scenarios and associated analyses. On the other hand, if we do not also provide them with tools for managing this work, their chances of success are greatly diminished.

In other work, we have developed the Scenario Browser, a tool for supporting some aspects of scenario-based design for the case of Smalltalk application development [Rosson and Carroll 1993, 1995a, 1995b; Rosson 1999]. The Scenario Browser provides simple hypertextual tools for creating and editing a set of user interaction scenarios (organized by the typology described in Section 2.2.2; see Table 2.1) and for creating the associated POV and claims analyses (Figure 2.3).

The Scenario Browser provides some support for consistency management. POVs in the Scenario Browser include a specification of parts and of collaboration relationships among objects (for example, an introductory overview is part of a project, and a project collaborates with a user profile to produce a custom update). These logical relationships among objects can be graphed, either for a single scenario or across groups of scenarios. The graphs help designers see if objects are being used in a consistent fashion within and across scenarios. When a designer identifies an object in POV analysis, the Scenario Browser provides an alert if this name has been used in other scenarios. The analyst can then decide whether she or he is in fact modeling the same object at this point.

The Scenario Browser also supports later phases of software development through its tools for instance-centered development [Gold and Rosson 1991, Rosson and Carroll 1993]. After developing POVs for a scenario, the analyst can classify each object as an instance of a class that will be used during implementation (through either reuse or construction). Some or all of an object's attributes and behaviors can be implemented at any point. As multiple objects are implemented, a scenario-specific prototype begins to emerge. Depending on how much code is developed (or reused), such a prototype may involve the model objects only (such as a science project that collaborates with a notice

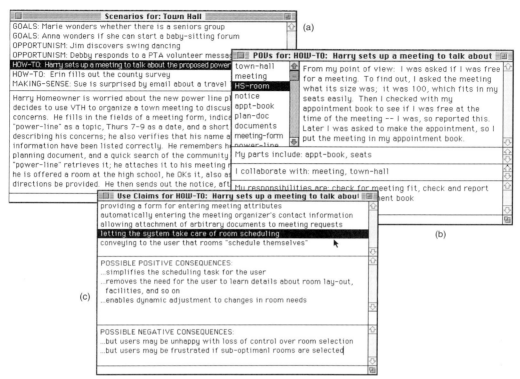

FIGURE 2.3 Some of the major tools provided by the Scenario Browser environment. (a) Scenario view, with list of user-interaction scenarios that can be edited as simple text. (b) POVs for selected scenario. (c) Claims editor used to identify features (upper pane) hypothesized to have both positive (middle pane) and negative (lower pane) impacts on the user's task.

class to create a notice initialized with the right information), or it may involve interactive objects (such as an interactive notebook that can be used by actual end users).

Claims analysis is again used to think about design decisions, but in this case it focuses on the trade-offs implicit in implementation decisions. These trade-offs are then used to refine or transform the OM, user scenarios, and so on. Throughout, refinement of the software abstractions takes place *within the usage contexts* that motivated their development in the first place.

To this point, the Scenario Browser has been used only for exploratory Smalltalk programming projects. We do not yet know whether it would be useful in large-scale software development projects. However, similar hypertextual tools have been successfully deployed in commercial environments [Kaindl 1997]. It seems clear that some level of tool support will be critical to the success of qualitative, analysis-intensive methods like scenario-based design.

2.4 Conclusion

We have explored the possible contributions that an object-oriented perspective might make in user interface design. Our example has demonstrated how analyzing the responsibilities of objects in scenarios can suggest enhancements to users' tasks. We have further demonstrated how claims analysis can aid in reasoning about the trade-offs associated with object-oriented task features. An object-oriented perspective can also play a role in the selection and application of user interface details to the task scenarios by encouraging the user interface designer to reflect on how much of an object model to reveal to users through their perception and manipulation of user interface elements. Claims analysis can again be used to capture and think about these implications for user-system interaction. Taking an object perspective on user scenarios helps designers organize users' tasks in terms of salient problem domain entities and their relationships. At the same time, the computational metaphor can help to extend a task model beyond the one currently implied by the problem domain. Finally, the parallel development of an object model and associated user interaction techniques may reduce the gap between the conceptual model implied by the user interface and the software that implements a design.

2.5 References

[Beck and Cunningham 1989] K. Beck and W. Cunningham. A Laboratory for Teaching Object-Oriented Thinking. *Proceedings of OOPSLA '89*. New York: ACM/SIGPLAN, 1989, 1–6.

[Booch 1994] G. Booch. *Object-Oriented Design with Applications*. 2nd Ed, Reading, MA: Addison-Wesley, 1994.

[Card et al. 1983] S. K. Card, T. P. Moran, and A. Newell. *The Psychology of Human Computer Interaction*. Hillsdale, NJ: Lawrence Erlbaum Associates, 1983.

[Carroll 1995] J. M. Carroll. Introduction: The Scenario Perspective on System Development. In J. M. Carroll, ed. *Scenario-Based Design: Envisioning Work and Technology in System Design*. New York: John Wiley and Sons, 1995, 309–336.

[Carroll 1996] J. M. Carroll. Becoming Social: Expanding Scenario-Based Approaches in HCI. *Behaviour and Information Technology*, 15 (4), 1996, 266–275.

[Carroll 1999] J. M. Carroll. Five Reasons for Scenario-Based Design. *Proceedings of the 32nd Hawaii International Conference on the System Sciences*, Los Alamitos, CA: IEEE Computer Society, 1999 (published as CD-ROM).

[Carroll 2000] J. M. Carroll. *Making Use: Scenario-Based Design of Human-Computer Interactions*. Cambridge, MA: MIT Press, 2000.

[Carroll and Rosson 1990] J. M. Carroll and M. B. Rosson. Human-Computer Interaction Scenarios as a Design Representation. In B. D. Shriver, ed. *Proceedings Volume II of HICSS-23: 23rd Hawaii International Conference on System Sciences, Software Track*. Los Alamitos, CA: IEEE Computer Society, 1990, 555–561.

[Carroll and Rosson 1992] J. M. Carroll and M. B. Rosson. Getting Around the Task-Artifact Cycle: How to Make Claims and Design by Scenario. *ACM Transactions on Information Systems,* 10 (2), 1992, 181–212.

[Carroll and Rosson 1994] J. M. Carroll and M. B. Rosson. Putting Metaphors to Work. In *Proceedings of Graphics Interface: GI '94,* Toronto: Canadian Information Processing Society, 1994, 112–119.

[Carroll and Rosson 1999] J. M. Carroll and M. B. Rosson. The Neighborhood School in the Global Village. *IEEE Technology and Society,* 17 (4), Winter 1998/1999, 4–9, 44.

[Carroll and Rosson 2000] J. M. Carroll and M. B. Rosson. Scenario-Based Usability Engineering. Notes from tutorial presented at *CHI 2000,* The Hague, Netherlands: ACM, April 2000.

[Carroll et al. 1994] J. M. Carroll, R. L. Mack, S. P. Robertson, and M. B. Rosson. Binding Objects to Scenarios of Use. *International Journal of Human-Computer Studies,* 41 (1), 1994, 243–276.

[Carroll et al. 1998] J. M. Carroll, M. B. Rosson, G. Chin, and J. Koenemann. Requirements Development in Scenario-Based Design. *IEEE Transactions on Software Engineering,* 24 (12), 1998, 1156–1170.

[Chin and Rosson 1998] G. Chin and M. B. Rosson. Progressive Design: Staged Evolution of Scenarios in the Design of a Collaborative Science Learning Environment. In *Proceedings of Human Factors in Computing Systems, CHI '98 Conference,* New York: ACM, 1998, 611–618.

[Chin et al. 1997] G. Chin, M. B. Rosson, and J. M. Carroll. Participatory Analysis: Shared Development of Requirements from Scenarios. In *Proceedings of Human Factors in Computing Systems, CHI '97 Conference,* New York: ACM, 1997, 162–169.

[Coad et al. 1997] P. Coad, D. North, and M. Mayfield. *Object Models: Strategies, Patterns, and Applications.* Upper Saddle River, NJ: Prentice Hall, 1997.

[Collins 1995] D. Collins. *Designing Object-Oriented User Interfaces.* Reading, MA: Addison-Wesley, 1995.

[Constantine 1995] L. L. Constantine. Essential Modeling: Use Cases for User Interfaces. *Interactions,* April 1995, 33–46.

[Constantine and Lockwood 1999] L. L. Constantine and L. A. D. Lockwood. *Software for Use: A Practical Guide to the Models and Methods of Usage-Centered Design.* Reading, MA: Addison-Wesley, 1999.

[Cox 1986] B. Cox. *Object Oriented Programming: An Evolutionary Approach.* Reading, MA: Addison-Wesley, 1986.

[Dourish and Bellotti 1992] P. Dourish and V. Bellotti. Awareness and Coordination in Shared Workspaces. In *Proceedings of the ACM CSCW '92 Conference on Computer Supported Cooperative Work,* New York: ACM, 1992, 107–113.

[Gold and Rosson 1991] E. Gold and M. B. Rosson. Portia: An Instance-Centered Environment for Smalltalk. In *Proceedings of OOPSLA '91: Conference on Object-Oriented Programming Systems, Languages, and Applications,* New York: ACM, 1991, 62–74.

[Goldberg 1990] A. Goldberg. Information Models, Views, and Controllers. *Dr. Dobb's Journal,* 66, 1990, 54–61.

[Jacobson 1995] I. Jacobson. The Use-Case Construct in Object-Oriented Software Engineering. In J. M. Carroll, ed. *Scenario-Based Design: Envisioning Work and Technology in System Design*. New York: John Wiley and Sons, 1995, 309–336.

[Jacobson et al. 1992] I. Jacobson, M. Christersson, P. Jonsson, and G. Övergaard. *Object-Oriented Software Engineering—A Use-Case Driven Approach*. Reading, MA: Addison-Wesley, 1992.

[Kaindl 1997] H. Kaindl. A Practical Approach to Combining Requirements Definition and Object-Oriented Analysis. *Annals of Software Engineering,* 3, 1997, 319–343.

[MacLean et al. 1991] A. MacLean, R. Young, V. Bellotti, and T. Moran. Questions, Options, and Criteria: Elements of Design Space Analysis. *Human-Computer Interaction,* 6 (3 and 4), 1991, 201–250.

[Moran and Carroll 1996] T. Moran and J. M. Carroll. *Design Rationale: Concepts, Methods and Techniques*. Hillsdale, NJ: Lawrence Erlbaum Associates, 1996.

[Mylopoulos et al. 1992] J. Mylopoulos, L. Chung and B. Nixon. Representing and Using Non-functional Requirements: A Process-Oriented Approach. *IEEE Transactions on Software Engineering,* 18 (6), 1992, 483–497.

[Noble et al. 1999] J. Noble, L. Constantine, and L. Lockwood. Usage-Centered Design with Essential Use Cases. Notes from tutorial presented at *OOPSLA '99,* Denver, 1999.

[Norman 1986] D. A. Norman. Cognitive Engineering. In D. A. Norman and S. Draper, eds. *User-Centered System Design*. Hillsdale, NJ: Lawrence Erlbaum Associates, 1986, 31–61.

[Robertson et al. 1994] S. R. Robertson, J. M. Carroll, R. L. Mack, M. B. Rosson, S. R. Alpert, and J. Koenemann-Belliveau. ODE: A Self-Guided, Scenario-Based Learning Environment for Object-Oriented Design Principles. In *Proceedings of OOPSLA '94: Conference on Object-Oriented Programming Systems, Languages, and Applications,* New York: ACM, 1994 51–64.

[Rosson 1999] M. B. Rosson. Integrating Development of Task and Object Models. *Communications of the ACM,* 42 (1), 1999, 49–56.

[Rosson 2000] M. B. Rosson. Object-Oriented Design of User Interfaces. Tutorial presented at *ECOOP 2000,* Sophia-Anatoles and Cannes, France, 2000.

[Rosson and Alpert 1990] M. B. Rosson and S. R. Alpert. The Cognitive Consequences of Object-Oriented Design. *Human-Computer Interaction,* 5 (1), 1990, 345–379.

[Rosson and Carroll 1993] M. B. Rosson and J. M. Carroll. Extending the Task-Artifact Framework. In R. Hartson and D. Hix, eds. *Advances in Human-Computer Interaction*. New York: Ablex, 1993, 31–57.

[Rosson and Carroll 1995a] M. B. Rosson and J. M. Carroll. Integrating Task and Software Development in Object-Oriented Applications. In *Proceedings of Human Factors in Computing Systems: CHI '95,* New York: ACM Press, 1995, 377–384.

[Rosson and Carroll 1995b] M. B. Rosson and J. M. Carroll. Narrowing the Gap Between Specification and Implementation in Object-Oriented Development. In J. M. Carroll, ed. *Scenario-Based Design: Envisioning Work and Technology in System Development*. New York: John Wiley and Sons, 1995, 247–278.

[Rosson and Gold 1989] M. B. Rosson and E. Gold. Problem-Solution Mapping in Object-Oriented Design. In N. Meyrowitz, ed. *Proceedings of OOPSLA '89: Conference on Object-Oriented Programming Systems, Languages, and Applications.* New York: ACM, 1989, 7–10.

[Scriven 1967] M. Scriven. The Methodology of Evaluation. In R. Tyler, R. Gagne, and M. Scriven, eds. *Perspectives of Curriculum Evaluation.* Chicago: Rand McNally, 1967, 39–83.

[Wirfs-Brock 1995] R. Wirfs-Brock. Designing Objects and Their Interactions: A Brief Look at Responsibility-Driven Design. In J. M. Carroll, ed. *Scenario-Based Design: Envisioning Work and Technology in System Development.* New York: John Wiley and Sons, 1995, 337–360.

[Wirfs-Brock and Wilkerson 1989] R. Wirfs-Brock and B. Wilkerson. Object-Oriented Design: A Responsibility-Driven Approach. In N. Meyrowitz, ed. *Proceedings of OOPSLA '89: Conference on Object-Oriented Programming Systems, Languages, and Applications.* New York: ACM, 1989, 71–76.

[Wirfs-Brock et al. 1990] R. Wirfs-Brock, B. Wilkerson, and L. Wiener. *Designing Object-Oriented Software.* Englewood Cliffs, NJ: Prentice Hall, 1990.

CHAPTER 3
Designing with Idiom

Mark van Harmelen

Abstract

Idiom is an object model based interactive system design method that supports the design of system scope, content, functionality, and interactivity. The method encompasses scenario generation; task modeling and description; referent identification; construction of object models of the system domain, the system core and its user interface; and concrete user interface design.

The design process involves visualizing the system and its envisioned use, abstracting models of user behavior and system content and functionality, using these models to systematically design and model significant aspects of the user interface, and using the system and user interface models to design the concrete user interface. These activities (and others) are performed in an interative and opportunistically ordered fashion to accommodate the (mutual) informing, discovery, and learning that characterizes interactive system design.

The current version of Idiom, described here, provides significant support for interactive system designers over and above the more specification-oriented features of an earlier version of Idiom.

3.1 Introduction

Idiom is a design method that incorporates both user interface and object modeling techniques. The development of Idiom started in 1991; the method was later used in several small projects and one larger project (ten people for one year). After the method was described [van Harmelen 1994], the development of Idiom was suspended. In 1997, the method was presented at a CHI workshop [van Harmelen et al. 1997] on object modeling and user interface design, and as a result of strands that arose there, Idiom was redesigned during 1999. Changes included introducing much more support for interactive system designers during the early stages of design, and development of a systematic way of identifying task execution spaces and the objects needed for support of user tasks in such spaces. This chapter describes the development of Idiom circa 1999 and represents a rational reconstruction of a single experimental design study, together with conclusions from that study.

The new Idiom has subsequently been used, with greater emphasis on participative design and paper prototyping than is recorded here, for an Idiom tool support project where two designers worked together, sometimes in participatory design sessions with users, for one month. This was followed by a one-person, seven-month implementation phase.

Having been influenced by a rigorous model-based specification method [Jones 1986], the previous emphasis in Idiom was largely on system and user interface specification rather than on support of the activities of interactive system designers. The current enhancements to Idiom incorporate design techniques that reflect modern human-computer interaction (HCI) design practice, particularly emphasizing scenario- and task-based design. The description provided here is a snapshot of a second stage in the development of the method. As such, it does not incorporate descriptions of participatory design techniques or field studies. Both participatory design and some kind of contextual data gathering process need to be formally introduced into the method in the near future.

The development of the first version of Idiom (called Idiom94 here) was driven by two observations. The first observation was that besides expressing the core functionality of a proposed system, object models can also convey significant amounts of detail about the interactivity of the system. Object-oriented specifications of core functionality and interactivity are useful in recording and conveying design information during an interactive system design and serve as references during implementation. The second observation was that it is possible to link renditions of proposed user interactions with the object models explicitly, using pre- and post-conditions over the model state, sometimes in combination with invariants over the model state.

As originally developed, Idiom94 did the following:

- It covered the design of both the core and interactive facilities of an interactive system.
- It accommodated the mutual informing that occurs during user interface design.
- It used graphical and object modeling notations for its modeling component and for specifications of user interaction.
- It bound (task analysis-based) user interaction to the object model using pre- and post-conditions.
- It allowed different degrees of formality in its models and conditions over those models.
- It was designed for use in specifying interactive system scope, content, interactivity, and concrete user interface for systems which were to be implemented with a graphical and/or windowed user interface.

In response to Idiom94's emphasis on interactive system *description and specification*, the current version adds methodological support for *design*, particularly by increasing the emphasis on upstream user-centered design activities.[1] In addition, some of Idiom94's more formal specification-based approach is removed. Idiom still retains Idiom94's model-based approach to designing and describing interactive systems.

The next section presents a general introduction to and description of Idiom. Sections 3.3 to 3.7 illustrate the use of Idiom, and Section 3.8 presents conclusions and discusses some of the structure of the method.

3.2 Idiom

Figure 3.1 shows the design activities that make up Idiom, together with arrows indicating the major paths through which activities provide informing design data to other activities. Activities can be and are performed in an interleaved fashion. There is a notion of a completion order to activities, roughly downward in the middle and right of Figure 3.1. Idiom accommodates opportunistic design practices and informing and iterative design. In *opportunist design*, design activities are chosen on the basis of prior experience with similar situations and on the basis of new design opportunities provided by discoveries made during ongoing design. Design opportunities occur in problems characterized by ambiguity, ill-formedness, and multiple sources of knowledge. These are all characteristics of early interactive system design. Multiple sources of knowledge characterize much, if not all, of interactive system design activities. The process in which one activity provides design information as input to another is known as *informing;* activities that supply information to each other are *mutually informing* [Henderson 1991]. *Iterative design* occurs when a designer repeats a design activity, often in light of new knowledge about the design problem. The new knowledge might, for example, have been generated by another design activity, as a result of a user evaluating a prototype, or as a result of a designer reframing the design problem.

The overall process of using Idiom includes the following:

- User categorization, scenario generation, and task modeling as a basis for further user interface design work.
- Construction of domain and core models. The choice of types (classes)[2] for these models is based on the objects that are required for task performance. Design of the core model is conceptual design in many user interface design methods.

---

[1] User-centered design is described in Chapter 10.

[2] In some object-oriented circles, "type" is used where "class" might normally be used. A *class* describes or specifies the implementation of a type level construct. Any type may be implemented using one of a number of equivalent classes. Use of this distinction here serves to underline the abstract—or essential [Cook and Daniels 1994, Fowler 1997, Constantine and Lockwood 1999] (and see also Chapter 7 in this volume)—nature of some of Idiom's object models.

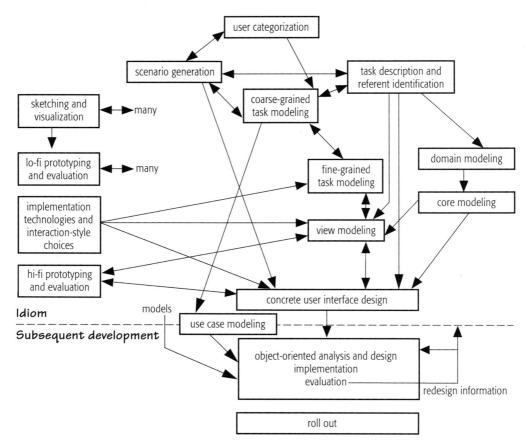

FIGURE 3.1 Design activities and major information flows in Idiom, together with subsequent development activities

- Construction of the view model, an abstract specification of the component parts of views, and of how views are dynamically created and destroyed. The view model is derived from the task model and the core model. Views provide the context for task execution. In a windowed environment, views are implemented as windows.
- Design of the concrete details of the user interface to the interactive system within the constraints of the choice of a particular implementation platform and interaction style. The resulting concrete user interface design includes the user-perceivable representations of objects in the core model, how the user interacts with these representations, selection mechanisms and their use, commands and their means of invocation, dynamic feedback during interactive

operations, interaction techniques,[3] cursor design, screen/window/panel layout, and error and exception handling. The design hopefully includes a help system design, user documentation, and perhaps training aids.
- Development of prototypes of the system and evaluation of those prototypes. The evaluation is a formative evaluation, where the evaluation informs redesign.

Together, the view model and the concrete user interface design specify the design of the user interface, and are, together with the task and core models, primary inputs to the rest of the development process. If the development employs use cases, these can be generated from the task model before development activities start.

The following object models, shown in Figure 3.2, are used in Idiom.

- The *domain model* specifies the application domain that is of interest to the users and designers.
- The domain model is the basis for the *core system model* (or, simply, the *core model*) of the computer system that is being designed; the types in the core

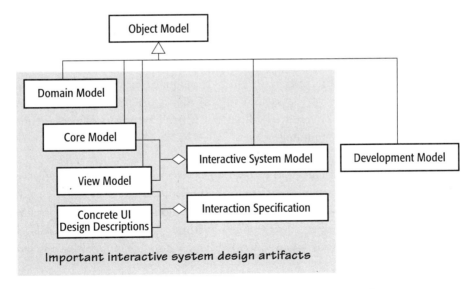

FIGURE 3.2 Some models in Idiom (task models not shown here)

---

[3] An *interaction technique* is a means of transforming user input into a form that can be used in a program. Examples include menus, palettes, text fields, buttons, sliders, and so on. Interaction techniques may be chosen from an existing set offered, for example, by a style guide or they may be designed from scratch.

model are close to a subset of those in the domain model. Core modeling has similarities to conceptual design, system analysis, and object-oriented analysis.
- The types in the domain and core models represent referents (objects used by users in their task-based behavior) that are important to users in their (future) task-based behavior in the application domain.
- The type definitions in the core model must eventually contain operations that correspond to abstractions of user interactions.
■ The core model is augmented with a *view model,* which specifies aspects of user interaction with the system. The view model, combined with non-object-oriented user interface design artifacts, forms part of a larger *interaction specification.*
- The use of the term "view model" does not imply limitations only to the design of GUIs; in Idiom, a view is simply a modeling construct that is useful in designing presentation and interaction.
■ Together, the core and view models form the *interactive system model.*
■ Idiom also includes an extra object model that is not used in the method, but exists to emphasize the abstract nature of the previously mentioned models. The *development model* is a derivation of the interactive system model that preserves the interaction specification while adding extra detail needed for system implementation purposes. The development model may go through several derivation steps en route to the final model of the implementation. The process of development modeling can be usefully thought of as the construction of object-oriented models of the system for (a) object-oriented analysis (OOA) activities that are not covered by Idiom and (b) all technical object-oriented design level (OOD-level) modeling.

Within any design-implementation-evaluation cycle in Idiom, the completion order for modeling is first the domain model, then the system and interaction models, and then the development model(s). The process of development modeling may be performed with any development method, object development methods being more compatible with Idiom than with other methods. Consequently, the development model is shown as an object model in Figure 3.2.

The general emphasis in the domain, core, and view models is on the structural view [OMG 1999] of the system. Taking a formal point of view, Idiom does not use an approach based on internal interactions (message passing) within these models. Rather, Idiom uses a model-based specification approach with optional pre- and post-conditions to specify the dynamic behavior of the system in response to user interactions. Message passing can subsequently be used to depict internal model and system behavior, thereby allowing the possibility of a smooth transition to fully developed OOA models. Use cases are not used; instead a task model is used to describe envisioned user behavior. Use cases can be easily produced from task information to ensure compatibility with conventional use case based object-oriented analysis and development (OOAD). Finally, notwithstanding Idiom's eschewal of internal interactions for design purposes, it is assumed that the normal way of ensuring consistency and viability of object models, analysis of dynamic behavior, and generation of UML interaction diagrams, would be performed as a background activity, *if* needed.

3.3 Designing and Specifying User Interfaces with Idiom

In what follows, the use of Idiom is illustrated by the partial development of an example. Design activities are divided into early design-related work and early design, later abstract design, and later concrete design.

- "Early" design-related work characterizes users, their tasks, and the application domain. Early design work includes exploring early ideas and visions of the system (see Section 3.4).
- "Later" abstract design is concerned with designing and abstractly specifying the interactive system, including its core structure and aspects of its user interface, the latter by developing a view model (see Section 3.5).
- "Later" concrete design is concerned with designing, describing, and specifying the detail of the concrete user interface design (see Section 3.6).

This time- and abstraction-based division is only one of convenience; activities may be ordered concurrently and opportunistically. It is likely that (a) system visualization is performed throughout the design cycle, (b) the "early" work will be revised later on, and (c) abstract and concrete design activities will be interleaved while the abstract structure is being firmed up.

To illustrate both Idiom's process of design and the resultant design artifacts, an example of an Internet-based chat system is developed in the next three sections. A simple and open-ended specification for this system is that the chat program enables users to communicate by typing messages to each other in the context of conversations that they initiate, participate in, and leave. The example illustrates the design of a single user's user interface to a distributed multi-user system.

This example was in an application area in which the author/designer had not used applications since using primitive UNIX chat utilities. It was felt that working in an unknown domain and choosing representative future users who were not current chat system users might illuminate interesting properties of Idiom when the final design was compared with current chat systems such as ICQ and Instant Messenger. For related experimental reasons there was a conscious decision to avoid some activities that would *normally* be part of good user interface design practice—namely, observation of the use of existing systems, discussions with existing users, and use of prototypes by existing users. Results show that these are essential activities: without performing them, there is a strong risk of not supporting the current activities of existing users.

In addition, the example has a development model that expresses a client-server architecture that, for users of the chat service, need not be considered in the domain, core, and view models. This serves to emphasize the fact that Idiom is concerned with the users' experience of the system, rather than the invisible implementation architecture and technology.[4]

3.4 Early Work with Users and the Domain

Seven mutually informing activities take place in parallel during the early stages of the design: user categorization and profiling activities, scenario generation, building of a relatively coarse-grained task model, task description and referent identification, early domain modeling, generation of design sketches, and generation and evaluation of low-fidelity prototypes. User categorization and profiling is not discussed except for a consideration of its consequences in Sections 3.4.2, 3.4.5, and 3.5.1, and low-fidelity prototypes are not discussed, except for a brief mention in Section 3.6.2.

Throughout much of the early design activities, there is a strong emphasis on opportunistic design practice while seeking to avoid over-commitment to early design artifacts. Some of the early design activities are concerned with finding visions and paths for the design—sometimes by looking in detail at the real world and sometimes through the formulation of tentative and partial design solutions that might be very concrete in nature. Subsequent early design activities abstract away from these details. Later, in Section 3.5, the resultant abstract models are used to systematically develop aspects of the user interface design. The processes of abstraction and subsequent model-based design can help in avoiding the retention of early concrete design ideas that might limit the concrete user interface design. In practice, this process must, at the least, be accompanied by user evaluation of the developing design.

---

[4] Of course, this paints an ideal picture. Implementation technology may have a profound effect on the user interface. In the chat example, a user might not, as a result of some temporary conditions, be able to communicate with other users. However, the effect of this can be expressed in the concrete design in relatively simple terms without delving into implementation technicalities. For example, if a server is down, "Sorry, I can't reach Sushila and Tom at the moment, shall I try later?" Problems are likely to arise in cases where underlying technology is inappropriately exposed to users; this is to be avoided if at all possible.

Early on, it is often a challenge to formulate abstract descriptions; sometimes it is easier to adopt the design tactic of formulating a description that includes some less than desirably abstract detail, and then to remove the non-abstract detail.

3.4.1 Scenario Generation

In Idiom, *scenarios* are stories, natural language descriptions of use of the system, written in user terms and language. Since scenarios are expressed in user language, they may be written, reviewed, and modified by both users and designers. Scenarios can be constructed for identified types of users, or scenario data can inform the identification of user types in user profiling activities. Scenarios can be written to capture user goals, expectations, and some of the context in which the users work. Scenarios can also be used for requirements capture, for illustration and visualization of system use, and to facilitate communication between designers and users. Later, in a process of abstraction away from the concrete detail of scenarios, the scenarios provide data that is used in task modeling and referent identification. More generally, scenario generation and task modeling and description are all mutually informing.

Much of the subsequent chat example is centered around a simple scenario depicting the initiation of a conversation, shown in Figure 3.3. Some of the detail in this (monitoring the agreement of invitees) changes as the design progresses.

> Ali wants to start a conversation about use-case notation with Tom and Sushila. He requests a new conversation and asks for Tom and Sushila to be invited to chat.
>
> While he does this he notices that Sushila is offline but, even so, he asks for her to be invited when she comes online. Ali submits the invitation.
>
> Tom, who is online, gets asked if he wants to join the conversation. He agrees and is then automatically provided with a chat window for typed chat. Ali is given a similar chat window and a window that monitors the agreement of each invitee.
>
> Sushila will be invited to join the conversation when she goes online, but for now she is shown as offline to the participants.

FIGURE 3.3 A scenario illustrating conversation initiation

3.4.2 Coarse-Grained Task Modeling

Idiom approaches the functional side of system specification via an abstract *coarse-grained* (or *high-level*) *task model* that is constructed with the users' goals in mind. A task model is required for each category of user. The level of abstraction utilized within at least the top-level tasks is similar to that of essential use cases—a kind of task model that is free of technology and implementation detail [Constantine and Lockwood 1999] (and see also Chapter 7). As with OVID [Roberts et al. 1998, p. 62], Idiom is not prescriptive as to the notation used for task modeling. Simple textual task decomposition styles are effective for both abstract and more detailed task models. One such style is used throughout this chapter. Collins [1995] recommends a similar, but slightly simpler technique that does not incorporate some of the control structures used here.

For the chat example, a simple high-level task model for a user who communicates with other users is shown in Figure 3.4. This is a rendition of a particular stage in the development of the model, along with comments, introduced with //, to the author and readers. The top-level task, Communicate, is motivated by the user goal to communicate with other users. Some sub-tasks that help realize this goal, such as address book–related tasks, are not included in the model in order to simplify and reduce the size of the example. Similarly, the task model omits the consideration of many exception conditions, such as everyone else leaving a conversation. The high-level task model in Figure 3.4 was constructed with extra detail that was then removed, as suggested in the preamble to Section 3.4.[5] The scenario in Figure 3.3 illustrates the InitiateConversation and RespondToConversationInvitation tasks in Figure 3.4.

A key to successfully using a textural form like the task model in Figure 3.4 is to accept some degree of informality in indicating interleaved task flow and thereby gain a way of indicating unordered sequences of optional activities while still using a relatively tractable syntax. The third (loop . . .) and fourth (start or resume . . .) lines in Figure 3.4 express a user-driven choice of interleaved concurrent task execution, as might be performed by users in a modern windowed environment with different windows providing different task execution contexts. Beyond this, there is no task model consideration of the sequencing of interleaved tasks, such as communicating with two sets of users via two different and simultaneously ongoing conversations.

---

[5] In passing, an alternative approach to formulate even more abstract, task-related models is Work Objective Decomposition [Monk 1998]. This approach uses a hierarchical structure to represent goal states (task post-conditions), thereby removing the need for task-sequencing information in the model.

```
Communicate
    Connect
    loop as often as needed for concurrent subtasks until desire to disconnect    // define concurrent subtask
        start or resume one of
            RespondToConversationInvitation
            create conversation and chat
                InitiateConversation
                if conversation successfully set up
                    ChatUntilFinished
    Disconnect

Connect

InitiateConversation                    // can be successful or unsuccessful (all invitees refuse)
    choose and invite participants

ChatUntilFinished
    loop as often as needed
        Chat                            // e.g., view conversation transcript (scrolling later?)
        LeaveConversation

Chat
    activities interleaved in some way
        read chat
        compose chat
        send chat

LeaveConversation                       // permanent leaving

Disconnect                              // temporarily suspends the local user from the conversations until the next
                                        // connect. In this simple case, just like temporarily leaving the locale of a spoken
                                        // conversation, one misses out on the intervening conversation.
                                        // A replay of missed material would be possible to implement if needed.

RespondToConversationInvitation         // this could be when the conversation starts up (for online users) or
    one of                              // when an invited user, previously offline, goes online to the chat system
        accept conversation invitation  // "notice use of chat system" rather than "chat server"
        reject conversation invitation
```

FIGURE 3.4 Coarse-grained task model

As in Idiom94, task models can incorporate the notion of system feedback, as in

$$\text{choose and invite participants}_{feedback}$$

This is similar to user action notation's (UAN's) use of an exclamation mark [Hartson et al. 1990, Hix and Hartson 1993].

3.4.3 Interaction Exploration Using Sequence Diagrams

UML interaction diagrams (sequence and collaboration diagrams) are normally used to illustrate use cases and depict details of inter-object interaction within the object model [Booch et al. 1999]. As noted in Section 3.2, while very useful for software engineering purposes, the documentation of internal object interactions is not generally useful for interactive system design (Constantine and Lockwood also note this in Chapter 7).

However, sequence diagrams can be used to visualize and illustrate interaction between users and a system. This technique is experimental; it seems useful as a way of *selectively* visualizing and exploring some aspects of user interaction. UML sequence diagrams that depict user-system interaction can be drawn at a high level of abstraction, or they can have increasing amounts of detail added to them. At a high level of abstraction, with both user and system actions illustrated by message sends as in Figure 3.5, the notation is close to essential use case notation [Constantine and Lockwood 1999] (and see also Chapter 7).

The addition of task information to sequence diagrams can be useful in the visualization of the developing task model. Here, these sequence diagrams tend to show only one

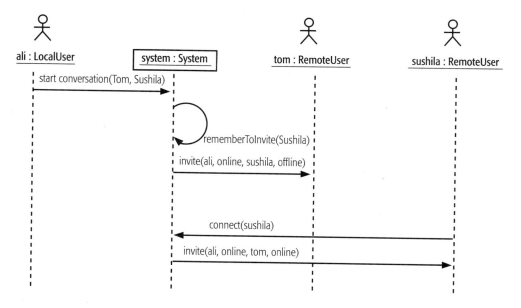

FIGURE 3.5 Sequence diagram showing the initiation of a conversation and the associated issuing of invitations

user, by reflecting the single-user nature of task models. Examples are illustrated in Figures 3.6 and 3.7. The advantages of such task-sequence diagrams *seem to be* that they do the following:

- Combine user tasks with depictions of interactions between the user and the system, and thereby start to "bring the task model to life" as part of the developing user interface and system design.
- Help in the examination and further development of the envisioned task model.

While this diagramming technique can be used to illustrate increasingly fine-grained task models, indications are that the point at which to stop this activity is when the high-level task model has been satisfactorily explored. However, since sequence diagrams are notationally heavyweight and have only limited applicability for high-level system visualization purposes, they may either be omitted from future versions of Idiom or only be used for occasional task-model visualization. Certainly, the technique would be tedious and time-consuming in use at fine-grained detail for large systems, or even all the way across a set of high-level tasks.

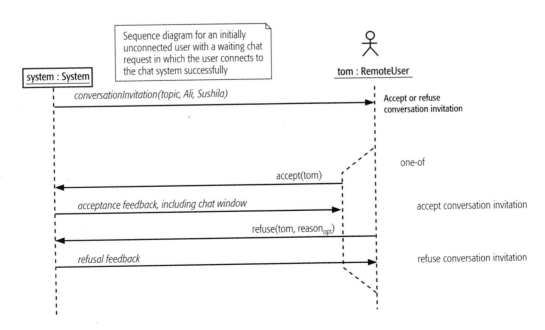

FIGURE 3.6 Task-sequence diagram for a response to a conversation invitation when already online

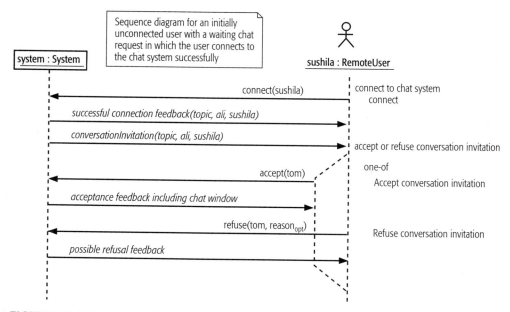

FIGURE 3.7 Task-sequence diagram for online connection to the chat system and a response to a pending conversation invitation

3.4.4 Describing Tasks and Identifying Referents

Users have goals that they attempt to realize by task performance. During task performance, users manipulate *referents,* which are user-world objects that are of interest or utility to users in the performance of their goal-directed task behavior. (See the CHI97 framework in [van Harmelen et al. 1997] or see Chapter 10.) Idiom encourages the discovery of referents from scenario data as part of the process of extracting task descriptions from scenarios. These referents are later represented by types and attributes in the domain and core models and are used in the identification and design of a set of contexts for task execution to be implemented in the interface.

The procedure for describing tasks and recording referents in Idiom is to list selected tasks defined in the task model, to describe these tasks in user language (some of this detail may appear in enacted form in the scenarios), and then to find and describe the referents used in each task from the task description. Referents appearing in the task description are underlined and are listed after the task description. Focusing on nouns in the task description is one good way to find potential referents. Each referent description includes (a) a resolution of any naming ambiguities in the task descriptions (if those ambiguities have not, for one reason or another, already been resolved) and (b) a user language description of the referent.

In Figure 3.8, a task has been rendered as a brief textual description; the underlined words refer to objects or relationships. Referents used in the task are listed below the task, together with a resolution of any ambiguities in terminology, the chosen names being unbracketed. Not all of the extracted referents are model objects in themselves. For example, invitee status could be represented in a domain or core model using a UML-association class, or by the use of different associations, as shown in Figure 3.9; the former is the more elegant solution.

This phase of referent identification is not the only source of referents. Scenarios and business input may provide referents, as may users, domain experts, and designers. Whatever the source, referents should be recorded against the task descriptions in which the referents are used. This information will be used to discover if any task execution contexts can be merged during later user interface design (see Section 3.5.3.1).

Initiate Conversation

The local user uses photographs or names or nicknames of other users to choose individuals (the invitees, some of the other users, remote users) to communicate with in a conversation. The local user sends the invitations after making invitee choices. Invitee status (no acceptance yet, accepted, rejected) is shown for all invitees as a result of the conversation initiation. A chat window appears before or as a result of the first user accepting a conversation invitation.

remote user (other user, invitee) = a user who is known to the chat system, who may or may not be connected to the chat system, but who is available to be invited to a conversation. If/when connected, the remote user may accept or refuse the conversation invitation.

user representation (photograph or name or nickname of other user) = something representing a remote user. Displayed in some way that enables choice of invitees while initiating a conversation.

conversation = ongoing distribution of messages from users in the conversation to the other users in the conversation.

invitee status = invited and not replied, replied and accepted and connected now, replied and accepted but unconnected now, replied and refused.

chat window = place to send and receive communications with remote users who have accepted a conversation invitation.

FIGURE 3.8 A task description together with referent descriptions

86 | **CHAPTER 3** Designing with Idiom

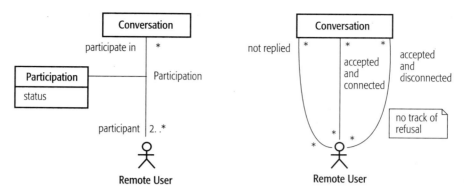

FIGURE 3.9 Modeling invitee status (with the preferable solution on the left)

3.4.5 The Domain Model

The domain model uses *referent types* to represent referents in the users' world and uses associations to represent relationships between those referents. First versions of the domain model should be developed as soon as possible to encourage the designer to rapidly understand the contents and structure of the application domain. Skilled object modelers may wish to start modeling almost immediately, using the later output of the referent identification as an additional source of information for their modeling activity, while less experienced object modelers may wish to start modeling only after the referent identification has produced some output, without worrying too much, at first, about cardinalities. Whichever approach is taken, the domain model must articulate the users' understanding of the domain before the core model is constructed (see Section 3.5.1).

Should users be modeled in the domain model? A domain model for an architectural CAD system would not include the users of that system [van Harmelen 1994]. However, in systems in which users need to communicate and interact with each other, users appear in the domain model. However, it should be noted that modeling provides only a very abstract representation of interactions between users; modeling is no substitute for field work that leads to a rich understanding of ways in which the user activity can be supported.

The chat example includes users who communicate with each other. For these users, initial referent identification leads to the model shown in Figure 3.10(a). Figure 3.10(b) shows a slightly enlarged domain model incorporating another referent—an address book or "buddy list" that provides referents for use while initiating a conversation.

Different types of users may use different kinds of referents in distinct domain models. Thus, if there were chat system administrators who were responsible for chat server

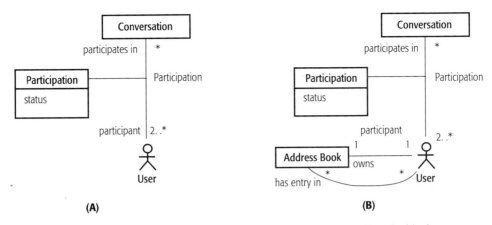

FIGURE 3.10 (A) Basic domain model and (B) the domain model used later in this chapter

administration, their domain model would have to include referents representing servers and provide operations on those types to enable and support the administrators' activities. To accommodate different kinds of users, designers can think in terms of different compatible domain models, or in terms of different aspects of a single domain model.

3.4.6 Visualization Using Sketches

There is a strong need for the users and designers to gain a feel for a system, and how it might operate, very early in design. *Sketches*—freehand drawings of the system's appearance—can be used to depict user interfaces while exploring system functionality, behavior, and use. The process of drawing sketches by hand is direct and immediate, without the overhead of computer use. Sketches can be combined to form *storyboards,* which are sequences of depictions of the system over time, or *interaction sequences* [van Harmelen 1994], which are sequences of renditions of the screen state separated by depictions of user interactions that cause the transitions between the renditions, see Section 3.6.1. For user interface design, sketches can include ideas of interaction along the lines of the example shown in Figure 3.11. All of these sketching techniques provide user interface representations that can be discussed, compared, mutated, redrawn, and even used as prototypes, all without any need for polished drawing skills. As such, the technique is simple, useful, and laudable. Winograd [1995] makes some similar observations about sketching for software design.

Unfortunately, there is a danger that, as an early design activity, sketching can lead to (a) inappropriate assumptions on the part of the designers and (b) incorporation of premature and inappropriate low-level interaction detail into the developing design. Once

88 | **CHAPTER 3** Designing with Idiom

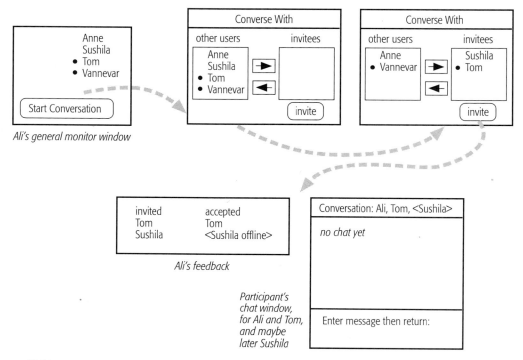

FIGURE 3.11 Rough early design ideas about interaction flow copied from a sketch on a whiteboard

recorded in an early sketch, there can be a strong tendency for ideas of system appearance, interactive characteristics, and functionality to continue unrevised in the developing design. As pointed out by Constantine [2000], avoiding these problems is a good reason for proceeding directly to an essential view of the system. Idiom's approach involves retaining sketching and early concrete visualization while being aware of their limitations.

The original version of Figure 3.11 was drawn on a whiteboard within an hour or two of starting this design study. The figure provides examples of the kinds of problems that early sketches can introduce:

- *Inappropriate assumptions:* The rendition uses, to a computer-literate designer, a useful interaction technique that allows for revision of choices while formulating a list of conversationalists. Interestingly, in showing just how wrong designer choices can be, the very first user who was asked how to initiate conversations rejected this approach in favor of manipulating (in some unknown way) photographs of the users with whom he wanted to chat.[6] Yet other users might want a shortcut in order to chat with a single online user.

- *Sub-optimal concrete design choices:* The status window was soon abandoned as polluting the view space, because, if it were needed, the status of conversationalists (accepted, refused, not online) could be shown in each user's chat window, given a likely-to-be-found solution to the problem of displaying invitee status for a set of invitees.

Even with the danger of these kinds of problems, sketching is extremely valuable and can be used effectively *if* designers are prepared to revise solutions. Involving users, working with user-derived information in the design process, abstracting and then using the resultant models in further design, and testing prototypes with users are all ways of encouraging suitable revision while gaining a deeper understanding of and feel for the developing interactive system design.

3.5 Formulating Abstract Descriptions of the Interactive System

Descriptions generated from the early design material include the core model, a finer-grained task model, and the view model. It is useful to categorize these models together as abstract descriptions, even though the task and view models start to articulate some concrete user interface design choices and therefore the descriptions incorporate some non-essential interaction detail. The general categorization as *abstract* descriptions distinguishes these models from the *concrete* user interface design.

3.5.1 The Core Model

The *core model* of a system or application represents the part of the domain that is of interest to users of that system [van Harmelen 1994] and that is (to be) represented by the computer system. Like the domain model, the core model is a structural model that is concerned with referents and relationships between them, independent of user interface concerns.[7]

---

[6] This example is not quite as good as it might have been. When later using a partial prototype of a dialog box, the same user found this to be a satisfactory way of choosing users, given that (a) there was a way of detecting which users were connected (unlike the sketch shown in Figure 3.11, the prototype did not distinguish between connected and unconnected users) and (b) that it was used only to set up certain kinds of conversations, such as those between groups of business users.

[7] Pedantically, the core model contains implementation referents of interest and use to a user during that user's goal-directed behavior, and excludes those referents that are concerned with the user interface and the user's manipulation of the core model referents.

The core model is based on a subset of the domain model. For the example here, the core model is a slight transformation of a subset of the domain model.

Different kinds of users will have different tasks to perform using the facilities offered by the system and may only be concerned with different, possibly overlapping, parts of the system. Identifying the boundaries of concern delimits and focuses subsequent user interface design. Idiom can use different core models with referents derived from user-specific sets of tasks for different kinds of users and would name these by preceding "core model" with an appropriate actor name. Thus, for example, assuming that normal users of the chat system use only the chat facilities and will not need to know about chat clients and chat servers, there is no mention of clients and servers in the normal user's core model. Chat system administrators would have server objects in the administrator's core model, thereby allowing the subsequent design of a user interface that enables the administration of servers. Such partitioning is discussed by Collins [1995, p. 190] as "partitioning the analysis model into system models for different types of users." Clearly, designers should assure themselves that different core models are compatible and conform to the corresponding domain models.

Here we call normal chat users local users. In developing the local users' core model, the starting point is the domain model, as shown in Figure 3.12. Because the design is for a single local user's interface, a local user is emphasized. In Figure 3.13, only the local user's address book is considered, and not those of other users. The model is then transformed, as shown in Figure 3.14, into a representation of a chat system for the local user. In Figure 3.14, other users are represented as address book entries called User.

Early core model decisions strongly influence the resulting interactive system. Giving each local user access to only a personal address book is a design decision that illustrates how the interactive system can be limited from an early stage by particular design choices. In this case, the local user is limited to the use of entries in only one address book. The

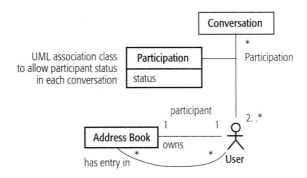

FIGURE 3.12 Chosen domain model

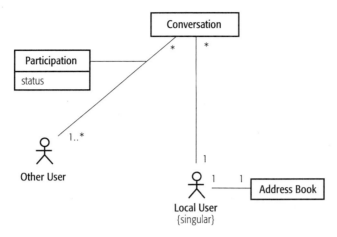

FIGURE 3.13 Intermediate model

core model would have to be revised in order to model the use of other address books, such as shared corporate address books.

A singular System type is introduced in Figure 3.14 to encapsulate systemwide functionality and to act as an anchor for the other objects in the model. Any types participating in associations with the local user can instead be safely associated with the system type, because both types are singular and, at this level of consideration, there is implied reachability from the user to all core objects, including the system object. System is often referred

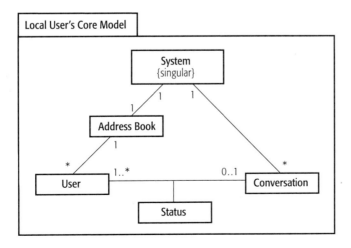

FIGURE 3.14 The local users's core model—this package is later represented as a type (in Figure 3.21)

to simply as "the system object" in the context of the core model. The system object serves as:

- A place for useful system operations, such as setting systemwide preferences, initiating major system functionality, or exiting the application.
- A place for operations that create core objects, typically for those core objects that are directly linked to the system object.
- An anchor for other objects in the model. In conjunction with relations between objects, the anchor ensures navigability to all objects in the model.

3.5.2 Finer-Grained Task Models

The coarse-grained task model in Figure 3.4 was limited to tasks that could be expressed without introducing tasks that reflect concrete interaction details. The task model is now extended to include more details of user interaction by moving the task model toward a finer level of granularity that expresses some concrete design choices. These choices are exemplified here by the implied use of dialog boxes in LeaveConversation, as shown in Figure 3.15.

3.5.3 The View Model

Whereas a core model is an abstraction representing a user's view of the deeper contents of the system, a view model provides a specification of how the user interacts with the system and provides the basis for subsequent concrete user interface design. A view model is composed of a static and a dynamic view model.

A *static view model* specifies the structure and contents of the user interface. The model is divided primarily into top-level views, each of which is implemented as a window or dialog box in a windowed environment. Top-level views are used to provide users with the information and the interactive facilities necessary for task performance. A view is composed of view objects that may be for internal view use or that may be rendered and provide interactive behavior at the user interface: some view objects exist to represent core objects or other view objects,[8] and some view objects exist purely to specify interactive capability. In a static view model, top-level views and view objects provide an abstract specification of the composition of the interface and of some aspects of interaction. They do not reflect how the interface will be implemented.

---

[8] The terms "top-level view" and "view object" may be shortened to "view" where the context of use is clear.

3.5 Formulating Abstract Descriptions of the Interactive System | 93

```
Communicate
    Connect
    loop as often as needed for concurrent subtasks until desire to disconnect    // define concurrent subtask
        start or resume one of
            RespondToConversationInvitation
            create conversation and chat
                InitiateConversation
                if conversation successfully set up
                    ChatUntilFinished
    Disconnect

Connect
    connect

InitiateConversation                              // can be successful or unsuccessful (all invitees refuse)
    invoke start conversation operation
    while not completed
        one of
            choose participant
            remove participant
    invite all chosen participants                // see addition below line across page as a result
                                                  // of re-reading this subtask

ChatUntilFinished
    loop as often as needed for concurrent subtasks until decide to leave conversation
        Chat                                      // e.g., view conversation transcript (scrolling later?), draw,...
    LeaveConversation

Chat
    activities interleaved in some way
        read chat
        compose chat
        send chat

LeaveConversation         //permanent leaving
    invoke leave conversation operation
    if one of last two in the conversation
        answer confirm and end conversation dialogue
    else
        answer leave confirm dialogue

Disconnect
    answer confirm disconnect dialogue  // temporarily suspends the local user from the conversations until the next
                                        // connect. In this simple case, just like temporarily leaving the locale of a
                                        // spoken conversation, one misses out on the intervening conversation.
                                        // A replay of missed material would be possible to implement if needed.

RespondToConversationInvitation         // this could be when the conversation starts up (for online users) or
                                        // when an invited user, previously offline, goes online to the chat system
    respond to request                  // "notice use of chat system" rather than "chat server"
```

FIGURE 3.15 A more detailed (or fine-grained) task model

A *dynamic view model* articulates the run-time view behavior of the system by describing the way in which top-level views are created and destroyed as a result of user interactions and system events.

3.5.3.1 Identifying Top-Level Views

Because top-level views displayed as windows provide contexts for task execution, they should support the user in his or her task-based behavior by making available (a) representations of the application objects that the user needs to refer to and/or manipulate during task performance, (b) controls to invoke suitable operations, and (c) feedback during and after the operation invocation. Unless there are strong motivating reasons not to do so, the user interface design should cater to task execution without the user having to manipulate multiple top-level views in order to complete a task (see also Chapter 8). As such, all task-related information and functionality should appear in or be easily accessible from the view supporting the performance of that task. To further reduce view switching by users, views should, whenever possible, support the performance of related tasks.[9] The analysis described here enables designers to (a) extract task contexts from task models for implementation as windows, dialog boxes, and tool palettes; and (b) inform the static and dynamic view modeling described in Sections 3.5.3.2 and 3.5.3.3. The techniques used here provide low-cost, low-commitment choices which allow for easy revision of existing choices.

The initial step is to choose tasks to be executed within particular task execution contexts that will be realized as windows. To choose task execution contexts, it is useful to annotate a task model: Figure 3.16 shows boxes drawn on a task model to represent contexts within which the boxed tasks can be executed. Overlapping boxes are necessary for tasks envisaged as being implemented with cross-window drag-and-drop operations.[10] The core objects and attributes that are used in task execution (revealed by referent identification from task descriptions in Section 3.4.4) can be recorded inside the corresponding boxes. This annotation enables the detection of any tasks using the same or similar information and, possibly, merging of the task execution contexts.

It is also possible to use the annotated task model to record how task execution contexts are created by users prior to use. Arrows are used to show how new contexts are created. This information is later recorded more formally in the *dynamic view model* (see Section 3.5.3.2).

---

[9] The example here does not readily demonstrate multiple tasks per view, but this is an inherent part of the Idiom approach.

[10] View identification is concerned with making decisions that affect the concrete design. The choice of drag-and-drop operations during view identification is an aspect of this general process.

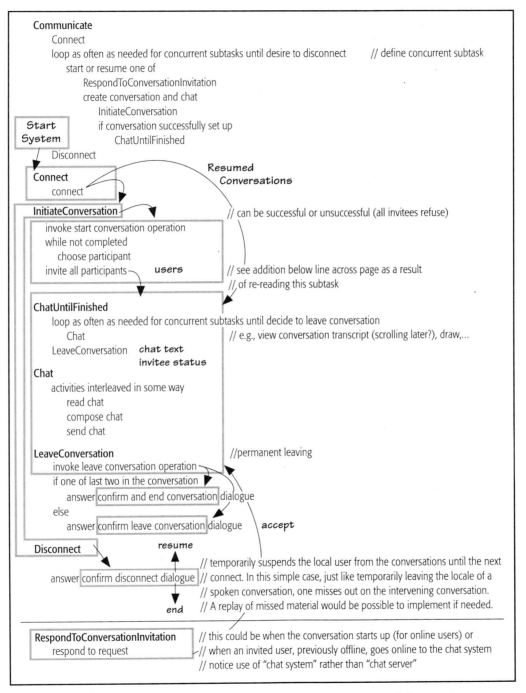

FIGURE 3.16 Tasks mapped to views (implemented as windows and dialog boxes)

96 | **CHAPTER 3** Designing with Idiom

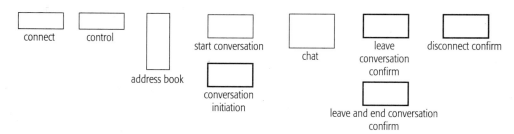

FIGURE 3.17 Potential windows and dialog boxes for task-execution contexts

The next step is to depict the boxes on the task analysis in a separate diagram. This is done in Figure 3.17. Moded dialog boxes are drawn with a heavy outline. One of these—the conversation invitation dialog box—is worth discussing here. Its modedness is a pragmatic choice that anticipates the prevention of unnecessary interaction when disconnecting at a later time, should an unmoded version of one of these views still be open. This is a design choice that needs to be evaluated with users; as an alternative, users might prefer unmoded invitations that can be left open so that a conversation can be joined later.

The consideration of exceptional cases is important for user interface coverage in the developing design. Thoughts about the exceptional case of all invitees refusing the invitation to a conversation prompted the invention of an extra dialog box (see Figure 3.18).

all refused

FIGURE 3.18 Extra dialog box

This pointed to a failure in the scenario generation process and the need for subsequent reconciliation of the new dialogue with the scenarios, task models, and task descriptions.

Users of the method may wish to experiment with rendering views as shown in Figure 3.19.

start conversation

task: InitiateConversation
referents: user representations
in invited and uninvited categories
subtasks: move user representation between categories
invite all in invited category

FIGURE 3.19 Alternative view rendition

3.5.3.2 View Behavior and the Dynamic View Model

Designers of systems need to be able to plan, communicate, and improve designs for the creation, deletion, lifetimes, and multiplicity of top-level views. A *dynamic view model* models this top-level view behavior.

Dynamic view modeling can be performed in a style that shows the particular paths of use and how each window, dialog box, or palette is created from another in a way similar to that shown in Figure 3.11. Constantine and Lockwood [1999] are two of the proponents of this kind of style. In their version, top-level views are represented by unadorned boxes. This kind of representation represents the description domain relatively directly, and it is easily understood by a wide variety of stakeholders. As such, it is noteworthy and significant.

However, there may be difficulties in using this form of representation to model all possible paths of view usage. Idiom solved this problem with, in retrospect, an overly complex form of parallel state machine called a *view transition machine*. Of primary interest to designers who like rigorous notations, a view transition machine (a) models the dynamic aspects of the existence of top level views and (b) specifies, at an abstract level, events leading to top-level view creation and destruction using *threads* akin to threads in a UML state machine. Details of this approach are omitted from this chapter, but the basic style of rendition, devoid of many annotations, appears in Figure 3.20.

3.5.3.3 View Structure and Static View Models

The *static view model* augments the core model with views and their contents based on previously formulated design information. Figure 3.21 shows the most abstract form of the chat example's view structure. The figure contains the core model, three views, and the user, who interacts with the core via the views. dialog boxes have not been shown, but they could be attached to the model via the views, thereby indicating the place from which they are "created."

The abstract form shown in Figure 3.21 is useful to record and convey an overall picture of the multiplicity of different types of top-level views. In the figure, we can easily see that there is a single system control view but an unlimited (at this stage, without machine constraints) number of Chat or Start Conversation views.

The composition of the top-level views is recorded by adding more detail to the model, as depicted in Figure 3.22. dialog boxes are again omitted; at this level of detail, they would be attached to the model via the source view and via any core or view types that act as information sources for the dialog box.

The types which appear in static view models represent top-level views or view objects. They may be populated with operations that correspond to user actions. Thus the type Start Conversation View in Figure 3.21 could contain operations like:

- selectParticipant()
- chooseParticipant()
- deselectParticipant()
- inviteAllParticipants()
- cancel()

In Figures 3.21 and 3.22 these operations could only appear in the Start Conversation View. However, placing an operation in a view object that constitutes part of a top-level view removes the necessity to list the operation in the top-level view type. Thus if the selection panel in Figure 3.11 had been modeled in Figure 3.22 with a Selection Panel type that was a constituent part of the Start Conversation View and that was associated with the User View type via associations labeled with the roles invited and not invited, then the first three of the above operations could be positioned in the Selection Panel with optional replication in Start Conversation View.

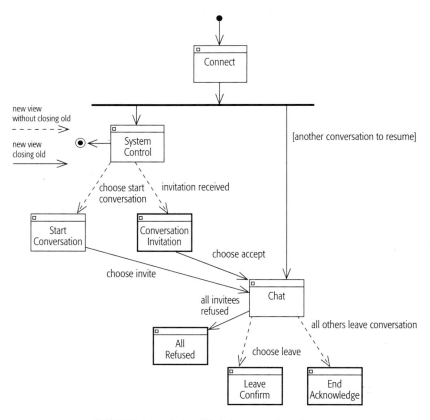

FIGURE 3.20 A simplified view transition diagram

3.5 Formulating Abstract Descriptions of the Interactive System | 99

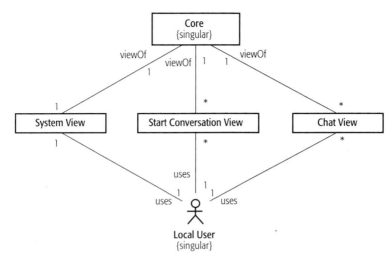

FIGURE 3.21 Abstract view structure

Sometimes, in making the transition between an abstract form like that of Figure 3.21 and a more detailed form as shown in Figure 3.22, the cardinalities become less than clearly expressive. This occurs for cardinalities on associations between core objects and view objects for those top-level views that may optionally exist once or more than once at a given moment at run time. In such a case it may be more useful to express the view structure as it is (partially) developed in Figure 3.23. There the larger boxes represent the core model type and a Start Conversation top-level view type, and the association between these boxes represents the optional "instantiation" of the top level view one or more times. The cardinalities between User and User View are now more reflective of the desired situation, that each of the users in the local user's address book (each of the set of instances of User in the core) is represented once in the Start Conversation View.

In terms of an abstract-to-concrete continuum, static view models provide intermediate-level descriptions; they articulate aspects of choices that specify concrete user interface design features. Imagine two different ways of initiating a conversation: (a) by using a dialog box (as illustrated in Figure 3.11) and (b) by dragging user photographs from an address book view to a chat view using drag-and-drop interaction techniques. These different forms of interaction would be articulated differently in the view model; in scheme (b), the Start Conversation view would be omitted from the view structure shown in Figure 3.21, and the user would interact by using a view displaying photographs of other users and a conversation view. Corresponding changes would be made at the more detailed level of Figure 3.22.

The construction of the view model can easily lead to re-evaluation of existing aspects of concrete design decisions. The positioning of invitee status feedback (accepted,

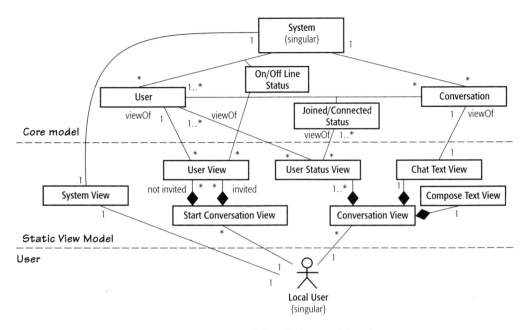

FIGURE 3.22 Core model, static view model, and user

refused, and so on) in the chat example was revised, in part, as a result of the informing role played by a static view model level consideration of the chat system.

3.5.3.4 More Complex View Models

Idiom incorporates a general model of interactive system structure that can cater for *transactions*[11] on the core model to enable query and interactive updates of the model [Wills 1988, van Harmelen 1994]. Transactions can be modeled with views and view objects.

The motivation for transactions in Idiom is derived from the observation that humans are limited in the things that they can do at one time and that under certain circumstances (for example, in editing an engineering drawing) modifications of core objects via the view model must be done one step at a time. This may perhaps leave the user's data in a temporarily inconsistent state. To avoid an inconsistent state, the changes are performed using a transaction that is a less stringently constrained copy of (part of) the core. When the transaction is again consistent in respect to the core's more stringent

---

[11] Here, transactions are modeling constructs and have nothing to do with database transactions. One could talk about transaction patterns being used in a model.

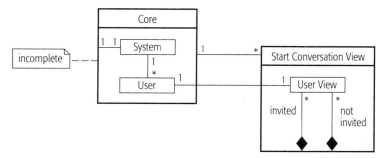

FIGURE 3.23 Partial refinement of a detailed static view structure

constraints, a change can be made to the core in a single transaction completion operation, and the transaction can be discarded. Thus, a transaction is a model-level representation of interactive capability.

There are three kinds of transactions, which are classified according to how they work:

- A *creation transaction* first gathers all the information needed to perform a change in the core and then invokes an update operation on the core. This is a kind of *change transaction*; it changes the core. If the chat system gathered a transcript of a conversation and, when the conversation was finished, saved that copy to an archive maintained by the core, the system would implement a creation transaction.
- A *copy transaction* is a less constrained "copy" of (part of) the core in which intermediate inconsistent core states are allowed and supported. To change the core after one or more changes have been made to the copy, a consistency check is run to see if the transaction is consistent with regard to core constraints, and, if so, an update operation is invoked on the core. This is a kind of *change transaction*.
- A *read transaction* simply presents copy information drawn from the core model without the possibility of changing that information.

Transactions may contain a range of objects that have nothing to do with the domain of interest per se. Thus, a typical change transaction might contain objects representing whatever the transaction is being used to edit, as well as objects required for interaction, such as cursor position, selection markers, and cut-copy-paste buffers. (See [van Harmelen 1994].) If this detail is recorded in a static view model, the purpose is to articulate interactive behavior, not to specify implementation mechanisms.

A top-level view or a view object may also be a *view* in the Model-View-Controller (MVC) [Krasner and Pope 1988] sense, or, less confusing terminologically, an observer in the Observer pattern [Gamma et al. 1995] sense. Such an *observer* reflects the state of a *subject* that the observer watches; the observer is dynamically notified of changes in the subject and updates itself accordingly. The subject might be changed by one of its observers as a consequence of user interaction with that observer, or the subject may be changed as the result of a system event. The pattern is useful in the specification of interfaces which dynamically display changing system data (control systems, for example), and for the specification of interfaces where the same user-manipulated data is displayed potentially multiple times, possibly in different forms, and needs to be kept up to date each time it is displayed.

3.6 Concrete User Interface Design

A *concrete user interface design* is a detailed description or specification of the appearance and interactivity of the user interface to an interactive system, including the core object representations and the system behavior at the user interface. Concrete user interface design is the activity of producing such a description or specification.

Inputs to concrete user interface design include:

- User profiles
- Scenarios
- Task models
- Sequence diagrams, if they are used
- The core model
- The view model: static and dynamic
- Interaction style and implementation technology choices

Outputs include:

- Window, dialog box, and alert layouts; interaction techniques used in these layouts; and the resultant system actions during and after use of the interaction techniques
- Core object representations, interaction with core object representations including any selection and dynamic feedback
- Menu and palette layouts, system actions on menu item and button choices, shortcuts, and undo facilities

Hopefully the outputs also include:

- Help facilities
- User documentation
- Training aids

These outputs may be represented using

- Text and diagrams
- Sketches and storyboards
- Interaction sequences
- Tool-generated layouts
- Prototypes

An aspect of the outputs is to show how user interactions affect the state of the core and view models. Interaction sequences, which are defined and discussed in the next section, allow designers, if they so desire, to tie prototypical user interactions to changes in model state.

3.6.1 Interaction Sequences

Interaction sequences show graphical depictions of *prototypical* interactions that are representative of user interactions and associated system responses. Thus while an interaction sequence might depict a user drawing a line of a particular length and direction, the interaction sequence is interpreted as depicting all line drawing situations. Interaction sequences can be used in three kinds of situations:

- Interaction sequences may be used early in and throughout the design cycle for many visualization and design purposes, often quite informally, and almost certainly without the use of pre- and post-conditions (discussed below in this section). Interaction sequences are both expressive and easy to use for visualization and design; on a whiteboard they provide a fluid medium for redesign.
- Interaction sequences may be used to specify interactions where the pre- and/or post-conditions are important for design and/or subsequent development purposes.
- Interaction sequences may be used to document and specify concrete user interface design details, particularly for detailed specification where cursor changes, cursor movement, alignment, and dynamic feedback are important.

An interaction sequence is composed of screen shots or sketches of screens or fragments thereof, interspersed with renditions of user interactions that may vary in scale from a simple button depression to more complex interactions such as the use of a menu or dialog box. An interaction sequence may optionally include a pre-condition that characterizes conditions that are required to undertake the interaction, and may optionally include a post-condition that specifies what will be true after the interaction is completed. Pre- and post-conditions can be expressed using different levels of formality. Natural language is sufficient for most interactive system and user interface design purposes, and the Object Constraint Language (OCL) [Walmer and Kleppe 1999] can be used if precision is required. The pre- and post-conditions are expressed in terms of core and/or static view model states. In post conditions it may be useful to adopt the convention that overlines are used to refer to system state before the interaction, and non-overlined state information refers to systems state after the interaction. An example interaction sequence that belies the ease of informal use of interaction sequences appears in Figure 3.24. In fact the example illustrates use of the notation at a formal extreme, more suited for detailed specification, rather than design, purposes.

Although interaction sequences are useful for the three purposes outlined above, it would be counterproductive to attempt to use interaction techniques to describe all interaction with a medium or large sized development; if only because working out which interaction sequences are applicable at a given point in time requires evaluation of all pre-conditions. In such cases designers should consider sketches, storyboards, and prototypes to convey design information, and selectively limit their use of interaction sequences to interesting, complex, or otherwise important aspects of interaction.

Interaction sequences draw on unpublished user interaction and screen depictions used by Stephanie Wilson and myself in the period 1984 to 1986. Pre- and post-conditions were added later by myself circa 1991.

3.6.2 Prototypes

Lo-fi prototypes were not used in this study, although they could, and indeed, should have been used at various stages from soon after the inception through the concrete user interface design stage.

A small number of medium-fidelity prototypes were tested by prospective users. The prototypes provided partial functionality along a scenario path of initiating and terminating a conversation. Two screen shots from one version appear in Figure 3.25. Users were introduced to the task, to communicate with other users, and were asked to use the prototype to initiate a conversation, to imagine a typed conversation with other users, and to leave the conversation. The users were asked to verbalize briefly their reactions to or feelings toward the system as they used it, and to mention if things were hard or easy

Interaction Notation

mouse button	⌐▶ ⌐▶ ⌐▶
menu selection	File>Save File>Save As…
cursor movement	DRAG
equality (not assignment)	=
logical and	∧
logical or	∨
grouping	( )

in post-conditions old values (values at the time of the pre-condition) are $\overline{\text{overlined}}$

Choose Pointing

pre: cursor.location inside menu.pointingModeButton.area

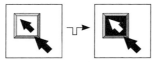

post: interactionMode = POINTING

Selecting a Line

pre: cursor.location inside line.selectionArea ∧ interactionMode = POINTING

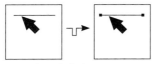

post: selected = line

Moving a Line

pre: selecte = line ∧ cursor.location inside line.selectionArea ∧ interactionMode = POINTING

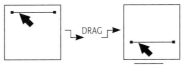

post: selected = line ∧ line.pos = $\overline{\text{line.pos}}$ + dragVector

FIGURE 3.24 Examples of interaction sequences. Normally, these interaction sequences would be used with natural-language pre- and post-conditions. The detail shown here illustrates the level of fine-grainedness that can be achieved if the system description demands it, and the way in which a formal link can be made to core and static view model states. From [van Harmelen 1994].

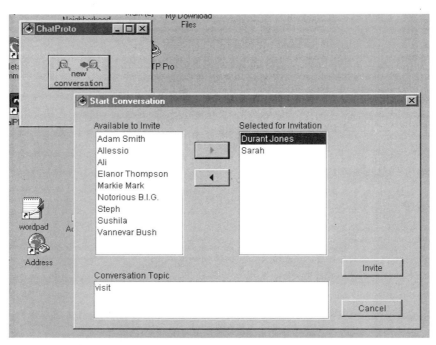
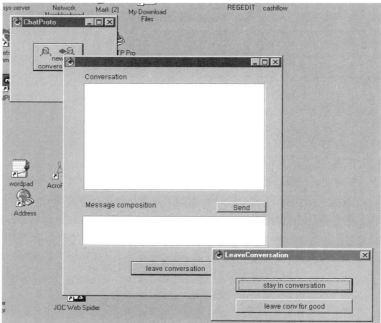

FIGURE 3.25 Initiating and terminating a conversation

to do. Sometimes the users were prompted in a non-directed fashion to express their feelings toward and reactions to things that they had noted as being easy or hard, as well as the reasons why they thought those things were easy or hard.

User feedback on the prototypes ranged from comments about functionality (for example, "It would help if I knew who's online when I'm using this") to questions and comments about the context of use of the system (for example, "Is this for business or personal use or what? If it's for . . .").

3.7 Generation of Use Cases

A use case model can be generated from the high-level task model. The kind of result that can be obtained is shown in Figure 3.26. This allows use cases to be used in subsequent OOA and OOD activities.

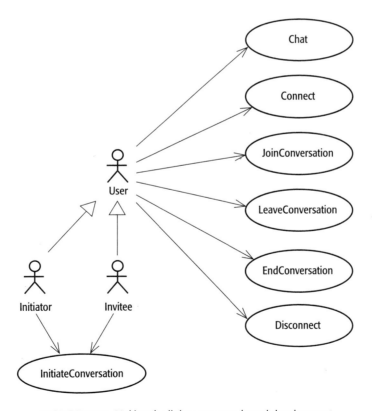

FIGURE 3.26 Making the link to use case-based development

3.8 Conclusions

In comparison to Idiom94, the new version of Idiom provides a better foundation for interactive system *design* by incorporating a thread of development that considers scenarios of system use, task and referent identification and extraction, and interactive system design based, in part, on task execution contexts. In this respect, some of the notable features of Idiom are:

- The use of task analyses and scenarios to generate task descriptions (different in approach to Rosson and Carroll's use of scenarios to generate POV analyses and thence object models; see Chapter 2).
- The use of task descriptions to identify referents and populate the domain model and its derived core model with referents.
- The use of a task analysis together with referents that are identified by task to identify and merge task execution contexts.
- The use of task execution contexts and the core model to guide the discovery and composition of views.
- The use of the view model to determine some aspects of the concrete user interface, for example, the contents of top-level views implemented as windows.

The enhanced method has been used sparingly, and more method development is anticipated, particularly with regard to participatory design. So far the enhanced method has been used in small studies, successfully applied by post-graduate computer science students to design problems in extended exercises, and used by the author and a colleague in a tool construction project. For the latter project, the method was mutated (making the method fit the problem and the resources, including the designer skill set, as recommended in Chapter 10). The domain and core models were drawn almost immediately and an envisioned task model was constructed rapidly.

Competing concrete user interfaces were designed and paper prototyped. The prototypes were iteratively re-designed with user participation during prototype evaluation and redesign. A horizontal computer-based prototype with only limited functionality was then built and tested, but due to the complexity of some of the underlying functionality for the design, a full evaluation of the resultant design could not be performed until the implementation phase was completed.

3.8.1 How Does Idiom Perform?

In developing the new method, the following five methodological concerns had to be addressed.

- *Coverage:* Are all the relevant sources of design information incorporated into the method? Do the outputs adequately convey the interactive system design, particularly for subsequent object development?

  Idiom now accommodates a wider range of inputs, incorporating upstream scenario-based design, and strong encouragement for user involvement. Participative approaches still need to be formally introduced into the method to more fully and effectively base the method on a deeper knowledge of user world phenomena. The outputs have been somewhat refined, incorporating a view transition model, and lessening the reliance on interaction sequences to specify dynamic behavior. A combination of task, use case, and object models, together with prototypes and concrete user interface design information, serve as a specification for subsequent development.

- *Process:* Are the design techniques capable of being used in a process framework of an opportunistic and informing design practice? Can activities be scheduled in a commercial environment?

  Supporting opportunistic design has always been an aim from the earliest days of Idiom. This is now well established at a method level. The ability to schedule work is provided by imposing a completion order on Idiom's design techniques.

- *Notation:* Do the notations used in the design techniques support the creation, recording, and communication of the design information? Do they support reasoning about designs, including competing designs? Do they support the transfer of informing design information to other techniques?

  The move to scenario-based design and the increased role of task-based design have been promising with regard to the use of these descriptions to create further design information. Textual representations of scenarios and tasks are used for object identification and extraction prior to the formation of object models. Task models lead to the identification of task contexts and windows and to the construction of the dynamic view model. For those that understand object modeling notation, object models successfully record and convey system structure and behavior for design purposes. As a pre-development hand-over activity, use cases can be generated from the task model. The representations support reasoning about the current state of design, development of the design, and the ability to express competing designs. The view transition notation requires further development to facilitate rapid and easy use.

- *Completeness:* Is there at least one path from inputs to outputs?

  Idiom provides a design path that spans from scenario generation to the specification of an interactive system and supports designers in moving to the interaction design level.

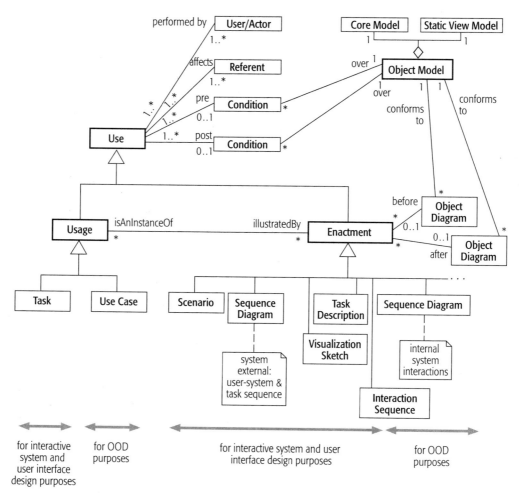

FIGURE 3.27 Use and model binding in Idiom

As yet, however, there is little to guide the detailed concrete design. When proceeding from the core and view model to a concrete design (as opposed to proceeding in the "opposite" direction by, say, abstracting view and perhaps core model features from a paper prototype), Idiom takes the designer as far as realizing that certain objects or features of objects and their associations have to be displayed together, but it provides no systematic guidance on the final stages of mapping the models to a concrete user interface design. This lack of process, including its aspects of participatory design and evaluation, must be addressed in future versions of Idiom.

- *Usability:* How usable is the new version of Idiom? The new version of Idiom requires more use before questions about its usability can be answered. Preliminary results indicate that sequence diagrams need to be replaced, or, at least, used with discretion, and that the dynamic view modeling notation needs to be simplified or replaced.

My feeling, and this is no more than a feeling, is that scenario-based design is relatively heavyweight when compared to participatory design approachs. An observation is that to be able to use the method, a mix of user interface design and object modeling skills are needed. This has team-structure implications. In common with Gulliksen et al. (Chapter 8) current and future method work will concentrate on a greater participatory emphasis.

3.8.2 Idiom as an Accommodating Framework

The more Idiom is developed, the more it comes to reflect a particular style of framework for user interface design and object modeling activities. This is neither the only framework nor a complete framework for the kinds of methods discussed in this book (see Chapter 10 for the latter). The "Idiom framework" involves the binding of user interactions to object models by means of pre-and post-conditions. It is flexible enough to accommodate a wide variety of different specifications of system use by optionally deploying the binding mechanism. The framework is shown in Figure 3.27.

3.9 Acknowledgments

Acknowledgments are due to Alan Wills, who collaborated with me circa 1992 on some early object modeling and user interface design integration, thereby helping to establish the path to Idiom; Dr. Katsura Kawakami, who gave me time to develop the first version of Idiom while I was employed at Matsushita's Tokyo Research Laboratory; Stephanie Wilson, who was largely responsible for initiating the redesign of Idiom by pointing out that the earlier version of Idiom was largely a specification-based approach that did not adequately support the process of user interface design; and Mary Beth Rosson, who made me aware of the possibilities of object extraction from scenarios [Rosson 1997]. The Department of Computer Science at the University of Manchester supported me by providing me with office space, colleagues to talk to, and computational facilities during a series of honorary positions. Cliff Jones and Brian Warboys are particularly to be thanked for their help in facilitating my appointment to those positions. Finally, John Artim, Larry Constantine, and Nuno Nunes kindly commented on the contents of this chapter.

3.10 References

[Booch et al. 1999] G. Booch, J. Rumbaugh, and I. Jacobson. *The Unified Modeling Language User Guide*. Reading, MA: Addison-Wesley, 1999.

[Carroll 1995a] J. M. Carroll, ed. *Scenario-Based Design: Envisioning Work and Technology in System Development*. New York: John Wiley and Sons, 1995.

[Carroll 1995b] J. M. Carroll. Introduction: The Scenario Perspective on System Development. In J. M. Carroll, ed. *Scenario-Based Design: Envisioning Work and Technology in System Development*. New York: John Wiley and Sons, 1995, 1–17.

[Collins 1995] D. Collins. *Designing Object-Oriented User Interfaces*. Menlo Park, CA: Benjamin-Cummings, 1995.

[Constantine 2000] L. L. Constantine. E-mail to author, 2000.

[Constantine and Lockwood 1999] L. L. Constantine and L. A. D. Lockwood. *Software for Use: A Practical Guide to Models and Methods of Usage-Centered Design*. New York: ACM, and Reading, MA: Addison-Wesley, 1999.

[Cook and Daniels 1994] S. Cook and J. D. Daniels. *Designing Object Systems: Object-Oriented Modelling with Syntropy*. Hemel Hempstead: Prentice Hall, 1994.

[Dayton et al. 1998] T. Dayton, A. McFarland, and J. Kramer. Bridging User Needs to Object Oriented GUI Prototype via Task Object Design. In L. Wood, ed. *User Interface Design*. Boca Raton, FL: CRC Press, 1998.

[DSDM 1995] The DSDM Consortium. *Dynamic Systems Development Method*. Version 2. UK: Tesseract Publishing, 1995.

[Fowler 1997] M. Fowler with K. Scott. *UML Distilled: Applying the Standard Object Modeling Language*. Reading, MA: Addison-Wesley, 1997.

[Hartson et al. 1990] H. R. Hartson, A. C. Siochi, and D. Hix. The UAN: A User-Oriented Representation for Direct Manipulation Interface Designs. *ACM Transactions on Information Systems,* 8 (3), 1990.

[Helander et al. 1997] M. Helander, T. K. Landauer, and P. V. Prabhu, eds. *Handbook of Human-Computer Interaction*. 2nd Ed., New York: Elsevier, 1997.

[Henderson 1991] A. Henderson. A Development Perspective on Interface Design and Theory. In J. M. Carroll, ed. *Designing Interaction: Psychology at the Human-Computer Interface*. Cambridge, UK: Cambridge University Press, 1991.

[Hix and Hartson 1993] D. Hix and H. R. Hartson. *Developing User Interfaces: Ensuring Usability Through Product and Process*. New York: John Wiley and Sons, 1993.

[Jones 1986] C. B. Jones. *Systematic Software Development Using VDM*. Englewood Cliffs, NJ: Prentice Hall, 1986.

[Monk 1998] A. Monk. Lightweight Techniques to Encourage Innovative User Interface Design. In L. E. Wood, ed. *User Interface Design: Bridging the Gap*. Boca Raton, FL: CRC Press, 1998.

[Muller et al. 1997] M. J. Muller, J. H. Hallewell, and T. Dayton. Participatory Practices in the Software Lifecycle. In M. Helander, T. K. Landauer, and P. V. Prabhu, eds. *Handbook of Human-Computer Interaction*. 2nd Ed., New York: Elsevier, 1997.

[OMG 1999] Object Management Group. *OMG Unified Modeling Language Specification.* Version 1.3 R9, 1999.

[Randall et al. 1994] D. Randall, J. Hughes, and D. Shapiro. Steps Toward a Partnership: Ethnography and System Design. In M. Jirotka and J. Goguen, eds. *Requirements Engineering Social and Technical Issues.* Orlando, FL: Academic Press, 1994.

[Roberts et al. 1998] D. Roberts, D. Berry, S. Isensee, and J. Mullaly. *Designing for the User with OVID: Bridging User Interface Design and Software Engineering.* Indianapolis, IN: Macmillan Technical Publishing, 1998.

[Rosson 1997] M. B. Rosson. Designing Object Oriented User Interfaces from Usage Scenarios. Workshop on Object-Oriented User Interfaces, CHI97, found at *http://www.cutsys.com/CHI97/Rosson.html,* 1997.

[Schneiderman 1987] B. Schneiderman. *Designing the User Interface: Strategies for Effective Human Computer Interaction.* Reading, MA: Addison-Wesley, 1987.

[Stapleton 1997] J. Stapleton. *Dynamic Systems Development Method: The Method in Practice.* Reading, MA: Addison-Wesley, 1997.

[van Harmelen 1994] M. van Harmelen. Object Oriented Modelling and Specification for User Interface Design. In F. Paterno, ed. *Interactive Systems: Design, Specification and Verification.* Proceedings of First Eurographics ISDV Workshop, Berlin: Springer, 1995.

[van Harmelen et al. 1997] M. van Harmelen, J. Artim, K. Butler, A. Henderson, D. Roberts, M. B. Rosson, J.-C. Tarby, and S. Wilson. Object Models in User Interface Design: CHI97 Workshop Summary. *SIGCHI Bulletin,* New York: ACM, October 1997.

[Walmer and Kleppe 1999] J. Walmer and A. Kleppe. *The Object Constraint Language: Precise Modeling with UML.* Reading, MA: Addison-Wesley, 1999.

[Wills 1988] A. Wills. *Structure of Interactive Environments in Software Engineering Environments,* P. Brereton, ed. Ellis Horwood, 1988.

[Winograd 1995] T. Winograd. From Programming Environments to Environments for Designing. *CACM,* 38 (6), June 1995.

CHAPTER 4

Entity, Task, and Presenter Classification in User Interface Architecture
An Approach to Organizing HCI Practice

John M. Artim

Abstract

As with any engineering discipline, human-computer interaction (HCI) practitioners are concerned with identifying standards of practice that lead to the production of safer, less expensive, and more effective systems for our customers. To gain the maximum effect from our standards of practice, we must understand how these practices relate to each other. We must also cooperate with professionals in many other disciplines to effectively complete the construction of useful and usable systems for our customers. The Entity, Task, and Presenter[1] (ETP) classification scheme provides a means of organizing the artifacts created and manipulated in the course of HCI activities. This chapter describes, from a practitioner's point of view, how this classification scheme, along with the activities of user task analysis and concept modeling, can be used both to facilitate individual HCI activities and then to coordinate HCI activities over time and throughout the development life cycle. This explicit classification of HCI artifacts can guide the user interface design process and help address the cost of performing impact analysis within the users' domain. The Unified Modeling Language, or UML [Rumbaugh et al. 1999], is used as the basis of a notation for the key HCI activities discussed in this chapter: the ETP classification scheme combined with UML modeling can be used to bridge the gap between HCI activities and artifacts and those of the development community.

---

[1] Formerly known as Entity, Task, and Interface [Artim et al. 1996].

4.1 Introduction

The human-computer interaction (HCI) literature of today is rich in theory and observation. An HCI practitioner, rather than being starved for ideas on how to proceed with a project, is faced with the sometimes daunting problem of determining which methods are most appropriate for a given project. That determination is based partly on the type of system to be created and partly on the project staff's mix of skills and experience including the total number of HCI professionals on staff. Even if an appropriate HCI method can be found for a given aspect of a project, it is likely that fitting that method into a comprehensive project methodology will be much more difficult.

This is especially true when one considers that the HCI professional is often a part of a larger team whose members reflect the stakeholders and developers of the system in question. On the one hand, this diversity of professional background and practice is needed to create today's systems, but on the other hand it means that the HCI professional's choice and use of methods are further constrained by the practices of the other participants in the system construction process. To create large software systems effectively, diverse professionals must adapt to each other's practices and languages [Christman and Artim 1997].

To further complicate matters, the role of the HCI professional is often understaffed. Although I have worked on projects staffed at approximately one HCI professional to ten developers, I have also worked in situations in which the ratio was as high as one to twenty-five for extended periods of time.

This chapter is concerned with the organization of HCI work so as to increase the effectiveness of HCI professionals. It is also concerned with coordination between HCI professionals and other members of extended system development teams. Beginning with a discussion of the CHI97 workshop framework (Section 4.2), this chapter discusses the notion of an organized process of system development (Section 4.3) and the role of architecture in this organization (Section 4.4). Next comes an overview of the Entity, Task, and Presenter (ETP) architectural approach (Section 4.5). Section 4.6 provides an extended discussion of key HCI processes and the pragmatics of performing those processes. Section 4.6 also provides an overview of task analysis, concept modeling, and user interface analysis and design. These activities are bound together using the fundamental units of HCI work: the user's task, the domain concept, and the problem-space representation. Although this approach was developed through experience on a number of large-scale system projects (systems supporting activities on the scale of a medium-size to large enterprise), many of the lessons are equally applicable to small-scale project work. Section 4.7 is a summary that includes a consideration of the problem of ontological drift. Section 4.8 concludes this chapter.

4.2 CHI97 Workshop Framework

The CHI97 workshop that discussed task and object analysis in user interface design created a framework to help the participants understand each other's perspectives and methods [van Harmelen et al. 1997]. This framework is illustrated schematically in Figure 4.1. The left side of this figure depicts the real focus of all HCI work: the users who are accomplishing work goals within some environment. To a user, this work consists of a set of tasks. These tasks involve the manipulation of referents, objects used by users, in the users' world. The HCI practitioner is participating in an effort to craft new referents to be introduced into the users' world along with modified versions of the users' tasks. The HCI practitioner's goal is to improve the quality or quantity of work that the users complete and, if at all possible, improve the quality of the users' experience of working.

To accomplish this goal, the HCI practitioner, in collaboration with other project team members, will create a set of descriptions. The descriptions document the users' world. They document the referents the users manipulate, the tasks users perform with these referents, the new or altered tasks these users wish to accomplish, and the additional referents they will need for these new tasks. These various descriptions are generally created and evolved in parallel. As users achieve a better understanding of one description, the content of related descriptions will evolve.

Likewise, the non-HCI members of the project team will be developing additional descriptions culminating in the creation of new system-supported referents. Also, as pointed out by Henderson [1993] and van Harmelen (see Chapter 10, Section 10.2.6), these descriptions are largely mutually informing. That is, an elaboration in the content of

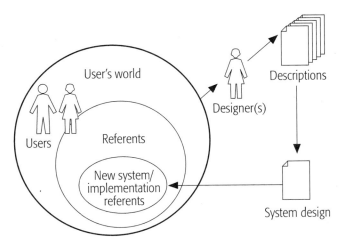

FIGURE 4.1 Overview of the CHI97 workshop framework

one description leads to improved understanding of, and, ultimately, changes in, other descriptions. Although often depicted as a cascade (or, to use a now-defunct metaphor, a "waterfall"), this mutualism guarantees the practitioner that description content will not just flow one way through the set of descriptions.

At the beginning of a project or when starting a new HCI organization, an HCI practitioner chooses a set of HCI methods. These methods must often be integrated into the practices of a system development team. To facilitate smooth, cooperative effort between the HCI team and the development team, the practitioner must understand several things about each method that will be used. First, what description content must be available to begin and to complete the work of a given method? Second, what description(s) will a method generate and evolve? Third, how will the description(s) created by a method relate to the descriptions created by the methods used by non-HCI team members? Finally, given a change in any of the descriptions that a method depends on as a source of information, how should the method be applied to further evolve the content of its descriptions? In answering these questions, the practitioner is elaborating on Figure 4.1 to indicate specifically what descriptions are to be created and what their relationships to each other will be.

Although a project may rely heavily on a published method in drawing this pattern of relationships among descriptions, every project is different. Some projects may require adaptation of existing methods to cope with novel situations. New methods will arise as the character of software organizations and their projects evolve over time. The practitioner who can analyze an HCI method and understand how it relates to other HCI methods and to the larger software engineering process can be more adaptable in the face of novel situations.

The next section discusses the division of descriptions into those that specify the problem a system addresses and those that specify a solution to that problem. This division can help to clarify an overall picture of HCI methods and the software engineering process.

4.3 Organizing Descriptions

Systematically addressing questions of method and methodology requires a framework for organizing the descriptions used throughout the development process. This system development world-view can be broken into two major pieces. The first is a specification of a goal or problem that needs to be solved (what the user must accomplish with the aid of the system). The second piece is the specification of a solution to that problem (a design of how the solution is to be implemented). Each of these chunks of specification implies its own set of descriptions. Figure 4.2 illustrates this world-view.

A problem specification describes the work and knowledge of a group of users. This specification is subject to forces related to the ways in which people think and act both as

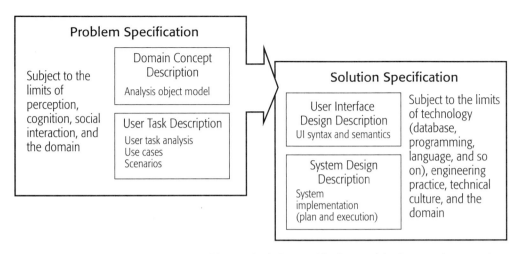

FIGURE 4.2 Relationship between problem and solution specifications and the forces acting on each

individuals and as collectives. HCI practice uses a domain concept description to organize our understanding of the users' knowledge and a task description to organize our understanding of the users' work. These descriptions of the users' problem space are required if software systems are to form effective partnerships with human workers. The problem specification includes the specification of the functionality that a system will be required to provide as well as the context in which the system will be placed.

Object-oriented development practice also splits the specification of problems into two interrelated descriptions. The first description consists of a set of use cases and scenarios that provide a structured description of examples of the domain activity to be supported. This description is, at least in part, a model of user tasks. The second description is an analysis object model that simplifies and summarizes the specification by the example provided in the scenarios. This division nicely corresponds to HCI's use of task descriptions and concept descriptions.

The solution specification can be broken into two design descriptions. These two descriptions will specify how the requirements from the problem specification are to be satisfied by an implemented system. The first solution description is the design of the user interface and the user's interaction model. The second solution description is the design and implementation of the system from a software (and, possibly, from a hardware) perspective. These descriptions specify two separate but interdependent design aspects of the one system.

Whether or not to separate the problem specification from the solution specification is a matter of ongoing debate in the object-oriented community. Many practitioners would use the domain concept description as a first draft of a system design description. Others would separate the two.

Within the HCI community, there are many views on this point. OVID (Object, View, and Interaction Design) [Roberts et al. 1998] maintains the separation of the interface design description from the system design description. At the same time, OVID tends to blur the distinction between analysis and design. Idiom (see Chapter 3), on the other hand, provides a set of descriptions that separate analysis from design and separates the user interface specification from the system specification.

Two basic approaches to the partitioning of information among descriptions are commonly used [Artim 1997]. The first approach is to merge the object model used to represent the domain concept description with the object model used to represent the system design description. The second approach maintains a separation of the domain concept description and the system design description but provides loose coupling between them to aid in impact analysis and model maintenance. Both of these approaches can be useful depending on an individual project's circumstances. In general, the larger and more diverse the staff, the more important these description distinctions can be. For large projects, separation of the descriptions of the problem space from the descriptions of the solution space is advisable. The next section discusses the role of architecture in orchestrating the activities of a large or diverse staff.

4.4 Architecture

However one chooses to organize the descriptions representing the analysis of a user-problem domain and the design of a system solution for that domain, it is clear that a great deal of information must be authored, evolved, and maintained. Architecture is one mechanism we can employ to tame the use of descriptions throughout the development process.

The *Random House Compact Unabridged Dictionary* defines architecture as "the action or process of building; construction *or* the structure of anything" [Random House 1996]. Though the use of the term "architecture" in discussions of software engineering varies, most usage conforms to these two definitions. When we discuss architecture, we are speaking of some set of guidelines or other organizing structure designed to facilitate the successful completion of a system. Section 4.4.1 expands this definition of architecture to describe the specifics the practice of software system construction.

4.4.1 System Architecture

A *system architecture* provides a conceptual framework for organizing and compartmentalizing a software system to better coordinate its evolution and better monitor its development. Although relatively unimportant in small projects (fewer than ten people), system architectures grow in importance as a project grows in size, scope, or projected life span.

Projects with more than 25 staff members or more than two to four applications in parallel development, projects whose target domains span multiple organizational units, and projects whose projected life spans are longer than two years can all benefit from a more systematic organizational framework. A system architecture is all about structuring communication artifacts (design documents, design discussions, and the like) and system artifacts (code, for example). Large projects build many system artifacts and in doing so generate a great deal of communication. Usually, less communication is achieved than is really required to keep things going smoothly. The structure of a system architecture makes it easier to exchange information and build these many system artifacts.

A system architecture consists of four parts:

1. A partitioning of the system into its constituent parts
2. A set of rules governing the interfaces between partitions in a system
3. A set of rules governing the content of each partition within the system
4. A set of guidelines concerning the methods and descriptions used to construct the system

In practice, most designers and developers think of a system architecture as the set of high-level constraints that embody the first three of these four parts. These constraints allow the system to be built cooperatively without every design decision within a partition requiring the attention of the team members concerned with the other partitions.

The utility of this partitioning and of the rules that define the partitions' content and relationships is not limited to enabling independent construction within the partitions. In the proper organization of the construction process itself, the fourth part of a system architecture should make conformance to the construction constraints of a system the path of least resistance for developers and designers. This adherence to process constraints is especially important for HCI activities that, by their nature, are more focused outward into the users' world than they are focused inward toward the construction of the system. Guidelines for methods and descriptions and their organization help to make the outward focus of HCI practice an implicit part of everyone's work without disrupting the necessarily inward-looking activities of development. Section 4.4.2 provides an explicit definition of user interface architecture. This is the working model of user interface architecture that is applied throughout the remainder of this chapter.

4.4.2 User Interface Architecture

User interface architecture is an approach to development processes, organization, and artifacts that enables both good user interface practices and better coordination with the rest of the development's activities. A user interface architecture should take into account the best practices of user modeling, visual formalisms, user interface design patterns, and usability assessment to provide a framework for binding these practices to a system architecture. To be effective, a user interface architecture *must* facilitate a flow of understanding from requirements to analysis and on to design, implementation, and maintenance and back again.

A user interface architecture is a set of principles that guide the construction of a system that features a significant user interface. The guidance starts with requirements and continues through system testing and deployment. These principles help to organize the understanding of the descriptions directly related to the user interface. They also help to organize the understanding of the impact of these user interface related descriptions on the rest of the system architecture and, of course, the effects of the system architecture on the user interface descriptions.

A user interface architecture has no lasting value if there is no clear mapping between the design of the user interface's semantics and syntax and the implementation of that user interface as a working body of code. Equally, a user interface architecture has diminished value if it does not facilitate building of the desired system either with less resource or with greater useful functionality.

If good user interface design practice rests on user modeling, visual formalisms, user interface design patterns, usability assessment, and code design approaches, a user interface architecture is a thread that weaves these HCI aspects together. A user interface architecture also weaves through these components and binds them to the other blocks of a system's architecture. The ETP user interface architecture, which is described in Section 4.5, is one such architecture.

4.5 An ETP-Based User Interface Architecture

At the heart of the ETP user interface architecture is the assumption that the HCI artifacts that form our descriptions can be classified into three major groups: entities, tasks, and presentation elements (or simply presenters) [Artim et al. 1996]. This classification is an elaboration of Jacobson's division of entity, control, and interface [Jacobson et al. 1992]. In ETP, entities correspond to the users' domain concepts—the users' understanding of the referents in their world. Tasks in some way capture the procedural knowledge that manipulates those domain concepts. The presenters serve as the problem-space representations that display a set of entities in a way that is optimized for aiding someone in completion of one or more tasks. Although most of the techniques discussed in this chapter do not require explicit use of the ETP architecture, manifesting this categorization of entities, tasks, and presenters in the descriptions for each technique serves as a basis for coordinating all of these techniques. Section 4.6 provides a tour of key HCI techniques augmented by the ETP architecture.

Jacobson's entity, control, and interface classification was meant to promote stability in design: "Why do these three object types give us a stable system? The basic assumption is that all systems will change. Therefore stability will occur in the sense that all changes will be local, that is, affect (preferably) only one object in the system" [Jacobson et al. 1992]. The ETP classification provides the same emphasis on system stability but refines this approach with the following benefits:

- In requirements documentation, ETP classification helps organize scenarios to aid in user concept and user task analysis.
- In analysis, ETP classification structures the concept model of tasks to maximize stability. For example, tasks that recur in relation to entities are modeled as entity rules—tasks that are bound to and used exclusively with one domain entity. Tasks that encapsulate business logic beyond one entity in scope and not directly bound to a single entity are modeled as domain rules—tasks that are bound to two or more entities and that are used by (triggered from) other tasks. Finally, tasks that manipulate the presentation are compositionally bound to the tasks that are responsible for creating the presentation.
- In design and implementation, ETP classification provides traceability at a granularity that is sufficiently coarse so that model maintenance costs are minimized but sufficiently fine so that impact analysis costs can be minimized in the face of requirements or design change.
- Most ETP structuring criteria are based on human concept modeling and problem solving. As a consequence, clear boundaries are established between analysis of the users' problem space and design of the solution space.

Because ETP classification is based on cognitive principles, it can be applied to the classification of real-world concepts, but ETP applies equally well to the classification of software constructs. It is this dual application of ETP classification that bridges HCI and object-oriented software engineering practice.

Section 4.6 discusses how a few key HCI processes can be enhanced to achieve these benefits.

4.6 Key Processes in Practice

This section provides a detailed discussion of the key HCI-related descriptions outlined earlier in this chapter. It describes a working set of artifacts and processes that have proven to be essential to pursuing usability in user interface design for medium-sized to large organizations. This minimum working set of HCI artifacts and processes, organized using the ETP architecture, provide an organizational framework for the custom configuration of artifacts and processes. Such customization is essential for meeting the variability inherent in the everyday practice of HCI.

The examples discussed in this section, although extremely simple, are consistent with each other. The content of these examples is presented as it might evolve over the span of a project.

4.6.1 User Task Modeling: Requirements

User task modeling is at the core of current HCI practice. Task analysis is the means of understanding the procedural knowledge of our key user populations. This information drives the segmentation of the user interface into discrete pieces (individual windows in the current paradigm) and our understanding of the flow among these pieces. It drives the user interface design within each piece of interface. This information also provides us with explicit grounds for discussions with business process engineers when business strategies occasionally need to be modified to accommodate the pragmatics of end-user tasks.

A user task description depicts who does what and how. For each key user population, a user task description should describe what tasks that population performs and with what frequency. This user task model is important in system design because it specifies, with minimal analytical assumptions, what users must accomplish in the real world to satisfy the users' goals (even though those goals must often be put into the context of some larger organization's goals). In particular, how does an envisioned system aid in accomplishing these goals? This task model defines the task requirements that must be met in order to construct the envisioned system successfully.

Sections 4.6.1.1 through 4.6.1.6 describe an approach to representing a user task model using Unified Modeling Language (UML) modeling constructs.

4.6.1.1 Users' Work Context: Implied Requirements

One important aspect of a user-centered design approach is to have an overall description of the affected user populations. This description should be a relatively complete profile of these populations, including their general work characteristics. This *user profile* should include work context information such as frequency of task interruption, noise and distraction levels in the office environment, size of the physical workstation layout, size and resolution of the monitor, typical educational level, typical experience within the domain, and so on. Some of the more easily summarized information (monitor resolution, for example) should be kept in a separate profile document or as UML tagged values on actors in a use case model. The less easily quantified information (noise and distraction levels are good examples) may simply be documented on video for later reference or for use in briefing development team members.

The essential information about the *users' work context* is really the list of user populations. When supporting the design of enterprise software, even a relatively small company may have upwards of 15 to 20 distinct user populations. It is critical that when system development proceeds independently for many separate applications, someone must have an overall view of how each user population will work across the task domains represented by the applications. If this information can be made accessible to everyone on the project, so much the better.

4.6.1.2 Defining Individual Tasks

Task modeling often begins with interviews of individual users. As discussion progresses, the users will talk about the tasks they perform. Descriptions of each of these tasks should be captured as operational definitions. These definitions should be one sentence to perhaps a short paragraph in length. The value of an operational definition is that it provides a compact description of the essence of the task. Since each task is a problem space (or a part of a larger problem space), the operational definition provides an overview of that problem space. To complete each task effectively and efficiently, the user requires an effective problem-space representation to traverse that task's problem space. The job of the user interface designer will be to engineer at least one problem-space representation that supports each task.

4.6.1.3 Providing an Overview of Each User's Task

One graphically effective way of listing the tasks that each user population performs is to create a *use case diagram* for each actor [Artim et al. 1996]. In typical HCI practice, each *actor* corresponds to a role or population of users. The use case diagram provides a compact way to visualize the relationships among the user's tasks. Figure 4.3 shows an example of a use case diagram. This example illustrates one of the key shifts in perspective from object-oriented application design to HCI (or business analysis).

When providing an overview of one user's role, the application designer will ordinarily consider only those tasks within the scope of the application under discussion, whereas the HCI professional must consider the broader context of the user's work. For example, the diagram in Figure 4.3 includes a use case, Fill Out Time Card. In this fictitious example, the Fill Out Timecard task probably would not be of interest to an application designer working on an order-entry system. The HCI professional, however, will be interested in knowing that this user has a recurring task to fill out their timecard. Even the HCI professional's interest will probably be limited to an operational definition of this task. Scenarios for the Fill Out Timecard use case need only be created if a timecard application is to be developed or if the task model must support detailed work descriptions such as those used to support ISO 900X process descriptions. The level of detail captured at a particular point in an analysis model should reflect the purpose that that portion of the model must support.

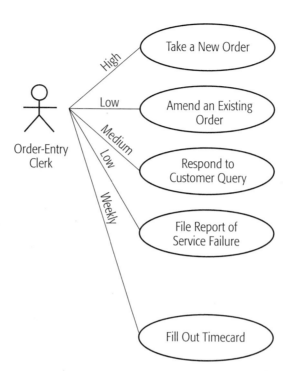

FIGURE 4.3 Use case diagram showing the tasks performed by an actor

In addition to this listing of who does what, the use case diagram also documents how often an actor performs each task and what goals are associated with each task. This task-frequency information provides a basis for prioritizing design work and understanding the design constraints. UML provides a mechanism called "tagged values" that can be used to capture information such as frequency data and associate it with a model element such as the relationship between an actor and a use case. As Computer Assisted Software Engineering (CASE) tools better support UML, the HCI professional will be in a better position to extend existing diagramming tools in support of HCI methods [Artim et al. 1998a]. Even prior to the advent of UML, some CASE tools provided enough extensibility to support these HCI-related extensions such as frequency data [Artim 1997].

In cases in which two or more individuals perform a sequence of interrelated tasks, the system is implicitly supporting communication between users. For example, one user role, Order-Entry Clerk, may be responsible for the task Take a New Order or Amend an Existing Order. Another user role, Shipping Clerk, may be responsible for the tasks Prepare Order for Shipment and Ship Order. These two user roles are communicating about customer orders via the system. Specifically, when the Order-Entry Clerk takes a new order, they are communicating the need for a Shipping Clerk to prepare an order for shipment.

The more spatially or temporally separated these user roles are, the greater the system's communication support role will be. When such a situation arises, it can be helpful to visualize the system-mediated interaction in an additional use case diagram. The diagram can make explicit the scope and content of this information interchange. Or, if such mediated user-to-user interactions are especially numerous or complex, consider employing the user-system sequence diagrams from Idiom (see Chapter 3).

A related and very useful lightweight HCI technique is the Soft Systems Methodology (SSM) *rich picture*, also described later by Andrew Monk [Monk 1998, Monk and Howard 1988]. The rich picture artifact is worth close scrutiny and, given the low cost of creating one, worth some experimentation by the practitioner. Rich pictures depict the context of work for one type of actor by describing a combination of goals, concerns, user-to-user interactions, user-to-system interactions, and user-artifact flow. A rich picture is essentially a snapshot of the user's world from one user's perspective. Very high level task responsibilities may also be appropriately captured in a rich picture. UML is sufficiently extensible so that the content of a rich picture could be added to a use case model.

The goals associated with a task reveal the motivational forces that may selectively bias the user toward some task solutions over others. For example, if a company rewards salespeople for their numbers of sales transactions, it will be most rational if the salespeople structure task completion so that they can complete many easy (perhaps small) sales transactions. But what if responding to customer queries in a prompt and accurate fashion is identified as the most important goal of the business? Then the user may have the incentive to work away from the task that most needs his attention. To better understand how the user perceives and addresses the task space, a simple goal statement should be associated with each user task.

It is often advisable to document the business's goals independently so that conflicts between the business's strategies (business goals) and tactics (the business practices that are reflected in the users' goals) can be made explicit and easier to understand. Where such conflicts exist, their alleviation requires business process reengineering.

Use case diagrams provide a broad overview of user tasks, but most especially they provide a view of how a system's users communicate with each other through the system in order to get their work done cooperatively.

4.6.1.4 Scenarios

Use case diagrams document who does what, but they do not document how it gets done. *Scenarios* document tasks as narrative descriptions structured as a sequence of steps. (These scenarios are defined differently than those described in Chapters 2 and 3.)

A scenario is a description of one concrete occurrence of a task, not an abstract description of all possible ways to complete the task. Scenarios describe concrete examples of specific tasks and are usually in no way exhaustive. Each task should have at least one scenario describing a typical occurrence of the task. Additional scenarios may describe exception cases or alternative ways of completing the task.

The UML sequence diagram can be used to document scenarios for a use case. In this use, a sequence diagram shows an actor interacting with one or more referents. The actor and the referents are represented by vertical lines spaced across the diagram. Each interaction or task step is an event drawn between the actor and an object or between two objects (see Figure 4.4). If a tagged value is used to associate a text description with each event, and your CASE tool has a reporting tool with sufficient flexibility, both a diagrammatic version of the scenario and a narrative version can be maintained side by side (see Figure 4.5). Although this is a cumbersome way to author narrative text, it allows the analyst to compile a CASE tool-managed object model while keeping both the object

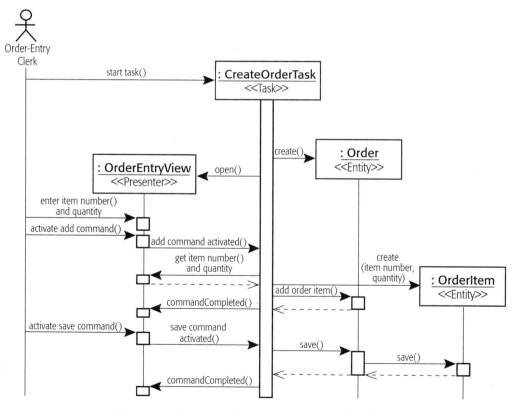

FIGURE 4.4 Sequence diagram used as a formal representation of a task scenario

Take a New Order—Normal Course

Step 1: Start the Create Order task.
Step 2: Create a new Order with a system assigned sequence number.
Step 3: Open the Order-Entry View using the new Order and display it to the user.
Step 4: Enter an "item number and quantity."
Step 5: Activate the "add" command.
Step 6: Inform the Create Order task that the "add" command was activated.
Step 7: Get "item number and quantity" and validate the value.
Step 8: Create an Order Item using item number.
Step 9: Add the newly created item to the Order.
Step 10: Activate the "save" command.
Step 11: Inform the Create Order task that the "save" command was activated.
Step 12: Tell the Order to save itself.

FIGURE 4.5 Structured narrative representation of the task scenario shown in Figure 4.4

model and the scenario narrative text in synch. Ultimately, the savings in impact analysis costs outweigh the cost of keeping these two descriptions synchronized.

Figure 4.4 also illustrates a use of the ETP architecture. The referents identified in the scenario are stereotyped[2] according to whether they are categorized as an entity, a task, or a presenter. Since these referents will also be materialized in an analysis model as objects, this marking can be used throughout analysis as a means of coordinating HCI activities and providing tool support through either programmed constraints or simple reports. The role of the entities in this scenario is apparent, but it is worthwhile to examine the task and presenter referents in more detail.

The Order-Entry View presenter in the scenario shown in Figure 4.4 is, at this stage of work, a simple collector of display requirements needed to support successful completion of this task. The description of this referent should include a listing of all the information that must be displayed to complete this task, along with display structure information. This information must be detailed enough to lead to effective problem-space representation choices. The chunking of interface units (combining similar presenters into a single interface specification) will be examined in Section 4.6.2.2.

The Create Order task documents the sequencing of events as the actor uses the Order-Entry View to complete the Create Order task. In effect, the task, as it appears in the sequence diagram, documents the mapping of the presenter (problem-space representation) onto

---

[2] If this use of stereotypes interferes with other uses of class stereotyping, such as abstract versus concrete class marking, a tagged value denoting ETP classification can be used instead.

the domain concepts. This information will play a crucial role in a later analysis phase as the HCI professional first segments the interface into discrete units.

One word of caution is in order here. The scenario described in Figures 4.4 and 4.5 depicts one envisioned task in the user's system-augmented world. While I argue that such a scenario should reflect real practice and experience (that is, the user's real working context), it will not richly illustrate an extended scenario in the user's daily work life, as the scenarios in Chapters 2 and 3 might do. Section 4.6.3.7, Prototyping and Storyboarding, discusses this latter, larger sense of scenario.

The scenarios described in this section provide a concrete portrayal of each task. Guiding the description of each task with one or more scenarios grounds a task model in concrete reality. If the scenarios make sense and the task model is faithful to its scenarios, the task model will be a faithful description of the users' world.

4.6.1.5 Guiding Task Decomposition

The goal of scenario-based modeling is to specify and elaborate on a set of tasks. If you think of the task description as a task decomposition going from the very general, high-level tasks of the user down to the minutiae of completing those high-level tasks, the tasks described in the course of task analysis correspond to the upper portion of this task decomposition. When development performs use case driven scenario modeling, the use cases capture the lower portion of this task decomposition. Since use case modeling is a form of task analysis [Artim et al. 1998a], the more detailed tasks captured as use cases can be incorporated as lower-level tasks in the overall user task description. Use cases can be represented in scenarios as additional referents in sequence diagrams. This will implicitly reference the decomposition within the scenario diagrams and narrative text.

Ordinarily, it is not user tasks that fill the upper apex of the task decomposition. The most abstract tasks in a decomposition hierarchy are, in many work contexts, a business process decomposition. Organizational units with strategic goals of their own perform these abstract, high-level tasks. If your project has a business process analyst, it can be invaluable to maintain a model of business processes side by side with user task information. A single task description enables the HCI professional to assess more efficiently the effect of a change to the business process or system assumptions on the user.

This three-way distinction between business goals, user goals, and system goals is often uniformly captured in UML as use cases. The resulting cases are sometimes labeled business cases, use cases, and system cases.

Given a three-layer (business, user, and system) task description, the greatest risk is that the task decomposition will become arbitrarily deep and complex. At any level in the decomposition, task detail must be specific to the goals the task must support, and the description of the goals must be appropriate to the actor (role or organization) who must accomplish them. If the practitioner pays close attention to this pairing of goal to task and stays focused on the appropriate goals, the pitfalls of task decomposition can be avoided.

4.6.1.6 User Questions: A Model of Discrete Task Goals

The lowest level of the task decomposition that is essential to HCI techniques corresponds to a description of the problem-space representations needed by the users to complete their tasks and, just above this point in the task decomposition, the major tasks that define the manipulation of these representations. The *user question,* a simple, structured description of the problem-space representation, provides an indication of when the user task description has reached the problem-space representation level of detail.

A user question identifies three things: the object of the task, what it is about the object of the task that must be displayed, and how to structure this display to facilitate task completion. The Create Order task shown in Figure 4.4 would have the following user question associated with it: "For a given Order, which Customer placed it, which Employee is fulfilling it, and what are the Order Items comprising it?" The user question does not address the task goal directly; instead, it describes the problem-space representation needed to reach the goal.

Compound user questions are also possible. Take, for example, the Windows Explorer in Microsoft's Windows operating systems. The user question corresponding to the Windows Explorer would be: "For a given Desktop, what is the hierarchical arrangement of Folders and Devices on that Desktop? For a given selected Folder or Device on that Desktop, what are the contents of that selected object?" This compound user question for Windows Explorer provides a description of both of the fundamental parts of this design—the ability to explore the nesting of folders and the ability to see the contents of one folder in detail. This compound user question corresponds closely to a domain description informed by knowledge of user interface conceptual patterns [Tidwell 1999].

The value of user questions lies in their deceptively simple description of relatively coarse chunks of user interface. When a task model has driven down to this level of detail, concept analysis can begin. If system analysis and design are done in an iterative fashion, with short, complete spirals through the steps, the process becomes more self-correcting. This can be helpful in avoiding analysis paralysis. What is more, the user question structures these concepts into a unit that will be reflected in later analysis: an object (entity), a view of that object, and a description of the entities that must be presented in that view.

Section 4.6.1.4 shows how to define a task concretely by describing scenarios that illustrate that task. Implicit in these scenarios are the concepts manipulated by the user. Section 4.6.2 describes a process for extracting these concepts and documenting them.

4.6.2 Extracting a Domain Concept Description: Analysis

As soon as some of the scenarios describing user tasks have been drafted, preliminary work on the domain concept description can begin. The purpose of this analysis is to provide a simplified static description of the domain; the *domain concept* should represent the users' domain concepts as described within the scenarios. The domain concept description includes the categorization of concepts into subordinate and superordinate groupings, the key associations among concepts, and the construction of concepts out of component concepts.

This concept description can be represented using an object model depicted as a UML class diagram. The classes correspond to concept types in the domain concept description. The latter corresponds to Idiom's domain model (see Chapter 3). The domain concept description includes an object representation of the tasks as concepts.

The activity of concept modeling is analysis in the software engineering sense in that the resulting model is a description of the problem domain. The domain concept description should be free of all design content. This includes both description of code design and description of the design of the user interface. The distinction between user interface analysis and design can be a subtle one. Although we will touch on this point throughout Section 4.6.2, the distinction is made more explicitly in Section 4.6.3.4.

Section 4.6.2.1 discusses how to capture this concept model. Section 4.6.2.2 describes how to organize the description of presentation concepts in this model. These presentation concepts represented as classes correspond to Idiom's view model. Section 4.6.2.3 describes a user interface paradigm that simplifies mapping from concept model to user interface design. Section 4.6.2.4 describes the relationship between concepts in the concept model and the structure of user navigation in the user interface, and Section 4.6.2.5 discusses an approach to describing the dynamic aspect of concepts in the concept model.

4.6.2.1 Defining the Concepts

Operational definitions provide an excellent, lightweight starting point for understanding concepts in the users' domain. Most CASE tools provide some means of associating a text description with a class. Displayed in a glossary format, these definitions provide an excellent resource for all project members, particularly those new to the domain. Even those participants with extensive domain experience will benefit from the added coherence these operational definitions can impose.

A concept should always be labeled with its preferred term. The label should be one to a few words in length. Each concept should be defined by an operational definition. This definition describes the essential meaning of the concept in one to a few sentences.

Concept labels should always be checked against the content of operational definitions using dictionary definitions. This serves two purposes. The first purpose is to check to be sure that the label and the operational definition make sense in isolation. The second purpose is to avoid concept descriptions that are brittle and difficult to evolve. By adhering as much as possible to standard language usage, the concept description will at least retain the adaptability of the language in which it is drafted. Although this heuristic of checking content against a dictionary applies to all operational definitions, it is especially important for the domain concept description. This may seem to be an obvious thing to do, but it is seldom done in practice.

Similarly, encyclopedia articles (*Britannica* is my favorite) can be used to monitor the structure of a concept description. An encyclopedia article's author has expended much effort summarizing an entire domain into a few paragraphs or pages. The author's insight into the structure of the domain can often strengthen the HCI practitioner's structuring of the concept description. This includes the emphasis put on associations among domain concepts as well as the chunking of the domain into related subparts.

The use of the dictionary and encyclopedia help to avoid brittle analyses. An analysis is brittle when extensions of the analysis, usually from a change in requirements, leads to extensive changes in the existing model. When using a dictionary or encyclopedia, the modeler is relying on the robustness of the general use of the language to avoid brittle (and breakable) models.

The UML inheritance relationship is used to represent categorization within the concept types. The categorization terminology here is adopted from Rosch [Rosch et al. 1976]. A basic-level category would be represented as a concept type and shown as a class in the model. A subordinate category would also be represented as a concept type but would be shown as a class associated with the basic-level category with an inheritance relationship. Thus, for example, the concept Document is a basic level category and Order is a subordinate category in the concept diagram in Figure 4.6.

Categorization in concept modeling deserves close scrutiny. Wherever possible, try to be faithful to the users' language. Depending on context, users will often, but not always, shun the use of superordinate category labels in normal discussion. Wherever possible, use basic- or subordinate-level terminology in the interface design. Be especially careful when creating and introducing a superordinate term.

In Figure 4.6, the UML inheritance relationships depicted represent a categorization structure and not an inheritance structure. An inheritance structure reflects a pattern of common behavior shared by a set of classes and indicated through a common superclass. A categorization structure should reflect the use of domain concepts by users or, at the very least, an intended use of concepts by users.

Associations help to document the overlap between one concept and another. Take, for example, the concept Order. The *Random House Compact Unabridged Dictionary* [Random House 1996] defines an order as, among other things, "a quantity of goods or items purchased or sold." This definition expresses and implies associations with other

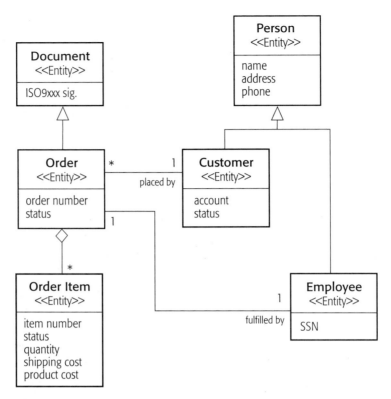

FIGURE 4.6 UML class diagram representing the entities in a user concept description

concepts. The implication is that for there to be a sale of goods, the order must have someone who has placed the order and someone who is fulfilling it. The purchasing party is represented by the placed by association between Order and Customer. The selling party is represented by the fulfilled by relationship between Order and Employee. The quantity of goods or items is represented by a special kind of association between Order and Order Item—an aggregation. The aggregation—in this case a composition—represents a whole-part relationship between the two concepts. In this example, Order represents the whole, while Order Item represents the part. The asterisk next to the part end of the association is the UML cardinality marking for many.

From a practical standpoint, the key to concept modeling is brevity. The dictionary definitions are concise. If a concept's operational definition and associations with other concepts are similarly concise, the concept description will be much more understandable. When needed, greater detail can be captured either implicitly in the task scenarios or explicitly as operations (responsibilities) in the concept description.

Ordinarily, one does not need much more detail than that shown in Figure 4.6. Each concept, attribute, association, and, if present, operation should also have an operational definition. Additional detail is usually not needed to support HCI analysis activities. Any extraneous detail imposes model maintenance burden. If later on you find that you must have additional detail, add it only as it is needed.

Creating this description of user concepts provides a lexicon of the entities that will be presented to the user by the system. Starting from this lexicon provides the HCI practitioner with a means of staying self-consistent from the very beginning of the analysis and design process. In the case of a large evolving system with many pieces of user interface, this may be the only practical way of maintaining a usable level of user concept level consistency over longer time scales.

Figure 4.6 depicts the entity concepts only. In the next section, we will begin to describe the declarative aspects of the domain tasks and the display requirements that these tasks impose.

4.6.2.2 Initial Segmentation of the Interface

The concepts described in the task scenarios are not limited to entities. As we saw in Figure 4.4, these concepts also describe the tasks and presenters that appear in the scenarios. Initially, the tasks and presenters identified in this way are chunked in a somewhat coarse fashion corresponding to the chunking of the task decomposition. A concept description depicting the content of the event diagram in Figure 4.4 is shown in Figure 4.7. This diagram shows the presenter, Order-Entry View, along with the task this presenter supports (Create Order), the entities displayed in this presenter (Order Item, Customer, and Employee), as well as the entity being viewed in the presenter (Order). Each of the three parts of the concept description, the domain entities, and task, and the conceptual definition of the presenter are appropriately marked with the UML stereotypes for entities, tasks, and presenters.

The Order-Entry View presenter supports only one task: the Create Order task. At this point of analysis, the user interface segmentation simply pairs presenters with corresponding tasks. Until the presenter and task concept definitions have been examined in more detail, there is no basis for combining more than one task under a single presenter.

The next association in which Order-Entry View participates is provides a view of. This association is unidirectional and points to the entity that the view will be displaying. Some views may provide the ability to present more than one type of entity. If this is the case, use multiple provides a view of associations with an XOR constraint across them.[3]

Various associations labeled views in context connect the Order-Entry View with associations between Order and its associated entities. A views in context assocation should always

---
[3] See the example on page 102 of [Rumbaugh et al. 1999].

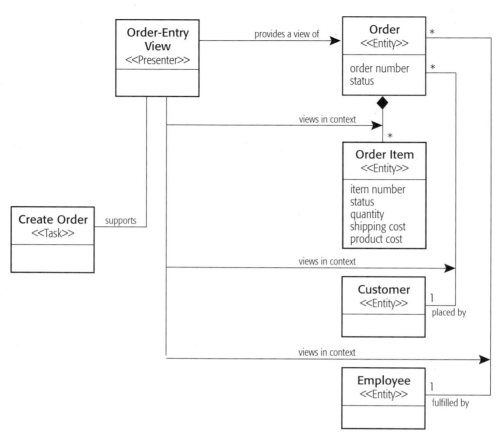

FIGURE 4.7 Concept diagram for one task and corresponding presenter prior to interface chunking

have a presenter as its source object. The target of this association is an entity to be displayed in the presenter, but since an entity can engage in many associations, simply pointing to the entity itself is relatively unhelpful. By pointing to a specific association, the diagram reader can see not only which entity is being displayed but also what role that entity is playing in the task. For example, to complete the Create Order task, the user must view the set of Order Items that constitute the Order. Similarly, the instance of Customer who placed the Order and the Employee who fulfilled the order are also displayed. Use of this association-to-association notation for display requirements is also seen in OVID [Roberts et al. 1998].

The views in context associations can be used to capture a more detailed description of display requirements. If, for example, all four attributes of Order Item should be displayed, an annotation describing this requirement can be attached to the corresponding views in context association. The attributes of Order Item to be displayed can be selectively shown in the class diagram. However, this is not a substitute for the annotation on the views in context association. Also, remember to encapsulate information where it belongs. If quantity can be an integer with a range of values between 0 and 99, this information should be an annotation on the quantity attribute (and not on the views in context association).

The first step in segmenting the interface into pieces that are more optimal for task completion is to examine the list of user questions associated with the tasks. In the case of the Create Order, Amend Order, and Browse Order tasks, the user questions associated with them are identical.

The next step is to compare the concept diagrams for each of these three tasks. If the display requirements are compatible, the individual presenters can be combined and used to support each of the separate tasks. Figure 4.8 shows a concept diagram that generalizes the presenters that appeared in separate scenarios. The Order Editor presenter, like the Order-Entry View in Figure 4.7, also displays an Order's Order Items, the Customer who placed the Order, and the Employee who is fulfilling the Order. In addition, we can now see the complete set of tasks serviced by the Order Editor presenter. This diagram defines an abstract specification for the initial segmentation of this portion of the user interface, including the mapping of the presenter to task responsibilities.

The views in context associations in Figure 4.8 imply display requirements for the Order Editor presenter. If display requirements for a set of tasks are very similar but not identical, the views in context associations should reflect the union of display requirements.

Moreover, the supports associations will imply requirements for presenter mechanisms (eventually implemented by command buttons and menu items) to allow the user to access each of the corresponding tasks. Finally, each entity type that can be the object of the presenter's user question should have a corresponding provides a view of association to the presenter.

The Order Editor presenter in Figure 4.8 is a description of a problem-space representation supporting the tasks with which it is associated. Good problem-space representations should make the user's choice of solution obvious. They should avoid displaying unnecessary information, because this can distract the user from formulating solutions. The driving force in the concept model's description of problem-space representation is cognitive principles [Greeno and Simon 1988] and not software engineering practice.

Capturing the formal model of these presenters is not really what this process is about. It is really about finding tasks that require the same problem-space representation to support the user's timely completion and treating these tasks as one unit. In this way, the task space becomes a more manageable place for the analyst to live.

This segmentation of what can sometimes seem to be an arbitrarily large and complex collection of user tasks and entities into a manageable set of future presentation units can be the most daunting part of analysis and design. The beauty of this approach is that it can

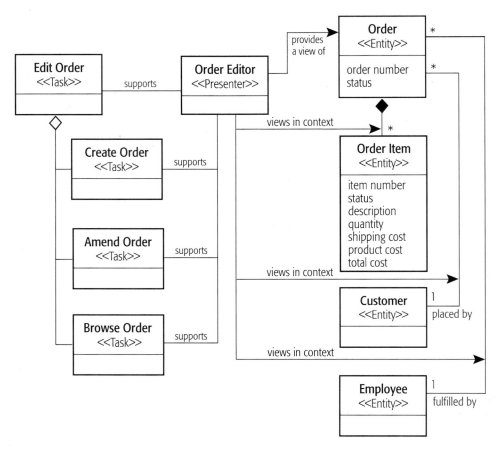

FIGURE 4.8 Concept diagram for a related set of tasks sharing a common presenter

start virtually anywhere in the task space. The approach is, by its nature, iterative. It will take many passes through the task space to arrive at a satisfactory segmentation.

The focus of the presenters, such as Order Editor, described in this section is to define the primary views provided by an application or system. A *primary view* is a chunk of UI that supports an independent task or collection of tasks. Primary views are the focus of user interaction. *Secondary views* implemented with secondary windows, or dialogues, are used to perform small supporting tasks whose meaning is dependent on a task being performed in the context of a primary view. Section 4.6.3.8 discusses independent tasks in more detail. Section 4.6.3.9 describes alternative windowing approaches in terms of primary view characteristics. For a detailed discussion of primary and secondary views, please see [IBM 1992].

The treatment of preliminary user interface analysis described in this section is similar to the process described in Section 3.5.3.

4.6.2.3 The Object-View Paradigm

The purpose of describing tasks in terms of user questions is now more apparent. First, user questions help guide the process of combining tasks with highly similar display requirements under one presenter. Second, user questions guide task decomposition to an appropriate level of granularity. Once task decomposition has reached the point at which one (or a few closely related) user questions are associated with each task, design has reached an appropriate depth of analysis for all but detailed user interaction analysis.

The third reason for making use of user questions in the course of task analysis is that it guides the design toward coherency. Once tasks with similar display requirements have been combined, the resulting set of user questions for the associated tasks serves as an operational definition of a presenter. This simple structured definition, especially when used in a user interface architecture that incorporates the object-view paradigm, leads to modular, understandable pieces of user interface that can be readily combined and applied to real-world problem solving. Tasks whose solution can be facilitated by the same or similar problem-space representations share the same presentation context.

The provides a view of association between the Order Editor presenter and the Order entity shown in Figure 4.8 illustrates the use of the IBM Common User Access (CUA) object-view paradigm [IBM 1992], which is an optional user interface architectural element. The object-view paradigm describes the user interface as a set of objects representing the users' entities and a set of views on those objects that provide the means of browsing and manipulating their content and relationships. Any one view of an object provides a coherent presentation of information about that entity object.

In Figure 4.8, the Order Editor presenter with its views in context associations is an analysis-level description of a view. The provides a view of association between the Order Editor presenter and the Order entity documents the entity type or types that can be viewed using the Order Editor presenter.

Although the object-view paradigm is realized by look-and-feel design elements, it corresponds to a description of user concept semantics that, when properly stated, is free of lower-level design descriptions. Limiting the description of object-view relationships to provides a view of associations in the concept model keeps the analysis model free of design contamination.

4.6.2.4 User Navigation

User navigation requirements come in two forms: requirements that can be anticipated before the fact and requirements that cannot be anticipated.

Fixed Navigation

Those navigation requirements that can be anticipated are modeled using an association from one task to another. The navigation is the usually optional triggering of one task from within another. The triggered task is often not a subtask (in the task hierarchy) of the triggering task. A good role name for these associations is navigate to. These navigation paths are known as fixed navigation paths (or, alternatively, hard-coded navigation paths in reference to the implementation consequences). At design time, these navigation associations will imply the need for a widget in the design, such as a button or menu item, that can be used to trigger the pathway.

An example of a fixed navigation requirement is shown in Figure 4.9. The user interface analyst has determined that the user must frequently look up stock item information to complete the order. A Browse Stock Item task is connected to the Edit Order task via a navigate to association. An interface mechanism to start the Browse Stock Item task must appear somewhere in the ultimate design of the Order Editor presenter.[4]

Flexible Navigation

Obviously, those navigation requirements that cannot be anticipated cannot be explicitly modeled, at least in the conventional sense. If, with respect to the problem domain, a minimally spanning set of user questions is enabled, the user can create ad hoc compound user questions to address many novel problems. Since the object-view user interface design provides all pathways implied by the provides a view of associations in the concept description, the user can freely navigate the domain. These navigation paths are known as flexible navigation paths.

The domain entities and their associations can also imply some flexible pathways. In Figure 4.9, the placed by association between Order and Customer implies the potential need for a pathway to a Find Customer task and possibly to an Edit Customer task. If generic finders and editors can be provided for each type of entity in the concept description, these user task requirements can be met without further design effort. Similarly, tabular views of aggregations can be automatically anticipated irrespective of domain semantics.

Flexible navigation also highlights a fourth and most important advantage of documenting user questions during analysis. If the primary views of a system can each be described by a single user question, the architect can assess these views as user mechanisms for traversing the domain entities. Each user question describes one way of traversing part of the user concept model. The analyst can look at the user questions in aggregate to see if portions of the user concept model remain inaccessible.

---

[4] It is worth noting that conceptually the navigate to association should link the appropriate views in context association with the Browse Stock Item task. Unfortunately, this implies an association on an association on an association, which would lead to a diagram that is as difficult to read as this sentence.

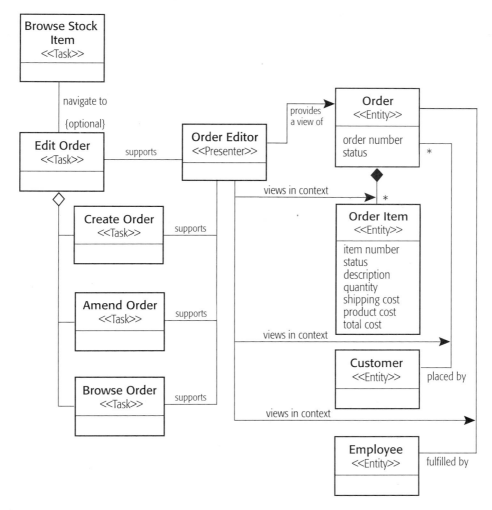

FIGURE 4.9 Capturing a fixed navigation requirement in the concept description

While design and implementation description have no part in a concept (analysis) model, if an analysis feature cannot be implemented, it is of no practical value. Consequently I diverge from the topic of analysis for just a moment, and discuss implementation of the object-view analysis pattern.

Implementing flexible navigation paths is less complex than it might at first appear. In the IBM OS/2 operating system, each view is registered with the system so that the operating system has knowledge of which entities can be opened with each view. It is a relatively simple matter for the operating system to create dynamically a cascaded menu based on an instance of one of the desktop's objects. From those views provided by the desktop, this cascaded menu is available as part of the pop-up menu for any desktop object. Microsoft Windows 95 and higher and Macintosh OS 8.0 and higher all provide a similar mechanism, although user access is more cumbersome.

Providing system support for flexible navigation in an enterprise system composed of many applications requires the creation of a system service. This service maintains a lookup table of view types available for each entity type as well as a registration mechanism and a dynamic menu cascade mechanism. This often requires only relatively minor adjustments to GUI code design.

These two navigation constructs, combined with a presenter segmentation that focuses on independent collections of tasks, provides a modular approach to analyzing the users' domain prior to user interface design. It is this modularity that promotes good iterative practice.

We have focused on static aspects of the concept model. The next section continues the discussion of analysis with a technique for adding some description of dynamic behavior to the concept model.

4.6.2.5 State Behavior

One object-oriented technique that can be extremely useful in concept modeling is the use of *statechart* to describe the state behavior of a class or, in our case, a concept. Some domain entities, such as an Order, will exhibit a strong state character. The entity behaves differently depending on its internal state. An Order might be new, confirmed, shipped, back-ordered, returned, and so on.

Understanding the state behavior of the entity is often linked to understanding and documenting the allowable sequence of task activities that can be performed on that object. The statechart for the Order entity is shown in Figure 4.10.

Although statecharts are helpful in characterizing the concepts themselves, this information really becomes useful during user interface design and during the design of the system implementation.

Many tasks can also be described in terms of their state behavior. Although a detailed explanation is beyond the scope of this chapter, the dynamic behavior of a piece of user interface, such as a primary view, can be described as a composition of tasks. Each task encapsulates knowledge of its allowable states. For example, the Order Editor must support (according to Figure 4.10) an action that triggers an add item event. The mechanism for this support, eventually a button or menu item, can be enabled only while the Order is in the New or Incomplete state. A composed task could model this simple state behavior and enable or disable the button or menu item as needed [Artim and Fulcher 1999].

More than any other part of analysis, state modeling can be very time-consuming work. What's more, because the kind of state behavior described in Figure 4.10 reflects

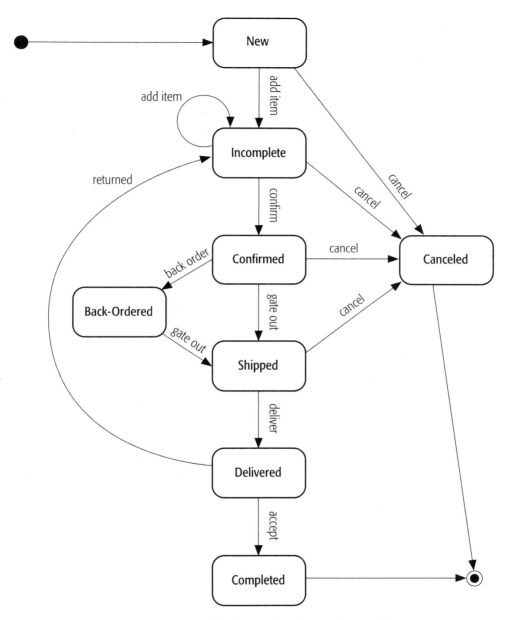

FIGURE 4.10 Example of a state-chart diagram for an Order

some degree of business process, the entire model is subject to evolution as business processes change. The visibility of business process and business process changes the value of a state model. While these models are not used as often as they should be, they can also be invaluable in making intractable requirements discussions more concrete. If stakeholders cannot come to an agreement, at least we can lead them to understand what they are disagreeing about.

4.6.3 User Interface Design

So far, we have discussed how to efficiently capture and represent a description of the problem space for a group of users. We've done this through user task modeling (Section 4.6.1) and user concept modeling (Section 4.6.2). Included in this description of problem space is a description of the presentation requirements. The essential activity of user interface design is to take our analysis description of presenters and translate it into a useful and usable concrete user interface design. This process of translation is the topic of Section 4.6.3.1.

4.6.3.1 User Interface Design Patterns

A *user interface design pattern* can be thought of as a canonical interface design. This canonical design consists of a prototypical combination of interface components used for a particular purpose. That purpose is defined by a description of the task characteristics that determine the applicability of the canonical design. To explore the implications of this definition, let's examine a widget choice example and then scale it up to an example of a canonical design.

The diagram in Figure 4.8 depicts a single presenter, the Order Editor. Initially, our interest is in the relationship between Order and Order Item. According to UML notation, this aggregation association indicates that each Order can have multiple Order Items associated with it. Let's assume from our task scenarios that we have also determined that as many of the Order Items as possible should be visible to aid task completion. We have two commonly available widgets that will satisfy these constraints: a scrollable list box and a scrollable table. The list box will display a list of objects (items) showing a single text attribute to identify each object. The table will display a list of objects showing one to many text or graphical attributes of each object. After a little more research into the task scenarios, we find that the employee who is taking the order must verify the item description with the customer after it is entered and must obtain a quantity desired value from the customer and inform the customer of the unit price and total item cost. This additional information determines our choice of a table as the appropriate widget for presenting the Order to Order Item whole-part association. Johnson et al. [1993] first described this particular use of cardinality markings in widget choice in their ACE work using selectors.

Now let's consider the overall description of the shows in context associations. This summary is expressed by the user question associated with the Order Editor presenter: "For a given Order, show the Customer placing it, the Employee fulfilling it, and the Order Items comprising it." This high-level description of the display requirements, when combined with a review of the associated task descriptions, tells us that a number of heterogeneous objects and attributes must be displayed simultaneously to complete the task. This leads us to choose a "Form" user interface design pattern. At this point, we would go through the display requirements in detail and for each item in the list determine the best widget to display that item. When done, we might have a design something like the one shown in Figure 4.11.

One way to approach this process of user interface design pattern and widget choice is to accumulate a list of task characteristics for each task in the concept description. These characteristics are captured as a set of tagged values. Guided pattern and widget choice support can then be provided via online user interface style guide documentation.

Tidwell [1999] provides an excellent discussion of user interface patterns with an emphasis on the definition and selection of patterns based on semantics.

4.6.3.2 Layout of the User Interface

Even the oversimplified user interface shown in Figure 4.11 demonstrates a few layout heuristics. For example, the form elements are arranged from top to bottom and left to right in approximately the order in which they would ordinarily be encountered in normal task execution. Related items are grouped together, such as when the various totals

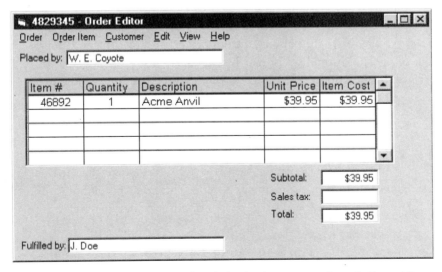

FIGURE 4.11 Prototype user interface design for the presenter shown in Figure 4.8.

are lined up below the Item Cost column in the table. Finally, where possible, the alignment of labels and fields is used to eliminate ragged edges, as with the placed by and fulfilled by fields.

In day-to-day practice, I have seen a bewildering number of useful layout heuristics. The problem for the practitioner is not that these heuristics are hard to express or learn. The problem is that in any design of significant (that is, real-world) complexity, the design will tend to be overconstrained with respect to layout heuristics. That is to say, no single layout exists that satisfies all of the heuristics. The practitioner ends up weighting these layout heuristics and attempting to satisfy as many heuristics as possible in the order of their importance within a particular context. The weighting of these heuristics is a matter of experience and judgment. Needless to say, a more systematic way of organizing layout heuristics would be very welcome in everyday practice.

4.6.3.3 Visual Formalisms and Problem-Space Representations

User interface design patterns are based largely on the notion of visual formalisms [Nardi and Zharmer 1993]. A *visual formalism* provides an abstract display semantic geared to support a particular type of problem-space representation. By "abstract display semantic" I mean the intended usage of display elements to provide a mapping of meaning between these elements and a concrete problem space.

For example, a table, such as the one shown in Figure 4.11, is a visual formalism that maps objects onto the table's rows and maps attributes of those objects (or associated objects) into the table's columns.[5] Other common visual formalisms include hierarchy displays, network diagrams (cyclic graphs), maps, forms, tables, point plots, hypertext, and much more. These formalisms are the basic elements of choice in user interface design and form the heart of a pattern language of user interface design.

Nardi and Zharmer [1993] discuss the importance of providing a command language equivalent of a visual formalism primarily as a mechanism for power users to extend a user interface. In the approach outlined in this chapter, the command language formalism is also used to understand how to map from a concept description to a user interface design description. Each visual formalism has its own specialization of the views in context association for identifying exactly which portion of the domain concept description is mapped to which aspect of the visual formalism. In the case of a table formalism, the association would be labeled views in context as a row. To the extent that a visual formalism describes an abstract type of problem-space representation, this elaboration of the views in context relationship leaves the concept description free of design assumptions.

---

[5] A table can also be used in a situation in which the rows of the table do not represent specific, user-identifiable objects. In such a case, the user's understanding of the meaning of the interface may be more at risk, depending on the context.

The value of viewing the user interface in this way is that it decouples the semantics of a well-engineered formalism from the look-and-feel design elements that support that semantics. This allows usability evaluation and tuning of the formalism's implementation to go on independently of work on the user-task (application) logic. The tasks can be described in terms of the formalism's semantics, not a look-and-feel design.

4.6.3.4 The User Interface as Visual Language

The notion of visual formalisms—that a visual presentation of information can be structured in much the same way as a language—gets to the heart of why HCI practice is important. If designers and developers viewed GUI design as the design of a visual language, they would approach this endeavor with more caution. Projects would be less likely to underestimate the cost of designing the user interface. Additionally, and perhaps most importantly, the real costs of analyzing and understanding the domain could be seen. Too many stakeholders in system development take the attitude that it is "just the user interface." As long as HCI is seen as nothing more than elaborate practices of graphic design,[6] we will be faced with this counterproductive attitude.

When considering the user interface as visual language, it can be even more instructive to consider that it is really two languages. The first is the language of interaction provided by the look-and-feel design elements with which the user manipulates the elements of a visual formalism. This language is the topic of conventional style guides. Specification of the look-and-feel language is largely an exercise in interaction design.

The second language is that of the user's problem domain. This language is manifested in a set of primary views and the objects and actions contained in and supported by those views. Describing this language is the focus of user concept modeling, as described in Section 4.6.2. We may structure a concept (analysis) model so that subsequent design of the user interface can be facilitated. This is the purpose of the ETP architecture, but the concept model must first and foremost be a straightforward description of the user's language.

The first of these languages—the look-and-feel language—should be intuitive (for the users) to the point that it recedes from the users' conscious awareness. The second language—the visual representation of the problem domain—is the explicit concern of the users and should be their nearly exclusive focus when using the GUIs we design for them. Both of these languages must be crafted with the care, and at least some of the formality, that we usually reserve for programming language design.

---

[6] Which is not to say that the graphic design practices that are a part of HCI are any less important. However, the graphic design practices without the cognitive engineering are simply not enough.

4.6.3.5 Compound User Interface Design Patterns

Just as user questions can form compounds, so too can visual formalisms be combined to create compound patterns. Typically, these compound patterns are useful when an abstract, compound task pattern is seen repeatedly either within a domain or across domains.

Consider the problem of finding things in a large system. Even in the absurdly small world described in the examples presented in this chapter, a user may need to find Customers, Orders, Order Items, or Employees. Each of these "finding" tasks requires a very similar user interface. The similarity can be expressed as a Finder pattern. A Finder must provide the user with the means of specifying some search criteria such as name, order or item number, address, description text, price, item category, and so on. These search criteria should be bundled into a form. Next, the Finder must provide the user with a table of found objects along with enough attribute information about each item so that the user can "find" the desired object among any similar "found" objects. Finally, the Finder should provide the user with a mechanism for navigating to some view of the found object so that the user can do work with that object. An example of this Finder pattern can be found in the Windows 95, 98, or NT File Finder.

4.6.3.6 Increasing Development Awareness of HCI

User interface design patterns can be an especially useful tool for communication both within a user interface architecture team and between the team members and the development staff they support. A user interface style guide can be built around a description of pattern and widget characteristics [Artim et al. 1998b]. As few as a dozen common patterns, along with about a dozen common widgets, form the core of information system interface design practice. By providing a description of the task characteristics that indicate usage of each pattern and widget, a style guide can improve development awareness of best practices. In my practice, we have made this style guide available online via an intranet. HCI practitioners can review user interface designs executed by development and annotate the review report with links to the appropriate patterns. The report should include an explanation of why a particular pattern is a good choice. Grounding the discussion in a design of immediate relevance to the developer capitalizes on a teachable moment and can help considerably in raising development awareness of HCI principles.

This task-based style guide approach also improves communication within a user interface architecture team. It provides the team members with a succinct but fairly powerful vocabulary for design discussions. At the same time, it provides a simple and extensible framework for sharing the results of the design discussions with the broader development community.

4.6.3.7 Prototyping and Storyboarding

For many practitioners and most of their users, there is little doubt that a picture is worth at least a thousand words. HCI practitioners depend on prototypes of a user interface design such as the simple one in Figure 4.11. These prototypes help to make concrete our initial efforts to model the concepts that users employ. As prototypes are refined, they help us communicate high-level user interface designs to end users, who often validate scenario content at the same time.

Although discussed near the end of this section on user interface design, prototyping and storyboarding often begin early in a project's life cycle. They are often done in tandem with user task analysis and may even precede the task analysis. However, whenever they are performed, prototyping and storyboarding must be viewed as the most iterative of processes. Prototypes and storyboards are informing for many other HCI and software engineering development processes. If they are not updated as the practitioner's understanding evolves, they can easily mislead.

Prototyping is a nearly pervasive HCI activity. Every chapter in this volume makes at least passing reference to prototyping. One small aspect of prototyping that does bear brief comment in this chapter is the management of prototype material over time. With large applications and certainly with large systems of applications, keeping an overview of prototype content is very important. This can best be done using screen shots of individual primary views organized by view name. For very large systems, it can be desirable to cross-reference these screen shots in the concept description (in the presenter corresponding to a particular primary view).

Storyboards, which are sequential user interface design sketches (that is, prototypical screen shots) illustrating an interesting story from one user's perspective, can be a tremendous tool in user interface design. Storyboards, also discussed in Chapter 3, can bring an envisioned system to life in a way that allows potential users to consider the impact of the envisioned system-based referents in their day-to-day work. Storyboards are one practical application of the kind of scenario-based design described in Chapter 2.

In large systems, storyboards also need to be kept organized, particularly by cross-referencing task descriptions to the storyboards. This consists of keeping track of which tasks and task scenarios are represented in which storyboards. For even moderate-sized projects this information is often fairly obvious and need not be formally maintained. However, consider explicitly tracking the correspondence between storyboards and the tasks and scenarios they illustrate when the storyboards will be accessed by project participants who are neither part of the user interface architecture team nor part of the application team that worked on a particular set of storyboards.

Although in principle the scenarios described in Section 4.6.1.4 could be automatically cross-referenced to content in storyboards or scenarios-in-the-large (as described in

Chapter 2), I am aware of no tool for facilitating this. If a task model, scenarios-in-the-small (as discussed in Section 4.6.1.4) and scenarios-in-the-large were managed by an XML markup based tool, maintenance of this related content would be simplified.

Much of this section has focused on how to organize prototypes and storyboards. This is because their true value is in translation of system analysis and design into terms that all users can share and understand. However, this value is greatly reduced if the prototypes and storyboards do not provide a test of the consistency and coherence of a system's analysis and design.

4.6.3.8 Units-of-Work, Transactions, and User Interface Design

Database designers are often (and quite rightly) concerned with the design of transactions and units-of-work. By "units-of-work" I refer to a set of object instances and changes that represent the result of a significant user task. A unit-of-work is often controlled or mediated by a database transaction, but in many cases this is an outer transaction composed of many nested transactions. The structuring of units-of-work will affect how well the user interface matches the user's expectations of task flow. Under almost all circumstances, it is highly desirable to localize the effects of a unit-of-work to a single primary window. Such a strategy will avoid confusing situations such as: if changes are outstanding in windows A and B and a transaction is initiated in window B, will the changes in window A also be saved to the database?

To make the concept of unit-of-work more concrete, let's assume that the domain shown in Figure 4.6 includes a Customer Editor. Sometime in the middle of making an order, a customer asks the employee to update the customer's phone number. If the employee saves and closes the Customer Editor window, should the partially completed order also be saved to the database? The answer is probably no, because the database should reflect only the change in the customer information (in this case, the changed phone number).

To make this decision, we would once again turn to the task description. Is the customer profile amendment task a part of the order creation task? If not, these two activities should not be included in a single unit-of-work. The task description should reflect the way the user thinks about her task space. If two tasks are thought of as independent of each other, they will appear in separate parts of the task hierarchy. If this is the case, these tasks should be included in separate units-of-work.[7]

Once again, the HCI practitioner employs her understanding of the user's tasks to inform her evaluation of another aspect of system design. The design of units-of-work in collaboration with database specialists can be one of the more difficult aspects of

---

[7] One exception to this generality occurs in cases in which a dependent task is included within a larger task, but in such cases the dependent task would be displayed in a secondary (dialogue) window rather than in a primary window.

collaborative software engineering. Database specialists are concerned with maintaining the integrity of the data for which they are accountable. HCI specialists are concerned that the users' day-to-day pragmatics are understood. It can be very helpful to have clear-cut explanations of these pragmatic issues framed in the context of the system as a whole. In this way, the users' pragmatic perspective is presented in the same overall context as data integrity issues.

4.6.3.9 Windowing Approaches Compared

The approaches to navigation—or, in Idiom terminology, "view behavior" (see Chapter 3)—described in this volume seem to fit into two broad camps. The first camp, illustrated in this chapter, assumes that user navigation is task-based and that fixed task-to-task transitions are not sufficient to cover the full range of user task requirements. The other camp increases usability by decreasing the number of primary views and therefore the number and depth of navigation links among them.

The ETP architecture described in this chapter can accommodate any reasonable navigation structure even though ETP, as presented here, is optimized to take advantage of the CUA Object-View paradigm. This chapter's example is similar to the predominant domain situations in which this author has worked. These task domains were characterized by diversity and flexibility in task sequencing coupled with pre-condition-restricted access to tasks (that is, the user cannot start a task until necessary domain preconditions have been met).

The CUA Object-View paradigm makes these assumptions about user tasks and nothing more. This makes for a very flat set of top-level views in that all primary views are assumed to be independent task representations. A few primary views act as domain object access points. Flexible navigation allows the user to chain through primary views to construct problem-space representations that were not considered by the designers. Although many primary windows may be open at one time, artificial (that is, not task-related) boundaries are avoided and so the potential for user confusion is greatly reduced. If the problem-space representations are carefully constructed, even complex ad hoc tasks will be presented in a reasonably minimal number of windows. Because window content can be directly mapped to the user's tasks, task-based window management can be provided to reduce further any user anxiety resulting from multiple windows open on the desktop.

If, however, such complex and ad hoc problem-space representations are deemed to be unnecessary (an assumption that should be closely compared with the user's world), an application type of user interface can be constructed. These user interfaces are typified by current personal productivity applications, and assume that the top-level view structure is shallow and that users typically do not need to navigate directly from one primary view to another, or that no more than one or two levels of navigation need to be supported and that these navigation paths are fixed. One such approach is described in the Rational Unified Process (Chapter 5).

One word of extreme caution concerns application-style view behavior: The Microsoft Multiple Document Interface (MDI) is frequently used when designing application-style view behavior. The MDI can be a poor choice of view behavior if you are deploying multiple applications and there is *any* chance that the user will need to use two or more of these applications in concert to complete any one task. Restrictions on screen real estate as the user tries to coordinate work across the MDI windows will frequently lead to an inability to view all relevant portions of the applications at the same time.

Whatever approach to windowing you adopt, the semantics of navigation must be faithfully captured in the concept model. Although analysis models should be free of design content, analysis descriptions must *specify* the content of design descriptions. When evaluating HCI methods, one pragmatic evaluation criterion is the absence of large gulfs between analysis content and design content. A group of experienced HCI practitioners might not agree with a design decision, but they all ought to be able to follow the chain of reasoning from analysis elements to design elements.

4.6.4 Implications for Usability Testing

Usability testing, a largely independent HCI activity, can benefit from an architectural approach to HCI. Whether a usability test or a more resource-sparing heuristic review is contemplated, the task model and scenarios provide an excellent basis for planning test activities. For usability testing, test problems or scripts will have to be prepared. These can and often should be based on task model scenarios. The test or heuristic review results will refer back to the task and concept description content. If possible, it is highly desirable to hyperlink usability report items to the description (task and concept model) content. As noted in Section 4.6.3.1, hyperlinking to an online style guide also stretches the utility of a usability report.

4.6.5 System Design and Implementation

If a user interface design cannot be implemented, it is of little value no matter how well its usability features have been designed. For this reason, user interface architecture must concern itself with the bridge between the design of the user interface and the design and implementation of the code underlying that interface. One area of interest is the analysis of the impact of a change in one description to the other artifacts maintained by a development project. The second area of interest is in structuring design to ensure more faithful implementation of user interface designs. First, we will discuss impact analysis.

4.6.5.1 Impact Analysis

Impact analysis is the process of analyzing the effects a change will have on schedule, resource, and requirements compliance. A change can be made to either requirements, the analysis of those requirements, the design of the system that will satisfy the requirements, or the implementation of the system.

The user concept model described in Section 4.6.2 provides a summary description of the user's requirements. In OOSE, an object model is similarly used to provide a summary description of the system's construction. The greatest cost of impact analysis is bridging from analysis (the problem description) to design (the solution description). The simplest way to reduce this cost is to provide some principled relationship between content in the analysis and content in the design.

One way to achieve this relationship is to provide some form of linkage between a concept in the user concept model and the set of one or more classes in the design that directly implement that user concept. One approach is to maintain in the design model a set of classes that directly correspond to the concepts in the user concept model. For example, the Order concept in Figure 4.9 would imply that the design should have a class derived from Order. Simple naming conventions can provide a bridge such that any change in requirements or requirements analysis that touches the Order concept implies the need to trace possible impact on the Order class in the design model. Similarly, a change to the Order class in the design implies the need to trace the effect of that change on the Order concept in the analysis model.

Impact analysis also extends from the design description to the implementation. Verifying that changes to the implementation do not adversely affect the design or the analysis (and therefore the requirements) is just as time-consuming as tracing the impact of design changes. In fact, the cost of impact analysis on code changes can be much greater. To trace the impact of implementation changes, you must potentially trace back twice through both the design description and the domain concept and task descriptions. Here again, impact analysis costs can be minimized if the analyst is able to trace bidirectionally between a class in the design description and a region of the implementation (typically, a set of classes often defined by some packaging unit in a source control library).

Impact analysis of code changes is becoming increasingly easier with the advent of better round-trip engineering tools. Many CASE vendors and most design tool vendors provide some round-trip and reverse-engineering abilities. With some of these products, a practitioner can freely move back and forth between design and code changes with little overhead. Of course, the programmer must leave those little embedded comments where they are—a requirement already placed on Java programmers who are using the Javadoc utility.

4.6.5.2 ETP Categorization and Framework Design

The ability to trace from concept to design region can be further augmented by carrying the ETP categorization through to the design phase. Roughly half of the code for a system that includes a GUI will be in support of the user interface [Myers and Rosson 1992]. The ETP classification scheme is a simple variation on the Entity, Control, and Interface (ECI) classification (ECI) proposed by Jacobson.[8] Carrying the ETP classification through to design can help organize a system design in much the same way that it organizes HCI artifacts. Various processes, rules, and heuristics can be applied to elements of the design description depending on their identity as entities, tasks, or presenters and on their relationships to each other.

When reflected in design, the ETP architecture can be elaborated into framework structures for GUI implementation. There are common patterns of interaction that can be simply expressed in terms of these three fundamental units. Here is a sample of the user interface framework patterns than can be expressed through the language of entities, tasks, and presenters alone:

- Presenters are often compositional in that complex problem-space representations can be constructed out of simple elements [Lovejoy and Mervine 1999].
- Tasks are also described compositionally and can often be modeled by nested state machines [Artim and Fulcher 1999].
- A presenter requires a matching task element to provide a mapping from a domain entity to the corresponding presenter [Lovejoy and Mervine 1999, Howard 1995].
- Tasks and presenters can behave as entities.

These framework design patterns can be equally useful during framework design or in evaluation of commercial frameworks. As with Jacobson's ECI, ETP provides encapsulation boundaries that better reflect system requirements. As requirements change, the object design evolves gracefully. Framework design can directly reflect ETP classification by providing classes in support of entity, task, and presenter. Adapter classes are implemented as task subclasses that affect the mapping of entity to presenter. Presenter subclasses encapsulate the mapping between the presentation elements of visual formalisms and their implementation using a widget toolkit embodying a set of look-and-feel design choices. The advantage of ETP is that it is a classification scheme more closely attuned to HCI conceptual frameworks. Frameworks such as Jaguar [Lovejoy and Mervine

---

[8] See also Figure 6.15 in [Jacobson et al. 1992].

1999], which indirectly embody ETP classification, provide a high degree of stability. Implementations based directly on ETP classification can be structured to match HCI analyses and design constructs at a much finer granularity, thereby providing a smoother evolutionary path for both framework and system.

4.7 ETP Summary

Using mostly "off-the-shelf" UML, we've traced a thread all the way through the range of descriptions of interest to the HCI practitioner. We started with task modeling, moved through concept modeling, analyzed and expanded the concept description to capture and understand the task and display requirements, and ended up in user interface design. The categorization of artifacts as entities, tasks, and presenters has been used throughout as a means of organizing descriptions and systematically understanding the connections and dependencies among these descriptions. Although described only in outline, ETP categorization can be carried through to code design and implementation as well [Artim and Fulcher 1999, Artim et al. 1996].

The CHI97 workshop paper described one difficulty that must be faced by any HCI approach: ontological drift. Although an architecture cannot offer a solution to the problem of ontological drift, the ETP architecture can help reduce the cost of coping with this drift. Section 4.7.1 discusses this problem and its relationship to ETP.

4.7.1 ETP and Ontological Drift

In the CHI97 workshop summary, Henderson raised the issue of ontological drift [van Harmelen et al. 1997]. Simply put, *ontological drift* is the natural process of evolution to which all languages are subject. Ontological drift can occur because of drift in usage within the language or because of evolution of the domain concepts. No architecture can do anything about the phenomenon of ontological drift because it is a property of the world, not of the descriptions we use to describe the world. However, architectures can and should be judged by how well they cope with realistic rates of drift. In the ETP architecture, drift is treated as any other change to a description would be. Changes to a description should trigger an iteration of impact analysis that ripples out from the change.

Ontological drift affects the specification of the entities in a concept description. These entity changes can be traced to the presenters in the concept description that show the entities. From here, the changes can be traced forward to a user interface design description and a system description. The changes can also be traced from the presenters to the tasks that are supported by the presenters. The changes can be further traced back to the scenarios in which the tasks are referenced. Changes to tasks and to presenters can be handled in a similar fashion. This approach to explicitly identifying and tracking ontological drift is especially useful when implementation relies on database technologies that require a static type schema.

4.8 Conclusion

I hope that in the course of reading this chapter you have been convinced of the efficacy of structuring your practice of HCI. The techniques I've described need not be heavyweight. Bits and pieces of this organizational approach can be used in any one project. In fact, I do not believe that there is any one right "methodology." Rather than "methodologies," we need to understand ever-evolving HCI methods well enough to know how to fit them together as new approaches are added to our repertoire. Each and every project we face has its own size, scale, domain, user populations, rates of domain evolution, development culture, business culture, and resources. Because of this diversity, each project we attempt requires that we tune our methods to meet these challenges. What's more, HCI practice must integrate with development practice if good design is to translate into useful systems. It is not primarily the methodologists and researchers, but each and every practitioner who must take up this challenge.

4.9 Acknowledgments

The author would like to thank Lillian Christman for having engineered the organizational context that brought this work to fruition. Thanks also to Jaclyn Schrier for pointing out the CHI97 workshop to me and for collaborating with me on user interface style guide and pattern work, and to my colleagues Richard Fulcher and Wenchi Yeh for putting these ideas into our day-to-day practice and making them far more robust than they could otherwise have been. The development of the "task" portion of ETP was accelerated tremendously through interaction with Charlie Bridgeford and through practice with Jan Jacobs and Debbie Escoto. I am grateful for the astute comments and guidance of my reviewers: Simon McGinnes, Nuno Nunes, and Mary Beth Rosson. Special thanks to Mark van Harmelen for making this work happen from CHI97 to the present volume. Most of all, thanks to Tony Leung and all my AD/Cycle colleagues for creating and compiling these ideas with me many years ago. The blame for any and all errors and omissions is, however, strictly my own.

4.10 References

[Artim 1997] J. Artim. Integrating User Interface Design and Object-Oriented Development Through Task Analysis and Use Cases. Position paper for the CHI97 Workshop on Tasks and Objects, found at http://www.cutsys.com/CHI97/Artim.html, 1997.

[Artim and Fulcher 1999] J. Artim and R. Fulcher. A Declarative Specification of UI Behavior and Presentation for a Thin Client Object-Oriented Application. Poster Presentation, *OOPSLA99 Proceedings,* 1999.

[Artim et al. 1996] J. Artim, C. Bridgeford, and L. Christman. Preliminary Experience Report on the Implementation of an Enterprise System Through Use Cases, Object Modeling and Task Analysis. Poster Presentation. *OOPSLA96 Proceedings,* 1996.

[Artim et al. 1998a] J. Artim, M. van Harmelen, K. Butler, J. Gulliksen, A. Henderson, S. Kovacevic, S. Lu, S. Overmyer, R. Reaux, D. Roberts, J. Tarby, and K. Vander Linden. Incorporating Work, Process and Task Analysis into Commercial and Industrial Object-Oriented Systems Development. *SIGCHI Bulletin,* New York: ACM, October 1998.

[Artim et al. 1998b] J. Artim, J. Schrier, and L. Christman. *Task-Based Organization of a UI Style Guide.* Unpublished manuscript, 1998.

[Christman and Artim 1997] L. Christman and J. Artim. *The Effect of Psychological and Sociological Factors in Collaborative Software Development.* Unpublished manuscript, 1997.

[Greeno and Simon 1988] J. G. Greeno and H. A. Simon. Problem Solving and Reasoning. In S. S. Stevens, ed. *Handbook of Experimental Psychology.* Vol. 2. New York: John Wiley and Sons, 1988.

[Henderson 1993] A. Henderson. A Development Perspective on Interface Design and Theory. In J. Carroll, ed. *Designing Interaction: Psychology at the Human-Computer Interface.* Cambridge, UK: Cambridge University Press, 1993.

[Howard 1995] T. Howard. *The Smalltalk Developer's Guide to VisualWorks.* New York: SIGS Books, 1995.

[IBM 1992] IBM. *Object-Oriented Interface Design: IBM Common User Access Guidelines.* New York: IBM, 1992.

[Jacobson et al. 1992] I. Jacobson, M. Christenson, P. Jonsson, and G. Overgaärd. *Object-Oriented Software Engineering: A Use Case Driven Approach.* Reading, MA: Addison-Wesley, 1992.

[Johnson et al. 1993] J. A. Johnson, B. A. Nardi, C. L. Zharmer, and J. R. Miller. ACE: Building Interactive Graphical Interactions. *Communications of the ACM,* 36 (4), 1993.

[Lovejoy and Mervine 1999] A. Lovejoy and F. M. Mervine. Jaguar: A UI Framework for Java. *OOPSLA99 Conference Proceedings,* New York: ACM, 1999.

[Monk 1998] A. Monk. Lightweight Techniques to Encourage Innovative User Interface Design, in *User Interface Design: Bridging the Gap from User Requirements to Design,* L. E. Wood, ed. New York: CRC Press, 1998.

[Monk and Howard 1988] A. Monk and S. Howard. Methods and Tools: The Rich Picture. *Interactions,* March and April.

[Myers and Rosson 1992] B. A. Myers and M. B. Rosson. Survey on User Interface Programming. *CHI92 Conference Proceedings.* New York: ACM, 1992.

[Nardi and Zharmer 1993] B. A. Nardi and C. L. Zharmer. Beyond Models and Metaphors: Visual Formalisms in User Interface Design. *Journal of Visual Languages and Computing,* 4, 1993.

[Random House 1996] Random House. *The Random House Compact Unabridged Dictionary.* 2nd Ed. New York: Random House, 1996.

[Roberts et al. 1998] D. Roberts, D. Berry, S. Isensee, and J. Mullaly. *Designing for the User with OVID: Bridging the Gap Between Software Engineering and User Interface Design.* Indianapolis, IN: Macmillan Technical Publishing, 1998.

[Rosch et al. 1976] E. Rosch, C. B. Mervus, W. D. Gray, D. M. Johnson, and P. Boyes-Bream, Basic Objects in Natural Categories. *Cognitive Psychology* 8, 349–382, 1976.

[Rumbaugh et al. 1999] J. Rumbaugh, I. Jacobson, and G. Booch. *The Unified Modeling Language Reference Manual.* Reading, MA: Addison-Wesley, 1999.

[Tidwell 1999] J. Tidwell. *Common Ground: A Pattern Language for Human-Computer Interface Design.* Found at *http://www.mit.edu/~jtidwell/common_ground_onefile.html,* 1999.

[van Harmelen et al. 1997] M. van Harmelen, J. Artim, K. Butler, A. Henderson, D. Roberts, M. B. Rosson, J. Tarby, and S. Wilson. Object Models in User Interface Design: CHI97 Workshop Summary. *SIGCHI Bulletin,* New York: ACM, October 1997.

PART III

Use Case Based Design

CHAPTER 5
User Interface Design in the Rational Unified Process

Philippe Kruchten
Stefan Ahlqvist
Stefan Bylund

Abstract

In this chapter, we first briefly introduce the major concepts used in the Rational Unified Process for process modeling, such as worker, activity, and artifacts. We then focus on the elements of this process that are related to user interface design. In particular, the Rational Unified Process utilizes the concept of *use case* as the starting point and the initial input for user interface activities. We introduce a *use case storyboard* to extend use cases with key information related to user interface, and we show how to model the user interface information structure with *boundary classes* and how this drives the realization of a user interface *prototype*.

5.1 The Rational Unified Process

The Rational Unified Process is a software engineering process developed and commercialized by Rational Software [Rational 1999]. It captures some of the best practices of the industry for software development. It is use case–driven and takes an iterative approach to the software development life cycle. It embeds object-oriented techniques, and many activities focus on the development of *models*, which are described using the Unified Modeling Language (UML) [Booch et al. 1999]. The Unified Process is a descendant of Objectory [Jacobson et al. 1992] and of the "Rational Approach," and has benefited over the years from many contributions by industry experts. For a short introduction to the Rational Unified Process, see [Kruchten 1999]. For a tutorial and the general philosophy behind the Unified Process, see [Jacobson et al. 1999]. This chapter is based on version 5.5 of the Rational Unified Process, released in 1998. Since then the

RUP 2000 has incorporated more guidance on user-centered design, in part due to a fruitful collaboration with some of the contributors to this book.

5.2 The Structure of the Rational Unified Process[1]

A process describes *who* is doing *what, how,* and *when*. The Rational Unified Process is represented using the following four key modeling elements (see Figure 5.1):

1. Workers (who)
2. Activities (how)
3. Artifacts (what)
4. Workflows (when)

A *worker* defines the behavior and responsibilities of an individual or of a group of individuals working together as a team. The behavior of each worker is expressed in terms of *activities* the worker performs; each worker is associated with a set of cohesive activities. "Cohesive" in this sense means those activities that are best performed by one individual. The responsibilities of each worker are usually expressed in relation to certain *artifacts* that the worker creates, modifies, or controls.

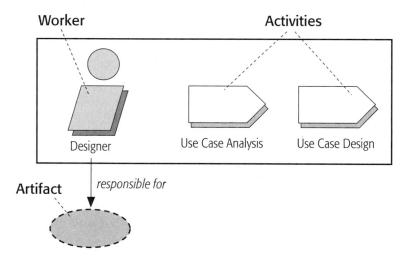

FIGURE 5.1 Worker, activities, and artifact

---

[1] This section was extracted from [Kruchten 1999], pp. 35–48, and has been reproduced with permission from the publisher.

5.2.1 Workers

A *worker* is like a "hat" that an individual can wear during the project. One individual may wear many different "hats." This is an important distinction because it is natural to think of a worker as an individual on the team, but in the Rational Unified Process the workers are simply the roles that define how the individuals should do the work. A worker performs one or more roles and is the owner of a set of artifacts. Another way to think of a worker is as a part in a play—a part that can be performed by many different actors.

5.2.2 Activity

An *activity* of a specific worker is a unit of work that an individual in that role may be asked to perform. The activity has a clear purpose that is usually expressed in terms of creating or updating some artifacts such as a model, class, or plan. Each activity is assigned to a specific worker. The granularity of an activity is generally a few hours to a few days, and it usually involves one worker and affects only one or a small number of artifacts. An activity should be usable as an element of planning and progress; if it is too small, it will be neglected, and if it is too large, progress will have to be expressed in terms of an activity's parts. Activities may be repeated several times on the same artifact, especially when going from one iteration to another and refining and expanding the system by the same worker but not necessarily by the same individual. In object-oriented terms, the worker is an active object, and the activities that the worker performs are operations performed by that object.

5.2.3 Steps

Activities are broken down into *steps*, which fall into three main categories:

1. *Thinking steps*, in which the worker understands the nature of the task, gathers and examines the input artifacts, and formulates the outcome
2. *Performing steps*, in which the worker creates or updates some artifacts
3. *Reviewing steps*, in which the worker inspects the results against some criteria

Not all steps are necessarily performed each time an activity is invoked, thus they can be expressed in the form of alternate flows.

5.2.4 Artifacts

An *artifact* is a piece of information that is produced, modified, or used by a process. Artifacts are the tangible products of the project, the things the project produces or uses while working toward the final product. Artifacts are used as input by workers to perform an activity, and are the result or output of such activities. In object-oriented design terms, just as activities are operations on an active object (the worker), artifacts are the parameters of those activities.

Artifacts may take various shapes or forms. An artifact may be:

- A *model*, such as a use case model or a design model
- A *model element*—that is, an element within a model, such as a class, a use case, a subsystem, or, as we will see in Section 5.5, a *use case storyboard*
- A *document*, such as a vision or business case
- *Source code*
- *Executables*, such as an executable prototype

5.2.5 Workflow

A mere enumeration of all workers, activities, and artifacts does not quite constitute a process. We need a way to describe meaningful sequences of activities that produce some valuable result and show interactions between workers. A *workflow* is a sequence of activities that produces a result of observable value.

In UML terms, a workflow can be expressed as a sequence diagram, a collaboration diagram, or an activity diagram. (For an example of a workflow, see Figure 5.4.) Note that it is not always possible or practical to represent all of the dependencies between activities. Often two activities are more tightly interwoven than shown, especially when they involve the same worker or the same individual. People are not machines, and the workflow cannot be interpreted literally as a program to be followed exactly and mechanically.

5.2.6 Additional Process Elements

Workers, activities (organized in workflows), and artifacts represent the backbone of the Rational Unified Process static structure. However, there are some other elements added to activities or artifacts that make the process easier to understand and use and that provide more complete guidance to the practitioner. These additional process elements are:

- Guidelines
- Templates
- Tool mentors
- Concepts

These elements enhance the primary elements, as shown in Figure 5.2.

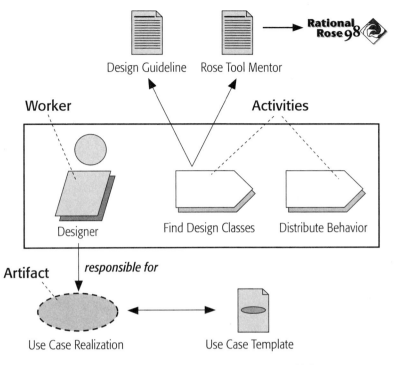

FIGURE 5.2 Adding templates, tool mentors, and guidelines

5.2.7 Guidelines

Attached to activities, steps, or artifacts are *guidelines*. Guidelines are rules, recommendations, or heuristics that support activities and steps. They describe well-formed artifacts and focus on qualities. Guidelines also describe specific techniques, such as transformations from one artifact to another or the use of the UML. Guidelines also assess the quality of artifacts in the form of *checklists* associated with artifacts or used for reviewing activities. We will show some guidelines for the use case storyboard in Section 5.5.

Activities and steps, by design, are kept rather brief and to the point, because they are intended to serve as references for what needs to be done. Therefore, they must be useful to the neophyte looking for guidance as well as to the experienced practitioner needing a reminder.

5.3 User Interface Design in the Rational Unified Process

In the Rational Unified Process, there is one *worker* involved in user interface modeling and prototyping: the user interface designer.

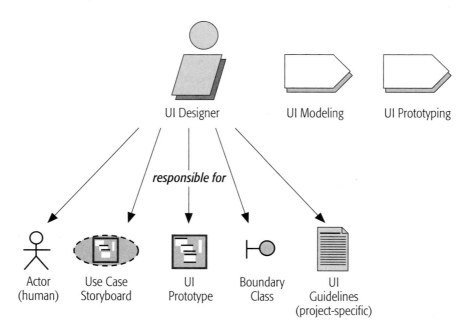

FIGURE 5.3 The user interface designer and the related activities and artifacts

The user interface designer is involved in two activities: user interface modeling and user interface prototyping.

There are two main artifacts that are developed during user interface modeling and protoyping: the use case storyboard and the user interface prototype.

In addition, as a side effect, the boundary classes (from an analysis model) are refined along with the user interface design guidelines that are specific to the project (see Figure 5.3).

5.3.1 Use Cases

The main input for the user interface design activities in the Rational Unified Process is an artifact called the *use case model,* which is organized around users of the system (represented as actors) and composed of all the *use cases* that show how the system is used. Use cases cover all possible usages of the system and do not overlap. The most important properties of a use case are the main flow of events and the alternate flow of events. A simplified version of the flow of events is what we will expand below with a *use case storyboard.* The use case model is also interesting because it allows the designer to ignore the use cases in which the actors are not human, to prioritize use cases (and flows) in order of decreasing frequency of use, and to focus more on the main flows of events than on the exceptional ones.

5.3.2 Analysis Model and Boundary Classes

In the Unified Process, the *analysis model* is an object-oriented model in which classes are assigned one of the following three stereotypes:[2]

- *«entity» class*. Models information that has been stored by the system, along with its associated behavior.
- *«control» class*. Models behavior that is specific to one or several use cases.
- *«boundary» class*. Models communication between the system's environments and its inner workings, and thus models the interactions between one or more actors and the system.

We will see in Section 5.9 that boundary classes play a key role in modeling the information structure, as well as the interaction and navigation, of the user interface. We have found that even in projects for which an analysis model is not fully developed, it is useful to identify and structure the boundary classes.

5.3.3 Workflow

The user interface design activities in the Unified Process are located in the *requirements workflow,* as shown in Figure 5.4. The primary reason for this location is that these activities relate very closely to the requirements artifacts—particularly use cases. In addition, requirements are often enhanced and refined with user interface prototypes. Finally, it is important to remember that because the Rational Unified Process is iterative, this workflow is revisited again and again at each iteration, including the user interface development activities, as needed.

---

[2] Stereotyping is an extension mechanism in UML that allows the creation of new kinds of building blocks that are derived from existing ones and specific to a certain problem domain.

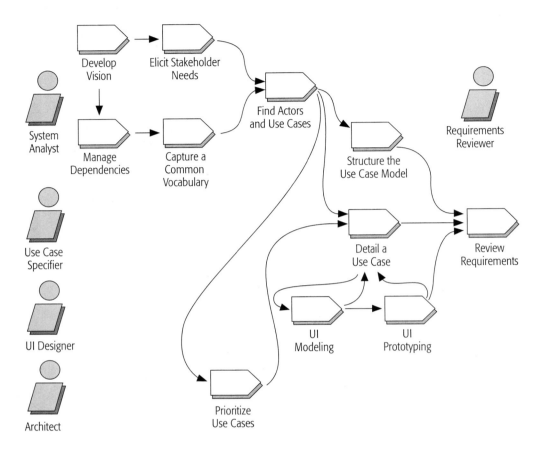

FIGURE 5.4 The requirements workflow, showing the user interface activities in context

5.4 Worker: The User Interface Designer

The user *interface designer* leads and coordinates the prototyping and design of the user interface by:

- Capturing requirements on the user interface, including usability requirements
- Building user interface prototypes
- Involving other stakeholders of the user interface, such as end users, in usability reviews and use-testing sessions

- Reviewing and providing appropriate feedback on the final implementation of the user interface (as created by other developers—that is, designers and implementers)

The user interface designer should not implement the user interface. Instead, the user interface designer should focus on, and devote time to, only the design and the "visual shaping" of the user interface. There are two reasons for this. First, the skills required by a user interface designer often need to be improved and optimized for the current project and application type (with potentially unique usability requirements), and this requires time and focus. Second, the risk of "mixed allegiances" should be limited—that is, the user interface designer should not become too influenced by implementation considerations (as opposed to usability considerations).

5.5 Artifact: The Use Case Storyboard

A *use case storyboard* is a logical and conceptual description of how a use case is provided by the user interface, including the interaction required between the actor(s) and the system. It is represented in UML [Booch et al. 1999] as a collaboration and is stereotyped as «use-case storyboard».

The following people work with use case storyboards:

- User interface designers, who build a model of the user interface.
- Designers of the boundary objects participating in the use case storyboard, who understand the objects' roles in the use cases and how the objects interact. Designers use this information to design and implement the boundary objects (that is, to construct the user interface).
- Designers of the next version of the system, who understand how the system carries out the flow of events in terms of boundary objects. For example, a change may affect a limited number of use cases, thus the designers need to see the realization of their flow of events.
- Testers, who test the system's use cases.
- Managers, who plan and follow up the analysis and design work.

5.5.1 Properties

Use case storyboard properties are shown in Table 5.1.

TABLE 5.1 Use Case Storyboard Properties

Property Name	Brief Description	UML Representation
Flow of events: storyboard	A high-level textual description of the interaction between the user and the system during the use case. This description is augmented with usability aspects of the use case to clarify and outline the allocation of usability requirements into boundary classes. This description can also be augmented with boundary classes for further clarification.	Tagged value of type "formatted text"
Interaction diagrams	The sequence and collaboration diagrams describing how the use case is realized in terms of collaborating boundary objects and actors	Participants are owned via aggregation "behaviors"
Class diagrams	The diagrams describing the boundary classes and relationships that participate in the realization of the use case	Participants are owned via aggregation "types" and "relationships"
Usability requirements	A textual description that collects all usability requirements on the use case storyboard that need to be taken care of during user interface prototyping and implementation. Examples are maximum execution time (for example, how long it should take a trained user to execute a scenario) and maximum error rate (for example, how many errors a trained user is allowed to make when executing a scenario).	Tagged value of type "short text"
References to the user interface prototype	To further clarify a use case storyboard, this can refer to the parts (such as windows) of the user interface prototype corresponding to its participating boundary classes.	Tagged value of type "short text"
Trace dependency	A trace dependency to the use case in the use case model that is storyboarded	Owned by the system via the aggregation "trace"

5.5.2 Timing

Use case storyboards are produced as soon as their corresponding use cases are prioritized for consideration from a usability perspective. Use case storyboarding is done before the user interface is prototyped and implemented (that is, both in the requirements workflow and in the analysis and design workflow).

5.5.3 Responsibility

A user interface designer is responsible for the integrity of the use case storyboard and ensures that the following requirements are met:

- Flow of events-storyboard is readable and suits its purpose.
- Diagrams describing the use case storyboard are readable and suit their purpose.
- Usability requirements are readable and suit their purpose, and correctly capture the usability requirements of the corresponding use case in the use case model.
- Trace dependency to the corresponding use case in the use case model is correct.
- Relationships, such as communicates associations, uses and extends relationships, of the corresponding use case in the use case model are handled correctly within the use case storyboard.

We recommend that the user interface designer responsible for a use case storyboard also be responsible for the boundary classes and relationships employed in the use case storyboard.

5.6 Activity: User Interface Modeling

The purpose of the user interface modeling activity is to build a model of the user interface that supports the reasoning about its usability and its enhancement.

The key input to this activity is the use case model, which is the set of use cases that define (most of) the requirements of the system. Each use case, prioritized for consideration from a usability perspective in the current development iteration, is treated as follows:

1. Describe the characteristics of related actors.
2. Create a use case storyboard.
3. Describe the flow of events-storyboard.
4. Capture usability requirements on the use case storyboard.
5. Find boundary classes needed by the use case storyboard.
6. Describe interactions between boundary objects and actors.
7. Complement the diagrams of the use case storyboard.
8. Refer to the user interface prototype from the use case storyboard. For the identified boundary classes, follow these steps:
    8.a. Describe the responsibilities of boundary classes.
    8.b. Describe the attributes of boundary classes.
    8.c. Describe the relationships between boundary classes.

8.d. Describe the usability requirements on boundary classes.
8.e. Present the boundary classes in global class diagrams.
9. Evaluate your results.

Note: These steps are presented in a logical order, but you may have to alternate between them or perform some of them simultaneously. Also, some steps are optional depending on the complexity of the specific user interface under consideration.

Step 1: Describe the Characteristics of Related Actors

Describe the characteristics of the (human) actors related to the use case. Focus on describing the primary actor of the use case, because the major part of the interaction involves this actor. This information is important for the subsequent steps.

Step 2: Create a Use Case Storyboard

Start by creating a use case storyboard for the use case and assigning a trace dependency between the two. The use case storyboard has various properties, such as text fields and diagrams, which describe the usability aspects of the use case.

Step 3: Describe the Flow of Events-Storyboard

The step-by-step description of each use case that is input to this activity needs to be refined and focused on usability issues. This refinement is captured in the flow of events-storyboard property of the use case storyboard, which is a simplified version of the flow of events from the use case. (We add "-storyboard" to mark the distinction.)

Start by creating an initial outline of the flow of events-storyboard using brief action statements to acquire an understanding of the use case. Then complement the flow of events-storyboard with the desired guidance, average values and volumes of objects, and average action usage for the different parts of the flow of events.

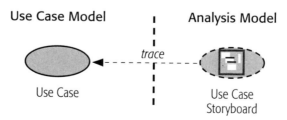

FIGURE 5.5 A use case storyboard in the analysis model can be traced to a use case in the use case model.

Step 4: Capture Usability Requirements on the Use Case Storyboard

Capture the usability requirements on the use case storyboard by defining how high the usability of the user interface must be. This step will be further described and illustrated in Section 5.9.

Step 5: Find Boundary Classes Needed by the Use Case Storyboard

In this step, we identify the central and primitive boundary classes needed to provide the user interface of the use case.

Identify Central Boundary Classes

Identify one central boundary class representing the primary window with which the actor is interacting. If such a class already exists, consider reusing it, because you should strive to minimize the number of primary windows a particular actor needs to interact with. However, you will, of course, have to compromise; primary windows should not be too complex or cluttered. These central boundary classes are often aggregates of more primitive boundary classes (see below).

> #### Example of a Central Boundary Class
>
> The central boundary class identified in a mail application is Mail Box.

Identify Primitive Boundary Classes

Study the flow of events-storyboard in detail, and any other use case descriptions at hand. Look for information interesting to the user and information that needs to be visible and managed in the user interface. Consider any business entity objects and any terms (especially nouns) in a glossary. Also consider entity objects if they exist. These are ways of gaining an understanding of which information is manipulated by the system and is therefore also interesting to the user. Then create one boundary class for each entity object manipulated by the actor through the user interface. When doing this, always consider reusing existing boundary classes. The result of this step will prepare you for the building of an object-oriented user interface—that is, an interface in which many of the entity objects are portrayed at the user interface and in which the user can interact with them.

> #### Examples of Primitive Boundary Classes
>
> The primitive boundary classes identified in a mail application include Mail Message Attachment.
>
> The primitive boundary classes identified in a document editor include Paragraph and Footnote.

Outline the Identified Boundary Classes

Describe obvious things about the boundary classes. At this stage, it is often possible to outline most of their attributes, aggregations and associations and some of their responsibilities. Recall that central boundary classes are often aggregations of more primitive boundary classes. Each class will be refined and described in detail in the following steps.

Relate the Boundary Classes to the Use Case Storyboard

The boundary classes participating in a use case storyboard need to be related to it. This is done by capturing the classes in class diagrams, including their relationships, attached to the use case storyboards.

Step 6: Describe Interactions Between Boundary Objects and Actors

This step is optional and is done if the interaction sequence (for example, the flow of windows and navigation paths) needs to be captured formally in an interaction diagram.

Step through the flow of events of the use case (or, more precisely, the subset of the use case under consideration in the current iteration) and identify the boundary objects responsible for the visible behavior of the use case. Note that these boundary objects are instances of the boundary classes as found in the preceding step. Illustrate the interactions between the participating boundary objects by creating one or more collaboration diagrams.

The collaboration diagram should also show interactions between the system and its actors. The flow of events usually begins when one of the actors requests something from the system, because an actor always invokes the use case.

Illustrate the interactions between objects by creating links between them; annotate the links with a short description of the intent of the invoking object—that is, what it wants to achieve in the interaction with the invoked object. These "intents" will then be integrated into responsibilities on each corresponding boundary class, as described in Step 8.a: Describe the Responsibilities of Boundary Classes.

Step 7: Complement the Diagrams of the Use Case Storyboard

Step 8: Refer to the User Interface Prototype from the Use Case Storyboard

Steps 7 and 8 are optional and are done if the diagrams and descriptions (as created above) need to be complemented and further clarified with references to an already existing user interface prototype. See Section 5.9.

The following steps (a to e) take place for each boundary class.

Step 8.a: Describe the Responsibilities of Boundary Classes

The approach to follow in this step is similar to the description of the responsibility of a class in analysis. The only difference is that the demands are extracted from use case storyboards rather than from use case realizations.

Note that a responsibility is a textual description of a cohesive subset of the behavior provided by a class. Given this, the responsibilities of boundary classes can be considered high-level descriptions of the operations provided by the user interface and its windows.

Step 8.b: Describe the Attributes of Boundary Classes

The approach to follow in this step is similar to the description of attributes and associations in object-oriented analysis.

Note that the attributes and their types should be conceptual and should serve as high-level descriptions of the properties of objects (such as windows) in the user interface. Also, these attributes may become classes themselves when the user interface is designed and implemented.

Step 8.c: Describe the Relationships Between Boundary Classes

In this step, we define aggregations, associations, and generalizations between boundary classes.

Step 8.d: Describe the Usability Requirements on Boundary Classes

Most of the usability requirements on the use case storyboard found in Step 4 should be distributed as requirements on the participating boundary classes and then refined at the class level if necessary.

Step 8.e: Present the Boundary Classes in Global Class Diagrams

The class diagrams created in Step 5 are local to the use case storyboard. However, in many cases it is of value to present the boundary classes in "global" class diagrams that are not local to any use case storyboard—for example, when used as input to the user interface prototyping activity. Such class diagrams can include the following:

- The most important boundary classes and their relationships. Diagrams of this type can function as a summary of the model and can be of great help in, for example, a review of the model or a prioritization of which parts of the model will be focused on in the current development iteration.

- Boundary classes that together constitute a specific user interface.
- Important or deep aggregation hierarchies of boundary classes.
- Associations between boundary classes in different aggregation hierarchies.
- Generalization hierarchies of boundary classes.

Step 9: Evaluate Your Results

The use case storyboards should be evaluated to verify that the work is headed in the right direction.

5.7 Artifact: The User Interface Prototype

A user interface prototype is a rough initial model of the user interface. For example, the prototype can manifest itself as any of the following:

- Paper sketches or pictures
- Bitmaps from a drawing tool, or design comps[3]
- An interactive executable prototype (for example, in Microsoft Visual Basic)

In most projects, you should use all three prototypes, in the order given here.

5.7.1 Purpose

The following people use the user interface prototype:

- Use case authors, to understand the user interface for a use case
- Object analysts, to understand how the user interface impacts the analysis of the system
- Designers, to understand how the user interface impacts the system and what it requires from the "inside" of the system
- Testers of the classes, to plan testing activities

5.7.2 Timing

The user interface prototype is built early—during the inception phase or at the beginning of the elaboration phase, and before the entire system (including its "real" user interface) is analyzed, designed, and implemented.

---

[3] Graphic designers' jargon for "compositions."

Note that the main purpose of creating a user interface prototype is to be able to expose and test both the functionality and the usability of the system before the real design and development begin. In this way, you can ensure that you are building the right system before you spend too much time and resources on development.

For this early testing to be achieved, the prototype must be significantly cheaper to develop than the real system, while still having enough capabilities to be able to support a meaningful use test.

5.7.3 Responsibility

A user interface designer is responsible for the integrity of the user interface prototype, thereby ensuring that the prototype will contribute to a usable user interface according to the requirements from use case storyboards and boundary objects.

5.8 Activity: User Interface Prototyping

The purpose of this activity is to create a user interface prototype. For each use case storyboard to be prototyped in the current iteration, you must perform the following steps:

1. Design the user interface prototype.
2. Implement the user interface prototype.
3. Obtain feedback on the user interface prototype.

Note that these steps are presented here in a logical order, but it is likely that you will need to alternate between them and perform them in parallel. Initially, you will spend most of your time designing the prototype; later, when you know more about the prototype, you will spend most of your time implementing and getting feedback on the prototype.

Step 1: Design the User Interface Prototype

The following aspects of the design of the user interface prototype must be considered:

1.a. Identify the primary windows.
1.b. Design the visualization of the primary windows.
1.c. Design the operations of the primary windows.
1.d. Design the property windows.
1.e. Design the operations involving multiple objects.
1.f. Design miscellaneous features.

However, you need not consider *all* of these aspects in the prototype, or at least not all at once. Instead, it is often appropriate to leave some aspects to the implementers and thus not deal with them in the prototype. In this case, we recommend that you focus on the aspects early in the list and leave the remaining aspects alone.

While you design the prototype, you should continuously implement your design (see Step 2: Implement the User Interface Prototype, below) and expose it to others (see Step 3: Obtain Feedback on the User Interface Prototype), and take into consideration any project-specific user interface guidelines or style guide.

Step 1.a: Identify the Primary Windows

Each boundary class aggregate yields a candidate for a *primary window* in the user interface. However, remember that one of our goals in building the object model (the boundary classes) was to make aggregation hierarchies as shallow as possible—essentially to minimize the number of primary windows and thus the length of the window navigation path connecting them. In addition to adding needless interaction overhead, a window navigation path that is too long makes it more likely that the user will "get lost" in the system. Ideally, all windows should be opened from a main primary window, thereby resulting in a maximum window navigation length of 2. Try to avoid window navigation lengths greater than 3.

The *main primary window* should be the window that is opened when the user launches the application. Normally, it is always open as long as the application is running, and it is the place where the user spends a considerable part of his "use time." Because it is always open and because it constitutes the user's first contact with the system, the main primary window is the foremost vehicle for enforcing the user's mental model of the system.

The most obvious candidate for the main primary window is defined by the top boundary class of the aggregation hierarchy—for example, the document class in a document editor. If there are several aggregation hierarchies, choose the one that is most important to the user—that is, the one in which the major part of the use time is spent.

When the main primary window is identified, you should consider the other aggregate classes that are part of the aggregation hierarchies and decide whether or not they should be designed as primary windows. The default recommendation is that they should be designed as composites instead of primary windows in their own right, if possible. Again, this is done to minimize both the number of primary windows and the length of the window navigation path connecting them. Moreover, a composite is often justified by the fact that its constituents need to be shown together and in spatial relation to the constituents of other composites. Note that this is hard to achieve if (primary) windows are used instead.

Examples of Primary Windows

The Paragraph aggregate in a document editor is designed as a composite instead of a primary window in its own right. This is done partly because the constituents of a Paragraph—that is, its Characters—should be shown together and in spatial relation to the Characters of other Paragraphs.

As an alternative design, imagine the usability of a document editor in which the user has to navigate to a separate (primary) window each time the contents of a specific paragraph are to be viewed.

However, it is often the case that not all aggregates can be designed as composites, because of limitations in screen area. If there is insufficient room for designing all aggregates as composites, try at least to design the following aggregates as composites:

- The aggregates that are central to the user's mental model of the system
- The aggregates in which the user will spend the greatest amount of use time
- The aggregates that provide the initiation of use cases

There is an important factor to consider in this step: the average object volume—that is, the number of objects that potentially need to be shown at once. Too many objects may imply that they cannot be designed as composites; instead, they may have a compact representation in the primary window in which they reside and then define primary windows of their own.

Step 1.b: Design the Visualization of the Primary Windows

The visualization of the primary windows, and of the main primary window in particular, will have a significant impact on the usability of the system. Designing this visualization means partly that you have to look at which parts (attributes) of the contained objects should be visualized. The flow of events-storyboard descriptions (especially when extended with the desired guidance needed) will help you prioritize which attributes to show. If the user needs to see many different attributes of the objects, you may implement several views of a primary window with each view visualizing a different set of attributes. Designing this visualization also means that you have to look at how the parts (attributes) of the contained objects should be visualized by using all visual dimensions.

If a primary window contains objects of several different classes, it is important to find "common denominators" for these classes—for example, attribute types that are contained in all or most classes. By visualizing common denominators by some dimension, the user can relate objects of the different classes with each other and start to see patterns. This greatly increases the "bandwidth" of the user interface.

Examples of Common Denominators

Assume that you have a customer service system in which you want to show such aspects as:

- The customer's complaints and questions over time
- Which products the customer has purchased over time
- How much the customer has been invoiced over time

Here, a common denominator is "time." Thus, displaying complaints/questions, purchases, and invoices beside each other on the same horizontal time axis will enable the user to see patterns of how these items are related (if indeed they are).

Step 1.c: Design the Operations of the Primary Windows

The responsibilities of the boundary classes specify the operations required by their corresponding windows. The operations of the primary windows and their contained objects are commonly provided as menu items in a menu bar and may be provided as alternatives via shortcuts and toolbars. If a primary window contains objects of several classes, and these objects have different operations, you can assign one menu for each class or one menu for each group of cohesive operations.

Example of a Primary Window Operation

In a document editor, there is an edit menu that groups cohesive operations such as cut, copy, and so on.

Note also that some operations may require complex interactions with the user, thereby justifying secondary windows of their own.

Example of a Secondary Window

In a document editor, there is a Print operation on a document that, owing to its complex interaction, justifies a separate dialogue window.

Step 1.d: Design the Property Windows

Property windows need to be designed for all boundary classes to make all their attributes available to the user. Note that some objects may be only *partly* visualized when they reside within a primary window (see Step 1.b: Design the Visualization of the Primary Windows), and yet their property windows will, on the other hand, visualize all their attributes. Note that any average attribute values are important inputs to this step, because they help in deciding the optimal visualization of a specific attribute.

Some of the simple responsibilities of boundary classes, such as setting the value of a specific attribute, are often provided as operations by the property window. In this case, such an operation either is unavailable in the primary window in which the object resides or can work as an alternative or complement to a similar operation in the primary window.

Also, if a boundary class is part of an association, this association (including the associated objects) is normally represented in the property window.

Step 1.e: Design the Operations Involving Multiple Objects

If a boundary class defines a large number of objects to be visualized in the user interface, it is often delicate to design operations involving these objects. Listed below are different variants of such operations:

- Searching among multiple objects
- Sorting of multiple objects
- User-controlled inheritance among multiple objects
- Management of browsing hierarchies of multiple objects
- Selection of multiple objects

Step 1.f: Design Miscellaneous Features

You must add the necessary dynamic behavior to the user interface. Most dynamics are given by the target platform, such as the select-operate paradigm, the open by double clicking paradigm, the pop-up menus on the right mouse button paradigm, and so on. There are, however, some decisions you need to make, including:

- How to support window management
- What session information, such as input cursor position, scroll bar position, opened windows, window sizes, relative window positions, and so on, to store between sessions
- Whether to support single- or multiple-document interfaces (SDIs or MDIs) for your primary windows

Also, you must evaluate other common features that can enhance usability, including:

- Whether "online help," including "wizards," should be provided
- Whether an "undo" operation should be provided to make the system safe for exploration
- Whether "agents" should be provided to monitor user events and actively suggest actions
- Whether "dynamic highlighting" should be provided to visualize associations
- Whether user-defined "macros" should be supported
- Whether there are specific areas that should be user-configurable

Step 2: Implement the User Interface Prototype

There are basically three kinds of implementations of a user-interface prototype:

- Drawings, which are created by the use of pencil and paper
- Bitmaps and design comps, which are created in a bitmap editor
- Executables, which are mock-up applications that can "run" and interact with end users

In most projects, you should use all three kinds of implementations, in the order given here, because this allows for the simple incorporation of changes early on, since their typical implementation times differ greatly (drawings are much faster to create and modify than executables). However, drawings do not properly reflect limited screen area; it is easy to put more in a drawing than there is room for on the screen.

In the end, a good way to specify the user interface is through a combination of bitmaps and executables. This should be done as soon as you need to expose the prototype to people other than user interface designers. A bitmap can specify the exact look of the primary windows, whereas the executables can approximate the look of the primary windows, and support their operations, as well as the look and behavior of the secondary windows. Naturally, it's better to implement the exact look of the primary windows in the executable, with a reasonably small effort, than to combine the executable with a bitmap. If you don't have enough resources to produce an executable, you can use bitmaps as the final implementation of the prototype. In this case, it can be useful to complement them with use case storyboards describing their dynamics; otherwise, chances are good that the implementers of the user interface will get the dynamics wrong.

Note that the focus should not be on achieving a good structure and modularization of the source code for the executable prototype; instead, the focus should be on creating a throwaway prototype that visualizes the significant aspects of the user interface and provides some of its significant operations. Moreover, a prototype is likely to change several times when it is designed and exposed to others, and these changes are often made as cheap patches. As a result, the source code of the prototype is often of very limited value, and not "evolutionary," when the real user interface is to be implemented.

In general, it is of value that an executable prototype is cheaper to implement than an implementation of the real user interface. The following are some differences between the prototype and the real implementation of the user interface.

- The prototype need not support all use cases and scenarios. Instead, only a small number of use cases and/or scenarios may be prioritized and supported by the prototype.
- The primary windows are often the most complicated to implement; if you make an advanced user interface that truly takes advantage of the visualization potential, it may be difficult to find ready-made components.

Rather than implementing new components, you can normally use primitive components, such as push, toggle, or option buttons, as an approximation of how the user interface will look for a certain set of data. If possible, make several prototypes showing different sets of data that cover the average values and object volumes. Simulate, or ignore, all operations on windows that are nontrivial to implement. Simulate, or ignore, the internals of the system, such as business logic, secondary storage, multiple processes, and interactions with other systems.

Step 3: Obtain Feedback on the User Interface Prototype

It is immensely important to expose the user interface prototype to others, but to get valuable feedback you don't have to go through full-blown use tests in which real users perform real tasks with the prototype. Most of the errors you find in use tests are simply flaws caused by a strange kind of "blindness" that makes you "not see" the obvious things that anyone who wasn't involved in the user interface design could have told you about.

As the design and implementation of the prototype progresses, you expose the design to increasing numbers of reviewers, including other project members, external usability experts, and users.

Exposing the Design to Other Project Members

This is an often underestimated way of exposing the design. It has a very fast turnaround time. Project members are already familiar with the application, and they are usually very available for a spontaneous demo. Do this continuously during the activity to cure your own "blindness."

Exposing the Design to External Usability Experts

A good usability expert, by virtue of the expert's skills and possibly a different perspective on the user interface, can facilitate development by pointing out obvious usability flaws. It can thus be of value to involve external usability experts during the first half of the activity so that you have time to work in the new direction, as suggested by the experts.

Exposing the Design to Users

Making demos for users is usually good use of your time. Do this as often as you can (access to users is often limited) to correct misperceptions made during requirements capture. However, don't expose the prototype to users before you have at least a decent bitmap prototype of the main primary window, and don't expose the same user to the prototype more than once, because the second time the user will be tainted by your earlier design ideas (similar to the "blindness" mentioned previously).

Also, be careful to set the expectations right. Many users will want to have the right behavior behind the user interface—that is, the windows—when the system is built.

How to Expose the Prototype

The best way to expose a prototype is often to sit together with the person you expose it to in front of a screen showing the prototype. Walk through a common scenario—for example, a use case's normal flow with normal values, as described in a use case storyboard. Encourage the person to ask questions and make comments. Take notes.

Another, rather overestimated, way of exposing the design is to perform use tests. In a use test, real users perform real tasks with the prototype. The problem with this is that to get reliable results you must do the following. First, you must have a very complete vertical prototype that is almost as functional as the final user interface. When you have reached this far in development, it is usually too expensive to make significant changes. Second, you must provide the user with sufficient training. Most users will be "improving intermediates," and if you want to determine how good the prototype is for these users, you will have to train them, in the worst case, for several weeks. For these reasons, and if you don't have a very generous budget for creating the user interface, use tests should be done at the end of the iteration in which the parts of the user interface are created.

5.9 Guidelines: Use Case Storyboard

The steps in the Rational Unified Process activities are rather terse. Most of the detailed guidance comes in the form of guidelines that explain the methods and provide heuristics, examples, and rules of "well-formedness" for certain artifacts. As an example, this section is extracted from the guidelines for the creation and updating of use case storyboards. It will also provide us with an opportunity to illustrate some of the points made earlier.

A use case storyboard is a logical and conceptual description of how a use case is provided by the user interface, including the interactions required between the actor(s) and the system.

Use case storyboards are used to understand and reason about the requirements of the user interface, including usability requirements. They represent a high-level understanding of the user interface and are much faster to develop than the actual user interface. The use case storyboards can thus be used to create and reason about several versions of the user interface before it is prototyped, designed, and implemented.

A use case storyboard is described in terms of boundary classes and their static and dynamic relationships, such as aggregations, associations, and links. Each boundary class in turn is a high-level representation of a window or similar construct in the user interface. The benefits of this approach are as follows:

- It provides a high-level view of static window relationships such as window containment hierarchies and other associations between objects in the user interface.
- It provides a high-level view of dynamic window relationships such as window navigation paths and other navigation paths between objects in the user interface.
- It provides a way of capturing the requirements of each window or similar construct in the user interface by describing a corresponding boundary class, because each boundary class defines responsibilities, attributes, relationships, and so on that have a straightforward mapping to the corresponding construct in the user interface.
- It provides a trace back to a specific use case, thereby providing a seamless integration with a use case driven approach for software engineering. As a

result, the user interface will be driven by the use cases that the system is required to provide and by the actors' (users') roles in, and expectations of, these use cases.

A use case storyboard in the analysis model is traced (one-to-one) to a use case in the use case model.

5.9.1 Describing the Flow of Events-Storyboard

The following are guidelines on how to describe a flow of events-storyboard:

1. Start by clarifying the use case itself, not its user interface. Keep the description independent of the user interface, especially if the use case is unexplored. Then, later on, as the use case is understood, the flow of events-storyboard can be augmented with user interface and usability aspects.
2. Keep action statements brief. The description does not necessarily have to be self-contained, because it does not have to be comprehensible to people other than user interface designers. Action statements that consist of brief steps give a better overview, because they make the use case descriptions shorter. For example, when you describe how the use case exchanges data with an actor, you should keep the description brief and comprehensive; you can list the exchanged data at the end of the line, within parentheses: "create person (name, address, telephone)."
3. Avoid sequences and modes. Human actors can often perform the actions of the use case in different sequences, especially in user interface-intensive systems in which the user is in control. Sequences often imply modes of the user interface, and you should avoid modes if possible. Thus, you should specify only the sequences that are mandatory in the use case. For example, specify that users must identify themselves before they can withdraw money from an ATM, or that the system must show invoices to users before they can accept or refuse them.
4. Be consistent with the use case. Because the use case storyboard can be described more or less in parallel with the corresponding use case, these two artifacts should be kept consistent with, and give feedback to, each other. In particular, the flow of events-storyboard of a use case storyboard should be kept consistent with the flow of events of the corresponding use case. Note that this often requires an extensive communication and feedback loop between the use case author responsible for the use case and the user interface designer responsible for the use case storyboard.

Example of an Initial Flow of Events-Storyboard

The following is an example of an initial flow of events-storyboard of a storyboard for the use case Manage Incoming Mail Messages before it is augmented with usability aspects:

a) The use case starts when the mail user requests to manage mail messages and the system displays the messages.
b) The mail user may then follow one or more of the following steps:
   1) Arrange mail messages according to sender or subject.
   2) Read the text of a mail message.
   3) Save a mail message as a file.
   4) Save a mail-message attachment as a file.
c) The use case terminates when the mail user requests to quit managing incoming mail messages.

Note that this initial flow of events-storyboard is similar to a step-by-step description of the corresponding use case as it may have been described in the Activity: Find Actors and Use Cases (see Figure 5.4). Thus, use the step-by-step description of the corresponding use case as input when creating the initial flow of events-storyboard description.

This initial flow of events-storyboard description is then augmented with various usability aspects, such as desired guidance, average attribute values and volumes of objects, and average action usage.

5.9.2 Desired Guidance

A really usable system not only helps the user by automating simple and repetitive tasks but also provides guidance, typically by (implicitly) providing information for the tasks that cannot be automated. Such guidance can, for example, be provided by "balloon help" or context-derived on-screen help.

This important input to the design of the user interface should be represented by identifying the need for such desired guidance at specific points in the flow of events of the use case.

The user-interface designer should walk through the flow of events and consider the following issues at each step:

- What guidance could the user possibly need?
- What guidance could the system possibly provide?
- What should be represented as desired guidance and what should not?

From the flow of events, the basic functionality of the system can be identified. From the desired guidance, you should be able to identify optional functionality that is not crucial for the user to be able to carry out her work but that might help her carry out the work by (implicitly) providing her with information that she needs. Thus, anything that could help you find such optional functionality should be represented as desired guidance. You should not, however, represent desired guidance that identifies only functionality that we would find anyway, just by using good user interface shaping practice. (For example, don't represent that the system should give the user feedback on his operations or show the user all the different options that she has, and so on).

Desired guidance can also tell you what not to show, thus enabling you to shape the user interface so that the user doesn't get swamped by irrelevant information.

Desired guidance is not an absolute requirement in the same way as the flow of events; it is more like "wishes," or "nice-to-haves." When you identify and describe desired guidance, you should not think in terms of what the system will eventually provide, but in terms of what else the user might need. If you do otherwise, you restrict our thinking. So, remember that the desired guidance is not absolutely necessary, but is merely a means of increasing usability.

Example of Desired Guidance

The following is an example of the flow of events-storyboard of a storyboard for the use case Manage Incoming Mail Messages, augmented with desired guidance (within []).

a) The use case starts when the mail user requests to manage mail messages and the system displays the messages. [**The user should be able to differentiate among new, read, and unread messages; the user should also see the sender, subject, and priority of each message.**]
b) The mail user may then follow one or more of the following steps:
   1) Arrange mail messages according to sender or subject. [**The user should see that there is a choice.**]
   2) Read the text of a mail message.
   3) Save a mail message as a file.
   4) Save a mail-message attachment as a file. [**The user should be able to see the file types of the attachments.**]
c) The use case terminates when the mail user requests to quit managing incoming mail messages.

Desired guidance is often required for actions in which the user has to make a decision. The following points often apply to such decisions:

- They are nontrivial to the user.
- They impact people's lives or businesses surrounding the system ("people's lives or businesses surrounding the system" usually means the business, the user, and the task the user is trying to carry out).
- They matter once the use case has terminated.

In the flow of events-storyboard of the use case Manage Incoming Mail Messages, deciding to save an attachment is an obvious decision made by the user. It therefore requires some guidance.

5.9.3 Average Attribute Values and Volumes of Objects

It is often important to capture average attribute values and volumes of objects that need to be managed by, or presented to, the user. The user interface can then be optimized for these average values and volumes. These are often just educated guesses that may require some validation and measurements later.

Example of Average Attribute Values and Volumes of Objects

The following is an example of the flow of events-storyboard of a storyboard for the use case Manage Incoming Mail Messages, augmented with average attribute values and volumes of objects (within { }):

a) The use case starts when the mail user requests to manage mail messages and the system displays the messages. {**An average of 100 unread mail messages are shown simultaneously; and in 90% of the cases, the subject line of a message is less than 40 characters.**}
b) The mail user may then follow one or more of the following steps:
   1) Arrange mail messages according to sender or subject.
   2) Read the text of a mail message. {**The message text contains 100 characters on average.**}
   3) Save a mail message as a file.
   4) Save a mail-message attachment as a file. {**In 95% of the cases, there are less than two attachments.**}
c) The use case terminates when the mail user requests to quit managing incoming mail messages.

5.9.4 Average Action Usage

Average action usage is captured to find actions that are heavily used, as opposed to actions that are seldom used. This is akin to task frequency statistics. As a result, we will find both common and uncommon sequences (flows) through the use case. This is important information that can be used to prioritize and focus on intensively used parts of the user interface and its navigation hierarchies (for example, by providing shortcuts or additional toolbars in the user interface to perform common actions). This is often more a case of educated guesses than real statistics.

Example of Average Action Usage

The following is an example of the flow of events-storyboard of a storyboard for the use case Manage Incoming Mail Messages, augmented with average action usage (within ()).

a) The use case starts when the mail user requests to manage mail messages and the system displays the messages.
b) The mail user may then follow one or more of the following steps.
  1) Arrange mail messages according to sender or subject. (**Done in more than 60% of the cases.**)
  2) Read the text of a mail message. (**Done in more than 75% of the cases.**)
  3) Save a mail message as a file. (**Done in less than 5% of the cases.**)
  4) Save a mail-message attachment as a file.
c) The use case terminates when the mail user requests to quit managing incoming mail messages.

The conclusion from this example is that Steps 1) and 2) need thorough user interface support.

5.9.5 Summary of the Flow of Events-Storyboard

The basic idea of the flow of events-storyboard is to augment the flow of events description with various usability aspects; this information is then used further on to design a usable user interface. Also note that the usability aspects as shown in the example below may be modified or extended with other aspects, depending on the needs of the particular application type or user interface technology in use.

Example of Various Usability Aspects

The following is an example of the final flow of events-storyboard of a storyboard for the use case Manage Incoming Mail Messages, augmented with the various usability aspects.

a) The use case starts when the mail user requests to manage mail messages and the system displays the messages. [The user should be able to differentiate

among new, read, and unread messages; the user should also see the sender, subject, and priority of each message.] {An average of 100 unread mail messages are shown simultaneously; and in 90% of the cases, the subject line of a message is less than 40 characters.}
b) The mail user may then follow one or more of the following steps.
   1) Arrange mail messages according to sender or subject. [The user should see that there is a choice.] (Done in more than 60% of the cases.)
   2) Read the text of a mail message. {The message text contains 100 characters on average.} (Done in more than 75% of the cases.)
   3) Save a mail message as a file. (Done in less than 5% of the cases.)
   4) Save a mail-message attachment as a file. [The user should be able to see the file types of the attachments.] {In 95% of the cases, there are less than two attachments.}
c) The use case terminates when the mail user requests to quit managing incoming mail messages.

If your tool supports it, you can enhance this by using color instead of [ ], { } and ( ), as done in [Rational 1999].

5.9.6 Creating Boundary Class Diagrams

A use case storyboard is realized by boundary classes and their interacting objects. To illustrate the boundary classes participating in the use case storyboard, together with their relationships, we create class diagrams and include them as part of the use case storyboard.

Example of a Class Diagram

Figure 5.6 shows a class diagram owned by the use case storyboard corresponding to the Manage Incoming Mail Messages use case.

5.9.7 Creating Boundary Object Interaction Diagrams

To illustrate the boundary objects participating in the use case storyboard and their interactions with the user, we use collaboration or sequence diagrams. This is useful for use cases with complex sequences or flows of events.

Example of a Collaboration Diagram

Figure 5.7 shows a collaboration diagram owned by the use case storyboard corresponding to the Manage Incoming Mail Messages use case.

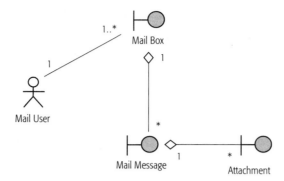

FIGURE 5.6 Class diagram, including the Mail User actor and the boundary classes Mail Box, Mail Message, and Attachment, participating in a use case storyboard corresponding to the Manage Incoming Mail Messages use case. We let it be understood from the context that a Mail User interacts with all objects contained in the aggregation hierarchy under Mail Box.

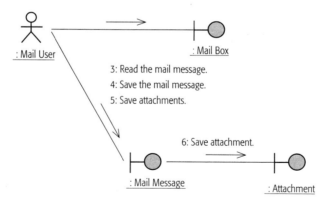

FIGURE 5.7 Collaboration diagram, including the Mail User actor and the boundary objects of Mail Box, Mail Message, and Attachment, participating in a use case storyboard realizing the Manage Incoming Mail Messages use case.

5.9.8 Complementing the Diagrams of a Use Case Storyboard

If necessary, the diagrams of a use case storyboard may be further clarified by using the flow of events-storyboard as a complementary textual description. This can be done by augmenting the flow of events-storyboard with the *boundary classes* involved.

Example of Boundary Classes

The following is an example of the flow of events-storyboard of a storyboard for the use case Manage Incoming Mail Messages, augmented with boundary classes (within " "):

a) The use case starts when the mail user requests to manage mail messages and the system displays the messages. [The user should be able to differentiate among new, read, and unread messages; the user should also see the sender, subject, and priority of each message.] {An average of 100 unread mail messages are shown simultaneously; and in 90% of the cases, the subject line of a message is less than 40 characters.} "Mail Box"
b) The mail user may then follow one or more of the following steps:
   1) Arrange mail messages according to sender or subject. (Done in more than 60% of the cases.) "Mail Box"
   2) Read the text of a mail message. {The message text contains 100 characters on average.} (Done in more than 75% of the cases.) "Mail Message"
   3) Save a mail message as a file. (Done in less than 5% of the cases.) "Mail Message"
   4) Save a mail-message attachment as a file. [The user should be able to see the file types of the attachments.] {In 95% of the cases, there are less than two attachments.} "Mail Message" "Attachment"
c) The use case terminates when the mail user requests to quit managing incoming mail messages. "Mail Box"

5.9.9 Capturing Usability Requirements on the Use Case Storyboard

Usability requirements may define how high the usability of the user interface must be. Such requirements may, for example, be found in another artifact of the Rational Unified Process, the Artifact: Supplementary Specifications. This means that the usability requirements should not be set to what you believe that the system can achieve, but to the lowest level of usability that the system must achieve in order to be used.

What the system must achieve in order to be used depends mostly on the alternatives to using the system. It is reasonable to require that the system should be significantly more usable than the alternatives. The alternatives can be to utilize:

- Existing manual procedures
- Legacy system(s)
- Competing products
- Earlier version(s) of the system

Usability requirements can also come from the need to justify the new system economically. If customer has to pay $3 million for the new system, he might want to impose usability requirements that imply that he will save perhaps $1 million per year because of decreased workload on his human resources.

Usability requirements on a use case storyboard typically specify

- Maximum execution time—how long it should take a trained user to execute a common scenario of the use case
- Maximum error rate—how many errors a trained user will average for a common scenario of the use case

The errors that are relevant to measure are those that are unrecoverable and will have negative effects on the organization, such as losing business or causing damage to monitored hardware. If the only consequence of an error is that it takes time to fix, this will affect the measured execution time.

The learning time should be measured as the time it takes before the user can execute a scenario faster than the specified maximum execution time.

Note that the usability requirements should not work as a target—that is, an upper limit. Usability requirements should define the absolute lowest acceptable system usability. Thus, you should not necessarily stop improving usability as soon as usability requirements have been fulfilled.

Example of Requirements on a Corresponding Use Case Storyboard

The following is an example of usability requirements on the use case Manage Incoming Mail Messages, as captured on its corresponding use case storyboard:

- The Mail User should be able to arrange Mail Messages with a single mouse click.
- The Mail User should be able to scroll Mail Messages texts by pressing single keyboard buttons.

- The Mail User should not be disturbed by incoming Mail Messages when reading existing Mail Messages.

5.9.10 Referring to the User Interface Prototype from the Use Case Storyboard

The use case storyboard can refer to the parts (such as windows) of the user interface prototype that correspond to its participating boundary classes. This can be useful if parts of the user interface prototype already exist when the storyboard is described.

Use case storyboards are primarily used in the initial stages of development, before the user interface is prototyped, as a "reasoning" tool to capture requirements on the user interface.

Use case storyboards are often considered to be transient artifacts and may be left unmaintained once the prototyping or implementing of the user interface is up to speed. However, in some cases it might be of value to maintain the use case storyboards through a number of iterations—for example, if there are complex requirements posed on the user interface that take time (over several iterations) to be understood.

The use case storyboards need not be described with any readers other than use case designers in mind, because the use case storyboards are conceptual and high-level and may appear ambiguous to other individuals. Instead, it is their concrete manifestation (that is, the user interface itself or a prototype of it) that is discussed, reviewed, and use-tested with other stakeholders such as end users. Still, the use case storyboards can be used by the user interface designer as a reference during use-testing to focus on the correct issues to test (complex interaction sequences, for example).

However, there is a compromise in the preceding recommendation. If it is significantly cheaper to develop the storyboards than to develop the actual user interface prototype, it might be worthwhile to have users review the storyboards directly before the prototype is implemented. Of course, descriptions of the storyboards need to be clear and self-contained so that they can be understood by the users, and creating such descriptions can require substantial development resources.

In cases in which use case storyboards are outlined in the requirements workflow and a user interface prototype is created, the corresponding boundary classes are good inputs to analysis activities. However, one sometimes also needs to create use case storyboards during analysis in order to drive the corresponding user interface design and implementation activities, for two reasons. First, in some projects no user interface prototype is created; instead, the user interface is designed and implemented directly, with no prototype as input. Second, in some projects a user interface prototype is created, but only for a small number of use cases; for the rest of the use cases, the user interface is not prototyped.

5.10 Conclusion

We have presented a subset of the Rational Unified Process dedicated to user interface design, based on use cases. The two main artifacts involved are the *use case storyboard* and the *user interface prototype,* and we have shown some of the activities, steps, and techniques involved for the user interface designer. Missing from this chapter are the general *user interface design guidelines* and the activities describing the development of the prototype, which can be found elsewhere [Rational 1999]. This approach is unique in the very tight integration that it provides among the requirements work, the general application design and development, and the user interface design, all in an iterative life cycle that over time leads to greater *consistency.*

As proposed originally by Larry Constantine [Constantine 1995], the user interface work is *driven* by the identification of the use cases. It focuses on extracting true user interaction requirements without diluting them with irrelevant requirements, by segregating them in the use case storyboard. The by-products of user interface design are not only the user interface prototypes but also analysis and design models used by analysts and designers, taking advantage of the UML.

5.11 References

[Booch et al. 1999] G. Booch. *UML User's Guide.* Reading, MA: Addison-Wesley, 1999.
[Constantine 1995] L. L. Constantine. Essential Modeling: Use Cases for User Interfaces. *ACM Interactions,* 2 (2), April 1995.
[Jacobson et al. 1992] I. Jacobson, M. Christerson, P. Jonsson, and G. Övergaard. *Object-Oriented Software Engineering—A Use Case Driven Approach.* Reading, MA: Addison-Wesley, 1992.
[Jacobson et al. 1999] I. Jacobson, G. Booch, and J. Rumbaugh. *The Unified Software Development Process.* Reading, MA: Addison-Wesley, 1999.
[Kruchten 1999] P. Kruchten. *The Rational Unified Process—An Introduction.* Reading, MA: Addison-Wesley, 1999.
[Rational 1999] Rational Software Corporation. *Rational Unified Process.* Version 5.5, Cupertino, CA: Rational Software Corporation, 1999.

CHAPTER 6

Wisdom—Whitewater Interactive System Development with Object Models

Nuno Jardim Nunes
João Falcão e Cunha

Abstract

This chapter presents Wisdom (Whitewater Interactive System Development with Object Models), an integrated, lightweight, Unified Modeling Language (UML)-based software engineering method. Wisdom is both a method for developing interactive software and an approach to software process improvement in small software developing companies (SSDs). Wisdom makes extensive use of object models to support user interface design within an evolutionary prototyping software process. Here we describe our approach and how it can be used for effective and controlled design of interactive systems by SSDs or small development teams within large companies or user organizations.

6.1 Introduction

For several years, we worked with SSDs to try to help them build a rational software development process. We learned how people in such environments build interactive software; developed an understanding of their methods, techniques, and tools; characterized the kinds of products they built; and studied how they worked together and with their customers. Wisdom is the result of our efforts to bring rational software development practices into these environments.

Wisdom originated from a simpler 1997 proposal called User-Centered Evolutionary Prototyping (UCEP) [Nunes and Cunha 1998, Nunes et al. 1998]. UCEP was a customized set of methods and techniques aimed at rationalizing a chaotic software process in a particular SSD on the Island of Madeira, Portugal. Our initial approach was applied to a medium-scale project involving a small team of six people. The project saw the development of a supervisory and decision support system for SITINA, the power management company in Madeira [Nunes and Cunha, 1998]. The UCEP set of methods, tools, and techniques that we adapted and transferred into the SSD were as follows:

- Object-oriented methods, which at the time were an adapted version of the Object Modeling Technique (OMT) [Rumbaugh et al. 1991]
- Visual modeling tools, initially Rational Rose and in the end a simple drawing package due to integration and platform restrictions
- Low-fi and high-fi prototyping [Rudd et al. 1996]
- Participatory techniques, which were used to support requirements discovery, introduce notation, and evaluate prototypes

Figure 6.1 illustrates the Wisdom genealogy. On the left-hand side of the figure are major software engineering influences; on the right-hand side are major human-computer interaction influences. From this illustration, we can see that Wisdom was inspired by Boehm's Spiral Model [Boehm 1988] and Kreitzberg's LUCID [Kreitzberg 1996]. From the Spiral Model, Wisdom got the evolutionary rhythm, and from LUCID the user-centered perspective.[1] From the beginning, our approach used an object-oriented analysis and design notation to specify and document the software system. We chose OMT because of its easy-to-learn notation and simple transformation rules for the relational schema. The OMT notation (essentially, the static model) played two major roles in UCEP. On the one hand, it worked as the common language for practitioners and between practitioners and users in participatory sessions and prototype evaluation. On the other hand, the working models stabilized the evolutionary process and documented the projects.

The success of several experiments with UCEP and the advent of the UML led us to rewrite our approach in late 1998 and early 1999. The UML provided new modeling constructs and built-in extension mechanisms that were essential to the formalization of some offhand modeling techniques used in UCEP, such as the ones that specify the user interface and task flows. Special care was also taken to improve UCEP's participatory techniques. Participatory techniques play a major role in our approach because they bring users to the development process, introduce the notation on a need-to-know basis, and take advantage of the SSD's enhanced communication capabilities [Nunes and Cunha 2000c]. For that purpose, we adapted some ideas from the Bridge method

---

[1] See Chapter 9 (Hudson) for a comparison of LUCID and other user-centered methods in system analysis and design.

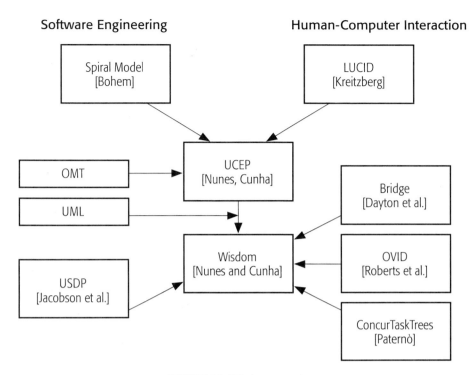

FIGURE 6.1 Wisdom genealogy

[Dayton et al. 1998]. Since our emphasis was not only to produce object-oriented user interfaces, such as in the Bridge method, we decided to detach the technique from this specific interaction style. To specify the dialogue model in Wisdom, we adapted the ConcurTaskTrees task formalism [Paternò 1999], hence providing support for reusable task structures, task patterns, and task-based evaluation of the user interface. Finally, we decided to use the Unified Process (UP) framework [Jacobson et al. 1999] as the process framework for Wisdom. Being also focused on process improvement for SSDs, we required a process framework that clearly mapped to the existing best practices on the object-oriented software engineering field.

Because of the degree of customization needed to integrate human-computer interaction techniques, Wisdom is not intended to develop non-interactive software. We have not tried Wisdom on large-scale projects, because our remit is not intended for such large projects or for large development teams. Furthermore, we have only used Wisdom on custom or in-house projects. We have never tried our approach in off-the-shelf and contract-based development contexts [Grudin 1991]. Although we do not claim that Wisdom is a scalable method, we believe that it can be applied within other contexts and that it represents a good step toward a large-scale industry process like the Rational Unified Process

(RUP)[2] [Kruchten 1999] or Catalysis [D'Souza and Wills 1999]. Wisdom is strongly based on the UML, and it uses several models and views that exist in such large industrial processes. Thus, an organization can start implementing Wisdom and then incrementally introduce new workflows, models, and views using the UML, to ultimately reach an industry-scale process (see Figure 6.2).

Wisdom is a lightweight software engineering method. It is lightweight in the sense that it can be learned and applied in a couple of days or weeks. Wisdom is object-oriented; it uses the UML to specify, visualize, and document the artifacts of the development

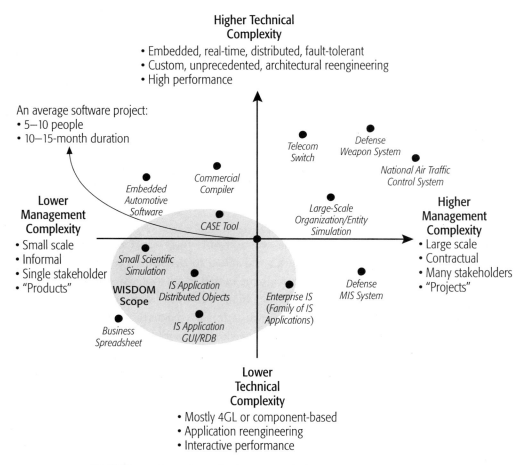

FIGURE 6.2 Dimensions of software complexity and Wisdom [Royce 1998]

---

[2] See Chapter 5 (Kruchten et al.) for a description of user interface design and RUP. See also Chapter 8 (Gulliksen et al.) and Chapter 9 (Hudson) for discussions of RUP and user-centered design.

project. Wisdom is specifically adapted to develop interactive systems because it uses and extends the UML to support human-computer interaction techniques. Finally, Wisdom is evolutionary in the sense that the project evolves in a sequence of incremental prototypes that ultimately lead to the end product.

6.1.1 The Working Context: SSDs and Lightweight Techniques

SSDs are recognized as the backbone of the software industry. According to several studies, both in the United States and Europe [Brodman and Johnson 1994, Choust et al. 1997], they account for 80% of the companies in the IT sector. They are also responsible for about 18% of the employment and sales in this sector. The same studies also show that 70% of the software departments contain fewer than 50 people. A Western European survey of SSDs and software improvement identified the major problems to be in the areas of requirements specification (> 50%), customer requirements (> 40%), documentation, testing, lack of high-quality system and structured approaches, and project management (between 30% and 40%) [Ibanez and Rempp 1996].

Software process assessment and improvement models such as the Capability Maturity Model (CMM) and the Quality Improvement Paradigm (QIP) are not suitable for SSDs [Cattaneo et al. 1995]. Research surveys and case studies concluded that SSDs are concerned with being measured against a model whose requirements they cannot meet [Brodman and Johnson 1994]. Such companies want to improve, but they also want their own tailor-made methods to be accepted by process improvement paradigms. To accomplish this goal, we have to accept that most SSDs are at very low maturity levels and that their ascension process might, or should in fact, be quite different from what process improvement models recommend. The main problems faced by SSDs are in fact related to managerial and practitioner cultural barriers and to the required customization of complex methods, tools, techniques, and standards. Additionally, process improvement must comply with existing practices and tools to minimize training costs and avoid decreases in short-term productivity—hence the need for pragmatic, lightweight methods that build on the idiosyncrasies of SSDs [Nunes and Cunha 2000c].

Our own studies about the way companies work and think about software revealed a strong urge toward implementation. This urge ultimately leads them to chaotic, tailor-made processes, also known as the Nike ("just do it") approach to software engineering. An informal survey on SSDs' software engineering practices in Portugal [Nunes et al. 1998] showed that these companies are in fact at very low maturity levels. The survey concluded that 80% of the surveyed companies don't use formal process models but instead either "just do it" or use tailor-made methods. The same study showed that 80% of the companies use fourth-generation languages (4GLs), either as their sole development tools or in conjunction with third-generation languages (3GLs). People working in small companies or within user organizations tend to focus their activities on custom or in-house development [Grudin 1991]. This development context is deeply focused on user interaction, because it usually concerns developing (or adapting) small software systems to meet specific user needs not covered by large, "shrink-wrapped" systems—hence the increasing importance of human-computer interaction techniques to support user interface design, participatory techniques, and user-centered design in SSDs. SSDs are typically *closer* to end users and, owing to their limited resources, increasingly dependent on the quality of the user interface to satisfy client needs. It is also well known that user interfaces are responsible for a significant share of the development effort. An informal survey on user interface programming [Myers and Rosson 1992] concluded that, on average, 48% of the code is devoted to the user interface. Respondents estimated that the average time devoted to user interface development during the various phases was 45% during the design phase, 50% during the implementation phase, and 37% during the maintenance phase.

We may conclude that small teams (of ten or fewer people) working in SSDs or within large user organizations are often in the same situation as that of SSDs. Our own experience, and case studies made available in the current literature, illustrate that such people have no specific technical functions within their organizations. They work simultaneously on small-scale projects (from a couple of weeks to several months), and they follow no formal process models. They are typically fairly skilled and highly motivated, and they also have good access to the end users throughout the entire development process. However, because their resources are very limited, they tend to be quite dependent on their development tools, typically 4GLs, and they also have limited knowledge (or no knowledge) of analysis and design methods. Although our surveys and experiences have been limited to SSDs working in Portugal, we believe, on the basis of several cited studies in other countries, that similar situations exist in other European and North American countries.

6.1.2 Chapter Structure

The remainder of this chapter is divided into four parts. Section 6.2 describes the key issues in Wisdom: process, architecture, and notation. We present the Wisdom evolutionary process and address the issues related to the process improvement nature of our approach. We also explain why Wisdom is driven by use case and task flows, justify the Wisdom architecture, and present the proposed UML notational extensions. Section 6.3 presents the Wisdom method in terms of the three software development workflows: requirements, analysis, and design. We draw activity diagrams for each workflow and discuss the Wisdom activities involved. Section 6.4 relates the Wisdom architecture to the CHI97 framework and discusses their similarities and major divergences. Following Section 6.4, we present our conclusion.

6.2 Wisdom: Process, Architecture, and Notation

We developed Wisdom to address the specific needs of small development teams who are required to design, build, and maintain interactive systems with the highest process and product quality standards [Nunes and Cunha 2000c]. The Wisdom lightweight software engineering method encompasses three important components, as follows:

1. A software process framework (the Wisdom process) based on a user-centered, evolutionary, and rapid-prototyping model specifically adapted for small teams of developers working in environments in which they can take advantage of (a) enhanced communication, both internally and toward external partners; (b) flexibility, in the sense that developers are encouraged to take initiative and are not obliged to follow rigid administrative processes; (c) control, meaning that teams and projects are easily manageable; and (d) fast reaction, in the sense that developers and managers are able to respond quickly to new conditions and unexpected circumstances.
2. A set of UML models (the Wisdom model architecture) that support the different development life-cycle phases involved in the Wisdom process and that are also required to build interactive systems in general. In addition, an extension of the UML analysis framework (the Wisdom interaction architecture) that captures the essential elements of well-known interactive systems' conceptual and implementation architectures.
3. A set of modeling notations (the Wisdom notation) based on a subset of the UML and enhanced with UML-compliant extensions specifically adapted to develop interactive systems. The UML extensions provide support for modeling the presentation and dialogue aspects of interactive applications.

In the following sections, we describe the three important components of our approach: process, architecture, and notation.

6.2.1 The Wisdom Process

The Wisdom process defines the steps for successfully implementing the Wisdom method in a software development organization. It is also an approach to software process improvement for SSDs with chaotic ways of working. By "chaotic ways of working," we mean that such companies develop software with a strong urge toward implementation, thereby evolving the product through a succession of consecutive prototypes. This way of developing software is usually called the Nike ("just do it") approach to software development. The Nike approach prevents repeated success, makes project management and measurement difficult, and tends to produce low-quality products with increasing maintenance and support costs. Although SSDs recognize the drawbacks of chaotic atmospheres, they have several problems that prevent them from improving their processes. One of the major problems is managerial and practitioner cultural barriers. Therefore, we need a model that seamlessly adapts itself to all SSD environments. The Wisdom process rationalizes the Nike approach and builds on factors that best characterize small software companies: fast movement, flexibility, and good communication. Our approach leverages those factors and smoothly evolves the chaotic atmosphere into a controlled evolutionary prototyping model [Nunes and Cunha 2000c].

Figure 6.3 illustrates the Wisdom process. The process is presented in a way similar to that in which iterative and incremental processes are presented in the object-oriented software engineering field [Jacobson et al. 1999, Kruchten 1999]. At the upper right in the illustration are the four phases of software development (inception, elaboration, construction, and transition), which are called "evolutionary phases" here because of the

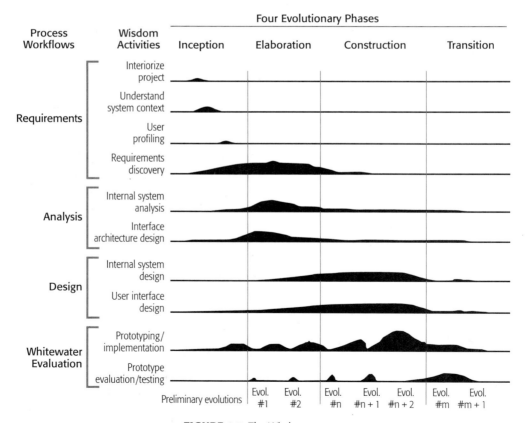

FIGURE 6.3 The Wisdom process

evolutionary character of Wisdom. At the far left are the process workflows. We use the term "workflows" to describe the activities that software engineers perform and the artifacts they produce in the context of the Wisdom process. Listed first are three of the well-known workflows of software engineering (requirements, analysis, and design). We use them for clarity when introducing our approach, because they are usually recognized by the common software engineer—even by those who work by random acts of hacking. The fourth workflow in our approach is renamed *whitewater evolution,* replacing *traditional* implementation. In this term, "whitewater" reflects the strong resemblance to the intense energy in rapid streams of water, in which the total (and apparently messy) energy makes the activity as a whole progress very quickly [Dayton et al. 1998], and "evolution" refers to the fact that the process evolves in a sequence of incremental prototypes, ultimately leading to the end product. To the right of the process workflows are the activities performed in the Wisdom method. They are presented in terms of the devoted effort usually required as time goes by. Finally, at the bottom of the illustration, we represent time in terms of evolutions. We consider an evolution to be a functional or non-functional prototype of a software system resulting from intentional (conceptual or concrete), incremental change made with the goal of achieving a desired end product.

In Chapter 8, Gulliksen et al. discuss the role of prototyping in iterative design. However, Wisdom emphasizes the use of prototyping for incremental development. There is an important distinction between using prototyping "as an effective technique for seeing if a proposed solution is adequate" (see Section 8.1.4) and evolving prototypes to reach an end product. Evolutionary prototyping requires special concerns to prevent end products from becoming badly structured, thereby increasing maintenance costs and preventing reuse. In addition, evolutionary prototyping is usually very sensitive to the impact of non-functional requirements, such as the ones that affect performance. As we discuss in the following sections, special care was taken in Wisdom to prevent these problems, while at the same time allowing users to benefit from the advantages of prototyping in iterative and user-centered design.

In the remainder of this section, we briefly present the main characteristics of the Wisdom process philosophy. We define and discuss the important concepts used in the Wisdom method and notation regarding evolutionary prototyping, use cases and task flows, model and interaction architectures, and the UML notation extensions. Wherever required, we contrast concepts and definitions with related approaches both from the object-oriented and human-computer interaction fields.

6.2.1.1 Evolutionary Prototyping

One can look at the Nike approach as nothing more than a performance of the whitewater evolution workflow as a process in itself. In fact, to implement Wisdom, we evolve this chaotic activity introducing the concept of iteration. In this way, we aim to preserve the whitewater nature of the Nike approach by recognizing the importance of maintaining the quick and powerful pace of development in order to seamlessly improve the existing process and prevent unnecessary barriers from hindering the development team. To do this, we ask the development team to state prototype objectives and perform adequate evaluation of those objectives at the end of the evolutionary iteration. This activity introduces a sense of completion and control, which is very effective in gaining the support of both developers and managers. The key idea is to enhance the importance of progress measurement and to permit identification of the major areas of intervention for the following process improvement techniques. It is imperative that the development team see a clear advantage and benefit of those techniques over the random acts of hacking they usually perform.

After successfully introducing the concept of iteration, we start introducing the Wisdom notation, which is a subset and extension of the UML, through participatory requirements discovery sessions with end users. Since the major process improvement problems faced by SSDs are in requirements specification and management, there is a clear advantage to starting with this activity. The participatory sessions use a reworked version of the Bridge method [Dayton et al. 1998]. Regarding process improvement, we are only concerned with using the participatory sessions as a way of seamlessly introducing the notation on a need-to-know basis. In this way, we are able to minimize training overload and overcome cultural barriers. Moreover, our model-based approach ensures that creating, managing, and maintaining documentation will become a consequence of the development process itself and not an additional support activity. We usually call this improvement approach a friendly *Trojan horse* approach because of the disguised way the techniques are introduced to the development team.

This goal-setting and evaluation cycle, anchored on a diagrammatic requirements model, forms the foundation of the Wisdom improvement process. By depending on different environment characteristics (team size, training, maturity, complexity of the project, tools, and so on), we introduce the remaining Wisdom activities, models, and required notation. By consistently following the same friendly Trojan horse approach, we enable the development team to expand the evolutionary cycle according to their needs.

6.2.1.2 Driven by Use Cases and Task Flows

Use cases are more than tools for capturing functional requirements; they drive the entire development process, thereby binding the core workflows together [Jacobson et al. 1999]. In Wisdom, they also serve as the major inputs for finding and specifying task flows, analysis classes, and interaction classes. In addition, they work as containers for non-functional requirements.

As mentioned in Section 6.2.1.1, we initiate process improvement with participatory requirements discovery sessions. We adapted the Bridge method [Dayton et al. 1998] and

Activity diagrams are then used throughout the entire development process to prototype and design the user interface. They ensure that the dialogue and presentation models focus on the task flows and don't get lost at lower levels of abstraction. These descriptions of task flows are also refined during analysis and design by using feedback from usability testing and prototype evaluation. In addition, they serve as the major inputs for finding and specifying analysis classes, tasks, and interaction spaces.

6.2.2 The Wisdom Architecture

One of the more important goals in software development is to establish the architectural foundation of the envisioned system. According to Shaw and Garlan [1996], a software architecture involves "the description of elements from which systems are built, interactions among those elements, patterns that guide their composition, and constraints on these patterns." Despite following the same principles as in this definition, a characterization of interactive system architecture should include other issues related to the interactive nature of the system. However, definitions in the literature are diverse in breadth and purpose.

In Chapter 4, Artim describes a user interface architecture as "an approach to development processes, organization, and artifacts that enables both good user interface practices and better coordination with the rest of development activities." This highly conceptual description focuses mainly on the process of building an interactive system and the need for collaboration and coordination between human-computer interaction and software engineering practices. Paterno [1999, p. 99] gives a definition that is more traditional (in the software engineering sense): "The architectural model of an interactive application is a description of what the basic components of its implementation are, and how they are connected in order to support the required functionality and interactions with the user." However, this definition still lacks some key aspects of software architectures, such as reuse and pattern composition. Kovacevic [1998] addresses reuse concerns and some key aspects of model-based approaches by observing that such an architecture should "maximize leverage of UI domain knowledge and reuse . . . providing design assistance (evaluation, exploration) and run time services (e.g., UI management and context-sensitive help)."

We consider that an architecture for interactive systems involves the description of the elements from which those systems are built, the overall structure and organization of the user interface, the patterns that guide their composition, and the way they are connected in order to support the interactions with the users in their tasks.

This characterization of interactive system architecture can be recursively decomposed into parts that interact through interfaces and are described with different models concerning different criteria—for instance, granularity, the nature of the entities, and usage. There

6.2 Wisdom: Process, Architecture, and Notation

gave it a broader scope within Wisdom. The Bridge is a comprehensive and integrated method for quickly designing object-oriented, multi-platform graphical user interfaces (GUIs). A typical Bridge session encompasses three explicit steps. Step 1 expresses the user requirements as task flows. Here the goal is to translate user needs for the task into requirements that reflect the task flows. The output of this step is a set of index cards and sticky notes describing what users will do with the new interface. In Wisdom, we use the same underlying participatory concept to perform other activities in the requirements workflow. Depending on the complexity of the project, the early participatory sessions are used to perform domain and business analysis, user profiling, and requirements discovery. Section 6.3.1, which is devoted to the requirements workflow, describes this approach in detail.

At the end of the participatory sessions, the development team translates the index cards and sticky notes into UML diagrams. Cards expressing actors and use cases are translated into corresponding UML classifiers. The Bridge-originated task flows are used to detail use cases and are translated into UML activity diagrams. An activity diagram or chart is a special case of a state machine used to model processes involving one or more classifiers. Action states in such a graph represent atomic actions [OMG 1999]. Similar actions can occur in the user profiling activity with user role maps [Constantine and Lockwood 1999] (see Section 6.3.1 for details). Wisdom also uses notes to attach non-functional requirements to use cases at the model level (general requirements), at the use case level, or at the activity level (annotating actions in activity diagrams). This approach reduces the number of artifacts to manage and keeps non-functional requirements at the hierarchical level they ought to be considered at [Cockburn 1997]. Our approach enables developers to manage several types of constraints, including technical, usability, and organizational ones. Therefore, the outcome of participatory sessions becomes the Wisdom requirements model, and little additional effort is required to produce a workable specification of the requirements [Nunes and Cunha 2000c].

However, a use case-driven process doesn't guarantee the required user-centered development of interactive systems. In fact, long before the advent of the UML, Constantine, in his proposal for essential use cases [Constantine 1992], argued about the system-centric nature of use cases. Essential use cases enabled the connection between the structure of use and the structure of the user interface, thus providing a way to connect the design of the user interface back to the essential purpose of the system and the work it supports. Refer to Chapter 7 (Constantine and Lockwood) for an in-depth discussion of this issue. Task flows play the same user-centered role in Wisdom. While use cases structure the functionality (services) of the system, task flows arrange the structure of use, thereby ensuring that the user interface will ultimately reflect the desirable and realistic task flows. Thus, Wisdom is not only use case driven but also task flow driven. Activity diagrams represent desirable and realistic task flows [Dayton et al. 1998] performed by the actors.

are two major architectural descriptions for interactive systems. Higher-level models, such as PAC [Coutaz 1987] and MVC [Goldberg and Robson 1983], concern entities (for example, the notion of dialogue control) and how they relate to each other in the design space. Implementation models, such as Seeheim [Pfaff 1985] and Arch [Bass 1992], concern software components (for example, a dialogue controller) and the relationship between the components. In implementation models, the components and relationships are driven by practical software engineering considerations such as reusability, maintainability, and performance.

These approaches have adopted the separation of concerns between the entities that model the task domain and those involved in the perceivable part of the system. On the one hand, this distinction enables the entities that depend on the task domain (functional core) to be reused with different interpretations and rendering functions. On the other hand, interpretation and rendering entities define a software component (the user interface) that can be maintained independently of the functional core [Coutaz 1993]. Due to practical engineering issues, this separation of concerns is further refined in implementation-oriented models. The Seeheim model [Pfaff 1985] (illustrated in Figure 6.4) proposes a simple three-layer model (application, dialogue, and presentation) of an interactive system that roughly couples the semantic, syntactic, and lexical functionalities of the user interface. The application component models the domain-specific components, the dialogue component defines the structure of the dialogue between the user and the application, and, finally, the presentation component is responsible for the external to internal mapping of basic symbols. The Arch model [Bass 1992] (also shown in Figure 6.4) goes one step further, including run-time considerations with a five-layer approach balanced around the dialogue component. The components of the Arch model are as follows:

- The interaction toolkit component implements the physical interaction with the end user.
- The presentation component provides a set of toolkit-independent objects.
- The dialogue component is responsible for task-level sequencing, multiple interaction space consistency, and mapping between domain-specific and user interface-specific formalisms.
- The domain adapter component implements domain-related tasks required but not available in the domain-specific component.
- The domain-specific component controls, manipulates, and retrieves domain data and performs other domain-related functions.

Figure 6.4 depicts the Seeheim and Arch architectural models, which influence the two architectural descriptions emphasized in Wisdom: Wisdom model architecture and the Wisdom interaction architecture.

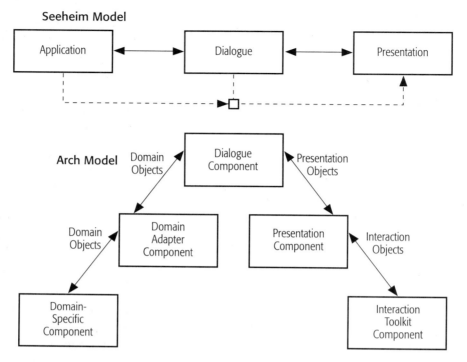

FIGURE 6.4 User interface architectural models

6.2.2.1 Wisdom Model Architecture

A model is an abstraction of a physical system with a certain purpose. In the UML, models have two goals: (a) to capture the semantic information of a system through a collection of logical constructs (for example, classes, associations, use cases, and so on) and (b) to present that information in a visual notation that can be manipulated by developers. Models can take different forms, aim at different purposes, and appear at different levels of abstraction. However, specific models should be geared toward a determined purpose. For instance, models can guide the thought process, guide the abstract specification of the essential structure of the system, completely specify the final system, partially describe the system, or exemplify typical solutions [Rumbaugh et al. 1999]. A model architecture defines a set of models with a predefined purpose. An example of a model architecture is defined in the UML standard profile for software development processes [OMG 1999], which defines the use case, analysis, design, and implementation models. Another example is the CHI97 framework (depicted in Figure 6.18), which defines the task, business, interactive system, interaction, domain, and core models.

The Wisdom model architecture specifies the different models of interest for effective development of an interactive system under the framework of the Wisdom method. This model architecture guides the thought process in Wisdom from the high-level models built to capture requirements to the implementation models that fully specify the final system. The Wisdom model architecture leverages both the internal and user interface architectures. Software engineering methods traditionally focus on the organization of the internal components and their relationships—the internal architecture of the software system. Wisdom also focuses on the external or user interface architecture. Just as the internal architecture is more than a set of internal components, the user interface architecture is more than a set of user interface components. In Wisdom, the external architecture not only concerns individual user interface components but also (and essentially) the overall structure and organization of the user interface.

Figure 6.5 illustrates the Wisdom model architecture. Seven models are developed in Wisdom, but not the implementation model, which represents all the artifacts generated to deploy the system (databases, code, user interface, and so on).

At the upper left in Figure 6.5 is the first inception model, the *business* or *domain model*. According to Jacobson et al. [1999], a domain model "captures the most impor-

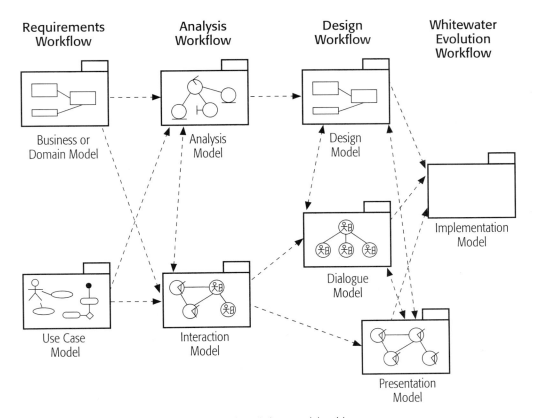

FIGURE 6.5 The Wisdom model architecture

tant types of objects in the context of the system. The domain objects represent *things* that exist or events that transpire in the environment in which the system works." In contrast, Jacobson et al. characterize the business model as describing "the business processes of a company or organization in terms of its workers, clients and entities they manipulate." For user interface design, a domain model should also include the users and the objects of interest to them [Nunes et al. 1999]. In Wisdom, we represent the domain model using a class diagram. If required, the business process model is built using the standard UML profile for business modeling. A UML profile is a predefined set of stereotypes, tagged values, constraints, and notation icons that collectively specialize and tailor the UML for a specific domain or process [OMG 1999].

The second inception model is the *use case model*. A use case model specifies the services that a system provides to its users [OMG 1999]. As we mentioned in Section 6.2.1.2, our approach enriches that specification by detailing use cases with activity graphs and hence focusing on user needs for the tasks reflected in task flows. The use case model is represented with a use case diagram and several activity graphs—typically, one per use case. There is no obvious logical dependency between the business/domain and use case models, but as the arrows (logical dependencies) in Figure 6.5 suggest, they both influence the following models.

Whereas the requirements models (business/domain and use case) are an external view of the system described in the language of the customer, the *analysis model* is an internal view of the system described in the language of the developers. This model structures the system with stereotypical classes (and packages, if required) that outline how to realize the functionality within the system. Therefore, the analysis model shapes the internal architecture of the system by defining how different analysis classes participate in the realization of the different use cases. To specify the analysis model in Wisdom, we use an adapted version of the UML standard profile for software development processes [OMG 1999]. We describe the notation in Section 6.2.3.2.

As mentioned at the beginning of this section, there is common agreement over the clear advantage of separating the user interface from the functional core in conceptual and implementation architectural models for interactive systems. Such conceptual (but not necessarily physical) separation leverages on user interface knowledge by providing design assistance (evaluation, exploration) and run-time services (user interface management, help systems, and so on) [Kovacevic 1998]. This approach should support implementation of internal functionality independent of the user interface by fostering reuse, maintainability, and multi-user interface development, which is an increasingly important requirement with the advent of multiple information appliances [Norman 1998].

The Wisdom *interaction model* is an external view of the system from the user interface perspective. This model structures the user interface, thus identifying the different elements that compose the dialogue and presentation structure of the system, and how they relate to the domain-specific information in the functional core. The different elements that compose the Wisdom analysis architecture are described in the next section. To specify the interaction model in Wisdom, we use the Wisdom UML profile. Section 6.2.3.2 describes this profile.

The *design models* in Wisdom reflect the same separation of concerns between the internal functionality and the user interface at a lower level of abstraction. The design model defines the physical realization of the use cases and focuses on how functional and non-functional requirements—and other constraints related to the implementation environment—impact the system [Jacobson et al. 1999]. Hence, the design model is more formal than the conceptual analysis model and is specific to an implementation. To specify the design model, we can use any number of stereotypical language-dependent classes.

The *dialogue model* specifies the dialogue structure of the interactive application, thereby focusing on the tasks that the system supports and the temporal relationships between tasks. The dialogue model specifies task-level sequencing and provides relationships that ensure multiple interaction space consistency while mapping between domain-specific and user interface-specific formalisms [Bass 1992]. There is general agreement that dialogue models are fundamental models in user interface design because they help developers to specify the dialogue structure of the application without low-level implementation details [Paternò 1999]. The Wisdom dialogue model serves this purpose while refining the analysis architecture and ensuring the separation of concerns between the user interface and the functional core, and also between the presentation and dialogue aspects of the system. To specify the Wisdom dialogue model, we use a UML extension based on the ConcurTaskTrees task formalism [Paternò 1999]. This extension and the main features of the formalism are discussed in Section 6.2.3.3.

In Chapter 9, Hudson presents task analysis as a common activity in user-centered design. Considering task analysis in a broader sense, this activity is performed in Wisdom by detailing use cases as activity diagrams which are expressed in the use case model. However, the Wisdom dialogue model isn't concerned with task analysis per se; it is concerned with the specification of the dialogue component of the interactive system using a task-based formalism. In this way, the dialogue model presents a form of task synthesis.

The *presentation model* defines the physical realization of the perceivable part of the interactive system (the presentation), focusing on how the different presentation entities are structured to realize the physical interaction with the user. The presentation model provides a set of implementation-independent entities (interaction spaces) for use by the dialogue model, thereby leveraging the independence of the interaction techniques provided by the user interface technology (for example, the user interface toolkit). Interaction spaces are responsible for receiving and presenting information to the users supporting their tasks. Interaction spaces are typically organized in hierarchies, and containment relationships can occur between interaction spaces. According to Nunes et al. [1999], an interactive system architecture should "support the separation of the user interface specifics (look and feel) from its (conceptual) specification, independent of the type of interaction and technology." Such separation leverages automatic user interface implementation from conceptual (abstract) models [Nunes et al. 1999]. We specify the presentation model using the Wisdom UML profile described in Section 6.2.3.3.

6.2.2.2 Wisdom Interaction Architecture

The other architectural description in Wisdom is the interaction architecture, which addresses the refinement and structuring of the system's requirements. This architecture encompasses three types of stereotyped classes: entity, task, and interaction space.

The information space for the Wisdom interaction architecture is illustrated in Figure 6.6. The new information space contrasts with the information space of object-oriented software engineering (OOSE) [Jacobson et al. 1992], the Unified Process [Jacobson et al. 1999], and UML standard profile for software development processes [OMG 1999], and introduces two new dimensions for the dialogue and presentation components. In addition, the presentation dimension of the Unified Process (and of the corresponding UML profile) is restricted to non-human interfaces. Note that the information dimension is shared between the two information spaces, leading to a total of five dimensions if we consider both information spaces as a whole. Such combined information space spans the analysis model and the interaction model, which are described in Section 6.2.2.1.

This Wisdom interaction model encompasses the information, dialogue, and presentation dimensions of the information space, clearly mapping the conceptual architectural models for interactive systems described in Section 6.2.2. Accordingly, the analysis model accommodates the existing analysis dimensions, and also includes the shared information dimension. Note that the presentation dimension in the analysis model is

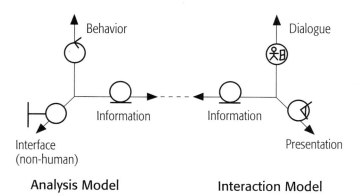

FIGURE 6.6 The Wisdom interaction model architecture

reduced to capture the interface (not the presentation) to external systems. In this way, we are able to tie the internal and interface architectures, thus leveraging the required separation of concerns while maintaining the necessary relationship among them. Moreover, the two information spaces accommodate the domain knowledge of both the OOSE and human-computer interaction communities.

The Wisdom architecture—like the MVC, PAC, and Unified Process analysis architectures—is a conceptual architecture. Therefore, it should not take into consideration design or implementation criteria as the Seeheim and Arch models do (see Section 6.2.2). However, the Wisdom architecture is at a higher granularity level than that of the MVC and PAC models, and thus it will eventually be reified during object-oriented design and implementation. Therefore, the Wisdom architecture should support such reification, maintaining qualities such as robustness, reuse, and location of change while leveraging the mediating nature of the domain adapter and interaction toolkit components of the Arch model (see Figure 6.4).[3]

The elements of the analysis model are analysis classes, standardized in the UML as class stereotypes. The three stereotypes are as follows:

- <<Boundary>> *class stereotype.* The boundary class in the Wisdom architecture models interaction between the system and external systems (non-human actors). The interaction involves sending and receiving (not presenting) information to and from external systems. Boundary classes clarify and isolate requirements in the system's boundaries, thus isolating change in the communication interface (not the human interface). Boundary classes often represent external systems—for example, communication interfaces, sensors, actuators, printer interfaces, APIs, and so on.
- <<Control>> *class stereotype.* The control class represents coordination, sequencing, transactions, and control of other objects. Control classes often encapsulate complex derivations and calculations (such as business logic) that cannot be related to specific entity classes. Therefore, control classes isolate changes in control, sequencing, transactions, and business logic that involve several other objects.

---

[3] The process of reification is typically achieved through precise allocation of information objects (entity classes) to the domain adapter and domain-specific components at design and implementation time. Such allocation enables semantic enhancement (dividing or joining objects in the domain adapter component) and semantic delegation (enhancing performance by preventing long chains of data transfer to objects in the domain-specific component) [Coutaz 1993]. The same applies to the interaction toolkit component—at this level, with presentation objects (interaction space classes). For a detailed description and discussion of the Wisdom architecture, refer to Nunes and Cunha [2000a].

- *<<Entity>> class stereotype.* The entity class models perdurable (often persistent) information. Entity classes structure domain (or business) classes and associated behavior, often representing a logical data structure. As a result, entity classes reflect the information in a way that benefits developers when designing and implementing the system (including support for persistence). Entity objects isolate changes in the information they represent.

The elements of the interaction model are interaction classes, defined as stereotypes of UML class constructs. The two stereotypes proposed in the Wisdom architecture are as follows:

- *<<Task>> class stereotype.* The task class models the structure of the dialogue between the user and the system. Task classes are responsible for task-level sequencing, multiple interaction space consistency, and mapping back and forth between entities and interaction space classes. Task classes often encapsulate complex behavior that cannot be related to specific entity classes. Therefore, task classes isolate changes in the dialogue structure of the user interface.
- *<<Interaction space>> class stereotype.* The interaction space class models interaction between the system and the users (human actors). An interaction space class represents the space within the user interface of a system in which the user interacts with all the functions, containers, and information needed for carrying out some particular task or set of interrelated tasks. Interaction space classes are responsible for the physical interaction with the user, including a set of interaction techniques that define the image of the system (output) and the handling of events produced by the user (input). Interaction space classes isolate change in the user interface of the system and often represent the abstraction of windows, forms, panes, and so on.

In Chapter 4, Artim describes a user interface architecture similar to the one proposed for the Wisdom interaction model. According to Artim, the Entity, Task, and Presenter (ETP) architecture is based on the common assumption that "the HCI artifacts that form our descriptions can be classified into three major groups: entities, tasks, and presentation elements." Artim's approach is also an elaboration of the original analysis framework from Jacobson and colleagues [Jacobson et al. 1992]. However, there are differences between the elements that establish the Wisdom interaction model and the presenter and task elements of the ETP architecture. Refer to Chapter 4 for contrasting definitions and corresponding examples.

6.2.3 The Wisdom Notation

The Wisdom notation is a subset and extension profile of the UML, which is the standard object-oriented language for visualizing, specifying, constructing, and documenting the artifacts of a software-intensive system [OMG 1999]. According to a recent study based on charts of concepts, UML Version 1.1 has 84 basic concepts and 149 diagram concepts, for an overwhelming total of 233 concepts [Castellani 1999]. This large number of concepts leads to a need to reduce complexity by tailoring UML for the explicit context of a method. In Wisdom, we use a subset of the UML and extend the language using its built-in extension mechanism to provide some additional modeling constructs that are useful in designing interactive systems. For a detailed description of the Wisdom notation, refer to [Nunes and Cunha 2000b].

Figure 6.7 represents the four software development workflows and the corresponding Wisdom activities, models, and diagrams used to specify the models. As you can see from the illustration, Wisdom, in its full form, is based on seven models and uses four types of diagrams (two types of structural diagrams and two types of behavioral diagrams). According to Castellani's study of the UML concepts [Castellani 1999], we estimate informally that our selection of diagrams and concepts contains about 39 basic concepts and 29 diagram concepts, for an overall total of 68 concepts (29% of the total number of concepts in UML Version 1.1).

6.2.3.1 Notation for the Requirements Workflow

The requirements workflow in Wisdom defines three models. The domain model uses class diagrams and the business model uses the standard UML profile for business modeling, together with activity diagrams to specify the business processes. The use case model is expressed with use case diagrams and activity diagrams that detail task flows.

6.2.3.2 Notation for the Analysis Workflow

To specify the analysis model, we use an adapted version of the UML profile for software development processes [OMG 1999], as described in Section 6.2.2.2. The two alternative notations for the entity, control, and boundary analysis stereotypes (see Kruchten, Chapter 5, for a contrasting definition of boundary class) are shown at the far left in Figure 6.8.

The UML profile for software development processes also defines the following association stereotypes:

- <<Communicate>> is an association between actors and use cases denoting that the actor sends messages to the use case or the use case sends messages to the actor [OMG 1999]. This stereotype can also be used among boundary, control,

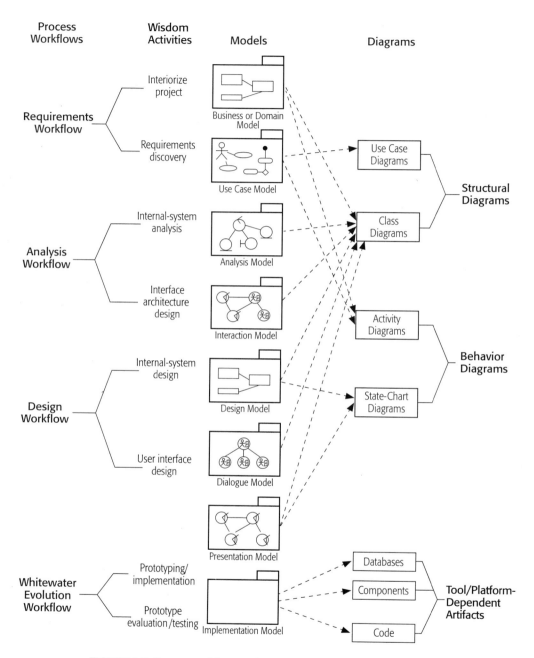

FIGURE 6.7 Process workflows, activities, models, and diagrams in Wisdom

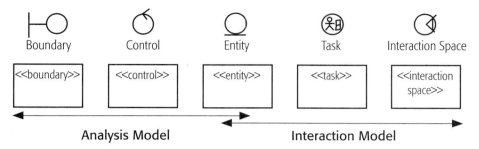

FIGURE 6.8 Alternative notations for the class stereotypes of the UML standard profile for development processes and the Wisdom interaction model

and entity. In addition, it can be used between actor and boundary, with the Wisdom-specific restriction that actor is an external system. The direction of communication can be one way or two ways.

- *<<Subscribe>>* is an association between two class states, meaning that objects of the source class (subscriber) will be notified when a particular event occurs in objects of the target class (publisher). Subscribe can be used from boundary, entity, and control to entity. The direction of subscribe is one way.

The Wisdom interaction model, as described in Section 6.2.2.2, defines two additional class stereotypes: task and interaction space. The alternative notations for the Wisdom-specific stereotypes of the interaction model are depicted at the far right in Figure 6.8. Class stereotypes of the Wisdom interaction model support communicate and subscribe associations. In addition, Wisdom defines more associations; thus the five associations used are as follows:

- *<<Communicate>>* can be used between entity and task, and between task and interaction space.
- *<<Subscribe>>* can be used from task to entity.
- *<<Refine task>>* is an association between two tasks denoting that the target class (subtask) specifies the source task (parent task) at a different (lower) level of detail. The refine task association is unidirectional and can be used only between task classes.
- *<<Navigate>>* is an association between two interaction space classes denoting a user moving from one interaction space to another. The navigate association can be unidirectional or bidirectional; the latter usually means that there is an implied return in the navigation. Users navigate in interaction spaces while performing complex tasks. A change between interaction spaces usually requires a change in thinking on the part of the user.

- <<*Contains*>> is an association between two interaction space classes denoting that the source class (container) contains the target class (content). The contains association can be used only between interaction space classes and is unidirectional.

The refine, navigate, and contains association stereotypes are usually employed in the dialogue and presentation models. At the interaction model level—that is, at the process level of analysis—only communicate and subscribe associations are used among the different class stereotypes (entity, task, and interaction space). This usage of associations reflects the specific detail of each model—that is, relationships between task and interaction spaces reflect the details of the corresponding interaction components (dialogue and presentation).

6.2.3.3 Notation for the Design Workflow

The design workflow in Wisdom defines three models: the design model, the dialogue model, and the presentation model. To specify the design model, we can use any number of stereotypical development environment-dependent classes. To specify the dialogue and presentation models, we use the Wisdom-specific association stereotypes that were defined previously.

As we mentioned in Section 6.2.2.1, the dialogue model specifies the dialogue structure of the application using a UML-based adaptation of the ConcurTaskTrees visual task formalism [Paternò 1999]. Until recently, Wisdom supported only the specification of the presentation aspects. This strategy scattered dialogue responsibilities among entity, presentation, and control depending on their complexity. Despite its simplicity and usefulness for simple applications, this approach exhibited problems with complex applications, specifically those supporting collaborative work. In addition, the lack of expressive task formalism prevented reuse of successful task structures while not supporting evaluation and description of task patterns.

According to Paternò, the main purpose of ConcurTaskTrees is to support the specification of flexible and expressive task models that can be easily interpreted even by people without formal backgrounds. ConcurTaskTree is an expressive, compact, understandable, and flexible notation that represents concurrent and interactive activities by task decomposition and by supporting cooperation between multiple users. ConcurTaskTrees defines four types of task allocations: user tasks (tasks performed by the user), application tasks (tasks completely executed by the application), interaction tasks (tasks performed by the user interacting with the system), and abstract tasks (tasks that require complex activities whose performance cannot be univocally allocated). Task allocation, if required, is supported by defining tagged values for task classes—that is, by defining the following tagged values: {user task}, {application task}, and {interaction task}. A

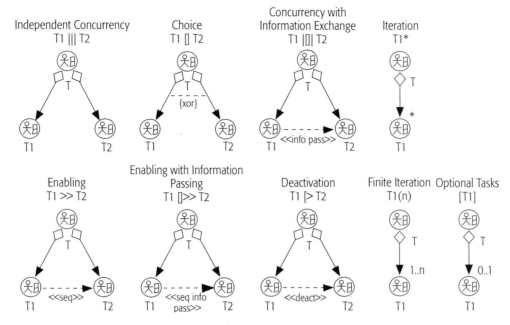

FIGURE 6.9 Notation for temporal constraints between tasks in the dialogue model

discussion of the implications of task allocation in the task model is beyond the scope of this chapter; refer to Paternò [1999] for details.

An important ConcurTaskTrees feature that is essential in bringing detail to the dialogue model is the ability to express temporal relationships between tasks. In our adaptation of the formalism, we use the UML constraint extension mechanism and stereotyped dependencies to express such temporal relationships between tasks. A constraint is a semantic relationship among model elements that specifies conditions and propositions that must be maintained as true [OMG 1999]. The temporal relationships in ConcurTaskTrees that are adapted in Wisdom are illustrated in Figure 6.9 and are described as follows:

- *Independent concurrency* (T1|||T2) denotes that actions belonging to two tasks (T1 and T2) can be performed in any order without any specific constraint.
- *Choice* (T1[]T2) denotes that it is possible to choose from a set of tasks and, once the choice has been made, to perform the chosen task, while other tasks are not available.
- *Concurrency with Information Exchange* (T1|[]|T2) is equivalent to independent concurrency, but the tasks have to synchronize in order to exchange information.
- *Deactivation* (T1[>T2) denotes that the first task (T1) is definitely deactivated once the second task (T2) terminates.

- *Enabling* (T1>>T2) denotes that the second task (T2) is activated once the first task (T1) terminates.
- *Iteration* (T*) denotes that the task (T) is performed repeatedly until the task is deactivated by another task.
- *Finite Iteration(s)* (T1(n)) is equivalent to iteration, but the task (T) is performed n times.
- *Optional Tasks* ([T]) denotes that the performance of a task is optional.

For a complete description of ConcurTaskTree involving all the possible uses of such formalism, specifically for evaluation and pattern expression, refer to Paternò [1999].

To specify the presentation model, we use the <<navigate>> and <<contain>> association stereotypes defined in Section 6.2.3.2. Such associations define the navigation and hierarchy of the presentation aspects of the system. The interaction space stereotype in Wisdom has two types of stereotyped attributes and one type of stereotyped operation. They are usually employed in the presentation model to refine the top-level interaction spaces identified in the interaction model. They are:

- *Input element* denotes information received from the user—that is, information the user can manipulate.
- *Output element* denotes information presented to the user—that is, information the user can perceive but cannot manipulate.
- *Action* denotes something a user can do in the physical user interface that causes a significant change in the internal state of the system—that is, a change in the long-term information of the system (entities), a request for signification functionality, a change in context of the user interface, and so on.

Interaction spaces in Wisdom have similarities with the concept of boundary classes in UDSP [Jacobson et al. 1999] and with View in OVID [Roberts et al. 1998]. For a detailed comparison of these concepts in UDSP, OVID, Usage-Centered Design, and Wisdom, see Figure 6.10.

6.2.3.4 Notation for the Implementation Workflow

Wisdom does not specify workflows for implementation and testing. Our experience with SSDs [Nunes and Cunha 1998] showed that they are highly dependent on development tools that support these specific workflows. They frequently use fourth-generation languages (4GLs) as their single development tool, sometimes in conjunction with 3GLs. 4GLs usually integrate a database management system and a user interface design toolkit [Myers 1995], which leads to strong dependence on the relational schema and the GUI design toolkit of the 4GL. Additionally, conceptual models at these levels of development

Concept	USDP Boundary [Jacobson et al. 1999]	Ovid View [Roberts et al. 1998]	Usage-Centered Design Interaction context [Constantine and Lockwood 1999]	Wisdom Interaction space [Nunes and Cunha 2000b]
Representation	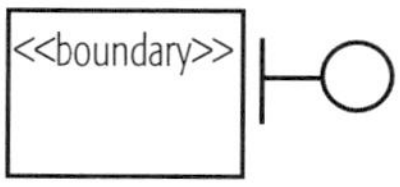 «boundary»	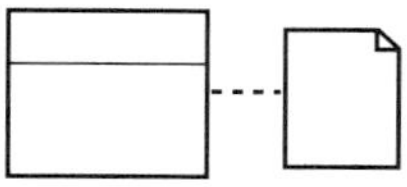	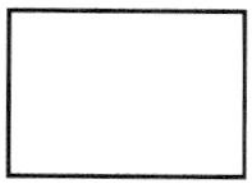	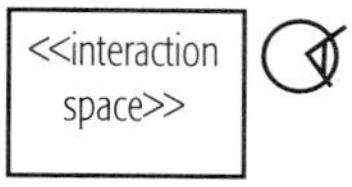 «interaction space»
Definition	Models the parts of the system that depend on its actors (users and external systems)	Presents information to users and allows them to use information to accomplish desired tasks	Represents the places within the user interface of a system in which the user interacts with all the functions, containers, and information needed for carrying out some particular tasks	Responsible for the physical interaction with the user, including a set of interaction techniques that define the image of the system (output) and the handling of events produced by the user (input)
Classification	Abstractions of windows, forms, panes, communication interfaces, printer interfaces, sensors, terminals, and APIs	Classified in composed, contents, properties, and user assistance (help)	Classified in any, screen or display, window, dialogue or message, panel, or page within tabbed or compound dialogue	No specific classification; stereotyped attributes (input and output) elements, operations (actions), and associations (navigational and containment)
Organization	Organized in the analysis model in class, sequence, collaboration, state-chart, and activity diagrams	Organized in designers and implementation models in class, sequence, and state-chart diagrams	Organized in navigation maps	Organized in the presentation model in class and activity diagrams

FIGURE 6.10 Presentation elements in USDP, OVID, Usage-Centered Design, and Wisdom

are hard to maintain without the support of a modeling tool, and there is still a lack of support for such tools to integrate with mainstream 4GLs. Therefore, it is our belief that the UML will play a major role in expanding the modeling tool market and lead to increased usage and integration of high-end CASE tools and 4GLs.

6.3 The Wisdom Method

In the introduction (Section 6.1), we explained why Wisdom was specifically designed for interactive systems development by SSDs. In Section 6.2.1, we discussed Wisdom's whitewater nature—which means that the development process moves very quickly toward its goal owing to the intense energy involved in the sequence of evolving prototypes. We saw why this whitewater nature seamlessly fits the SSD environment by reducing cultural barriers while ensuring short-term productivity. Sections 6.2.2 and 6.2.3 presented the main aspects of the Wisdom architecture and notation, which led to the extensive use of object models in our approach. This section presents the Wisdom method in detail and introduces the specific activities involved in each of the three major workflows for software development: requirements, analysis, and design. In the following subsections, we describe the activities for each workflow, present the main techniques used in Wisdom, and illustrate the application of the method with a simple hotel reservation system.

The three Wisdom software development workflows presented in this section are depicted as UML activity diagrams in Figures 6.11, 6.13, and 6.15. Despite the problems in representing evolutionary processes with sequential notations, we recognize the importance of such representations to clearly present the method. To overcome some of those problems, we introduce several graphical notations to better express Wisdom's whitewater evolutionary nature. Each graph represents one well-known software development workflow. The Wisdom-specific activities, introduced in Figure 6.3, are illustrated with three cogwheels (stereotypes of activities). Subactivities are illustrated as two cogwheels and, where required, are grouped in a rounded rectangle to detail a specific Wisdom activity. Owing to the whitewater nature of Wisdom, several activities can occur in parallel; forks and joins are depicted with short horizontal bars. Output artifacts of the Wisdom activities are illustrated with icons and are related to the producing activities with a dashed arrow pointing to the artifact. We recognize this arrow notation to be non-compliant with the UML specification, but we use it for better clarity.

We believe that the activity diagrams in Figures 6.11, 6.13, and 6.15 represent a *hypothetical* implementation of the Wisdom method and should work only as a framework. The flow of events can vary, depending on the complexity of the project, the maturity of the development team, and other factors. For instance, some activities can be eliminated in simple projects, while others can be added for different purposes (for example, quality procedures, process management, and so on). This can happen within teams, projects, or even iterations in the same project performed by the same team. To better illustrate this whitewater nature of Wisdom, suppose you draw each activity of a specific workflow on a separate sheet of paper and throw all the sheets of paper into rapidly moving water (whitewater). What usually happens is that some sheets encounter obstacles and reach the target later (or never) than others that are able to find quicker paths. If you repeat (iterate) the experience, the pace will differ each time, and sheets that moved slowly (or failed to reach the target) the first time may perform exceptionally well on a different turn. In the end, you'll find that the overall outcome is quite beneficial in comparison with having the sheets in a neat line in a narrow canal along which they travel at the same speed.

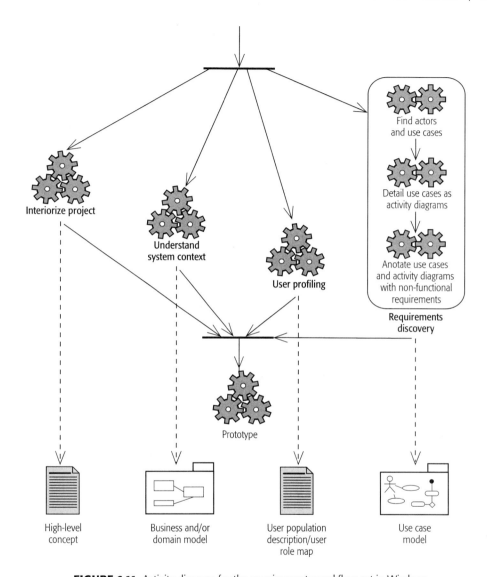

FIGURE 6.11 Activity diagram for the requirements workflow set in Wisdom

As we mentioned at the beginning of this section, we use a simple hotel reservation system to illustrate our method. Similar examples can be found in the literature [Roberts et al. 1998, Dayton et al. 1998]. We define the problem as follows.

The guest makes a reservation with the hotel. The hotel will take as many reservations as it has rooms available. When a guest arrives, he or she is processed by the registration clerk. The clerk will check the details provided by the guest with those that are already recorded. Sometimes guests do not make a reservation before they arrive. Some guests want to stay in non-smoking rooms. When a guest leaves the hotel, he or she is again processed by the registration clerk. The clerk checks the details of the staying and prints a bill. The guest pays the bill, leaves the hotel and the room becomes unoccupied. [Nunes et al. 1999]

In the following section, we use this apparently simple description of a hotel reservation system to explain how our method can be used in practice to support the development of a hypothetical interactive application.

6.3.1 Requirements Workflow

The purpose of the requirements workflow is to aim development toward a system that satisfies the customers (including the final end users). At this level, Wisdom differs from mainstream object-oriented software engineering process frameworks by introducing several activities in the requirements workflow that support the participatory user-centered perspective.[4] Figure 6.11 represents a UML activity diagram describing the main activities in the requirements workflow.

The *interiorize project* activity (at far left in Figure 6.11) is aimed at raising some initial brainstorming over the scope of the envisioned system. In this activity, the end users and the team devise a high-level concept of the problem. This short textual description, usually a single paragraph [Kreitzberg 1996], should clearly indicate what the system should and should not do and what the potential benefits and anticipated risks are. One can see this description as an initial user manual of the system. For more information on this approach, see [Norman 1998].

The *understand system context* activity aims at understanding the domain of the problem by focusing only on the *things* involved either in the problem domain or in the users and their work processes. The former, simplified version usually happens when the problem domain is very simple or the development team is experienced in the domain. The resulting artifact is then a domain model of the problem, usually a UML class diagram describing the business or real-world objects manipulated in the problem domain and their relationships. The latter, more complex version happens when the problem domain is complex or when the development team has little or no knowledge of the domain, which occurs frequently in SSDs because of their flexibility. In such cases, the development team produces a business model describing the workers, the work processes they

---

[4] Refer to Hudson (Chapter 9) and Gulliksen et al. (Chapter 8) for discussions of RUP and user-centered design.

perform, and the business entities they manipulate. The outcome is again a UML class diagram, which uses the business process profile of the UML, and several activity diagrams describing the business processes. It is beyond the scope of this chapter to discuss this standard profile. Refer to OMG [1999] for further details.

The purpose of the *user profiling* activity is to describe the users who will be supported by the system. Here, the goal is to describe who the prospective users are, how they are grouped, and what their relevant characteristics are (sex, age, computer experience, important disabilities, and so on). Depending on the complexity of the project, the outcome of this workflow can be a simple textual description of the users or a complete user role map [Constantine and Lockwood 1999]. This recent proposal, from the authors' Usage-Centered Design approach, profiles the users in terms of their needs, interests, expectations, behaviors, and responsibilities. The user role map is a diagrammatic representation that captures how all the various roles fit together in defining who will use the system and how. It is a map because it represents the relationships among the roles that users can play. Users can be interrelated by affinity, classification, or composition. Refer to Constantine and Lockwood [1999] for a detailed description of this approach.

The *requirements discovery* activity aims at finding and capturing the functional and non-functional requirements of the envisioned system. Being a use case-driven method, Wisdom relies on use cases to capture functional requirements. Because of the evolutionary nature of the method, non-functional requirements can largely influence the quality and stability of the end product. We attach non-functional requirements to the use case model at different levels of abstraction. The requirements discovery activity encompasses several subactivities (at far right in Figure 6.11): (a) finding actors and use cases, (b) detailing use cases as activity diagrams, and (c) annotating use cases and activity diagrams with non-functional requirements. At this level, there are several differences between Wisdom and the Unified Process (UP) [Jacobson et al., 1999]. Our approach uses activity diagrams to detail use cases that express desirable and realistic task flows [Dayton et al. 1998]. These task flows drive the later user interface design process, ensuring that the interaction model supports the actual perceived tasks of the users. For an in-depth description of this process using participatory techniques, see Dayton et al. [1998]. Our approach also encourages the use of annotations to express non-functional requirements in the actual use case model. This approach [Cockburn 1997] reduces the number of artifacts the development team must master and maintain. Also, non-functional requirements can be placed at the hierarchical level best suited to them—that is, annotating an activity in the activity diagram, annotating an entire activity diagram, or even annotating the entire use case model for high-level, non-functional requirements.

Usually, an evolutionary prototyping approach ends the requirements workflow with one or several prototypes. At this stage, prototypes are typically low-fi and non-functional [Rudd et al. 1996]. However, functional prototypes are sometimes useful for illustrating a novel technology or jump-starting requirements discovery. We have witnessed several successful experiences in which a functional prototype was useful for demonstrating to clients the potential of a given novel solution, thereby fostering a better understanding of the impact of the envisioned system.

Figure 6.12 represents three artifacts from the requirements workflow. At the upper left is the use case model annotated with one non-functional requirement. At the right is an activity diagram expressing the make reservation use case. The first two swim lanes illustrate which actor performs which activity. Finally, at the lower left is a domain model showing the most important *things* in the problem domain and how they relate to each other. As a simple example of the importance of participatory techniques in creating requirements models, we asked several experienced practitioners to build a domain model from the problem description in Figure 6.12. We also worked the example into a short participatory session with domain experts. The former considered the hotel the universe of discourse and omitted the class from the domain model. The latter included

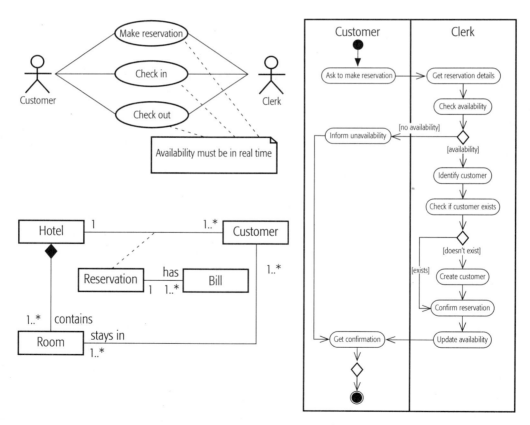

FIGURE 6.12 Artifacts from the requirements workflow for the hotel reservation system

the hotel class because it is clearly a user-perceivable object and therefore is important from the user interface perspective.

In Chapter 8, Gulliksen et al. present a list of weaknesses in RUP regarding usability aspects and user-centered design. In our attempt to avoid comparisons between Wisdom and large-scale industrial processes like RUP, we proceeded with the participatory and user-centered perspectives as they are explicitly stated in the requirements workflow. On the one hand, all the activities in the requirements workflow are performed (to different degrees) with end users and through participatory sessions. On the other hand, usability aspects are explicitly part of the artifacts produced during the workflow.

6.3.2 Analysis Workflow

The analysis workflow refines and structures the requirements described in the previous workflow. The purpose is to build a description of the requirements that shape the structure of the interactive system. Whereas the use case model is an external view of the system, described in the language of the users, the analysis model is an internal view of the system in the language of the developers.

The activity diagram for the Wisdom analysis workflow is illustrated in Figure 6.13. The major activities in this workflow reflect the incremental construction of structured, stereotypical classes and package diagrams. The separation of concerns between the internal architecture and the user interface architecture is reflected in the two concurrent flows of activities in the illustration. The flow at the far left is concerned with the construction of the internal architecture of the system and how analysis classes are organized to realize the different use cases. The flow at the far right structures the interaction model in terms of task and interaction space classes and how they are organized to support the user interface of the system. Note that the activity at the far right is itself divided into two concurrent flows that support the separation between the dialogue and presentation structures of the interactive system. (Refer to Section 6.2.2 for details on the Wisdom architecture.)

The *internal system analysis* activity aims at structuring the requirements in a way that facilitates their understanding and management. Analysis classes represent abstractions of domain concepts that are captured in the requirements workflow and are focused on functional requirements, postponing the further handling of non-functional requirements to later design. Analysis classes contain attributes, operations, and associations at a high level of abstraction—that is, attributes are conceptually typed, operations are informal descriptions of responsibilities, and associations are more conceptual than their design and implementation counterparts. There are two subactivities in this internal system analysis: identify analysis classes and structure analysis classes. There are several techniques for extracting analysis objects from the requirements model. Wisdom does not define any special technique for doing this; instead, we recommend a lightweight version of the Class

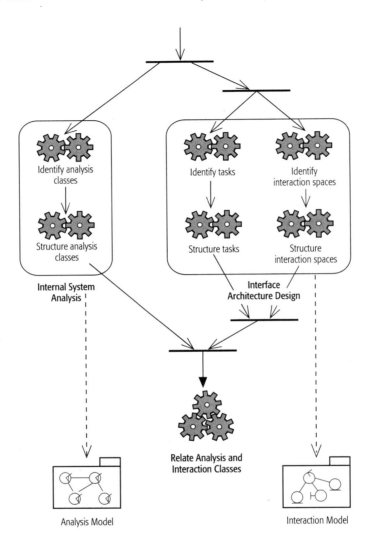

FIGURE 6.13 Activity diagram for the analysis workflow in Wisdom

Responsibility Collaboration (CRC) card method [Beck and Cunningham 1989]. We found out that this method, because of its close resemblance to the participatory nature of the Bridge method, can be easily introduced as an effective way to extract analysis classes and corresponding responsibilities from the requirements model. The next subactivity is to structure the identified classes into analysis stereotypes and distribute responsibilities to build the internal architecture. This subactivity usually takes several iterations, prototypes, and performances of other activities in the requirements workflow before a stable architecture is reached.

The *interface architecture design* activity is concerned with the design of the external architecture of the system—that is, the part of the system that is responsible for user interface support of the users performing envisioned tasks. This activity compromises two concurrent flows of activities corresponding to the dialogue and presentation models of the user interface. Similar to the internal architecture activity, these two flows of activities also have two subactivities: identify and structure interaction classes (task and interaction space). As we discussed in Section 6.2.2.2, Wisdom defines two stereotypes for interaction classes. The task class stereotype is the element of the dialogue component, and the interaction space class stereotype is the element of the presentation component. While devising the interaction architecture, we should concentrate on the desirable tasks rather than on a particular user interface design solution, which is the role of the design-level models (presentation model and dialogue model) in the design workflow. To identify both the task and interaction space classes, we use the task flows from the requirements workflow as the main source of information. Tasks usually have a clear mapping to the task steps in the task flows. The major problem at this level is to identify a set of tasks that support the task flows while ensuring that there is robustness and reuse in the interaction structure. Regarding the presentation component, identifying and structuring interaction spaces includes a choice between the number of interaction spaces and the number of transitions between interaction spaces. This is usually done by producing several versions of the architecture and testing this abstract representation in usability sessions with end users. As in the previous activity, the interface architecture usually takes some performance of the requirements workflow activities before a stable architecture can be achieved.

The final activity in the analysis workflow is to relate the internal and external architectures to see how they collaborate in realizing the use cases. This activity is very important in balancing both architectures and ensuring that the design and implementation models can seamlessly build on them. This subactivity creates associations between classes in the two models and usually communicates or subscribes association stereotypes between entities in the analysis model and tasks in the interaction model (see Section 6.2.3).

If required, there is an additional activity in this workflow. This optional step is packaging of analysis classes and interaction classes into smaller, more manageable pieces. Because use cases capture functional requirements, they are the natural basis for packaging. Therefore, packaging should allocate groups of use cases, preferably those related in the same domain or business model, to analysis packages. These packages will then fulfill the use cases' functionality accordingly.

Figure 6.14 illustrates three artifacts from the analysis workflow for the hotel reservation system. At the left is an activity diagram (task flow) expressing the *make reservation* use case. To the right of the activity diagram is a possible interaction model with stereotyped interaction classes (interaction spaces and tasks) and corresponding associations. The arrows between the two diagrams represent mappings used to identify

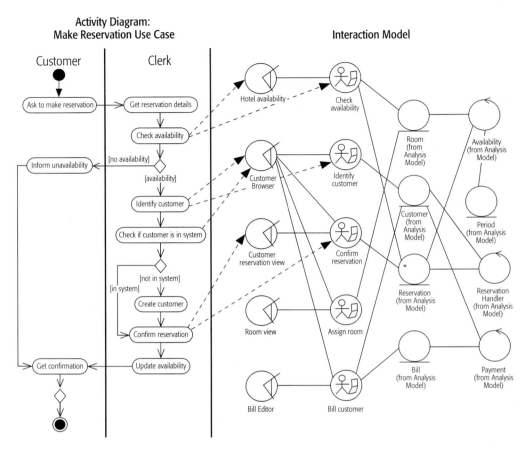

FIGURE 6.14 Artifacts from the analysis workflow for the hotel reservation system

interaction spaces and tasks from the task flow. As you can see, the mapping is simple and straightforward. At the right is a possible internal architecture model with stereotyped analysis classes (control and entity) and corresponding communicate associations. The relationships between tasks, classes, and entity classes tie both architectural models together and correspond to the relate analysis and interaction classes activity in Figure 6.13. A comparison between this analysis model and the domain model in Figure 6.12 clearly points out the goal of the internal analysis activity. The analysis model is a model of the problem domain whereas the domain model is the architecture of a solution. Although this is a simple example, note that not all the entities identified in the analysis model are user-perceivable objects (objects of interest to the users). This example also depicts multiple analysis and interaction classes collaborating in the realization of one or more use cases. For instance, the customer browser interaction space, the Identify Customer task, the customer entity, and the availability control, among others, realize the make reservation use case. In addition, except for the availability control, they all realize the Check in and Check out use cases (see Figure 6.14).

6.3.3 Design Workflow

The design workflow drives the system to implementation by refining its shape and architecture. Although analysis focuses only on functional requirements, design also focuses on non-functional requirements. At this level, the constraints related to the development environment (languages, databases, GUIs, operating systems, and so on) are also considered. The system is then broken up into manageable pieces that are possibly allocated to different development teams.

The activity diagram for the design workflow is illustrated in Figure 6.15. The major activities in this workflow reflect the incremental refinement of the analysis and interaction models. The separation of concerns initiated in analysis continues during the design workflow. Since the design workflow tends to progress through a succession of incremental prototypes, two activities usually take place simultaneously: the internal system design and the user interface design. One of the major improvements of Wisdom at this stage is enabling careful planning of design (and consequent implementation) by prioritizing the evolutionary process based upon use cases and interaction classes—that is, the architectural building blocks. The internal and user interface architectures devised in the previous workflow guarantee that the incremental construction brings muscle to a coherent skeleton.

The *internal system design* activity is illustrated at the left in Figure 6.15. Because design is highly dependent on the development environment (tools, technologies, programming languages, and so on), we will describe its goal only briefly. The first subactivity is to prioritize and select candidate use cases for design. As we saw in Section 6.2.1.2, use cases drive the development process by binding the workflows together. At this stage, information from the use case model, including the desirable and realistic task flows, gives cadence to the evolutionary process. The unified process places this activity in the early phases of the development process; in our approach, such a decision is done in design, because experience has shown that SSDs tend to move faster in the early phases of development. Prioritizing decisions is often achieved well after an in-depth understanding of the system under development. The subsequent design of the use case classes accomplishes the refinement of the stereotypical analysis classes, at both the responsibility and association levels. Refinement is achieved once the integration of the non-functional requirements has taken place. The earlier annotation of the requirements model with non-functional requirements is important at this stage. Because the requirements accompany the use cases that drive the development process, the risk of leaving

234 | **CHAPTER 6** Wisdom—Whitewater Interactive System Development with Object Models

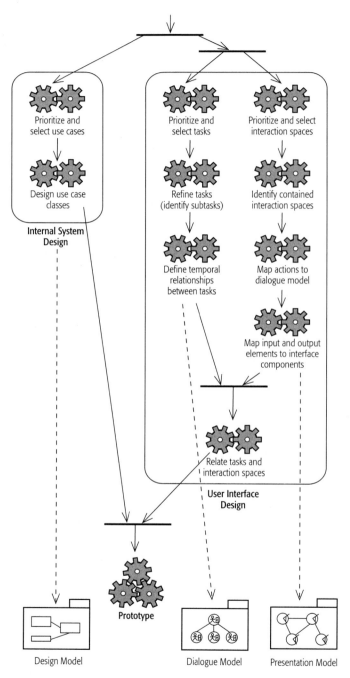

FIGURE 6.15 Activity diagram for the design workflow in Wisdom

out such requirements is minimized. This leads to better design decisions. Also, this refinement process in SSDs' environments can lead to a partial translation of the analysis model (typically, entity stereotypes) into a relational schema. The characteristics of the 4GLs used can increase the risk of deriving the user interface from the database schema. To prevent this, it is important to separate the user interface from the design model.

The *user interface design* activity is concerned with the realization of the interaction model as a concrete user interface. This activity usually encompasses two main design decisions or restrictions: the interface style and the user interface technology. They both influence each other—for example, a particular user interface technology can prevent the implementation of a specific interaction style. The construction of the presentation model, which is detailed at the right in Figure 6.15, encompasses two concurrent flows of activities that correspond to the dialogue and presentation components of the interaction model. The left-hand flow of activities corresponds to the refinement of the tasks identified and structured in the analysis workflow. This process usually involves three steps: (1) decide which tasks to refine, usually in coordination with the prioritization used for internal functionality; (2) identify which subtasks refine the top level; and (3) define the temporal relationships among the subtasks according to the options presented in Section 6.2.3.3. Whenever possible, task patterns should be used in steps (2) and (3). The right-hand flow of activities corresponds to the refinement of the presentation model defined in the analysis workflow. This process usually involves four steps: (1) decide which interaction space to refine, usually in coordination with the use case prioritization defined for internal functionality; (2) decompose complex interaction spaces in different contained or navigable interaction spaces, thus creating interaction spaces that easily map to the implementation toolkit and to presentation patterns that foster reuse; (3) map actions on interaction spaces to the dialogue model, hence establishing an initial correspondence between the dialogue and presentation models; and (4) map input and output elements to interface components, such as GUI widgets. The user interface design activity ends by relating both task classes to interaction space classes, thus completing the process of distributing responsibilities between the dialogue and presentation models.

Like the internal system design the user interface design is highly dependent on the development environment and on a large number of external factors. Our goal in Wisdom was to build a model-based framework that could accommodate different design techniques, user interface styles, and technologies. On the one hand, we have a UML model-based approach that detaches the user interface design techniques from a specific design context by using the abstract concepts of tasks and interaction spaces. On the other hand, those abstract concepts are refined during design time by supporting different design alternatives to create the concrete user interface; a good architecture enables the implementation of multiple user interfaces according to different design constraints.

The Bridge method [Dayton et al. 1998] is one alternative for designing concrete user interfaces in Wisdom, one that clearly fits the SSD environment. Hence, if the development team decides to design an object-oriented GUI, Parts 2 and 3 of the Bridge can be easily implemented within our approach. (Refer to Section 6.1 for a description of the Bridge, Part 1.) Part 2 of the Bridge is mapping task flows to task objects (task objects in the Bridge are objects used in the execution of a task). The goal is to map the user interface requirements into discrete units of information that users manipulate to do the task. In Wisdom, the task objects map to interaction spaces. Therefore, the specific behaviors and containment relations for task objects in the Bridge are, in fact, Wisdom-stereotyped interaction spaces with input and output elements, actions, and navigational and containment associations. In this object-oriented GUI context, we can use the Bridge task object design technique to discover, design, document, and perform usability tests on the task objects. Afterward, we can use Part 3 of the Bridge to map task objects to GUI objects. This third step of the Bridge guarantees that the GUI is usable for executing the task. For an in-depth description of the Bridge, refer to [Dayton et al. 1998]. The Bridge is also described in Chapter 10. For a brief illustration of this integration of the Bridge in Wisdom, see the example in Figure 6.17.

Iterations through the Wisdom design workflow usually reflect the actual implementation of the end product. At this level, prototypes are usually fully functional incremental evolutions of the end product that are typically organized in terms of prioritized use cases and interaction classes. This characteristic of development is very important for SSDs, because they are very reluctant to throw away functional prototypes. If adequately implemented, Wisdom provides the needed control over the evolutionary process to quickly and effectively produce high-quality products from this final Wisdom workflow.

Figure 6.16 illustrates two Wisdom design artifacts for the hotel reservation system. The upper diagram is part of the dialogue model—specifically, the refinement of the top-level task check availability (see the related example in Figure 6.14). This particular example uses the search task pattern from [Paternò 1999]. The lower diagram represents part of the presentation model. This example illustrates two advantages of the presentation model. While the left side of the diagram details the presentation structure that supports the top-level task check availability, the right side shows the top-level navigation structure. In this way, developers can zoom into detail while maintaining focus on the high-level structure, thus preventing the well-known problems of incremental approaches.

Figure 6.17 illustrates the process of mapping descriptions from the Bridge participatory sessions into the Wisdom model-based approach and the concrete user interface. At the far left is a Bridge task object with corresponding index cards showing the object identity, attributes, actions, and containment relationships. At the center is the Wisdom formalization of that information as stereotyped interaction spaces. Each of the different views of the Bridge task object maps to an individual interaction space in Wisdom. Then,

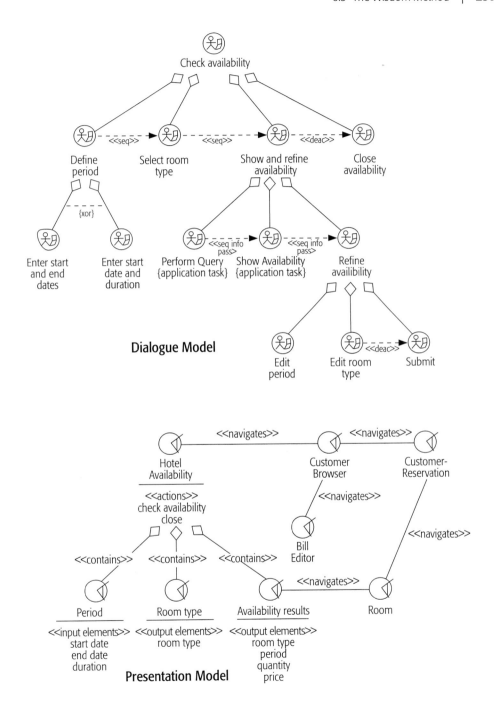

FIGURE 6.16 Artifacts from the design workflow for the hotel reservation system

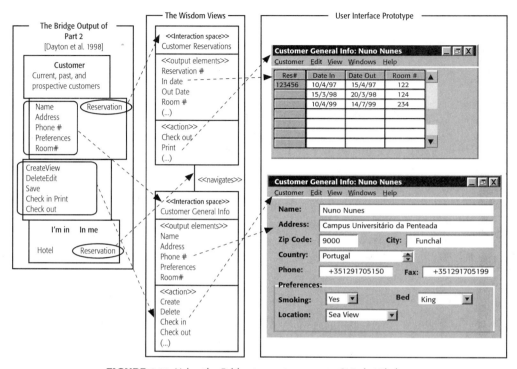

FIGURE 6.17 Using the Bridge to create concrete GUIs in Wisdom

attributes are mapped to stereotyped input or output elements, actions to stereotyped actions, and containment relationships to navigate or containment stereotyped associations. This mapping clearly shows how Wisdom interaction spaces realize the interface architecture. The final step in this process is to execute the Bridge, Part 3, to map the Wisdom interaction spaces to concrete GUI objects. This mapping is shown at the far right in Figure 6.17. Refer to [Dayton et al. 1998] for more details on the Bridge, Part 3.

6.4 Wisdom and the CHI97 Metamodel

Figure 6.18 illustrates the relationship between the Wisdom architecture and the CHI97 metamodel [van Harmelen et al. 1997]. At the top of the illustration are parts of the CHI97 metamodel, and at the bottom are the corresponding Wisdom models. Relationships are "illegally" shown as UML dependencies. This simplistic mapping shows how the models in Wisdom instantiate the conceptual CHI97 metamodel. In that sense, the domain model is mapped to our domain or business model. The use case model doesn't have a clear correspondence in the CHI97 metamodel, but because we use task flows to detail use cases, a correspondence to the task model exists. However, such correspondence

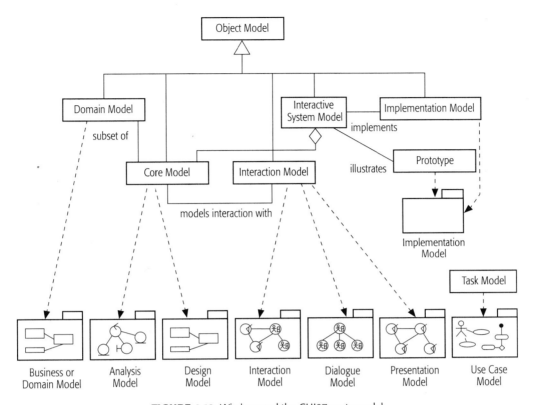

FIGURE 6.18 Wisdom and the CHI97 metamodel

lacks some of the inherent characteristics of the use case model, which clearly isn't present in a task model. The core model corresponds, at different levels of abstraction, to both the analysis and design models in Wisdom. The interaction model maps directly into our interaction model, thus showing how both models really specify the interaction at an abstract or highly conceptual level. Finally, the dialogue and presentation models map partially to the interactive system model. Variations on the CHI97 interaction model exist [Kovacevic 1998, Nunes et al. 1999].

6.5 Conclusion

The UML opened a window of opportunity for the human-computer interaction and object-oriented software engineering communities. We believe, and hope this chapter confirms, that the UML and its built-in extension mechanisms are powerful tools that will help you design better and more usable software. Moreover, staying within UML semantic constraints will ensure improved tool support and integration, which remain open issues recognized by both communities [Bomsdorf and Szwillus 1998, Iivari 1996].

We recognize that our approach is somewhat pragmatic. Wisdom is tailored for SSDs, but it doesn't (explicitly) support implementation and test workflows and it doesn't fully support task analysis [Artim et al. 1998, Kovacevic 1998]. However, Wisdom is the result of extensive experience and active observation from work with SSDs. Methods and techniques are hard to introduce in these environments. We need to reduce the number of concepts they have to manage and offer a more scalable method. The basics of such methods should be learned in a couple of days or weeks, and should not compromise future progress. We believe that our approach does just that by staying within UML and hopefully benefiting from future integration between modeling and development tools to support advanced stages of development.

We hope that our work with SSDs will persuade other researchers and practitioners to invest more resources in this inspiring field of software engineering "in the small." In the end, it's all about the users, but developers are also users of the modeling languages, tools, techniques, and methods. Ensuring that they have a proper set of manageable tools, methods, and techniques is the first step toward our quest for quality and usability in software.

6.6 Acknowledgments

Several people contributed in various ways and degrees to the development of Wisdom. We would like to acknowledge all the companies, organizations, practitioners, and students who used and contributed to our approach. In particular, we would like to thank Jaelson Castro, who worked with us on previous versions of our approach; Tom Dayton, for his inspiring comments about user interface design and the Bridge; and Dave Roberts, for providing resources and ideas about object views and model-based user interface design. We also want to thank Mark van Harmelen and John Artim for their comments on early drafts of this chapter.

6.7 References

[Artim et al. 1998] J. M. Artim, M. van Harmelen, K. Butler, J. Gulliksen, A. Henderson, S. Kovacevic, S. Lu, S. Overmeyer, R. Reaux, D. Roberts, J.-C. Tarby, and K. Vander Linden. Incorporating Work, Process and Task Analysis into Industrial Object-Oriented Systems Development. *SIGCHI Bulletin,* 30 (4), 1998.

[Bass 1992] L. Bass. A Metamodel for the Runtime Architecture of an Interactive System: The UIMS Developers Workshop. *SIGCHI Bulletin,* 24 (1), 1992.

[Beck and Cunningham 1989] K. Beck and W. Cunningham. A Laboratory for Teaching Object Oriented Thinking. *Proceedings of the OOPSLA '89 Conference,* New York: ACM, 1989.

[Boehm 1988] B. Boehm. A Spiral Model of Software Development and Enhancement. *IEEE Computer Society,* 21 (2), 1988.

[Bomsdorf and Szwillus 1998] B. Bomsdorf and G. Szwillus. From Task to Dialogue: Task-Based User Interface Design. *SIGCHI Bulletin,* 30 (4), 1998.

[Booch et al. 1999] G. Booch, J. Rumbaugh, and I. Jacobson. *The UML User Guide.* Reading, MA: Addison-Wesley, 1999.

[Brodman and Johnson 1994] J. Brodman and D. Johnson. What Small Businesses and Small Organisations Say about CMM. In *Proceedings of the ICSE '94 Conference. IEEE Computer Society,* 1994.

[Castellani 1999] X. Castellani. Overview of Models Defined with Charts of Concepts. *Proc. IFIP WG 8.1 Int'l Working Conf.* ISCO4, Dordrecht, Holland: Kluwer Academic Publishers, 1999, 235–256.

[Cattaneo et al. 1995] F. Cattaneo, A. Fuggetta, and L. Lavazza. An Experience in Process Assessment. *Proceedings of the ICSE '95 Conference.* 1995, 115–121.

[Choust et al. 1997] G. Choust, P. Grünbacher, and E. Schoisch. To Spire or Not to Spire—That Is the Question. *Proceedings of the EUROMICRO '97 Conference.* 1997.

[Cockburn 1997] A. Cockburn. Structuring Use Cases with Goals. *Journal of Object-Oriented Programming,* September–October and November–December 1997.

[Constantine 1995] L. L. Constantine. Essential Modeling: Use Cases for User Interfaces. *Interactions,* 2(2), New York, ACM, April 1995.

[Constantine and Lockwood 1999] L. L. Constantine and L. A. D. Lockwood. *Software for Use.* Reading, MA: Addison-Wesley, 1999.

[Coutaz 1987] J. Coutaz. PAC—An Object-Oriented Model for Dialogue Design. In *Proceedings of the INTERACT '87 Conference.* Stuttgart, Germany: Elsevier Science, 1987.

[Coutaz 1993] J. Coutaz. Software Architecture Modeling for User Interfaces. In *Encyclopedia of Software Engineering.* New York: John Wiley and Sons, 1993.

[Dayton et al. 1998] T. Dayton, A. McFarland, and J. Kramer. Bridging User Needs to Object-Oriented GUI Prototype via Task Object Design. In L. Wood, ed. *User Interface Design.* Boca Raton, FL: CRC Press, 1998.

[D'Souza and Wills 1999] D. D'Souza and A. Wills. *Objects, Components and Frameworks with UML: The Catalysis Approach.* Reading, MA: Addison-Wesley, 1999.

[Goldberg and Robson 1983] A. Goldberg and D. Robson. *Smalltalk-80: The Language and Its Implementation.* Reading, MA: Addison-Wesley, 1983.

[Grudin 1991] J. Grudin. Interactive Systems: Bridging the Gap between Developers and Users. *IEEE Computer Society,* 24 (4), 1991, 59–69.

[Ibanez and Rempp 1996] M. Ibanez and M. Rempp, European User Survey Analysis, ESPITI Project Report; http://www.sisu.se/projects/espiti/ESPITI.html, 1996.

[Iivari 1996] J. Iivari. Why Are Case Tools Not Used? *Communications of the ACM,* 39 (10), 1996.

[Jacobson et al. 1992] I. Jacobson, M. Christenson, P. Johnson, and G. Övergaard, *Object-Oriented Software Engineering: A Use Case Driven Approach.* Reading, MA: Addison-Wesley, 1992.

[Jacobson et al. 1999] I. Jacobson, G. Booch, and J. Rumbaugh. *The Unified Process*. Reading, MA: Addison-Wesley, 1999.

[Kovacevic 1998] S. Kovacevic. UML and User Interface Modeling. In J. van Leeuwen, ed. *Proceedings of the UML Workshop*. New York: Springer-Verlag, 1998.

[Kreitzberg 1996] C. Kreitzberg. Managing for Usability. In A. F. Alber, ed. *Multimedia: A Management Perspective*. Wadsworth, 1996.

[Kruchten 1999] P. Kruchten. *The Rational Unified Process*. Reading, MA: Addison-Wesley, 1999.

[Lillienthal and Zullighoven 1997] C. Lillienthal, and H. Zullighoven. Application-Oriented Usage Quality: The Tools and Materials Approach. *ACM Interactions,* 4 (6), 1997, 35–41.

[Myers 1995] B. Myers. User-Interface Software Tools. *ACM Transactions on Computer-Human Interactions,* 2 (1), 1995, 64–103.

[Myers and Rosson 1992] B. Myers and M. Rosson. Survey on User Interface Programming. *Proceedings of the CHI92 Conference*. New York: ACM, 1992.

[Norman 1998] D. Norman. *The Invisible Computer*. Cambridge, MA: MIT Press, 1998.

[Nunes 1999] N. Nunes. A Bridge Too Far: Can UML Finally Help Bridge the Gap? In M. Sasse and C. Johnson, eds. *Proceedings of the INTERACT '99 Conference*. Edinburgh, Scotland: IOS Press: Ohmsha, 1999, 692–693.

[Nunes and Cunha 1998] N. Nunes and J. F. Cunha. Case Study: SITINA—A Software Engineering Project Using Evolutionary Prototyping. In Keng Siau, ed. *Proceedings of the CAiSE '98/IFIP 8.1 EMMSAD '98 Workshop*. Pisa: Italy, 1998.

[Nunes and Cunha 2000a] N. Nunes and J. F. Cunha. Wisdom: A UML Based Architecture for Interactive Systems. In Fabio Paternò and Philippe Palanque, eds. *Proceedings of the DSV-IS 2000 Workshop on Design, Specification and Verification of Interactive Systems*. Limerick, Ireland, June 2000. New York: Springer-Verlag LNCS 1946, 2000.

[Nunes and Cunha 2000b] N. Nunes and J. F. Cunha. Towards a UML Profile for Interactive Systems Development: The Wisdom Approach. In Andy Evans, ed. *Proceedings of the International Conference on the Unified Modeling Language, UML 2000*. York, UK, October 2000. New York: Springer-Verlag LNCS, 2000.

[Nunes and Cunha 2000c] N. Nunes and J. F. Cunha. Wisdom: A Software Engineering Method for Small Software Development Companies. *IEEE Software,* 17 (5), 2000.

[Nunes et al. 1998] N. Nunes, J. F. Cunha, and J. Castro. Prototipificação Evolutiva Centrada nos Utilizadores: Um Estudo de Case para Melhorar o Processo de Desenvolvimento de Software em PMEs. In R. Heredia, F. Jaramillo, E. Bastidas, eds. *Proceedings of the CLEI '98 Conference*. Quito, Ecuador, Pontificice Universidad Calólica del Ecuador, 1998.

[Nunes et al. 1999] N. Nunes, M. Toranzo, J. F. Cunha, J. Castro, S. Kovacevic, D. Roberts, J. Tarby, M. Collins-Cope, and M. van Harmelen. Workshop on Interactive System Design and Object Models (WISDOM '99). In A. Moreia and S. Dbmbybn, eds. *ECOOP '99 Workshop Reader*. New York: Springer-Verlag LNCS, 1999, 267–287.

[OMG 1999] Object Management Group. OMG Unified Modeling Language Specification. Version 1.3, found at *http://www.omg.org*, 1999.

[Paternò 1999] F. Paternò. *Model-Based Design and Evaluation of Interactive Applications*. London: Springer-Verlag, 1999.

[Pfaff 1985] G. R. Pfaff, ed. *User Interface Management Systems.* London: Springer-Verlag, 1985.

[Roberts et al. 1998] D. Roberts, D. Berry, S. Isensee, and J. Mullaly. *Designing for the User with OVID.* Indianapolis: Macmillan, 1998.

[Royce 1998] W. Royce. *Software Project Management: A Unified Framework.* Reading, MA: Addison-Wesley, 1998.

[Rudd et al. 1996] J. Rudd, K. Stern, and S. Isensee. Low vs. High-Fidelity Prototyping Debate. *ACM Interactions,* 3 (4), 1996, 76–85.

[Rumbaugh et al. 1991] J. Rumbaugh, M. Blaha, F. Eddy, W. Lorenson, and W. Premerlani. *Object-Oriented Modeling and Design.* Englewood Cliffs, NJ: Prentice Hall, 1991.

[Rumbaugh et al. 1999] J. Rumbaugh, I. Jacobson, and G. Booch. *The UML Reference Manual.* Reading, MA: Addison-Wesley, 1999.

[Shaw and Garlan 1996] M. Shaw, and D. Garlan. *Software Architecture: Perspectives on an Emerging Discipline.* Upper Saddle River, NJ: Prentice Hall, 1996.

[van Harmelen et al. 1997] M. van Harmelen, J. Artim, K. Butler, A. Henderson, D. Roberts, M. B. Rosson, J-C. Tarby, and S. Wilson. Object Models in User Interface Design. *SIGCHI Bulletin,* 29 (4), 1997.

CHAPTER 7
Structure and Style in Use Cases for User Interface Design

Larry L. Constantine
Lucy A. D. Lockwood

Abstract

Although widely employed in both object-oriented software engineering and user interface design, use cases are not well defined. Relatively little attention has been paid to the various styles for writing the narratives that define use cases and their consequences for user interface design and software usability. In this chapter, common narrative styles are presented with examples and discussions of their relative advantages and disadvantages. Essential use cases, a variant employed within usage-centered design, are contrasted with conventional use cases and scenarios. For the most efficient support of user interface design, and particularly for large, complex projects, a highly-structured form of use case has evolved. New narrative elements and relationships among use cases are introduced. These include means for expressing the partial or flexible ordering of interaction, relationships with business rules, as well as a clarification of the often misunderstood concept of extension that recognizes two distinct forms: synchronous and asynchronous extensions.

7.1 Introduction

Since their introduction in support of object-oriented software engineering, use cases have become ubiquitous in both development methods and development practice. Part of this ubiquity can be attributed to their utility—use cases have proved to be versatile conceptual tools for many facets of design and development—but part may also be a consequence of a certain imprecision in definition. Most developers can say they are employing use cases because almost anything may be called a use case despite the enormous variability in scope, detail, focus, format, structure, style, and content. Further muddying these already turbid waters, idiosyncratic terminology has been promulgated that obfuscates important distinctions, such as those between scenarios and use cases.

As an effective bridge between usability engineering and user interface design on the one hand and software design and development on the other, use cases offer a chameleon-like adaptability. For requirements engineering, use cases provide a concise medium for modeling user requirements; in the hands of user interface designers, use cases can become a powerful task model for understanding user needs and guiding user interface design; for software engineers, use cases guide the design of communicating objects to satisfy functional requirements. Success in all these endeavors rests on the realization that user interface design is not software design. Models originally developed to support the design of software components and their interactions are not automatically and necessarily well-suited for organizing user interface components and the interaction between users and these components.

7.1.1 Use Cases Undefined

One of the more remarkable aspects of use cases is that they have achieved such wide currency despite an almost complete lack of precise definition. Entire books have been devoted exclusively or primarily to use cases without even so much as offering a definition [Schneider and Winters 1998, Texel and Williams 1997]. Jacobson's original definition is brief, broad, and barely descriptive:

> A use case is a specific way of using the system by using some part of the functionality. [A use case] constitutes a complete course of interaction that takes place between an actor and the system. [Jacobson et al. 1992]

Owing in part to imprecise definition and in part to the confusion and conflation of the various possible uses and purpose of use cases, many use cases, including published ones, intermingle analysis and design, business rules and design objectives, internals and interface descriptions, with gratuitous asides thrown in to cover all bases. So deep is the confusion that even the most unconstrained mishmash can be put forward as a use case.

Example 1

The guest makes a reservation with the hotel. The hotel will take as many reservations as it has rooms available. When a guest arrives, he or she is processed by the registration clerk. The clerk will check the details provided by the guest with those that are already recorded. Sometimes guests do not make a reservation before they arrive. Some guests want to stay in non-smoking rooms. [Roberts et al. 1998, p. 68]

What is the use case here, and what is its purpose? Is it to reserve a room or to obtain a room? Or is it to check in a guest? Who is the user and in what role do they act? Is the user a guest or a clerk or the telephone operator who takes the reservation? What is the interface to be designed?

To their credit, the developers of UML (the hubristically monikered Unified Modeling Language) have collectively chimed in along common lines in an attempt to narrow the scope of definition somewhat. For example, a use case is:

> The specification of sequences of actions, including variant sequences and error sequences, that a system, subsystem, or class can perform by interacting with outside actors. [Rumbaugh et al. 1999, p. 488]

In other works from the same group the definition has been qualified by the phrase "that yields an observable result of value to a particular actor" [Jacobson et al. 1999, p. 41; Kruchten 1999, p. 94].

Despite the addition of this slight nod to external significance, the current "official" definitions have actually moved away from Jacobson's original emphasis on use and have taken on what may legitimately be described as a more "system-centric" viewpoint: The focus is on what the system performs, not on what the user does or wants. In our opinion, this inside-out perspective, subtle though it may be, has actually contributed to problems in applying use cases to user interface design.

A somewhat more user-centric definition is offered by Fowler, in a popular introduction to UML:

> A use case is a typical interaction between a user and a computer system [that] captures some user-visible function [and] achieves a discrete goal for the user. [Fowler, 1997, p. 43]

However, for the most part, use cases have been defined not with reference to users but with reference to "actors"—external agents interacting with a system. For software design, actors may include other systems that must interact with the system being developed, but for purposes of user interface design, only the human users are relevant.

Most designers understand at some level that it is not so much users themselves but the roles that they play in relation to a system that must be taken into account in user interface design. The UML-sanctioned use of the term "actor" in this context is particularly unfortunate because it leads to such awkward and ultimately nonsensical formulations as the following:

> An actor is a role that a user plays with respect to the system. [Fowler 1997, p. 46]

In all other areas of discourse, the actor is not the role, but is distinguished from it. The linguistic legerdemain of calling a role an actor is particularly confusing to users and clients, but it can also cast an insidious spell on the minds of designers who can all too easily unconsciously confuse the characteristics of an occupant of a role—the incumbent—with aspects of the role itself. For this reason, we prefer to call the thing what it is and use the term *role* or *user role* to refer to a role played by human "actors," that is, users of a system. To avoid confusion and outright conflict with UML terminology, we distinguish *system actors*—other systems—from users in roles. A *role* thus constitutes a relationship between a user and a system and is defined by a set of characteristic needs, interests, expectations, behaviors, and responsibilities [Wirfs-Brock 1994].

7.1.2 Concrete and Essential Use Cases

As most commonly used, use cases have described the actual interaction between external users (or system actors) and a system through a particular interface. Because they are expressed in concrete terms, such use cases are best referred to as *concrete use cases*. For example, consider the beginning of the "Returning Item" use case for a recycling machine.

Example 2

> The course of events starts when the customer presses the "start-button" on the customer panel. The panel's built-in sensors are thereby activated. . . . [Jacobson et al. 1992, p. 157]

Use cases of this ilk are completely inappropriate for the design of user interfaces for the simple reason that they already assume some particular user interface and interaction design. To write use cases of this form, you must already have designed the user interface, at least in part. Why does the recycling customer press a button rather than touch a screen? Why does the customer have to do anything other than begin putting items in the recycler? The tacit assumptions built into such use cases can unnecessarily constrain the design and, in practice, often lead to inferior user interfaces with overly conventionalized and unnecessarily complex interaction.

It was precisely this dilemma of circular description that led us to devise a radically different kind of use case and to develop a systematic process for the creation and utilization of these use cases for user interface design. The secret for turning use cases into a truly effective tool for designing good user interfaces and enhancing usability is a shift in focus from interactions to intentions and from elaboration to simplification. Instead of modeling the interactions between users and a user interface, the focus shifts to the intentions of users. Instead of elaborating use cases with specific details and alternative courses of interaction, the focus is on simplification, on simplified descriptions that capture the essence of a case of use.

We termed these models *essential use cases* [Constantine 1994b; 1995; Constantine and Lockwood 1999] because they constitute essential models in the sense originally employed by McMenamin and Palmer [1984], that is, abstract, generalized, and technology-free descriptions of the essence of a problem.

We would now define an *essential use case* as a single, discrete, complete, meaningful, and well-defined task of interest to an external user in some specific role or roles in relationship to a system, comprising the user intentions and system responsibilities in the course of accomplishing that task, described in abstract, technology-free, implementation-independent terms using the language of the application domain and of external users in role. We were not alone in recognizing the need for such a teleocentric ("purpose-centered") approach to use case modeling and for a move toward abstraction in use case construction. Kaindl [1995] has proposed incorporating goals into use cases, as did Cockburn [1997, 2000], and Graham [1996] has argued the value of abstract use cases. A consensus in concept if not in details seems to be emerging: More recently, others have joined the chorus [Lee and Xue 1999], and even the architects of the self-styled Unified Process have recognized the limitations of concrete use cases and the advantages of the essential form [Jacobson et al., 1999, p. 164].

It is our intention in this chapter to help bridge the gap between software engineering and usability engineering by adding some clarity, precision, and depth to the discussion of use cases. Toward this end, we will explore variations in narrative style and their significance for user interface design. We will introduce the notion of *structured use cases,* which are use cases that are organized and described in a highly systematic form to enhance their utility both for user interface design and for integration with the rest of the development process.

7.1.3 Notation

We must also make a somewhat apologetic explanation regarding the idiosyncratic notation employed in this chapter. Although we recognize the hegemony of the UML, we have been somewhat tardy in reconciling our notation with that notation. While the UML pays close attention to defining the notational details of many of its models, almost nothing is specified regarding the notation for use cases, that is, for the specification that actually defines what a particular use case is and is about. This neglect of such a core issue has no doubt contributed to the confusion regarding what is and what is not a proper use case.

Like all usability specialists and user interface designers, we are also keenly aware that the utility of information is profoundly affected by how it is presented. Notation is, in truth, the user interface of models. We have long argued that the visual form of notation can significantly increase or decrease the effectiveness of those who create and interpret the models [Constantine 1994a; Constantine and Henderson-Sellers 1995a, 1995b; Page-Jones et al. 1990]. Although some of the ideas in this regard have been incorporated into the UML (largely without acknowledgment), the bulk of the arguments and recommendations of those of us who are interested in the communicative function of notation seems to have fallen on deaf ears. Modern-day modelers are thus left with the choice between notational anarchy and a standard notation that is itself riddled with serious usability defects. (Beyond issues raised here, see also [Henderson-Sellers 1999; Henderson-Sellers and Barbier 1999; Henderson-Sellers and Firesmith 1999]).

Two aspects of notation for use cases must be addressed. The first concerns the notation used within use cases—that is, the style of representation employed in the narrative body defining the use case. The second concerns how relationships among use cases are visualized in diagrams to convey the overall structure of the tasks being modeled through use cases. Each of these aspects will be addressed separately.

7.2 Usage-Centered Design

7.2.1 A Usage-Centered Process

Essential use cases evolved within the context of an orderly process for user interface design, and, although it is not our intention to dwell on methodology, it is worthwhile saying something about that process. The process is called *usage-centered design* [Constantine and Lockwood 1999] to highlight the fact that the center of attention is usage rather than users per se. Although our approach certainly partakes of a broadly user-centered design philosophy, in calling it usage-centered design we wanted to draw attention to those particular aspects of users that are most relevant to user interface design and to highlight the linkage to use cases as a model of tasks (or usage).

Usage-centered design is a flexible and scalable "industrial-strength" process that has been applied in business and industry to a wide variety of problems ranging in size from small-scale Web-site design to an eighteen-month industrial automation project involving a six-person design team and seventeen software developers. It has been used for software and Web-based applications in contexts as diverse as banking, publishing, manufacturing, and education as well as for designing consumer electronics and industrial automation tools.

As represented in Figure 7.1, usage-centered design is a model-driven process employing three primary abstract models: a user role model, a task model, and a content model. The *user role model* captures and organizes selected aspects of the relationship between particular users and the system being designed. The *task model* represents, in the form of essential use cases, those things that users in user roles are interested in accomplishing with the system. The *content model* represents the content and organization of the user interface apart from its appearance and behavior. These three core models are constructed both in terms of and interdependently with the *domain model,* which may take the form of a data model or an object model or even a simple glossary, depending on the nature and scope of the project. (The *operational model,* which captures aspects of the actual environment and operational context within which a system is deployed and used, is also developed concurrently with the core models but is beyond the scope of this chapter; interested readers should consult [Constantine and Lockwood 1999].)

Each of these three models consists of two parts: a collection of descriptions and a map of the relationships among those descriptions. Thus, the relationships among user roles are represented in overview by a *user role map*. The relationships among use cases are modeled in a *use case map* (corresponding to but not identical with the "Use Case Diagram" of UML). The content model represents the contents of the various *interaction*

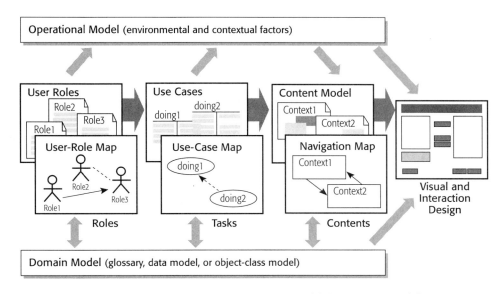

FIGURE 7.1 Logical relationships among primary models in usage-centered design

contexts (or "interaction spaces" as they are referred to in Wisdom (see Chapter 6) and in some other methods) within which users can interact with the system; the *navigation map* represents the interconnections among these interaction contexts. Together, the content model and the navigation map constitute what is sometimes called an *abstract prototype* [Constantine and Lockwood 1999]. (The "logical prototype" or "logical user-interface design" referred to in the Unified Process [Jacobson et al. 1999, pp. 161ff] is essentially the same concept, and reflects our work with Jacobson and his colleagues in the early 1990s [Ahlqvist 1996a, 1996b].)

Conceptually, a final visual and interaction design, usually in the form of an annotated paper prototype, is based on the abstract prototype, that is, the content and navigation models. These, in turn, derive from the task model, which itself depends on the model of user roles. In practice, however, the role model, task model, and content models are built more or less concurrently, with the attention of the modelers moving freely among them depending on the course of analysis and problem solving. The models themselves serve as holding places for the designer's fragmentary but evolving understanding, thereby helping to organize and systematize the process. This concurrent modeling approach makes for a more flexible and efficient process than traditional process models, which are more strictly sequential whether they are based on iteration or on a once-through "waterfall" cycle.

Usage-centered design is an "outside-in" approach in which the internal system design is devised to support the user interface, which supports external user needs. For this reason, essential use cases are considered the primary model, and concrete use cases, if needed for other purposes, are a derived model. In practice, use cases supporting system actors can be developed directly in concrete form and concurrently with the essential use cases supporting user roles.

Usage-centered design constitutes an adaptable agenda that can be practiced within almost any software-development process [Constantine and Lockwood 1999]. Key elements have, for example, been elegantly incorporated into the "lightweight" Wisdom approach (see Chapter 6). On the other hand, the "heavyweight" framework of the Unified Process [Jacobson et al. 1999] has proved more challenging. Among other things, the United Process perpetuates a long-standing practice of putting the cart before the horse by making user interface prototyping part of the requirements process. However, a user interface design in the form of a prototype is really a part of the solution description rather than the problem definition. A key to enhancing usability is to defer user interface design details by expressing requirements independent of their implementation and of their realization in a particular form of user interface. The problems in the Unified Process are not insurmountable, and with suitable improvements and refinements the process can serve as a context within which to practice usage-centered design. The details of such an integrated process are beyond the scope of the present discussion.

7.2.2 Task Modeling, Scenarios, and Use Cases

Task modeling is the pivotal activity in usage-centered design. User roles are a useful construct, but the user role model is not so much of interest in itself. It serves primarily as a bridge to the identification and construction of use cases and secondarily as a holding place for information about users and their work environment as it affects user interface design. Content models are another bridge—one that connects use cases to the user interface design. Both the role and content models facilitate the design process and promote the systematic development of effective user interfaces, but the models can be, under some circumstances, more or less dispensable. On the other hand, a task model is indispensable.

Use cases and essential use cases are, of course, only one of many potential ways of modeling tasks, ranging from rigorous and highly structured approaches that are of greatest interest to researchers and academics, to informal movie-style storyboards and free-form scenarios.

Scenarios have been widely used in design, in general, and in user interface design, in particular, to capture and represent tasks [Carroll 1995] (and see Chapters 2 and 3 in this volume). Although some writers [Booch 1994, Graham 1996, Wirfs-Brock 1993] have used the term "scenarios" more or less interchangeably with use cases, scenarios, as most commonly employed in design [Carroll 1995], are quite different from use cases. Scenarios are typically extended narratives forming a plausible vignette or storyline. They tend to be rich, realistic, concrete, specific, and often replete with gratuitous details for enhanced verisimilitude.

For example, a scenario for "Ian Smith gets help with his HyperCam software installation through our new Web-based technical support system" might read something like this:

Example 3

It is two o'clock in the morning, and Ian cannot get his new HyperCam software to install properly. He points his browser to *www.camerahype.com,* gets the splash page, and waits for the corporate home page to appear. He scrolls down the page and clicks on the tech-support link. On the provided form, he types his name, and then gets his customer ID off the packing slip for the HyperCam and types it in. He clicks the Submit button. He scans the Tech Support home page and finally clicks on the .GIF, which shows a befuddled user with a packing crate. This takes him to the Installation Help page, where he begins filling out the Incident Report form. Dissatisfied with the suggestion supplied by the system after the form is submitted, he goes to the Contact Us page and sends an e-mail message.

It is likely that the long-standing popularity of scenarios with traditionally trained human-computer interaction and user interface design professionals owes, in part, to this richness and realism. In contrast, use cases tend toward more stripped down and less interesting narratives, in which details are reduced and "variables" or class names replace more literal description, such as in this concrete use case for "getting installation help":

Example 4

The use case begins when the customer goes to the Customer Log-On page. There, the customer types in his or her name and customer ID and submits it. The system then displays the Tech Support home page with a list of Problem Categories. The customer selects clicks on Installation Help within the list, and the system supplies the Incident Report Form. The customer completes and submits the form, and the system presents a suggested resolution.

By contrast, a comparable essential use case for "getting help with specific problem" is even more spare:

Example 5

User Intentions	System Responsibilities
identify self as customer	
	present help options
select help option	
	request description
describe problem	
	offer possible solutions

As these examples illustrate, scenarios, conventional (concrete) use cases, and essential (abstract) use cases represent successive levels of abstraction and generalization. A scenario comprises a combination of use cases as they are actually enacted by some user.[1] In this example, for instance, the scenario includes enactments of use cases for logging on, for getting help with a specific problem, and for sending e-mail. Ignoring convention, the framers of the UML have declared that a scenario is a single thread through an instantiated use case; we prefer to honor accepted usage that is more common within the design

---

[1] In object-oriented parlance, a use case is instantiated, but the term makes little or no sense to the average user. Human beings in user roles do not "instantiate" use cases, they "enact" or "carry out" or "perform" them.

and human-computer interaction communities, which would make a scenario a composition of one *or more* enacted use cases, that is, a single thread through the instantiations of one or more use cases.

Thus a *scenario* is a composition of one or more enacted (instantiated) use cases expressed as an extended narrative or sequence of events or states forming a plausible vignette or realistic story line.

Of the three task models, essential use cases are the most robust, especially in the face of changing technologies, largely because they model tasks in a form closest to the essential nature of a problem and do not intermingle design solutions with problem description. As an illustration, Example 5, the essential use case for "getting help with specific problem," need not be rewritten or altered in any way should a later decision be made to implement the tech-support system as a menu-driven voice-response interface over the telephone. In contrast, neither the scenario in Example 3 nor the concrete use case in Example 4 would remain valid.

7.2.3 Use Case Decomposition

In usage-centered design, each essential use case represents incremental capability—a small piece of an aggregate set of tasks. Modeling with essential use cases favors a fairly fine-grained decomposition of tasks. The work to be supported by the system is partitioned into a collection of simple use cases interrelated by inclusion, specialization, and extension. Excessive decomposition of use cases has been denounced by some writers [e.g., Fowler 1997; Korson 1998], but decomposition in usage-centered design is not carried out for its own sake or to construct some sort of conceptually pure representation of a goal hierarchy.

Decomposition into relatively small, coherent units has several major advantages for usage-centered design. First, it leads to a smaller, simpler use case model in which each part of the overall model is comparatively simple and easy to understand in itself and in relation to a small number of other use cases. Second, the total model is simplified through reuse because common elements are factored out into separate use cases rather than being repeated in numerous places and variations.

When used as a guide to the design of the user interface and supporting internals, this form of decomposition promotes reuse of internal and external components and designs. Each piece of the problem can be solved once, and the solution can be recycled wherever the corresponding use case is referenced in the task model.

Our design experience also suggests a subtle but significant payoff in enhanced usability. A user interface that reflects a fine-grained, usage-centered task decomposition enables flexible re-composition by users into new combinations of tasks. In this way, designers can deliver powerful tools that support even unanticipated uses and usage patterns.

7.3 Use Case Narrative Style and User Interface Design

Scenarios, concrete use cases, and essential use cases are examples of varied styles of modeling and representation that have different relative advantages in different contexts. Usability inspections and usability testing usually require fairly detailed or specific scenarios that will exercise a variety of functions and expose a greater portion of the user interface to scrutiny. Nontechnical end-users are often most comfortable with the greater realism and specificity of scenarios or concrete use cases. For software engineering and the design of internal software architecture, however, the more traditional concrete use cases have proven particularly effective. Essential use cases can be too abstract to guide many important programming and program-design decisions, and scenarios informally intermix multiple functions, features, and threads of usage.

For user interface design, however, the abstraction of essential use cases is precisely what is needed because abstraction allows the designer to model the essential structure of tasks without hidden and premature assumptions about user interface design details. We have long argued that abstraction encourages creative innovation, and the recent experiences of several teams using essential use cases have supported this argument with a string of new software patents.

7.3.1 Language and Structure in Models

Because language influences thought patterns, the style of writing, the format, the wording, and even the grammatical form employed in use case narratives can all influence the value of use cases for designing user interfaces. Of course, the same must be true for the design of software architecture as well, but our concern here is with usability and user interface design more than the other issues in object-oriented software engineering.

Given that really good user interface design is so difficult, and real-world design problems are often so complex, the designer needs every bit of cognitive leverage and perceptual help that is attainable. Some styles of writing use cases facilitate good user interface design, while others are either indifferent or even interfere with it.

The more central and direct the role of use cases in the user interface design process, the more important becomes the issue of the form and style of representation. If, as in usage-centered design, the use case model directly drives and informs the user interface design, then narrative style and representation emerge as critically important.

7.3.2 Common Narrative Styles

Beyond the gross distinctions among scenarios, use cases, and essential use cases, we have found that the style in which use cases are written has a profound effect on their utility to designers and on the quality of the designs that result. In this section, we will illustrate some common styles in which use cases have been written.

The process or narrative body of a use case, what in UML is referred to as the "flow of events," constitutes the definition of a given use case. Use case narratives have been written in widely varying styles that differ in a number of significant ways. (For an excellent discussion of use case style and its consequences, see [Cockburn 2000].)

7.3.2.1 Continuous Narrative

Many writers and modelers have favored a continuous, free-form narrative—a style first introduced by Jacobson and his collaborators. Here is a recent example taken from the Web:

Example 6

A cash withdrawal transaction is started from within a session when the customer chooses cash withdrawal from the menu of possible transaction types. The customer chooses a type of account to withdraw from (e.g., checking) from a menu of possible accounts, and then chooses a dollar amount from a menu of possible amounts. The system verifies that it has sufficient money on hand to satisfy the request. If not, it reports a failure to the session, which initiates the Failed Transaction Extension to report the problem. If there is sufficient cash, it sends the customer's card number, PIN, chosen account and amount to the bank, which either approves or disapproves the transaction. If the transaction is approved, the machine dispenses the correct amount of cash and issues a receipt. If the transaction is disapproved due to an incorrect PIN, the Incorrect PIN extension is executed. All other disapprovals are reported to the session, which initiates the Failed Transaction Extension. The bank is notified whether or not an approved transaction was completed in its entirety by the machine; if it is completed then the bank completes debiting the customer's account for the amount. [Bjork 1998]

The problems with this style of narrative are numerous. There is no clear separation between the user side of the interchange and the system side. The narrative intermixes internal and external requirements and jumps erratically between external and internal perspectives. Elements that are essential to the nature of the problem (for example, "the machine dispenses the correct amount of cash") are comingled with implicit decisions about the design of the user interface (for example, "[the customer] chooses a dollar amount from a menu of possible amounts"). The lack of structure forces the reader to trace through the entire text just to get an idea of the general nature of what is happening. Portions of the narrative that are important for the design of the user interface are buried among descriptions that are irrelevant.

7.3.2.2 Numbered Sequence

Another common style is to write the narrative as a series of numbered steps. For example, consider another narrative for the same use case [Kruchten 1999]:

Example 7

Withdraw Money

1. The use case begins when the Client inserts an ATM card. The system reads and validates the information on the card.
2. System prompts for PIN. The Client enters PIN. The system validates the PIN.
3. System asks which operation the client wishes to perform. Client selects "Cash withdrawal."
4. System requests amounts [sic]. Client enters amount.
5. System requests type. Client selects account type (checking, savings, credit).
6. The system communicates with the ATM network to validate account ID, PIN, and availability of the amount requested.
7. The system asks the client whether he or she wants a receipt. This step is performed only if there is paper left to print the receipt.
8. System asks the client to withdraw the card. Client withdraws card. (This is a security measure to ensure that Clients do not leave their cards in the machine.)
9. System dispenses the requested amount of cash.
10. System prints receipt.
11. The use case ends.

One advantage of this style is immediately apparent: The separation into distinct steps makes it easier to skim the use case for an overview and to see the general nature of the interaction. However, it suffers from many of the same problems as the continuous-narrative style. Despite the segmentation into discrete steps, individual steps intermix system and user actions. The narrative exemplifies a systems-centric view: With one exception, each step begins with the system side of things.

Both Examples 6 and 7 also illustrate an aspect of narrative style that is all too common in use cases. They are wordy and filled with verbiage that is little more than noise. Despite the fact that the beginning and end of a use case are invariably self-evident, many writers seem compelled to announce pedantically, "The use case begins when . . ." or to declare, "The use case ends."

7.3.2.3 Partitioned Narratives

Because they have little or no structure, both the continuous and the sequenced narrative styles require, for clarity, that the perspective or focus be declared repeatedly (the system does this, the user chooses that, the system completes something else), which contributes to their wordiness. Even so, the boundary between what is inside the system and what is outside—the user interface—is not readily apparent and can only be discerned piecemeal through careful perusal of the entire narrative.

The simple solution to this is to separate the user and the system side of the interaction completely. For use cases, this separation was originally suggested by Wirfs-Brock [1993], although others have effected similar divisions in other forms of task models. Wirfs-Brock divides the narrative of concrete use cases into two columns: the user action model and the system response model. In this style, the boundary representing the user interface is obvious, and it is immediately apparent, without intrusive repetition, which part of the narrative refers to the user and which to the system. For example, here is another variant of the cash withdrawal use case expressed as a partitioned narrative:

Example 8

User Action	System Response
insert card in ATM	
	read card
	request PIN
enter PIN	
	verify PIN
	display option menu
select option	
	display account menu
select account	
	prompt for amount
enter amount	
	display amount
confirm amount	
	return card
take card	
	dispense cash if available

This format is so superior and more readable by all interested parties that it is hard to justify not using it in all cases. Of course, nothing prevents the use case writer from also numbering the actions and responses, which makes for even greater utility.

7.3.2.4 Pseudo-Code

Some writers of use cases employ varying amounts of so-called structured English or pseudo-code in the use case narrative. For example, constructions like these are commonly encountered:

```
until customer_done repeat
if valid_user_code then do...end_do else do...end_do end_if
```

Although such expressions seem to offer precision and may be comfortable and familiar to software engineers, they are seldom transparent to ordinary users, and the precision can actually obscure the real nature of the interaction.

In our experience, the more that use case narratives look like code, the more likely it is that they are just that. Programming is a necessary and noble activity, but it belongs as part of implementing a solution and not in modeling the problem, which is yet another argument for essential use cases as the primary task model.

7.3.2.5 Interaction Diagrams

Some designers substitute graphical models, such as the sequence diagrams and collaboration diagrams of UML, for the narrative text that more commonly models the flow of events defining use cases. Although arguably well-suited to the original software-engineering purposes for which they were conceived, interaction diagrams are a poor fit with the needs of user interface design. Instead of maintaining an external-user perspective and a focus on the essential nature of tasks, they plunge the designer into considering messages passed among software objects. Like pseudo-code, they introduce internal design considerations prematurely, but the notation and constructs are even more obscure and alien to nontechnical users and clients.

7.3.2.6 Pre- and Post-Conditions

One important exception to the rule against using programming constructs in use cases, particularly those intended for guiding user interface design, is the use of pre- and post-conditions, which have also become common in writing use case narratives. See, for example, [Schneider and Winters 1998]:

Example 9

Place Order

Preconditions: A valid user has logged into the system.

Flow of events:

Basic Path

1. The use case starts when the customer selects Place Order.
2. The customer enters his or her name and address.
3. If the customer enters only the zip code, the system will supply city and state.
4. The customer will enter product codes for the desired product.
5. The system will supply a product description and price for each item.
6. The system will keep a running total of items ordered as they are entered.
7. The customer will enter credit card information.
8. The customer will select Submit.
9. The system will verify the information, save the order as pending, and forward payment information to the accounting system.
10. When payment is confirmed, the order is marked Confirmed, an order ID is returned to the customer, and the use case ends.

Alternative paths

In step 9, if any information is incorrect, the system will prompt the customer to correct the information.

Post-condition: The order has been saved and marked Confirmed.

Although we initially resisted this seeming intrusion of programming into task modeling, we found that pre- and post-conditions serve significant purposes in supporting usage-centered design. For one, ordinary users often are more comfortable when preconditions are made explicit. In the absence of the precondition in Example 9, for instance, users and customers will often protest that the use case will not work or is incomplete without logging a valid user into the system. Indeed, many writers may be tempted to make such an action the first step of the use case, as was done in Examples 7 and 8. However, this shortcut has the disadvantage of making a discrete interaction a mandatory step in every use case dependent on it, which clearly can misrepresent the real task structure. (In most American ATMs, the user need not insert a card for each separate transaction, for example.) The precondition is left implicit in Example 6 ("A cash withdrawal transaction is started from within a session"), which is significantly less clear than an explicit declaration.

Preconditions also offer a non-procedural means for expressing necessary ordering among use cases. If "logging into system" is a use case modeled with an appropriate narrative, then a pre-condition expressed as "valid user logged in with 'logging into system'" appropriately fixes the order of usage. These relationships among use cases are equally transparent and useful to users, user interface designers, and software developers alike. Contrary to the opinions of purists, this practice does not represent an intrusion of procedural modeling into object-orientation but merely expresses the intrinsic ordering of certain interrelated tasks. In fact, use cases as the pre- and post-conditions of other use cases provide a straightforward and logical means for modeling workflow, which is an aspect of task structure often neglected by use case modelers. (An appropriate CASE tool would support tracing or highlighting workflow relationships.)

7.3.2.7 Abstraction

Use case narratives can be written at various levels of abstraction and to varying ends. In our own design work, we sometimes refer to a style we call "suitably vague," in which a certain amount of hand waving and disregard for precision proves useful, especially in the early stages of task modeling. For example, in a numerically-controlled machine-tool application, an early form of one use case might read as follows:

Example 10

User Intentions	System Responsibilities
enter setup parameters	
	present setup configuration
confirm setup	
	perform tool setup

Not only does this degree of abstraction omit concrete details of the user interface design, but it glosses over much of the content of the task in itself. There may be dozens of individual parameters that take on various forms and have various constraints. Presenting the setup configuration to the user may imply elaborate, unavoidable transformations guided by the user.

Nonetheless, such "suitably vague" modeling can be extremely useful in deferring a premature digression into distracting details. In many cases, even obscuring essential details can pay off by implying the possibility of a generalized solution, such as, for example, a common mechanism for entering setup parameters even though these are of varied form and format. Indeed, just such suitable vagueness led one team to a solution deemed by their legal advisors to be a patentable software innovation.

In essential use cases, we avoid the extra words and verbal padding that are so common to most use cases for two simple and compelling reasons. First, phrases and constructions that add meaningless words merely decrease the signal-to-noise ratio and generally make it harder for analysts and designers to extract the real content that is relevant to user interface design. Second, substantive but unnecessary elaborations and redundant constructions, if actually translated into design features or elements, result in user interfaces that are unnecessarily complex.

A simple and representative instance is the use case for recycling (Example 2), in which the first user action represents an unnecessary step imposed by the narrative. Pressing a Start button is not part of the problem as viewed from the user's perspective. Inserting an object to recycle is sufficient in itself to define the start of the use case. In practice, use case narratives reduced to an essential form can guide the designer toward dramatic overall reductions in user actions because every nonessential step in a use case model adds to the interaction design. One software tool for industrial automation, when redesigned through essential use cases, halved the total number of steps required to complete a representative mix of programming tasks. In fact, essential use cases have also proved an effective tool for workflow redesign and process reengineering owing to their parsimony in expressing the inherent nature of tasks.

7.3.3 Task Goals and User Intentions

The narratives of essential use cases are cast in terms of user intentions and system responsibilities. Earlier in this chapter, we cited work on goal orientation in use cases, but the distinction between goals and intentions is a subtle though important one for user interface design. A goal is a desired end-state of a system, and as such it is correctly described in static terms as the state and features of objects. For example, in a hotel registration application, one goal of the hotel clerk might be expressed as "guest checked into acceptable room." An intention, in contrast, is dynamic and represents direction or progress rather than an end state.

Goals are destinations, whereas intentions represent the journey, and it is the user's journey—the interaction—that is most directly related to the issues of interface and interaction design. Goals, being static, place the focus on objects or nouns, while intentions, being dynamic, bring the actions and verbs to the foreground, thereby implicitly admitting that interactions are alterable and divertible. Intentions may be satisfied short of reaching one particular final goal, and any number of intentions may support reaching a single goal.

Broadly speaking, both goals and intentions can be considered part of a broader "teleocentric" or "purpose-centered" perspective in use case modeling and user interface design. Beyond the immediate intentions of users, one can consider the contextual purposes of usage in a broader or larger perspective. In many applications, individual use cases are part of a larger framework of tasks, such as the work, profession, or job responsibilities of the user in a particular role that is being supported by the system. The larger purposes or functions of an essential use case are a part of the use case and need to be expressed within it.

In essential use case models, the complete hierarchy of goals and subgoals, as well as their tasks and subtasks, is expressed through interrelationships among use cases (see also [Cockburn 2000]). These interrelationships are either embedded within the body of the use case narrative or placed within specialized clauses or sections devoted to that purpose.

7.4 Structured Essential Use Cases

In any model-driven design process, the quality and character of the models shape the quality and character of the results. For this reason, we have evolved a highly structured form of use cases based primarily on our own work and that of our clients in the practical application of usage-centered design but also incorporating ideas from numerous sources, including some of the stylistic innovations referred to in the previous section. The structure is intended to create an orderly and easily understood framework for organizing the various parts of the use case and to ensure that all the relevant aspects of the use case have been defined—or at least considered.

Compared with the informality evident in most of the examples presented thus far, structured essential use cases form a more solid bridge between traditional requirements analysis and user interface design and between design and implementation. As a tool for managing complexity, they also increase the effectiveness of essential use cases for truly massive problems. Informal and relatively unstructured forms of essential use cases are quite serviceable for relatively small and simple problems that are designed and implemented by small teams working in close communication. As the number of use cases and project participants increases, however, more systematic, elaborate, and highly structured forms of modeling and communication are needed.

There is no hard and fast rule for choosing between informal and structured use cases. It depends as much on how the project is organized as upon the size of the problem. However, in general, modeling with informal use case narratives begins to break down with more than a few dozen use cases. Moreover, in any situation in which analysts, designers, and developers work separately and communicate primarily through models, greater formality is also demanded.

The overall organization of a structured essential use case is illustrated schematically in Figure 7.2. The use case is divided into three principal parts: identification, relationships, and process. The identification section uniquely identifies the use case and explains its purpose or function. The relationships section identifies other use cases related in some

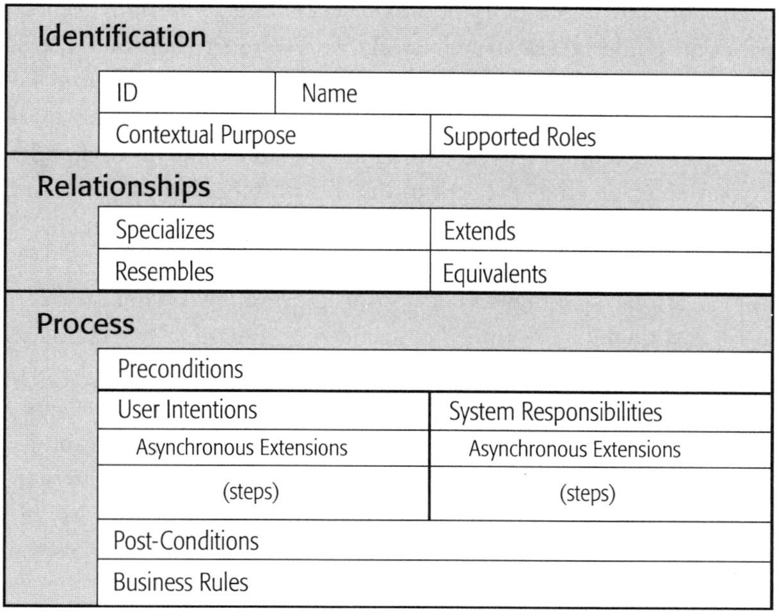

Identification			
ID		Name	
Contextual Purpose		Supported Roles	
Relationships			
Specializes		Extends	
Resembles		Equivalents	
Process			
Preconditions			
User Intentions		System Responsibilities	
Asynchronous Extensions		Asynchronous Extensions	
(steps)		(steps)	
Post-Conditions			
Business Rules			

FIGURE 7.2 Schematic framework for structured essential use cases

way to the use case. The process, the narrative body of the use case, defines its interaction process or dynamic aspects. Each of these will be explained in turn.

7.4.1 Identity and Purpose

The identifier of a use case is merely a sequence number or other unique and permanent identification code. While small problems may be modeled without resort to such codes, large projects will need them to help keep track of use cases and related models and documents.

The name of an essential use case should reflect its function or immediate purpose. An immediate purpose represents a single, discrete intention on the part of a user. Distinguishing intentions from goals leads to subtle differences in both description and definition of use cases.

We have found that present participles of transitive verbs—continuing actions taking a specific direct object—best capture the essence of user intentions. For example, getting cash from ATM or checking arriving guest into acceptable room. It is also important that the direct object be fully qualified by modifiers so as to distinguish it, as needed, from all other related or similar objects within the application. In general, especially as the problem size goes up, more specificity in the objects is safer. Especially to be avoided are use case names that could be construed as referring to more than one operation of the same name on more than one distinct and unrelated object of the same name. For example, deleting block is unacceptable for naming a use case in an application involving both deleting program block temporarily, meaning a reversible removal of a coding module, and the vastly different deleting execution-time block, meaning the disabling of a run-time debugging break. The boundary between suitably vague and dangerously ambiguous depends on the specifics of the problem at hand.

One useful variation on ambiguous or nonspecific naming is what we refer to as compound or cluster cases, which are named collections of functionally related use cases. For example, downloading modules/blocks/programs to simulator/controller is shorthand for what might eventually require six separate use cases or could potentially be covered by a single definition. Compound or cluster cases may be based on a common operation on varying objects or on multiple operations on the same object, as in entering/modifying patient background information. Compound cases are an especially useful shorthand notation in early modeling for applications with large numbers of use cases or for projects with extremely limited design time.

Having experimented with various orthographies for use case names, we now favor underlining and lowercase letters, with words separated by spaces. The underlining makes it easy to visually parse the use case name as a discrete whole that is distinct from the rest of the narrative in which it appears. Separating the words facilitates reordering and searching lists of use cases. Users also find this format to be "friendlier" and less "techie" than the strung-together, bi-capitalized style used in our book [Constantine and Lockwood 1999] and in some earlier work. The underlining is also suggestive of a hyperlink, which is precisely how a use case name should function in online documentation or models.

The Contextual Purpose section contains the description of the larger goals or working context in which the use case is employed. For example, the Contextual Purpose of browsing empty rooms by category in a hotel-reservation system might be as follows: "In order to complete guest registration, a suitable room must be located and assigned to the guest."

The Supported Roles section further qualifies the essential nature of the use case by listing the user roles that it is intended to support. For example, the use case browsing empty rooms by category might support the roles of Ordinary Desk Clerk, Desk Supervisor, and Self-Registering Guest.

7.4.2 Relationships

The Relationships section identifies other use cases to which the use cases is related. In usage-centered design, use cases may be interrelated in several ways:

- *Inclusion:* One use case is included (by reference) within or used by another use case.
- *Specialization:* One use case is a specialized variant of another more general case.
- *Extension:* One use case extends another by introducing alternative or exceptional processes.

In addition, we find the following other relationships useful on occasion:

- *Similarity:* One use case corresponds to or is similar to or resembles another in some unspecified ways.
- *Equivalence:* One use case is equivalent to another, that is, serves as an alias.

Similarity, a relationship often noted early in use case modeling, provides a way to carry forward insight about the relationships among use cases even when the exact nature of the relationship is not yet clear. For example, reviewing savings account summary and reviewing checking account summary might be modeled as separate but similar use cases before it is known whether one process can cover both or if two different approaches will be needed. Equivalence flags those cases where a single definition can cover what are, from the user's perspective, two or more different intentions. This construction makes it easier to validate the model with users and customers while also assuring that only one design will be developed. In the absence of such a relationship, the modeler would be forced to define the two use cases as trivial specializations of a totally artificial general use case.

Within the Relationships section, related use cases are listed in clauses labeled appropriately using the terms Specializes, Extends, Resembles, and Equivalents. Inclusions are omitted from this section for the simple reason that these cases are, as the name implies, included in other parts of the use case narrative.

For example, the use case browsing empty rooms by category might incorporate the following relationships:

- *Extends:* checking arriving guest into acceptable room; reviewing room utilization
- *Specializes:* browsing rooms

References within the Relationships section are reflected in the Use Case Map, which is discussed later in this chapter.

7.4.3 Process

The Process section of the use case begins with pre-conditions and ends with post-conditions. Both pre- and post-conditions can include explicit or implicit references to other use cases.

The narrative body of the use case is divided into User Intentions and System Responsibilities. Although we have primarily used the two-column format illustrated earlier in Examples 5 and 10, this arrangement can sometimes waste display space or present formatting difficulties, especially for use cases with more complex steps. An alternative format, shown in Example 11, uses indentation along with shading or distinct fonts to distinguish the System Responsibilities from the User Intentions:

Example 11

User Intentions	System Responsibilities
	1. present list of standard test setups
2. select standard test setup	
	3. display selected test setup
4. optionally [do modifying test setup]	
5. confirm test setup	
	6. run test as set up and report
7. optionally [print test results]	
	8. print and confirm

Although visually not quite as satisfying as the two-column format, this form is easier to create with word processors.

7.5 Elements of Style in Structured Essential Narratives

Within the process narrative describing user intentions and system responsibilities, the preferred primary language of expression is the natural language and vocabulary of the users and of the application domain. However, because essential use cases serve as the core model bridging between user requirements and the user interface design and between design and implementation, certain technical constructions and references are, of course, also required. These technical elements include references to objects and other use cases as well as idiomatic constructions for expressing conditional interaction, partial ordering, and extensions.

7.5.1 Objects

Ideally, the use case model, whether in concrete or essential form, is developed in tandem with an object model or another data model, as indicated earlier in Figure 7.1. The steps of the use case narrative can make explicit or implicit references to objects, their methods, or their attributes. Thus, for example "test results" may be a defined term or object class, with "print" as one of its methods. To highlight a reference to an object or data element as a defined term, italics or quotation marks can be used. A use case as a whole may also correspond to a method of a class, as might be the case with the use case <u>modifying test setup</u>.

7.5.2 Included Use Cases

The process narrative may include explicit references to other use cases that are used in the course of or become part of the interaction. As illustrated in step 4 of Example 11, the name of the use case is preceded by the word "do," which calls out the included use case and improves scansion, especially when being read by or reviewed with end-users or clients.

7.5.3 Conditional Interaction

Conditional interaction is presented with the word "optionally" followed by the optional actions in square brackets. Inclusions can be conditional, as in step 4 of Example 11. Conditional interaction is discussed further in connection with extensions in section 7.5.4.

7.5.4 Partial Ordering

One of the shortcomings of most conventional ways of writing the narrative body of use cases is that they provide no explicit way to express a very common situation in task modeling. Most published narratives, including all of the examples thus far presented, are fully-ordered and describe strictly sequential interaction: first the user does this, then the system does that and that, and then the user does something else. In these narratives, some actions may be optional, but the ordering is not.

Although some analysts add procedural richness through iteration and conditional expressions, the issue of optional or flexible ordering is seldom modeled explicitly. This oversight is a major shortcoming because many tasks can be performed in various orders and because allowing users to perform actions in various sequences is often a strong factor affecting usability.

In the past, many such cases were expressed in use case narratives as if they were strictly ordered even though it was implicitly understood that the order of interaction was actually flexible. In problems of modest size, one could trust that the final visual and interaction design would allow for the desired flexibility even though it was not expressed in the use case model. On large-scale projects, however, the chances are increased that important but implicit insights can be lost between analysis and design. The natural place to carry forward such information is as an intrinsic part of the use case narrative.

We have adopted the convention of using the phrase "in any order" followed by a list of actions or intentions, separated by semicolons and all enclosed in braces ("curly brackets"), as shown in Example 12.

Example 12

in any order {specify part number; specify quantity ordered}

This practice encourages the user interface designer to model as strictly ordered sequences only those interactions in which the order is actually fixed or required. The notation has proved easy and natural for users and nontechnical people to understand without instruction. The notation is designed to be distinctive enough that the words "in any order" can be omitted to form a shorthand that is convenient for specialists to use in rapid note taking or for communication among themselves.

7.5.5 Extensions

The notion of use case extensions has been a core concept in use case modeling since its introduction [Jacobson et al. 1992]. An extension is a distinct use case embodying alternative, conditional, or exceptional courses of interaction that can alter or extend the main "flow of events" embodied in some base use case. The base use case is said to be extended by the extension use case. The base case is the "normal" or expected interaction; the extension is an exception or alternative.

The primary advantage of extensions is that they make it possible to keep the narrative body of the base case simple and straightforward by separating out into distinct use cases the often numerous exceptional or unusual circumstances. Keeping the narrative for the base case clean is likely to lead to clean and simple operation of the user interface under normal circumstances. A second strong argument for extensions is that they encourage reuse—in models as well as in designs and implementation—since the extension case may modify or extend any number of other use cases.

Extensions pose a number of problems for methodologists and practitioners, however. One awkward aspect of the construct is the fact that the extension names the base case it extends, not the other way around as many people seem to expect. In other words, the extension is not visible in the base case, and diagrammatically, the arrow points from the extension to any use cases it extends. Although this convention seems backward to many people, it is an advantage in one sense because it allows extensions to be discovered or concocted after the fact without having to return to the base case and alter or rewrite the narrative body. Thus, initial attention is paid to the normal course of interaction and the special cases can be picked up later.

Although even some of the leading thinkers in the areas of object-orientation and use case analysis have struggled over agreement on the exact semantics of extensions, we have always taken a purely pragmatic approach. Because they simplify task models and therefore can lead to simplified user interaction, usage-centered design employs extensions freely without worrying too much over semantic precision or theoretical rigor.

However, as the scale of design problems rises with larger design teams and more and more use cases, the sort of "studied sloppiness" that can be beneficial for rapid design of modest problems begins to become a stumbling block. For this reason we have recently been rethinking the concept of extensions and how they are modeled in use cases and use case maps.

One of the problems is that the original concept of extension is actually a conflation covering two quite different kinds of exceptional or alternative courses of interaction which may occur either synchronously or asynchronously.

7.5.5.1 Synchronous Extensions

In the first variant, the extension use case can only occur at certain points in the course of the interaction, as in Example 11, in which the user may or may not choose to modify the test setup. This is clearly not a part of the normal or mainline course of interaction, so it is appropriate to consider it as a distinct use case that extends running a standard test. However, the user can enact the extension use case modifying test setup only after a predefined test has been selected and before the test setup has been confirmed for the system to run it.

This first form of extension is termed "synchronous" because its occurrence is synchronized with the use case it extends. In fact, a synchronous extension is nothing more than a conditional inclusion. It is a use case that will, under some circumstances, be included or used at a particular point in the course of the interaction. By definition it must be "visible" in the narrative for the base case because this narrative must specify at what point in the narrative the extension can occur.

7.5.5.2 Asynchronous Extensions

The other case covered by the original notion of extension refers to alternative or exceptional cases whose point of occurrence is unpredictable. Such asynchronous extensions operate like interrupts to the mainline interaction. For instance, in the use case of Example 13, the user might choose at any time to reset the system, thereby canceling the test and restoring all original values. Similarly, the system could at any time assume responsibility for informing the user that an unrecoverable exception has occurred. Because such extensions apply to the interaction as a whole but can occur at any point, they are most reasonably separated out and presented at the top of the narrative body, as in this example:

Example 14

User Intentions	System Responsibilities
Asynchronous Extensions	
optionally at point do {resetting test}	
	optionally at any point do {reporting fatal exception}
	1. present list of standard test setups
2. select standard test setup	
	3. display selected test setup
4. optionally [do modifying test setup]	
5. confirm test setup	
	6. run test as set up and report
7. optionally [print test results]	
	8. print and confirm

Cockburn [2000], among others, places extensions of either variety at the end of the use case narrative, but we find that arranging the asynchronous extensions as a prologue puts them where users, managers, and nontechnical people expect to find them. It is as if to say, "Before we start the details of our story, note that we could be interrupted at any time by certain occurrences." When showing use cases to nontechnical people, we would normally omit the heading "Asynchronous Extensions" from the section.

7.6 Use Case Maps

A use case map models the interrelationships among use cases by mapping the overall structure of the tasks to be supported by the system being designed. As noted earlier, problems with the UML Use Case Diagram have kept us from simply adopting its conventions wholesale. The large, complex models typically required for real-world applications can be particularly difficult to read and understand when expressed in UML. Integrating actors (user roles) with use case relationships in a single model leads to bewildering jumbles of lines for all but the most trivial problems of the sort found in books, articles, and tutorials. A suitable CASE tool would allow for selecting an actor or user role and seeing the associated use cases highlighted (or vice versa), but in paper or static diagrams, we would normally omit use roles from use case maps.

7.6.1 Representing Use Cases

Following Jacobson's lead, we have always represented each use case by an ellipse, but we have recently found that this convention, which seems adequate for academic or textbook problems in which all the use case names are short and simple, breaks down for many larger and more complex real-world problems. In particular, the elliptical shape does not as readily accommodate long names as do other geometric shapes. Two alternatives that do not abandon convention altogether are worthy of serious consideration (see Figure 7.3). One is to put the name outside the use case symbol, as Jacobson originally did. The other is to form a graphical hybrid that might be called an "elliptangle."

Compound cases, as we explained earlier, are portrayed as a graphical "stack," which visually suggests that the named case really covers a number of use cases (see Figure 7.4).

7.6.2 Representing Relationships

Because in UML the type of relationship represented by a given line is not clear from its appearance, one must trace a line to its endpoints and find an adjacent label somewhere in the middle to know exactly how two use cases are related. The guillemets (« and ») surrounding relationship labels in UML are nothing more than graphical noise that makes models harder to parse visually.

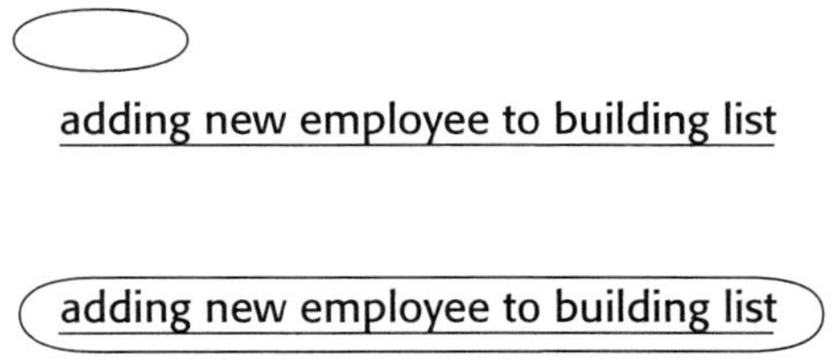

FIGURE 7.3 Alternative representation of use cases in maps

FIGURE 7.4 Representation of compound (cluster) cases in use case maps

As experience accumulates, especially with large, complex applications, we continue to revise usage-centered design notation to promote clarity and communication. For readability in complex models, we use different line styles to represent different relationships and employ labels for redundant communication. (See Figures 7.5 and 7.6.)

The distinction between synchronous and asynchronous extensions poses a notational challenge. The "extends" relationship is now reserved for asynchronous extensions. The fact that asynchronous extensions are referred to in the Asynchronous Extensions clause of the base use case is considered a form of optional visibility, and the arrow still points from the extension to the extended base use case.

Because synchronous extensions are merely conditional inclusions, they ought to be represented as some variation on the graphic for inclusion. We would prefer to model such relationships in a perfectly natural and expressive way by adding a decision diamond to the tail of the arrow normally used to show inclusion, which is precisely the way such relationships were represented in the structure chart notation in use around the world for more than twenty-five years [Yourdon and Constantine 1975]. Unfortunately, the UML somewhat arrogantly usurps the diamond—all but universally recognized as representing a decision or conditional operation—to represent aggregation, thus creating an arbitrary and nonintuitive notation made all the more obscure by the use of open diamonds and filled diamonds to represent (and, to many users, obfuscate) aggregation and composition of classes [Henderson-Sellers and Barbier 1999].

For conditional inclusion, other suggestions have been considered, including annotating the tail of the arrow with a question mark or with a cardinality, such as 0..1. We now favor a distinct line style with an informative label (see Figure 7.5).

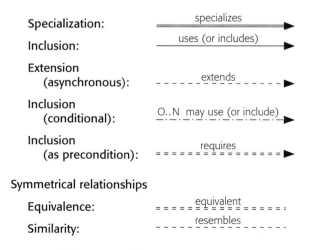

FIGURE 7.5 Relationships in use case maps

FIGURE 7.6 Example of a use case map

An example of a partial use case map using these conventions is shown in Figure 7.6.

7.7 Business Rules

In addition to functional requirements, almost all applications are defined in part by what are commonly known as "business rules." Business rules—or more simply, rules—are the policies, constraints, and conditions to be satisfied that underlie business processes [Gottesdiener 1999]. Such rules define the operational relationships or restrictions governing information and how it is processed within a system and, in some situations, within the larger organizational context. Although they have not figured prominently in academic and theoretical work on use cases and object-orientation, business rules are a critically important part of most real-world applications. Because they describe how "the business" or process is supposed to operate, the term is used even within technical areas that are not normally characterized in business terminology. For example, a rule might constrain the sequence in which various containers in a chemical process can be emptied and reloaded with other ingredients, or a rule might require that passwords contain a mix of digits and letters and must be updated at least every ninety days.

Although business rules are not functional requirements in themselves, they are often closely associated with the functionality embodied in use cases. Rules can apply to or be associated with any part of a use case, a use case as a whole, or the relationships among use cases. Clearly, the rules associated with use cases will have direct and important consequences for user interface design. A rule requiring the regular updating of passwords, for instance, mandates a means to inform the user when an update is needed and a means for changing the password that is accessible from within the log-in context.

To assure correct design and implementation and to facilitate tracing requirements, business rules should be clearly and directly connected with those parts of the analysis and design models to which they apply. On the other hand, business rules comprise a distinct collection of requirements that should not be scattered among various analysis and design models in which they can become buried, lost, or inadvertently duplicated. To resolve these conflicting needs, rules are compiled into a Business Rules Model that identifies, categorizes, and lists them. Business rules can then be referred to by annotating use cases and use case maps with references to the rules by name and/or identifier.

For example, a business rule may require that a credit limit increase cannot be authorized on an account for which an activity summary has not been requested in the same session, even though, in principle, there is otherwise no necessary sequential dependency between these two functions. The use case reviewing account activity summary therefore becomes a precondition of the use case authorizing credit limit increase. An annotation such as "(Rule: #27 Activity Review on Credit Increase)" is associated with the relationship between the two use cases and would appear on the relationship line in the use case map and in the Preconditions clause in a form like this:

Example 14

do reviewing account activity summary (Rule: #27 Activity Review on Credit Increase)

For those business rules applying to the use case as a whole, a clause is reserved within the Process section. Strictly speaking, a use case model is incomplete as a specification unless the associated business rules are included or connected in some manner.

7.8 Recommendations

For user interface design, extensive experience has demonstrated that an appropriate style of expression in writing use case narratives can support a more efficient design process, facilitate communication within a project, and lead to higher quality designs. A consensus may finally be emerging that use case narratives that are both abstract and purpose-centered offer demonstrable advantages as task models for user interface design. We propose, additionally, that a more highly-structured and systematic form of use case narrative is needed, especially to support larger and more complex projects. Structured essential use cases provide a rich and precise mode of expression that not only meets the needs of user interface designers and software engineers but is also easily understood and validated by end users and clients.

Such use cases improve modeling and communication through a refined and precise organization that includes the following: (1) a clear division separating user intentions from system responsibilities, thus highlighting the system boundary; (2) distinction between and separate presentation of asynchronous and synchronous extensions; (3) idioms for expressing partially ordered interactions; and (4) straightforward linking with related business rules. This structure strikes a balance that avoids both the informality and imprecision of continuous narratives and the inappropriate rigor of models such as interaction diagrams, which are better suited for object-oriented design and programming than for user interface design.

7.9 References

[Ahlqvist 1996a] S. Ahlqvist. *Objectory for GUI Intensive Systems*. Kista, Sweden: Objectory Software AB, 1996.

[Ahlqvist 1996b] S. Ahlqvist. *Objectory for GUI Intensive Systems: Extension*. Kista, Sweden: Objectory Software AB, 1996.

[Bjork 1998] R. C. Bjork. Use Cases for Example ATM System. Found at *http://www.cs.gordonc.edu/local/courses/cs320/ATM_Example/UseCases.html*, 2000.

[Booch 1994] G. Booch. Scenarios. *Report on Object Analysis and Design*, 1 (3), 1994, 3–6.

[Carroll 1995] J. M. Carroll, ed. *Scenario-Based Design*. New York: John Wiley and Sons, 1995.

[Cockburn 1997] A. Cockburn. Structuring Use Cases with Goals. *Journal of Object-Oriented Programming*, September/October 1997, 35–40; November/December 1997, 56–62.

[Cockburn 2000] A. Cockburn. *Writing Effective Use Cases*. Boston: Addison-Wesley, 2000.

[Constantine 1994a] L. L. Constantine. Mirror, Mirror. *Software Development*, 2 (3), 1994. Reprinted in L. L. Constantine. *Constantine on Peopleware*. Englewood Cliffs, NJ: Prentice Hall, 1995.

[Constantine 1994b] L. L. Constantine. Essentially Speaking. *Software Development*, 2 (11), 1994, 95–96. Reprinted in L. L. Constantine. *Constantine on Peopleware*. Englewood Cliffs, NJ: Prentice Hall, 1995.

[Constantine 1995] L. L. Constantine. Essential Modeling: Use Cases for User Interfaces. *ACM Interactions*, 2 (2), 1995, 34–46.

[Constantine and Henderson-Sellers 1995a] L. L. Constantine, and B. Henderson-Sellers. Notation Matters. Part 1: Framing the Issues. *Report on Object Analysis and Design*, 2 (3), 1995, 25–29.

[Constantine and Henderson-Sellers 1995b] L. L. Constantine and B. Henderson-Sellers. Notation Matters. Part 2: Applying the Principles. *Report on Object Analysis and Design*, 2 (4), 1995, 25–27.

[Constantine and Lockwood 1999] L. L. Constantine and L. A. D. Lockwood. *Software for Use: A Practical Guide to the Models and Methods of Usage-Centered Design.* Reading, MA: Addison-Wesley, 1999.

[Fowler 1997] M. Fowler. *UML Distilled: Applying the Standard Object Modeling Language.* Reading, MA: Addison-Wesley, 1997.

[Gottesdiener 1999] E. Gottesdiener. Business Rules as Requirements. *Software Development*, 7 (12), 1999.

[Graham 1996] I. Graham. Task Scripts, Use Cases and Scenarios in Object-Oriented Analysis. *Object-Oriented Systems*, 3 (3), 1996, 123–142.

[Henderson-Sellers 1999] B. Henderson-Sellers. OML: Proposals to Enhance UML. In J. Bèzivin and P.-A. Muller, eds. *The Unified Modeling Language: Beyond the Notation.* Berlin: Springer-Verlag, 1999.

[Henderson-Sellers and Barbier 1999] B. Henderson-Sellers and F. Barbier. Black and White Diamonds. In R. France and B. Rumpe, eds. *The Unified Modeling Language: Beyond the Standard.* Berlin: Springer-Verlag, 1999.

[Henderson-Sellers and Firesmith 1999] B. Henderson-Sellers and D. G. Firesmith. Comparing OPEN and UML. *Information Software Technology*, 41 (2), 1999, 139–156.

[Jacobson et al. 1992] I. Jacobson, M. Christerson, P. Jonsson, and G. Övergaard. *Object-Oriented Software Engineering: A Use Case Driven Approach.* Reading, MA: Addison-Wesley, 1992.

[Jacobson et al. 1999] I. Jacobson, G. Booch, and J. Rumbaugh. *The Unified Process.* Reading, MA: Addison-Wesley, 1999.

[Kaindl 1995] H. Kaindl. An Integration of Scenarios with Their Purposes in Task Modeling. *Proc. Symposium on Designing Interactive Systems.* Ann Arbor, MI: ACM Press, 1995.

[Korson 1998] T. Korson. The Misuse of Use Cases. *Object Magazine*, 8 (3), 1998, 18–20.

[Kruchten 1999] P. Kruchten. *The Rational Unified Process: An Introduction.* Reading, MA: Addison-Wesley, 1999.

[Lee and Xue 1999] J. Lee and N. Xue. Analyzing User Requirements by Use Cases: A Goal-Driven Approach. *IEEE Software*, 16 (4), 1999, 92–101.

[McMenamin and Palmer 1984] S. M. McMenamin and J. Palmer. *Essential Systems Analysis.* Englewood Cliffs, NJ: Prentice Hall, 1984.

[Page-Jones et al. 1990] M. Page-Jones, L. L. Constantine, and S. Weiss. Modeling Object-Oriented Systems: A Uniform Object Notation. *Computer Language*, 7 (10), 1990.

[Roberts et al. 1998] D. Roberts, D. Berry, S. Isensee, and J. Mullaly. *Designing for the User with OVID.* New York: Macmillan, 1998.

[Rumbaugh et al. 1999] J. Rumbaugh, I. Jacobson, and E. Booch. *The Unified Modeling Language Reference Manual.* Reading, MA: Addison-Wesley, 1999.

[Schneider and Winters 1998] G. Schneider, and J. P. Winters. *Applying Use Cases: A Practical Guide.* Reading, MA: Addison-Wesley, 1998.

[Texel and Williams 1997] P. P. Texel and C. B. Williams. *Use Cases Combined with Booch OMT UML.* Upper Saddle River, NJ: Prentice Hall, 1997.

[Wirfs-Brock 1993] R. Wirfs-Brock. Designing Scenarios: Making the Case for a Use Case Framework. *Smalltalk Report,* November–December, 1993.

[Wirfs-Brock 1994] R. Wirfs-Brock. The Art of Designing Meaningful Conversations. *Smalltalk Report,* February, 1994.

[Yourdon and Constantine 1975] E. Yourdon and L. L. Constantine. *Structured Design.* New York: Yourdon Press, 1975.

PART IV

User-Centered Design

CHAPTER 8

A User-Centered Approach to Object-Oriented User Interface Design

Jan Gulliksen
Bengt Göransson
Magnus Lif

Abstract

This chapter emphasizes user-centered design as the essential process for developing usable systems. User-centered design tries to strengthen the creative aspects of user interface design. However, this does not fit very well with the more structured, architecture-centered nature of object-oriented development methodologies. Several problems associated with object-oriented techniques have been observed in development projects in practice. In this chapter, realizing the increasing commercial market share of such software development processes, we set out to strengthen the user-centered design aspects of the Rational Unified Process (RUP) and the Dynamic Systems Development Method (DSDM). We describe the method of User Interface Modeling (UIM), which is based on object-oriented use cases, and establish task requirements that are specific to the user interface design process. We also introduce the role of the usability designer in vouching for the usability throughout the system development process. Finally, we describe our experiences in promoting user-centered design with object-oriented interface design techniques at the Swedish National Tax Board.

8.1 Introduction

8.1.1 Usability and User-Centered Design

The major goal of every professional involved in user interface development is, presumably, to develop systems that are usable. This should be especially important for user interface designers, because their efforts have the most immediate effect on system usability. We use the term *usability* as defined in the ISO 9241 standards *Software ergonomics for office work with visual display terminals, Part 11 Guidance on Usability:*

> Usability is the extent to which a product can be used by specified users to achieve specified goals with effectiveness, efficiency, and satisfaction in a specified context of use. [ISO 1998]

In order to reach these goals, a user-centered design and development process is a necessity, as argued by, for instance, Gould and Lewis [1983, 1985] and Gould et al. [1997]. In these reports, the authors claim that to be able to design usable systems, one needs to (a) have early and continuous focus on the users, (b) do empirical redesign, (c) do iterative design, and (d) do integrated design.

It is also well known that system development projects face a high risk of having their development plans thwarted, or even of being canceled. *The CHAOS Report* [Standish Group 1995] showed that out of 8,380 investigated projects in the United States, only 16.2 percent were completed successfully—that is, on time and on budget, with all features and functions as initially specified. There is no reason whatsoever to believe that this should be different now, five years later, or that the conditions should be different in other areas, such as Europe. For the successfully completed projects, the major success factor was active user involvement in the development process [Standish Group 1995].

This is why we feel that it is important to focus on aiding system development projects to produce better (more usable) results within the time and budget limits. To do this, we propose a user-centered design framework that promotes both active user involvement and greater focus on usability in the development process. Although a user-centered design approach is no guarantee of usable systems, we argue that without a user-centered design approach, genuine usability is usually nothing more than a coincidence.

Today, many companies are becoming aware of the advantages of user-centered design. However, it is extremely rare for a company to adopt a fully integrated user-centered design approach in one strategic shift. Rather, companies tend to adopt practices and methods in stages, or to adopt a particular method or practice only when a complex set of factors become aligned in a way that creates readiness [Dray and Siegel 1998]. There is a big market for companies that sell usability methods, but poor usability of systems and products is still very common, with vendors blaming it on factors outside their immediate influence. This is why we need to implement a user-centered design attitude as a major strategy in system and product development processes. Donald Norman argues for inclusion of usability professionals as peers in development organizations rather than the currently common practice of introducing usability resources only when they are deemed appropriate (and usually very late in the development process) [Norman 1998].

The problems of achieving an effective user-centered development approach are influenced by factors outside the actual system development project. It has been known for several decades that aspects of information technology (IT) cannot be changed without affecting the organization, work activities, and human beings and their skills [Leavitt 1958]. In fact, all of these factors influence one another, and thus a change in any one of them will inevitably result in a need to change one or more others. It is important to be aware of these effects in advance in order to meet them with appropriate actions in development projects. Such effects can include bad organizational structure, unclear work goals, lack of skills among workers performing new tasks, and so on. It is usually during IT development projects that these effects are brought to everyone's attention. These shortcomings are often blamed on the IT project itself. Working simultaneously with all four areas of development (IT, work, organization, and competence) is a formidable task for which few projects can find the required skills, time, and knowledge. We believe that user-centered design, in a context in which management commitment, user commitment and objectives, and goals are clearly specified, can make an important contribution to the success of such an undertaking.

This chapter will pursue a user-centered design approach to object-oriented design and development of usable user interfaces. It will describe various approaches to the design process; various aspects of object orientation, use cases, and scenarios; and how all these factors fit in with a user-centered system development process in a given context. It will then move on to describe the role of the usability designer and the method of User Interface Modeling (UIM) before finally describing the experiences we have had in an attempt to apply user-centered design at the Swedish National Tax Board.

8.1.2 Design Methods and Tools

The implementation of the user interface usually accounts for about 40 to 50 percent of the total amount of code in an interactive application [Nielsen 1993], but the time spent on this part of the code is much less than 40 to 50 percent. This is one of the reasons why we believe that usability and user interface design should receive much greater attention. In practical systems development today, a number of methods exist for systems analysis and evaluation with a human-computer interaction (HCI) focus. There are fewer methods or techniques that focus on the actual design work—that is, on producing the layout, style, and form of the user interface. Design is regarded as a creative process that does not need to be supported by methods and tools. Different approaches to HCI design exist; they all emphasize rather different views on how to analyze, develop, and maintain computer systems. We have found the following way of grouping the various approaches to user interface design appropriate in illuminating both the background sciences that have influenced these approaches and the methodological aids that have been developed [Wallace and Anderson 1993].

The *craft approach* views each design project as unique, in which software evolves under the guidance of a skilled human factors expert. Supporters of this approach tend to believe that a structured approach to interface design is impossible, because the esthetics of interface design cannot be achieved through analytical techniques. It focuses on the designer's need for talent rather than for method. The artistic aspects of user interface design are undoubtedly important, but using this craft view as an argument against methodologies or methodological aids for user interface design is clearly inappropriate.

The *enhanced software engineering approach* attempts to introduce HCI techniques into the repertoire of traditional systems engineering by various methods of task analysis. HCI aspects then become issues for the software engineers. Our experience (based on several observation interviews[1] with software engineers in their own work environments) is that the knowledge demands for efficient use of HCI techniques do not match the skills and knowledge of the software engineers. HCI issues will inevitably receive a lower priority. In order for a software engineer to apply HCI knowledge in the development process, that knowledge needs to be included in the development tool. The role of experience across projects is also central, but software development projects tend to be too time-consuming (it is not unusual for development time to be measured in years), and therefore it is often difficult for individuals to gain experience from a variety of projects.

To achieve "optimal" design, the *cognitive engineering approach* aims at applying theories from cognitive psychology to the problems facing the user interface designer. Cognitive metrics models, such as the keystroke-level model [Card et al. 1983], measure the user's performance and indirectly estimate the memory load for unit tasks to help predict the efficiencies of different design solutions. The grammar models, with formal grammatical notations, describe the mental models and their incorporation into the computer dialogue design. The knowledge methods try to make explicit the mental processes of the user when performing tasks. The user modeling methods describe not only what the user must know to perform a task but also how that knowledge is acquired and manipulated during the execution of a task. The problems of the cognitive engineering approach lie in its failure to be applicable in real-life development projects owing to the highly complex application of cognitive theories.

The *technologist approach* attempts to solve the problems of interface design by providing appropriate tools—especially the User Interface Management System (UIMS), which is both an interface development tool and an interface artifact. The UIMS consists of a special design environment, a linkage module, and a management function. It is useful for

---

[1] An observation interview is a semiformal interview with the purpose of interviewing a user in his own work environment as he performs work. The advantage of this technique is that tacit aspects and procedures that the user might not be aware of can be captured, such as the use of Post-it notes beside the screen display and the use of informal communication with peers.

prototyping and possibly even for interpretation of formal specifications. It is, however, no real design support, because design begins long before the first prototype is constructed; it is merely a tool that allows bad interfaces to be developed more rapidly.

Nevertheless, regardless of the selected approach, the result is far too often a user interface design solution that suffers from severe usability problems. Why?

The actual design of the user interface is, in practice, a phase of development that has a very unstructured nature. It is not uncommon for this phase to get little or no attention in the development work in practice. One of the reasons for this is that it is difficult to separate the creative design work from the programming. User interface design merely occurs as the result of a programming task without any specific individual taking responsibility for it. What we need to do is to visualize interface design as one important phase of the development process.

Should a well-functioning user interface design process follow a structured engineering model that identifies successive methodological steps, or do we intend to promote a shifting attitude in which the user interface evolves through the productive and creative efforts of a team? We want to arrive at a user-centered design and development process that bears similarities with the craft approach that emphasizes the creative abilities of the team. However, today's development teams consist mainly of engineers who, by tradition, require a structured development model. What we want to achieve in this chapter is the promotion of a user-centered design view into an engineering model such as the Rational Unified Process (RUP). This in itself is a very different approach compared with the four approaches listed above.

8.1.3 Learning Object-Oriented Design

Object-oriented techniques have become a fashion in development approaches and supply us with methods for analysis and design [Booch 1991, Rumbaugh et al. 1991]. Unfortunately, these techniques do not give enough support to the user interface design process. Object-oriented user interface design can be very appropriate for producing user interfaces for specific work activities, because objects in the user interface can correspond to objects in the real work environment, and have clear meanings for the users. However, our observation is that organizations that are adopting object-oriented techniques do not fully use them, or they produce design solutions that are not of an object-oriented nature, which then can be reflected in information systems with a low degree of usability. There is no support for object-oriented user interface design, which is treated in the same manner as object-oriented design in general. Usability requirements are not considered in object-oriented design.

The object-oriented way of thinking is not easy to acquire. It takes years for developers to switch from thinking in functional ways to thinking about objects, attributes, and methods

[Nielsen 1995]. Teaching developers to perform iterative design is equally difficult. The major obstacle to this process is time. To produce deliverable results, all people involved in the process tend to require more time than is allocated for analysis and design. Shortening the iterative life cycle could prevent delays in this process. RUP recommends less than six months as a turnaround time for the iterative development process [Kruchten 1998]. The Swedish National Tax Board (see Section 8.4) has decided on eight weeks for the iterative cycle. We believe that the development process can be significantly improved by employing a shorter iterative cycle in which more usable products can be manufactured. It could be reasonable to have a five-day iterative cycle—two days for analysis, two days for design, and one day for evaluation. If more time than this is allowed for the subprocesses, there is a great risk of what we call the "my baby syndrome,"[2] which involves excessively stubborn defense of a proposed solution. Therefore, we believe that the greatest challenge facing usability specialists is to teach and promote effective iterative user interface design (see Figure 8.1).

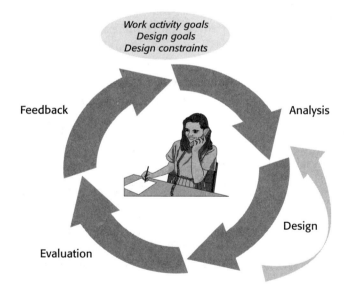

FIGURE 8.1 Teaching, or learning to adopt, a fully iterative user interface design and development activity has proven to be difficult. The darker arrows are the development phases. The lighter arrow indicates the small, informal design activities that are so important in the design phase.

---

[2] The "my baby syndrome" describes the situation in which a parent cannot see the faults and irregularities in his or her own baby. This phenomenon can be observed in the systems development process when project members spend a great deal of time and effort on a particular problem and tend to ignore critiques and comments from others.

8.1.4 Prototyping and Iterative Design

Prototyping can be used as an effective technique for determining whether or not a proposed solution is adequate, but this is only part of what prototyping is about. As a start, we can distinguish among the following different types of prototypes and their respective purposes [Preece et al. 1994]:

- *Requirements animation* demonstrates possible requirements to be assessed by users.
- *Rapid prototyping* collects requirements and the adequacy of possible solutions, "throw-it-away."
- *Evolutionary prototyping* strikes a compromise between production and prototyping, thus allowing the system to "grow" and change wherever necessary.
- *Incremental prototyping* builds the system incrementally, one section at a time.

It is important to define why a prototype is developed and to what purpose. In the computer software industry, we use the word "prototype" in a very broad and vague sense, whereas other disciplines, such as industrial design, have a very distinct interpretation of a prototype as the first fully functional version of a product. When we talk about prototyping, we actually mean anything from a rough paper mock-up to a fully functional product.

8.2 System Development Processes

In our experience, the system development process is central to the success of the final product. Various methods or techniques can always be applied to improve the final result of the product, but it is only when we view the entire process that we can predict where and when problems may occur. Today, when organizations decide to improve their system development processes, they often adopt a commercial system development process, such as RUP or DSDM, in the belief that every problem will be solved by the selected process. Unfortunately, not everything is specified in these processes, and these organizations do not see the need to specify complementary steps (it is a common strategy to ignore any issues that cannot be solved with the chosen method). They tend to avoid activities that are not explicitly specified in the new process, even if performing these steps was an established routine in their previous strategies. This is why we think that successful adoption of user-centered design with any of these commercial system development processes requires that the system development process be modified to meet the needs of the organization or even of individual projects. The organization needs to specify its own user-centered development process, based on the commercial processes, and it must specify which complementary activities are needed. In doing this, it can be advantageous to reuse the old methods or techniques previously established within the organization. A basis for the specification of an organizational system development process could be the ISO 13407 human-centered design processes for interactive systems.

8.2.1 ISO 13407: Human-Centered Design Processes for Interactive Systems

A successful user-centered development process should be based on a fairly well-defined and controlled iterative system development model. This is one of the key principles behind fully integrating a user-centered approach into an existing development framework. One aid in doing user-centered design is to use the international standard ISO 13407, *Human-Centered Design Processes for Interactive Systems* [ISO 1999]. ISO 13407 is an approach to human-centered software and hardware development that identifies four basic principles:

- Appropriate allocation of functions between users and system
- Active involvement of users
- Iterations of design solutions
- Interdisciplinary design groups

Human-centered design according to ISO 13407 involves (a) identifying the need for a human-centered design process, (b) understanding and specifying the context of use, (c) specifying organizational and user requirements, (d) producing design prototypes, and (e) evaluating the design prototypes according to the user and organizational requirements to determine how to further pursue the development (see Figure 8.2).

ISO 13407 states that the user-centered activities can be applied to any existing model, but we think that it is mandatory for this model to have a mature iterative process.

The traditional waterfall development model, or life cycle plan (for example, see [Boehm 1976]), describes the process of developing software as pure engineering work. This model was developed as an ideal strategy for project management, and the focus was on managing the different development phases one at a time in a logical sequence. This approach might have its advantages if we were limited to solving rather technical and well-defined engineering problems, but it doesn't take into account such things as the impossibility of a complete and permanently correct description of the system, formal and nonexecutable specifications that are largely unintelligible to users and developers, the need for user participation, and so on [Budde et al. 1992]. These are all aspects that are addressed in the ISO 13407 process, and the basic software development approach that will ensure this is to make the process iterative. This iterative process must still be predictable in the sense that we need controlled iterations to "ensure that we are not wandering aimlessly from iteration to iteration but are actually converging toward a product" [Kruchten 1998].

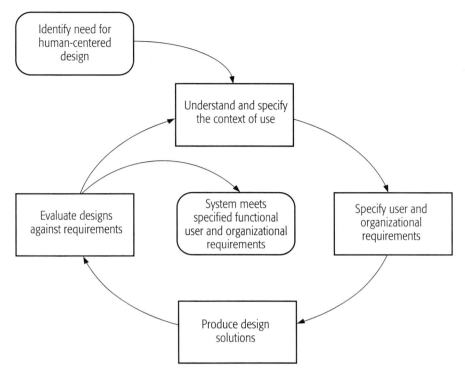

FIGURE 8.2 The principle behind a human-centered design process for interactive systems according to ISO 13407

8.2.2 The Rational Unified Process

The Rational Unified Process (RUP) [Kruchten 1998] and the Dynamic Systems Development Method (DSDM) [Stapleton 1997] represent two controlled iterative development processes. They have both emerged from what their inventors call "best practices." RUP grounds its iterative approach in the classic spiral model [Boehm 1988]. This model focuses on avoiding risks in the project by exploring the risks at an early stage.

RUP is an established commercial system development model. It is based on an object-oriented engineering view with a strong emphasis on system architecture as an "architecture-centric process" [Kruchten 1998]. RUP is based on what are known as "best practices." These are good habits that the developers/authors of RUP have acquired during decades of experience with object-oriented system development [Kruchten 1998]:

1. Develop software iteratively.
2. Manage requirements.

3. Use component-based architectures.
4. Visually model software.
5. Verify software quality.
6. Control changes in software.

RUP is divided into phases with workflows/activities and iterations (see Figure 8.3).

There are four phases in the development process: inception, elaboration, construction, and transition. These phases are oriented in time, and each of them contains iterations. The work within each phase is performed in workflows and subdivided into activities. The relative emphases on these different activities vary as time passes. For example, from Figure 8.3 we can tell that business modeling occurs mainly during the inception and elaboration phases.

8.2.2.1 RUP and Prototyping

It is interesting to study what the different development methods have to say about prototyping. Among other things, it will give us insight in what the different models emphasize. RUP defines four different types of prototypes:

- *Behavioral prototypes* are used to evaluate the behavior of a system from a user's perspective.

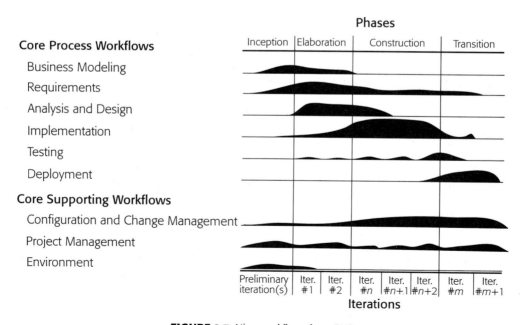

FIGURE 8.3 Nine workflows from RUP

- *Structural prototypes* are used to explore a system architecture or technique.
- *Exploratory prototypes* are used for experimentation and then are thrown away.
- *Evolutionary prototypes* are used to introduce stepwise development into the actual product.

From the perspective of RUP, the most important prototype is the structural prototype, which evaluates the system architecture. The purpose of this prototype is to verify that the proposed solution can be realized. Prototyping of the user interface is regarded as merely one activity in the requirements workflow, with the purpose of finding the requirements.

It is emphasized that the development of the system or product is supposed to be based on evolutionary prototyping. The other prototypes are used during shorter periods of development.

8.2.2.2 Studies of the Use of RUP in Practice

We have studied the use of RUP for user interface design in the context of user-centered design in several large in-house development organizations through observation interviews conducted with stakeholders at these organizations. Our findings have also been supported by experience reported by several consulting companies that were promoting user interface design with RUP. The in-house development organizations decided to purchase RUP—not for user-centered design reasons, but for other reasons, such as the following:

- Because of widespread use of Rational Unified Process, it has become a de facto standard.
- RUP makes it easier to hire external consultants.
- RUP is supported technically.
- RUP is based on object-oriented techniques, which are desirable for several reasons.
- Tool support and education are available.

We have seen organizations that have had problems discovering any explicit methodological support for performing user-centered design with RUP. RUP 2000 contains a concept paper that explains the foundations of user-centered design. This concept paper presents a good introduction to user-centered design, but its results are not fully integrated with RUP, which might explain why it does not give any real support in the actual performance of the user-centered design activities that use RUP. What evolves during development are the system architecture and the different classes and objects that form the basis for the object-oriented view. Usability, user interfaces, and users' ability to influence the system functionality and design are treated in the early phases of development.

From the user-centered perspective, we see a need to keep a continuous focus on users and users' tasks and to emphasize user participation in RUP.

Our experience, based on observations of several projects applying RUP in the user interface design process, is that successful adoption of user-centered design with RUP is the result of the participation of a person with high skills and experience in human-computer interaction. All projects with less-experienced staff using RUP in the user interface design process resulted in user interfaces with severe usability problems that could be related to the lack of support from the process itself.

RUP has its strengths in the controlled and iterative work processes. However, based on our studies of several organizations using RUP, we see several weaknesses in terms of how the usability aspects are taken care of and to what extent user-centered design can be performed. Examples of these weaknesses are as follows:

- The person responsible for applying RUP to user interface design thought that the model contained answers to all problems and stopped acting as a thinking person.
- In a user-centered design fashion, we want a development process that is focused more on usability. Usability must be regarded as a measurable entity containing both functional and nonfunctional demands and therefore must be supported in the entire development process and not only in relation to user interface design. There is little or no support for continuous, in-depth focus on usability beyond capturing requirements in RUP.
- User participation is vaguely expressed in terms of end users and domain experts. We know that users who are heavily involved in a project soon become biased in favor of the project; this is a danger for RUP's user participation.
- The only project role that has any relation to usability is called the user interface designer. This role has the responsibility of visually shaping the user interface (see Chapter 5) but does not necessarily provide any competence in usability.
- There is little support for the analysis of the user tasks or for the groups of users in the sense of context of use analysis. Context of use is fundamental in ISO 13407, because it gives invaluable information about users, tasks, equipment, and the users' physical and social environment [ISO 1999].
- There is an obvious risk that the users are introduced only at the beginning of the project and will be forgotten as the focus turns more and more to the system architecture.

8.2.3 The Dynamic Systems Development Method

The Dynamic Systems Development Method (DSDM) is a model (even though its name suggests that it is a method) that has been primarily developed in the United Kingdom by a consortium of several companies and individuals. There is an obvious trend among organizations and companies to show an interest in, and to use, DSDM. This is why it is interesting to examine DSDM together with RUP in terms of user centeredness. DSDM is also discussed in Chapters 1 and 10.

DSDM has nine principles that constitute the basis for the model:

1. Active user involvement is imperative.
2. DSDM teams must be empowered to make decisions.
3. The focus is on frequent delivery of products.
4. Fitness for business purpose is the essential criterion for acceptance of deliverables.
5. Iterative and incremental development is necessary to converge on an accurate business solution.
6. All changes during development are reversible.
7. Requirements are baselined (or frozen) at a high level.
8. Testing is integrated throughout the life cycle.
9. A collaborative and cooperative approach involving all stakeholders is essential.

The five phases of the model (see Figure 8.4) are as follows:

1. Feasibility study
2. Business study
3. Functional model iteration
4. Design and build iteration
5. Implementation

DSDM is to a great extent based on user participation. The users have also been categorized on the basis of the roles they have in the project. This shows insight regarding the ways that different user categories can contribute to the development work.

8.2.3.1 DSDM and Prototyping

DSDM argues for the following prototypes [Stapleton 1997]:

- *Business prototypes* test the functionality.
- *Usability prototypes* explore the user interface without influencing the functionality.
- *Performance and capacity prototypes* ensure the system's ability to handle different types of loads and so on.
- *Capability/design prototypes* test design solutions.

296 | **CHAPTER 8** A User-Centered Approach to Object-Oriented User Interface Design

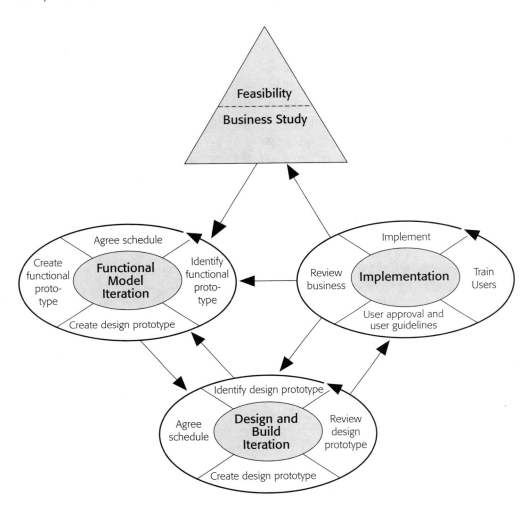

FIGURE 8.4 Phases and main processes in DSDM [Stapleton 1997]

The development of the system can be seen as incremental prototyping. Prototypes are important building blocks in the development work. The tight focus on the development time, the so-called "time boxing," is also important. The system can be divided into different deliverables, which often forces the development project to attempt to retain the development times rather than controlling them with the functionality. The effect of this is that, when the development team runs out of time, they often will start to "cut out" functionality instead of expanding the time box. DSDM is not at all as detailed and developed as RUP. Whereas RUP is based on the Unified Modeling Language (UML) and on development tools (such as Rational Rose), DSDM is a rapid application development framework which accommodates different development methods. There are, however, several activities within the consortium developing tools to support the process.

8.2.3.2 DSDM and User Participation

DSDM is based on user participation, and three user roles have been defined: ambassador user, visionary user, and advisor user. Each role has its own set of responsibilities and requires certain skills. The ambassador user can be considered to be the domain expert. The responsibility of this role is to represent the entire user community and supply the project with knowledge from the targeted business area. The visionary user is defined as having a high-level view of the overall goal and vision of the project. The advisor users are selected from the so-called end users. They are typically brought into the project whenever specific questions arise or when testing a prototype. Defining these different user roles is in itself a good idea, but merely using these roles does not constitute a representative sample of users. A representative sample is mandatory in order to cover all targeted user groups, including the users' backgrounds, experience, and knowledge. The DSDM user roles are defined with the purpose of creating effective work, especially through workshops.

Large parts of the development work in a DSDM project are based on so-called Joint Application Development (JAD) workshops [Stapleton 1997, p. 52]. These workshops are central to DSDM and can be seen as the most important methodological step in the DSDM process. According to DSDM, JAD workshops can be applied in almost any problem area. A workshop is considered an efficient tool for quickly arriving at results and decisions. However, there is an obvious risk that JAD workshops may be the only methods used. There is definitely a need for more analytical and structured methods, especially when it comes to analyzing users and tasks and specifying usability goals. Our observation is that it is very common that user representatives who have participated in the workshops no longer have strong connections with the work activity. You also miss a very important source of information gathering and analysis if you choose to bring in some defined user representatives and work with them exclusively without going out into the field and studying users firsthand.

When analyzing DSDM, we can see some shortcomings in the theoretical background and the practical application of the method. DSDM is based on experiences from several projects and companies, but it has no "modern" basis in usability or user-centered design. The full breadth of usability and user-centered design has not been fully realized or understood. The focus is much more on "time boxing" and JAD workshops and less on several of the important aspects of usability, such as the need to measure usability, the need to gather and visualize the requirements of all user groups, and the need for fully integrated design. We can also raise several doubts in relation to the user roles that have been specified—or perhaps, rather, in relation to the roles that are not there. We see a risk that the roles specified in the projects are expected to deliver all the answers to questions on the users' requirements, independent of the characteristics of the users in the target work domain.

Both RUP and DSDM have shortcomings in relation to the general notion of usability and user-centered design (as described in [ISO 1998] and [ISO 1999]). Nevertheless, we see the possibility that RUP and DSDM could be strengthened by adding activities (processes and methods) as well as roles within the models that could encourage the development of a usable product.

8.3 Design in Context

The user involvement and participation is often defined as bringing users, or user representatives, into the project. This is important, but it is equally important to make an effort to bring the developers closer to the users' working environments or situations. It is critical that the developers responsible for the design of the user interface actually spend time at the users' workplaces to discover the nature of the users' work environments and work activities, and especially the work activities and procedures that the users perform without being aware of them. This is true not only for the analysis phases of a project but also for the design and evaluation phases. The context of the users and their work situations is irreplaceable and must be experienced on-site. We recommend setting up a project with a "door-to-door" communication between the users and the developers. This means that parts of the developer organization, to some extent, "move in" to the users' workplaces and, whenever possible, run their portions of the development project in that context.

8.3.1 The Usability Designer

Usability is far too complicated to be left without giving anybody specific responsibility for it. It needs a specific caretaker in every systems development project. We have therefore found it necessary to define a specific role for usability—that is, the "usability designer." The usability designer is responsible for keeping the development process user-centered by focusing on usability aspects. It is crucial for the usability designer to take an active part in the design and development process and thus avoid becoming just another project manager. We emphasize the importance of one role player participating in all the user-centered activities in order to avoid losing valuable information in the transitions between the activities. The usability designer works closely with the user organization and participates in different analyses related to usability. The usability designer then transfers the results of these analyses into the design activities. The continuation is maintained as the usability designer participates in designing the prototypes. When the designer takes part in the succeeding evaluation activities, the iterative design cycle is closed. This role may specify usability goals and design criteria; conduct user and task analyses; elicit the user needs and requirements; design the user interface; or, in a large project, lead the design team and participate in the evaluation (see Figure 8.5).

A specific role for usability has the advantage of making sure that usability is explicitly brought to the agenda in the development work. The usability designer needs to be a human-computer interaction specialist capable of understanding system development techniques and tools. Interdisciplinary characteristics are absolutely necessary for this role. If feasible, the usability designer should work in conjunction with a graphical designer or other user interface designers who are skilled in visual and interaction design. Depending on the requirements for the visualization and the size of the project, the usability designer and the graphical designers will merge their activities. If the project is rather large, the usability designer will most likely focus more on the usability of the system, and the other designers will focus more on how to make the user interface attractive to the users.

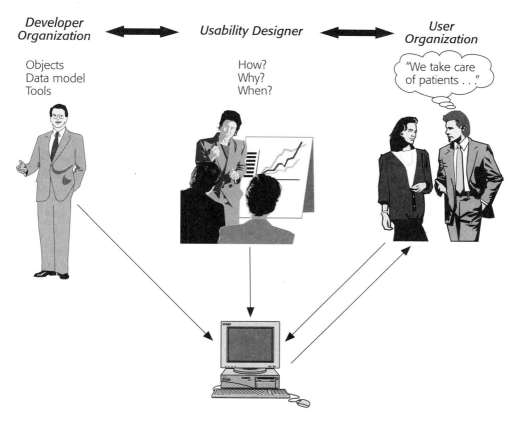

FIGURE 8.5 The usability designer as a new work role that manages and facilitates the user-centered design process

In summary:

- The usability designer is responsible for keeping the development process user-centered and focused on usability aspects. Planning and performing activities related to usability and making sure that the results of usability activities are further used in the development process are very important for the usability designer.
- It is crucial for the usability designer to take an active part in the design and development process and not to become just another project manager.
- We emphasize the importance of a person participating in all the user-centered activities to prevent valuable information from being lost in the transitions between the activities.

The role of the usability designer can to some extent be seen as a "discount" usability role, because it combines several skills in one role and manages the usability process in an efficient manner.

8.3.1.1 The Usability Designer in RUP

RUP defines different project roles called workers or "hats." We see a need to introduce the usability designer into RUP with the specific purpose of vouching for the usability of the resulting system. This role should support the roles of the use case specifier and the user interface designer in some of their tasks, but above all works as a usability authority throughout the development process. By moving some of the development tasks from the user interface designer to the usability designer, the remaining tasks for the user interface designer are best supported if they can be performed by a graphical designer. To be able to fulfill the goal of designing usable systems, the usability designer needs to take part in the specification of all aspects that contribute to the design from the very outset of the project when the business requirements are defined. This includes having an active role in the specification of the different artifacts that are produced in the early phases, such as the vision or use case model.

The usability designer does not necessarily have to produce any new artifacts. The major contribution is as a communication link between developers and users in the development process. This includes the responsibility for improving the use case storyboards and the user interface prototypes (see Chapter 5).

8.3.1.2 The Usability Designer in DSDM

DSDM is based on the best practices from several of the participating organizations in the DSDM consortium, and although it has realized the importance of the users in the process, DSDM has failed to realize the need to consider the entire mass of knowledge contained in the field of human-computer interaction.[3] The usability designer might be able to complement the development work in the sense of including human-computer interaction knowledge. Focusing on usability throughout the process is as essential for DSDM as it is for RUP.

8.3.2 User Interface Modeling

One of the goals of this book is to bridge the gap between object-oriented designers and user interface designers. However, the gap between object-oriented designers and users is bigger still. Use cases, scenarios, and user-centered system development models that focus on the definitions of object models that are close to the users' domain are very useful in the design of more usable systems. Every application domain has, however, its specific characteristics. This is why these methods and the user-centered development framework need to be adapted to the domain in question. In the following section, we will describe the method of User Interface Modeling that was originally developed in cooperation with the Swedish National Tax Board. This method has been further generalized during its application to other cases in other organizations. Then we will describe our experiences in the case of the Swedish National Tax Board as a way of showing how a user-centered design framework can be adapted to suit a specific organization.

Traditional systems development projects usually perform some kind of structured analysis and design in which the users' work is described with dataflow diagrams that show how data is processed within an organization and with data models that show objects and their relations [DeMarco 1978]. Such methods do not provide suitable support for developing the user interface, as observed by Floyd [1986]. Today it is becoming more common to use object-oriented modeling techniques such as RUP where the design of the system is driven by use cases: "A use case is a complete course of events in the system, seen from the user's perspective" [Jacobson et al. 1995, p. 157]. Use cases establish the requirements of the functionality of the system. Each use case is a description of how actors (groups of users, for example) interact with the application. It is a sequence of related transactions performed by an actor in dialogue with the system. The sum of all use cases defines the functionality of the entire system. RUP states that the inception phase produces an initial use case model covering about 10 to 20 percent of the expected total volume. We believe that user participation is critical in the inception phase.

In Chapter 7, Constantine and Lockwood claim that the concept of use case is not defined clearly enough. Because of this, there are huge variations in style for writing the narratives that describe use cases. They also emphasize that use cases can cause problems

---

[3] This is a conclusion based on a discussion with Jennifer Stapleton, the author of DSDM.

in user interface design if they are describing the interaction between the user and a particular interface. Instead, essential use cases are introduced when the focus is on the intention of the user rather than on the interaction, making essential use cases interface-independent. However, use cases as the only means of communication can be insufficient. Specifying the use cases together with users in workshops can be very useful, but there is a risk that these workshops will become too formal and less comprehensible for the users. Even though the use cases are expressed in natural language, they very soon become too complex to give the users a truly clear picture of what they can expect from the forthcoming system. We believe that it is absolutely necessary to complement the use cases with some sort of user interface prototype to illustrate how the system can support the users in their work.

Nonetheless, use cases are undoubtedly useful for communicating both internally and with clients and users about requirements. However, an object-oriented method employing use case modeling does not guarantee a usable information system. Such methods are suitable for developing software components of the information system, but they do not provide sufficient support for the design of the user interface. Instead, these methods invite the designer to create an interface in which each function or use case is represented by one window in the screen. Typically, the user has to interact with several such windows to complete a work task, which results in a fragmented interface with a large number of windows. This may affect the efficiency in performing the task and may also cause a potential increase in the mental workload [Lif et al. 2000]. During our research at the Swedish National Tax Board and in other projects, we have seen several examples of this. One could argue that this would not be a problem if the use cases were large enough to cover users' work tasks. However, according to our observations, many software engineers prefer smaller use cases because they are easier to handle when designing the software components.

User Interface Modeling (UIM) is basically a method for gathering user requirements that are directly applicable to user interface design for an information system [Lif 1999]. UIM is intended to be used as a complement to use case modeling in the system development process [Jacobson et al. 1995].

UIM specifies an *actor model*, a *goal model*, and a *work model* in sessions in which end users cooperate with software engineers and user interface designers. The actor model is a description of characteristics for each category of users that are important for the user interface design process. The goal model is a list of high-level goals that users want to achieve in order for the system to be usable. The work model is a specification of work situations, information objects and actions, and properties of attributes and operations that are suitable for the design. Each actor may handle one or more work situations (see Figure 8.6). There is a one-to-one mapping between a work situation and a workspace in the user interface [Lif et al. 2000]. In a typical workspace, the actor has access to

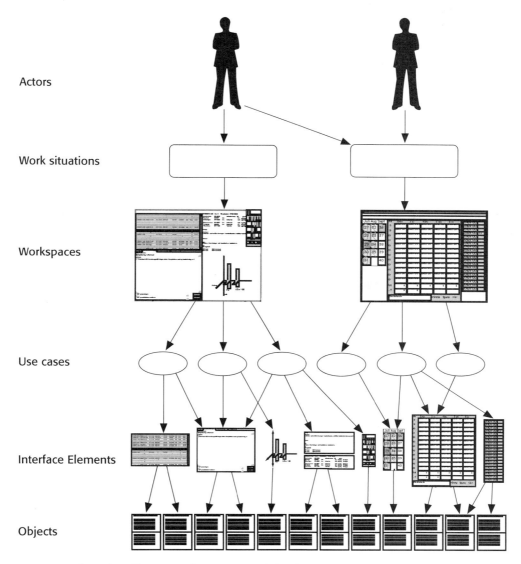

FIGURE 8.6 Illustration of how UIM relates actors, work situations, workspaces, use cases, interface elements, and objects that are useful for the process of user interface design

all information and all tools needed in one work situation—that is, when communicating with a set of related use cases. The same use case can sometimes be accessed from more than one workspace. In a banking application, for example, it should be possible to search for a customer's bank account from any workspace. On the screen, tools and information are parts of different interface elements.

UIM does not describe a step-by-step procedure for creating usable interfaces. Interface design is partially a creative process that cannot be completely described with a method. However, the design process can be facilitated if the design decisions are based on a substantial model that defines the user requirements for the interface. This model is created during UIM sessions.

8.4 Experiences in Promoting User-Centered Design at the Swedish National Tax Board

To be able to incorporate work, process, and task analysis into industrial object-oriented system design in practice, it is important to focus on all the factors that influence the development work. Such factors include the simultaneous development of information technology, users and their skills and experiences, the organization of the work, the work activity, and the physical work environment.

During the last five years, we have been performing action research in cooperation with the Swedish National Tax Board, which is an organization with about 15,000 end users and almost 400 different applications that run simultaneously. The organization used a variety of the commercially available techniques, such as mainframe systems, GUIs, and network-based applications. The development context is mainly in-house, but the organization has relatively ambitious development plans and a high degree of usability maturity.

Initially, our role was to serve as user interface consultants helping to improve the usability of systems that were undergoing revision. As time passed, however, our role became more strategic; we began adapting methods, introducing specific user interface design aids, and focusing on user-centered design in an object-oriented design environment. The specific tasks that we performed were as follows:

1. We established a methodological framework for the incorporation of domain knowledge into a user-centered development process.
2. We extended object-oriented use case modeling techniques with aspects relevant for user interface design.
3. We supported the user interface design process with domain knowledge by introducing a corporate style guide.
4. We enhanced the possibilities for designing systems that efficiently support the users' work through the workspace metaphor.

Currently, the focus of our research cooperation is improvement of the possibilities for efficient user participation in the development process.

8.4.1 Methods of Enhancing the User Interface Design Process

Six ways of enhancing the user interface design process are discussed here. All of these have been used (sometimes in a further elaborated form) at the Swedish National Tax Board discussed in Section 8.4.2.

One of the consequences of object-oriented design is the decline of the concept of applications in favor of reusable business objects with a mapping to the computerized information objects. As a prerequisite for achieving consistent and reusable system modules, we developed business processes of a general corporate nature and introduced them into the organization [Gulliksen 1996]. These business processes contained process descriptions, conceptual models, data models, and so on, for the work activity in general. The purpose was to establish a basis for the development of general modules for specific tasks such as data-entry handling, data transmission, case handling, evaluation, work distribution, and administration. Such a case-handling framework is, according to our view, a prerequisite for the design of general business objects. It is therefore an appropriate division of the work procedures to be able to divide the work activities into objects. The organization has recognized the need for such a case-handling framework without being fully aware of it as a necessity for user interface design. The organization has had difficulty in formally making the necessary decisions about such a framework, but it has more or less adopted such an object-oriented view of the business objects anyway.

Analysis of Information Utilization (AIU) [Gulliksen et al. 1997] and User Interface Modeling (UIM) [Lif 1999] address the problem of how to extract requirements on an appropriate level for the *design* of the user interface. AIU differs from traditional task analysis methods in that it reveals aspects of the use situation that the user might not be explicitly aware of. It covers not only the information entities that are used in each situation but also the way in which each information object is treated and manipulated. The observation is that users tend to be unaware of several of the operations they perform during their work as it becomes automated. AIU uses observation interviews to capture these aspects as they are performed. UIM focuses more on aspects relating to the user interface, and the extension of use case modeling [Jacobson et al. 1995], which focuses more on aspects relating to the user interface. UIM is a further elaboration of AIU that is specifically constructed to fit into an object-oriented development methodology, which is to be used in the types of modeling sessions that are typical of the development tradition of the Swedish National Tax Board.

The workspace metaphor [Lif et al. 2000] describes a new way of structuring the user interface in a work-oriented fashion. Instead of working with applications, the user has a number of workspaces that are carefully designed and customized computer screens to support the user in the performance of the different work situations. These workspaces become interface objects on a top level containing all the information objects needed in a specific work task.

A corporate style guide [Gulliksen and Sandblad 1995, Olsson and Gulliksen 1999] has proved to be an essential support in the design process, both as a documentation of domain-specific design guidelines and as a container for reusable interface objects. The style guide has been implemented as an interactive online document with the possibility of having electronic communication between the style guide users (that is, user representatives, system engineers, and system modeling experts) and the design experts in the organization.

Domain-specific evaluation [Lif and Sandblad 1996] is a method of evaluating the usability of interactive systems. This method consists of two parts: an expert evaluation and a cooperative evaluation. A user interface designer using a set of general heuristics performs the expert evaluation. The cooperative evaluation is done together with users performing a set of predefined scenarios. In the cooperative evaluation, the process is guided by a list of heuristics related to the users' domain.

All of these methods were developed before RUP and DSDM were available. However, these methods, in one form or another, could be used to enhance the system development process and to take usability and user-centered design into consideration when using RUP or DSDM.

8.4.2 Introducing User-Centered Design

A user-oriented perspective on development is undoubtedly important. Current research is forming a user-oriented view on the establishment of visions of the development of information technology, users and their competence, the organization, work activities, and the physical work environment. In the case of the Swedish National Tax Board, we pursued the notion that domain adaptation of the development models is very important to make them fit into the existing standard procedures within the organization.

To be able to justify efficiently a user-centered development process within the development organization, we decided to model the process using the current techniques that were well known to the participants at the organization. In short, these techniques meant modeling the current development processes and, based on these processes, establishing the future processes. This was performed in close cooperation with the user representatives that by Scandinavian tradition have a very important role in all development work. The participants in these modeling sessions included two representatives of skilled domain experts (professional user representatives), one skilled development project manager from the organization, one senior modeling leader from the organization, one usability analyst from the organization, and two usability designers who were also academic researchers.

8.4 Experiences in Promoting User-Centered Design at the Swedish National Tax Board

The work was performed in eight full-day meetings with a considerable amount of report and documentation work performed in relation to and after these modeling sessions. The development methods used were the organization's own methods that were adapted to the specific conditions of work. This work was complemented with observation interviews of the user interface developers within the organization.

The current status of the development process proved to be a very waterfall-like development method with clearly defined steps specifying the object model (data model) and business processes and subsequently engineering the user interface (rather than designing it). The future model (see Figure 8.7) describes only the user interface design process, although we observed the need to focus more on the steps taking place before this process, such as the development of the new work situations and the new business processes.

Listed below are some of the important requirements for an efficient and effective user centered design and development process at the Swedish National Tax Board.

- *Contextual aspects*. Emphasize the need to visit the workers in their own work environment rather than always bringing the users to the development organization.

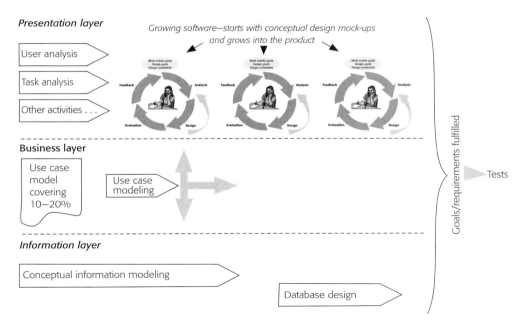

FIGURE 8.7 Results of the modeling of the user-centered design processes for user interface design as they turned out in our case at the Swedish National Tax Board

- *Prototypes.* Use prototyping to design and develop new interfaces.
- *Iterative cycle.* Reduce the duration of an iterative cycle to prevent the "my baby syndrome" and to minimize the risk of delays in the development project.
- *Prevent waterfalls.* Emphasize the need to teach the organization not to finalize every step before initializing the next step.
- *Integrated development.* Simultaneously develop the business layer, the information layer, and the presentation layer in the three-level client-server structure of the system.

Although there is much more to be achieved, at this stage the important result is to make the organization aware of the need to develop the procedures to make them more user-centered. When introducing object-oriented development tools and procedures, this is a good way of teaching the staff how to adapt these new tools to the specific characteristics of their organization.

8.4.3 Obstacles to the Development Work

One of the advantages of object-oriented design is the modularity that promotes reusability of screen objects. It is therefore necessary for interface objects to be directly mapped to information objects in the work tasks and to software objects in the computer system. This has several effects on the development work: the concept of applications becomes irrelevant and is replaced by objects that can be more easily developed and maintained, and the structure of development projects changes. This is why the introduction of an object-oriented view on information systems requires an object-oriented view on the work activity models and on the organizational structure.

Several lessons can be learned from the case of the Swedish National Tax Board. As an example of general work models that can be effectively used in the user interface design process, case-handling models were shown to be a necessary basis for deriving general, reusable work activity objects. UIM and AIU help to provide the basis for designing these objects. With a corporate style guide that has a library of reusable interface objects attached, the necessary support for a more efficient design process is available. In our case, the workspace metaphor became a substantial part of the corporate style guide.

However, incorporating user-centered design methods in an organization is not always a simple task. One of the main obstacles to doing this at the Swedish National Tax Board was a lack of support within the organization for working with user-centered design. Even though there is a supportive attitude higher up in the organization, it is not always evident among the people who are responsible for the user interface design process. This is illustrated by the following results that we received from an analysis of user interface design work within the organization.

- User interface programming is considered to be a problem-solving task. The developers want to have a programming task that can be solved within a couple of days and as a result deliver a piece of code that in some sense is the optimal solution to the task. However, developers seldom have the requisite ability, skill, or even interest to perform specific interface design prior to programming.
- For the programmers, design is not a conscious, esthetic activity for which they are responsible, but rather is the result of an engineering task. By writing the program code that was specified in the preceding item, they can solve their problem. The fact that the specific program code that they produce corresponds to a specific design of a user interface is not the result of a conscious activity; it just occurs. Programmers typically have a fear of doing user interface design.
- Interface prototyping could be performed very early in the development process, but this is very seldom done. Very often, a waterfall development model is used, which means that one activity must be finished before the next one can be pursued. This is a big mistake. A lot of work could be done using only 80 percent of the results of the previous activities. In order to be able to do truly iterative design, one must be prepared for frequent production of "deliverables" that are appropriate for user evaluation, according to some plan.
- A lack of development competence and/or experience is one of the biggest threats to the usability efforts in the process of designing user interfaces. One reason for this is that, as a low-wage government organization, the Swedish National Tax Board does not pay its employees competitive wages and therefore the hired developers may not always have the best available competency. First, the development organization relies heavily on the use of external consultants for most of the advanced development work. Second, external consultants have no incentive to support usability-related work, because this might lead to increased development times. Moreover, when the advanced development work is done solely by external consultants, there is no enhancement of the competence of the development organization.
- While frequent reorganizations aggravate attempts to achieve well-functioning procedures, performing a reorganization is a good way for a manager to prove results in an organization that has not yet achieved according to plans. Unfortunately, performing a reorganization does not always fulfill the goals that were anticipated.

The major problems that need to be solved at the Swedish National Tax Board include (a) the lack of organizational support for usability-related work and development tool dependencies and (b) the difficulty of maintaining work of a more general character in a constantly changing work environment.

8.5 Discussion

This chapter has focused on the need to create systems that have a high degree of usability. Object orientation is in itself no guarantee that usable systems will be designed. In fact, the tendency to design systems with severe usability defects is just as great when object-oriented techniques are used as when other techniques are employed. Even though the RUP and DSDM frameworks have managed to solve some of the difficulties of promoting iterative design in practice, there still is a need to complement these frameworks with specific methods and roles for the user-centered design process. As do many system development frameworks, the RUP framework ignores some of the most difficult problems inherent in the process of conducting a user-centered design project. Two such problems are as follows.

- *Communication with users.* Today, UML is the main communication language and is often complemented with use case storyboards. This is perhaps good for communication between system developers, but other representations are needed for communication with users. Educating users in the formal notation of UML and in use case modeling is a convenient and widely used solution, but this is not the right way to solve the problem.
- *Specific focus on usability.* Promoting user participation throughout the entire system development process and giving users the power to understand and influence the development of their working tools early in the development process will make the process more efficient and could improve the end result.

Thus, there definitely is a need for a framework for incorporating work, process, and task analysis into object-oriented design in real-life development settings [van Harmelen et al. 1997]. However, for such a framework to be effective in practice, it needs to put a certain emphasis on aspects that are relevant to the creative user interface design process. At the same time, users need to be efficiently introduced as active participants in the development work. Because the world of users is a world of objects, the mapping of such objects in the user interface should become fairly simple, and users should have greater opportunities to contribute while acting in a terminology that is familiar to them.

It is important to maintain a critical eye when deploying a commercial development process, particularly with respect to usability and user-centered concerns. However, in our experience, organizations do not critically evaluate such processes and do not perform the necessary process modifications to address their specific concerns. More generally we note that usability and user-centered design can of course be added when the commercial system development package is being customized, but we see no reason why these issues cannot be properly introduced into the general development models. Later, during projects, important aspects that are not properly introduced into a development model face a high risk of being ignored.

8.6 References

[Artim et al. 1998] J. M. Artim, M. van Harmelen, K. Butler, J. Gulliksen, A. Henderson, S. Kovacevic, S. Lu, S. Overmeyer, R. Reaux, D. Roberts, J.-C. Tarby, and K. Vander Linden. Incorporating Work, Process and Task Analysis into Commercial and Industrial Object-Oriented Systems Development. *SIGCHI Bulletin,* 30 (4), 1998, 100–101.

[Boehm 1976] B. Boehm. Software Engineering. *IEEE Transactions on Computers,* C25(12), 1976, 1226–1241.

[Boehm 1988] B. Boehm. The Spiral Model of Software Development and Enhancement. *IEEE Computer,* 21(5), 1988, 61–72.

[Booch 1991] G. Booch. *Object-Oriented Design with Applications.* Redwood City, CA: Benjamin Cummings, 1991.

[Booch et al. 1997] G. Booch, I. Jacobson, and J. Rumbaugh. *The Unified Modelling Language.* Version 1.0, found at *http://www.rational.com,* 1997.

[Budde et al. 1992] R. Budde, K. Kautz, K. Kuhlenkamp, and H. Züllighoven. *Prototyping—An Approach to Evolutionary System Development.* Berlin: Springer-Verlag, 1992.

[Card et al. 1983] S. K. Card, T. P. Moran, and A. Newell. *The Psychology of Human-Computer Interaction.* Hillsdale, NJ: Lawrence Erlbaum Associates, 1983.

[DeMarco 1978] T. DeMarco. *Structured Analysis and System Specification.* New York: Yourdan Press, 1978.

[Dray and Siegel 1998] S. M. Dray and D. A. Siegel. User-Centered Design and the "Vision Thing". *Interactions,* 5(2), 1998, 16–20.

[Floyd 1986] C. Floyd. A Comparative Evaluation of System Development Methods. In T. W. Olle, H. G. Sol, and A. A. Verrijn-Stuart, eds. *Information Systems Design Methodologies: Improving the Practice.* Amsterdam: Elsevier Science, 1986, 19–55.

[Gould and Lewis 1983] J. D. Gould and C. H. Lewis. Designing for Usability—Key Principles and What Designers Think. *Proceedings of the 1983 Computer-Human Interaction Conference,* 1983, 50–53.

[Gould and Lewis 1985] J. D. Gould and C. H. Lewis. Designing for Usability: Key Principles and What Designers Think. *Communications of the ACM,* 28(3), 1985, 300–311.

[Gould et al. 1997] J. D. Gould, S. J. Boies, and J. Ukelson. How to Design Usable Systems. In M. G. Helander, T. K. Landauer, and V. P. Prasad, eds. *Handbook of Human-Computer Interaction.* Amsterdam: Elsevier Science, 1997.

[Gulliksen 1996] J. Gulliksen. Case Handling Models as a Basis for Information System Design. In C. A. Ntuen and E. H. Park, eds. *Human Interaction with Complex Systems—II.* Norwell, MA: Kluwer Academic, 1996.

[Gulliksen and Sandblad 1995] J. Gulliksen, and B. Sandblad. Domain-Specific Design of User Interfaces. *International Journal of Human-Computer Interaction,* 7(2), 1995, 135–151.

[Gulliksen et al. 1997] J. Gulliksen, M. Lif, M. Lind, E. Nygren, and B. Sandblad. Analysis of Information Utilisation. *International Journal of Human-Computer Interaction,* 9(3), 1997.

[ISO 1998] International Standardization Organization. *ISO 9241. Ergonomic Requirements for Office Work with Visual Display Terminals (VDTs) Part 11: Guidance on Usability.* Geneva: ISO, 1998.

[ISO 1999] International Standardization Organization. *ISO 13407. Human Centred Design Process for Interactive Systems.* Geneva: ISO, 1999.

[Jacobson et al. 1995] I. Jacobson, M. Christerson, P. Jonsson, and G. Övergaard. *Object-Oriented Software Engineering, A Use Case Driven Approach.* Reading, MA: Addison-Wesley, 1995.

[Jacobson et al. 1999] I. Jacobson, G. Booch, and J. Rumbaugh. *The Unified Software Development Process.* Reading, MA: Addison-Wesley, 1999.

[Kruchten 1998] P. Kruchten. *The Rational Unified Process—An Introduction.* Reading, MA: Addison-Wesley, 1998.

[Leavitt 1958] H. J. Leavitt. *Managerial Psychology.* London: University of Chicago Press, 1958.

[Lif 1999] M. Lif. User-Interface Modelling—Adding Usability to Use Cases. *International Journal of Human-Computer Studies,* 3, 1999, 243–262.

[Lif and Sandblad 1996] M. Lif and B. Sandblad. Domain-Specific Evaluation, During the Design of Human-Computer Interfaces. In A. G. Sutcliffe, F. Van Assche, and D. Benyon, eds. *Domain Knowledge for Interactive System Design.* London: Chapman-Hall, 1996.

[Lif et al. 2000] M. Lif, E. Olsson, J. Gulliksen, and B. Sandblad. Workspaces Enhance Efficiency—Theories, Concepts and a Case Study. *Information Technology and People,* 30(4), 2000.

[Nielsen 1993] J. Nielsen. *Usability Engineering.* San Diego: Academic Press, 1993.

[Nielsen 1995] J. Nielsen. Teaching Experienced Developers Object Oriented Design. In K. Nordby, P. Helmersen, D. J. Gilmore, and S. A. Arnesen, eds. *Proceedings of INTERACT '95 Conference,* London: Chapman-Hall, 1995.

[Norman 1998] D. A. Norman. *The Invisible Computer.* Cambridge, MA: MIT Press, 1998.

[Olsson and Gulliksen 1999] E. Olsson and J. Gulliksen. A Corporate Style Guide That Includes Domain Knowledge. *International Journal of Human-Computer Interaction,* 11(4), 1999, 317–338.

[Preece et al. 1994] J. Preece, Y. Rogers, H. Sharp, D. Benyon, S. Holland, and T. Carey. *Human-Computer Interaction.* Wokingham, England: Addison-Wesley, 1994.

[Rumbaugh et al. 1991] J. Rumbaugh, M. Blaha, W. Premerlani, F. Eddy, and W. Lorensen. *Object-Oriented Modelling and Design.* Englewood Cliffs, NJ: Prentice Hall, 1991.

[Standish Group 1995] Standish Group. *The CHAOS Report.* Found at *http://www.standishgroup.com*, 1995.

[Stapleton 1997] J. Stapleton. *DSDM—Dynamic Systems Development Method.* Essex, England: Addison-Wesley, 1997.

[van Harmelen et al. 1997] M. van Harmelen, J. Artim, K. Butler, A. Henderson, D. Roberts, M. Rosson, J. Tarby, and S. Wilson. Object Models in User Interface Design: CHI 97 Workshop Summary. *SIGCHI Bulletin,* October 1997.

[Wallace and Anderson 1993] M. D. Wallace and T. J. Anderson. Approaches to Interface Design. *Interacting with Computers,* 5 (3), 1993, 259–278.

CHAPTER 9
Toward Unified Models in User-Centered and Object-Oriented Design

William Hudson

Abstract

Many members of the HCI community view user-centered design, with its focus on users and their tasks, as essential to the construction of usable user interfaces. However, user-centered design and object-oriented design continue to develop along separate paths, with very little common ground and substantially different activities and notations. The Unified Modeling Language (UML) has become the de facto language of object-oriented development, and an informal method has evolved around it. While parts of the UML notation have been embraced in user-centered methods, such as those in this volume, there has been no concerted effort to adapt user-centered design techniques to UML and vice versa. This chapter explores many of the issues involved in bringing user-centered design and UML closer together. It presents a survey of user-centered techniques employed by usability professionals, provides an overview of a number of commercially based user-centered methods, and discusses the application of UML notation to user-centered design. Also, since the informal UML method is use case driven and many user-centered design methods rely on scenarios, a unifying approach to use cases and scenarios is included.

9.1 Introduction

9.1.1 Why Bring User-Centered Design to UML?

A recent survey of software methods and techniques [Wieringa 1998] found that at least 19 object-oriented methods had been published in book form since 1988, and many more had been proposed in conference and journal papers. This situation led to a great deal of division in the object-oriented community and caused numerous problems for anyone considering a move toward object technology.

The picture today could not be more different. In classes that I teach, and when I'm working with my development customers, UML is the predictable answer to any question concerning process or notation. A simple comparison of methods and processes[1] mentioned on the Web (see Figure 9.1) shows UML outstripping its nearest competitor (Object Modeling Technique, or OMT) by a factor of four. A leading online book retailer lists no fewer than 64 titles on the subject, with new volumes seeming to appear at the rate of two or three a month.

The focus on a single object-oriented notation has numerous benefits. Skills are more readily transferred between projects, communication between designers and developers

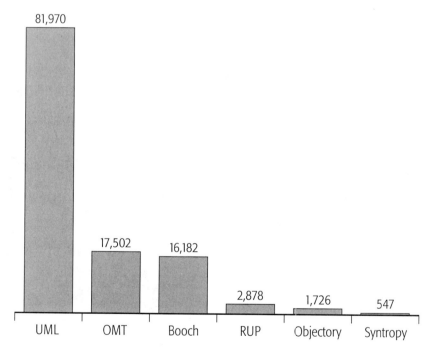

FIGURE 9.1 Web references to UML and object-oriented methods

Note: References were obtained by searching for each term (in English only) on *www.raging.com* in June 2000. Methods with commonly occurring names such as "OPEN" and "Fusion" could not be included for obvious reasons. "RUP" is the common abbreviation for the Rational Unified Process, which is discussed later in this chapter.

---

[1] There is quite a bit of disagreement over the meanings of "process" and "method" (compare Jacobson et al. [1992] and Olson and Moran [1995]). In this chapter, I have used the term "method" unless "process" has been used by the authors of the approach being discussed.

is easier, and development support in the form of software tools is steadily improving. Introducing user-centered techniques to UML would yield similar benefits, and also increase the awareness of developers to user-centered issues.[2]

This final point may seem both trivial and contentious. However, my own experience in developing interactive software and teaching for 30 years is that most systems are developed with little or no understanding of usability and user-centered issues. Raising awareness of these issues in a mainstream technology such as UML can only help to increase software usability.

9.1.2 Why Not Another New Method?

I argue against the introduction of another user-centered method for the following reasons.

- It perpetuates the object-oriented/user-centered divide. User-centered design needs to become a part of mainstream software development, not a collection of tributaries.
- Methods are not used in a formal way. Developers (object-oriented, user-centered or any other type) adopt techniques or notations that work for them. What most developers mean when they say that they are using a method is that they are using some parts of it. In the user-centered development survey presented later in this chapter, the most popular *technique* was used by 93.5 percent of respondents. In comparison, the most popular user-centered *method* was used by only 11.8 percent.[3]
- New methods are distractions to most development organizations. While some parts of the computer industry are perpetually searching for a new "magic bullet," most development managers live in dread of substantial technological change. Books, training, consultants, new staffing requirements, and reduced efficiency during the "learning curve" contribute to make this a stressful experience for all concerned.

Because UML includes use cases, it has the potential to be truly user-centered, given some appropriate adjustments. My premise is that introducing new or modified techniques to UML is, if nothing else, *psychologically* more acceptable to developers than introducing a new method. I also believe that this approach has a better chance of changing software development practice than the introduction of another new method.

---

[2] See Chapter 10 in this volume for a definition and discussion of user-centered design.

[3] Techniques are the constituents of methods and can be thought of as discrete high-level tasks for the user of a method.

9.1.3 How Can UML Be Made User-Centered?

A preliminary issue that I need to address is that UML is a language, not a method (hence UML, not UMM). Consequently, when developers state that they are using the UML method, they mean an informal method that has evolved around UML thanks largely to one of the earliest books on the subject: *UML Distilled* [Fowler 1997]. In addition, the UML notation draws heavily on the three *methods* that precede it: Booch [Booch 1994a], Objectory [Jacobson et al. 1992], and OMT [Rumbaugh et al. 1991]. The result is the informal method that I describe in Section 9.3.

Is UML a suitable basis for user-centered design? Like Objectory, the informal UML method is use case driven. It was Jacobson's original intention that use cases would allow systems to be built for their users [Jacobson 1987, p. 186]. However, it is now widely accepted [Cockburn 1997a, 1997b; Constantine 1994, 1995; Constantine and Lockwood 1999; Graham 1997] that use cases are too vague in their definition and varied in their use to be truly effective. Cockburn addressed this issue by trying to catalogue the variations and by focusing attention on a specific subset he called "goal-directed use cases." Constantine saw problems with unnecessary detail that led to premature design decisions and introduced a form of abstract use case he called "essential" (see Chapter 7). Meanwhile, Graham placed one foot firmly in the human-computer interaction (HCI) camp and suggested task scripts as an alternative (see [Graham et al. 1997]).

Not surprisingly, use cases top the list of problems that need to be addressed before the informal UML method can be considered user-centered. The complete list follows.

- *Confusion over use cases.* The purpose and content of use cases for user-centered design need to be refined and explained.
- *No separation of user and domain models.* Object-oriented methods in general do not acknowledge the difference between the problem domain and a user's understanding of the problem domain.[4]
- *No deliberate user interface design.* In many cases, design of the user interface is left to the developer who is responsible for the underlying functionality. This allows no proper opportunity to design the user interface as a whole.
- *Lack of contextual information.* User needs can vary dramatically according to context—that is, the set of circumstances and conditions under which a task is performed. In common with most other object-oriented approaches to software

---

[4] To be absolutely fair, it may be that some object-oriented methods intend the domain model to be a user's conceptual model, but few if any methods adequately explain what their domain models include.

development, UML does not take context into account, with the exception of brief task descriptions that may appear in use cases.
- *No usability evaluation.* This criticism is a little unfair but necessary. UML is primarily an analysis and design notation. It does not concern itself with how software is written and tested. However, as most usability practitioners will confirm, you can't have a user-centered approach without usability evaluation. (This is also the view taken by the ISO 13407 standard for human-centered systems design [ISO 1999].)

Usability evaluation is an example of one technique that we might incorporate into UML to make it more user centered. As there are dozens of techniques (see, for example, [Hackos and Redish 1998] and [Mayhew 1999]), how do we decide which are the most effective? After all, we can probably add only a small number to an existing method without appearing to hijack it.

The approach that I have taken is to conduct a survey of *effective* user-centered techniques and methods and then show how they could be combined with an informal UML method. The remainder of this chapter presents the survey, describes the current informal UML method, provides a unified approach to scenarios and use cases, introduces the "top ten" user-centered techniques to the UML method, discusses the application of UML to user-centered development, and compares the resulting method with other use case-driven approaches.

9.2 Survey of User-Centered Techniques and Methods

9.2.1 Description of the Survey

A self-selection survey[5] was conducted using three e-mail lists that focus on HCI and usability.

1. The ACM CHI Web list
2. A usability list operated by Clemson University
3. The British HCI Group News Service

Respondents were asked to rate the frequencies with which they employed a number of user-centered techniques, tools, and methods. They were asked to include only those that they found to be effective. These items are summarized in Table 9.1 and described in

---

[5] I am grateful to Nigel Bevan at Serco Usability Services for his help in drafting the questionnaire for the survey and for helping to make a charitable contribution for each response received.

detail in Sections 9.2.3 and 9.2.4. Section 9.2.2 presents the ten most popular techniques reported in the survey.

Sixty-five percent of the responses were from the United States; the remainder were international. The majority of respondents were usability practitioners. Slightly fewer

TABLE 9.1 User-Centered Techniques, Tools, and Methods Surveyed*

User-Centered Techniques and Tools	User-Centered Methods
Stakeholder meeting	Design for usability [John Gould 1997]
User analysis/profiling	GUIDE
Personas [Alan Cooper 1999]	LUCID
Task identification	OVID
Comprehensive (e.g., hierarchical) task analysis	STUDIO
Users' conceptual models (of the problem domain)	Usage-centered design/software for use [Constantine and Lockwood 1999]
Contextual analysis	
Evaluate existing system	
Set usability requirements	
Set quantitative usability goals	
Use case analysis	
Essential use cases [Constantine and Lockwood 1999]	
Scenarios of use	
Low-fidelity (e.g., paper) prototyping	
Use of style guides	
Visual interface design	
Navigation design	
Expert (heuristic) usability evaluation	
Informal usability testing	
Formal (e.g., quantitative) usability testing	
Usability checklists	
Attitude questionnaires	
Usability surveys	

*The lists are presented in the order in which they appeared in the questionnaire. For the techniques and tools, this coincides approximately with their order of use within the development process. Methods were presented alphabetically. Respondents were also free to write in other techniques or methods, although very few were mentioned by more than one or two respondents. The results are based on a total of 93 respondents.

than half of the respondents worked on Web development exclusively, with the bulk of the remainder splitting their efforts between Web and desktop applications. A small number worked exclusively on desktop applications and in other more specialized areas. Further results are shown in Tables 9.2 and 9.3.

TABLE 9.2 Respondents by Country and by Job Function

Respondents by Country, %		Respondents by Job Function, %	
United States	61.3	Usability practitioner	64.5
United Kingdom	12.9	Information architect	7.5
Netherlands	3.2	Developer	6.5
Sweden	3.2	Developer and usability/HCI	6.5
Belgium	2.2	HCI researcher	4.3
France	2.2	Project manager	3.2
Israel	2.2	Technical writer	2.2
Australia	2.2	Software testing/QA	2.2
Canada	2.2	Design director	2.2
Germany	2.2	Technology manager	1.1
Finland	2.2		
Ireland	1.1		
Iraq	1.1		
Italy	1.1		
Mexico	1.1		

TABLE 9.3 Respondents by Product Type and by Time Spent Applying Techniques and Methods

Respondents by Product Type, %		Respondents by Time Spent Applying User-Centered Techniques and Methods, %	
Web only	45.2	All or most	68.8
Mixed Web and desktop	33.3	Less than half	19.4
Desktop only	11.8	Occasionally	11.8
Other	5.4		
Consumer electronics	2.2		
Mobile comm's	1.1		
Multimedia	1.1		

The bulk of the questionnaire contained two lists. The first was a list of common user-centered techniques and tools; the second was a list of user-centered methods. Respondents were asked to rate the frequency of use for each technique, tool, or method that they found to be effective. The results shown in Figure 9.2 have been simplified and show only the percentage of respondents that used each technique or method.

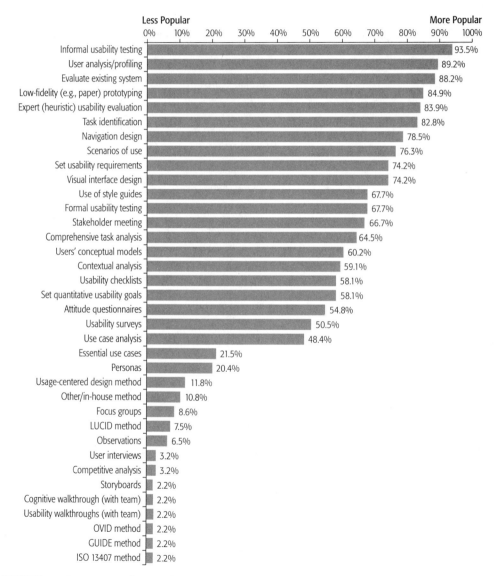

FIGURE 9.2 Percentages of respondents employing user-centered techniques and methods (excludes techniques and methods used by fewer than 2 percent of respondents)

9.2.2 The User-Centered Top Ten

Listed below are the ten most popular user-centered techniques reported in the survey. At least three-quarters of the respondents found them to be effective and reported having used them.

1. Informal usability testing (93.5%)
2. User analysis/profiling (89.2%)
3. Evaluate existing system (88.2%)
4. Low-fidelity (e.g., paper) prototyping (84.9%)
5. Expert (heuristic) usability evaluation (83.9%)
6. Task identification (82.8%)
7. Navigation design (78.5%)
8. Scenarios of use (76.3%)
9. Set usability requirements (74.2%)
10. Visual interface design (74.2%)

Interestingly, with only a few exceptions, these techniques were used in the methods surveyed, as shown in Table 9.4. However, the methods themselves were used infrequently in comparison with the individual techniques.

Listed below are the methods in reverse order of popularity:

1. Usage-centered design (11.8%)
2. Other/in-house method (10.8%)
3. LUCID (7.5%)
4. OVID (2.2%)
5. GUIDE (2.2%)
6. ISO 13407 (2.2%)
7. STUDIO (1.1%)[6]

Because some respondents used more than one method (one reported using six, which I think shows either a lack of perseverance or a surfeit of indecision), the total number using any method was 28 percent. (Bear in mind that respondents defined for themselves what they meant by "used." Many commented that they used only parts of a method.) In contrast, 100 percent of the respondents used one or more of the top ten techniques.

So, we have discovered two things. First, Table 9.4 shows that the techniques are not only important individually but also form an important part of user-centered methods (at least those considered here). Second, even though the methods make use of very popular

---

[6] STUDIO was omitted from Figure 9.2 because it fell below the 2 percent minimum.

TABLE 9.4 Techniques Used in User-Centered Methods

Technique	GUIDE	LUCID	OVID	STUDIO	Usage-Centered Design
Informal usability testing	Yes	Yes	Yes	Yes	Yes
User analysis/profiling	Yes	Yes	Yes	Yes	Yes
Evaluate existing system[a]					
Low-fidelity (e.g., paper) prototyping	Yes	Yes	Yes	Yes[b]	Yes
Expert (heuristic) usability evaluation	Yes	Yes	Yes[c]	No	Yes
Task identification	Yes	Yes	Yes	Yes	Yes
Navigation design	Yes	Yes[d]	Yes	Yes	Yes
Scenarios of use	Yes	Yes	Yes	Yes	No[e]
Set usability requirements	Yes	Yes	Yes	Yes	Yes
Visual interface design	Yes	Yes	Yes	Yes	Yes

[a] None of the methods explicitly mentions the evaluation of existing systems, although they all imply that this would be done as part of user and task analysis.

[b] STUDIO refers to these as superficial designs. They are subject only to heuristic evaluation [Browne 1993, pp. 129–131].

[c] Called a "walkthrough" or an "inspection" in OVID.

[d] LUCID is an approach rather than a method and is not fully specified. However, it does describe the design of the task flow, which is approximately equivalent to navigation design.

[e] Constantine and Lockwood prefer use cases to scenarios in the design phase of development. However, they do use scenarios in usability inspections.

techniques, the methods themselves are not popular by comparison. I am tempted to view this as an indication that more formal methods on the whole are not used, and adopt this as a motivation for incorporating the techniques into an informal UML method.[7]

9.2.3 User-Centered Techniques

The techniques are described below, in the order in which they appeared in the questionnaire and in Table 9.1.

- *Stakeholder meeting.* Normally held during project inception. A stakeholder is anyone with a vested interest in the project, such as a manager, designer, or user [Rouse 1991].

---

[7] Although many of the respondents were usability practitioners, they still would have been aware of performing their roles as part of a method if one was being used. Most of the other job functions listed in Table 9.1 would also have had direct involvement with or awareness of a method.

- *User analysis/profiling.* Covers a variety of techniques that involve understanding and describing users [Hackos and Redish 1998, Mayhew 1992].
- *Personas.* Alan Cooper uses this term to represent hypothetical archetypes of real users. Cooper argues that products should be designed for very specific personas, and this approach has been taken up with some interest by the HCI community [Cooper 1999].
- *Task identification.* Also task lists, inventories, and profiles. Identification of the tasks users need to perform, usually as part of task analysis. Task identification needs to be done by interacting with users. Profiling normally includes task frequencies and other characteristics [Hackos and Redish 1998, Mayhew 1999, Shneiderman 1998].
- *Comprehensive (for example, hierarchical) task analysis.* Rigorous analysis of user goals and tasks. Hierarchical task analysis (HTA) is one of the more common forms (see Task identification, above, for references).
- *Users' conceptual models (of the problem domain).* Sometimes referred to simply as a "user model" or, as in Chapter 10, as a "conceptual model." This model is intended to reflect users' understanding of the problem domain, often in the form of conceptual objects and the relationships between them [Norman 1986].
- *Contextual analysis.* Contextual inquiry, ethnography, and related techniques that involve understanding users in their environments [Beyer and Holtzblatt 1998, Mayhew 1999].
- *Evaluate existing system.* A common technique not limited to user-centered design. Sometimes performed as part of contextual analysis [Mayhew 1999].
- *Set usability requirements.* Usually qualitative, as in "The system should provide consistency across components" [Mayhew 1999].
- *Set quantitative usability goals.* Measurable goals, as in "Novice users (defined as first-time users) should take no longer than three minutes to fill in a certain online subscription form" [Mayhew 1999].
- *Use case analysis.* Ivar Jacobson's use cases, as found originally in Objectory and more recently in UML and RUP [Jacobson et al. 1992, 1999].
- *Essential use cases.* A form of abstract use case that focuses on the essence of an interaction between a user and a system [Constantine and Lockwood 1999].
- *Scenarios of use.* Descriptions in almost any form (for example, visual or narrative) of users performing tasks [Carroll 1995].
- *Low-fidelity (for example, paper) prototyping.* Crude mock-ups of user interfaces or portions such as windows, Web pages, or dialogues. Low-fidelity prototypes may be reviewed with users or form the basis of scenarios used to explore interactions [Nielsen 1993].

- *Use of style guides.* Style guides are generally recommended for desktop applications, because they provide consistency within the platform, organization, or product family. They are also becoming popular for Web site design [Mayhew 1999].
- *Visual interface design.* Any deliberate design of the visual aspects of an interface (as opposed to the interface evolving as a side effect of the development process). Visual design is often done in conjunction with low-fidelity prototyping [Nielsen 1995].
- *Navigation design.* This has become better defined with respect to the Web, but it has always been an important part of any user interface. Navigation design determines how users move between Web pages, windows, or dialogues [Hackos and Redish 1998, Fleming 1998].
- *Expert (heuristic) usability evaluation.* Review of a user interface by a usability practitioner familiar with design principles [Nielsen 1993].
- *Informal usability testing.* Usually direct observation, while asking users to think aloud [Tognazzini 1992, Nielsen 1993].
- *Formal (for example, quantitative) usability testing.* More planned or rigorous testing than informal direct observation. May be quantitative, may be set in a usability lab, or may involve detailed analysis of video tapes.
- *Usability checklists.* Primarily employed during evaluation and inspection, but may be used at other times in the development process. They are used to ensure that all desired aspects of usability have been considered [Nielsen and Mack 1994].
- *Attitude questionnaires.* Qualitative (rather than quantitative) questionnaires used to gauge user attitudes toward systems or system components, including individual Web pages or dialogues [Nielsen 1993].
- *Usability surveys.* Conducted to obtain more specific and frequently quantitative data on usability or factors directly affecting usability, such as environment, documentation, and training [Hackos and Redish 1998].

9.2.4 User-Centered Methods

The survey included five existing user-centered software development methods. This was done to determine the popularity of methods (as opposed to techniques).

The methods presented in the questionnaire are described briefly in the following sections. All have been developed from practical experience. Two are British in origin (GUIDE and STUDIO), two are American (LUCID and Usage-Centered Design), and one is Anglo-American (OVID). Most have been published internationally in book form.[8] The methods were presented in alphabetical order.

---

[8] LUCID is published on the Web and described in Shneiderman [1998]. See Section 9.2.4.2 for references.

9.2.4.1 Graphical User Interface Design and Evaluation (GUIDE)

GUIDE [Redmond-Pyle and Moore 1995] had its origins in the development of large Windows-based applications at LBMS[9] in the late 1980s and early 1990s. It is based largely on practical experience and the participation of one of the authors in the British government's Structured Systems Analysis and Design Method (SSADM) standards working group for graphical user interface (GUI) development.

Figure 9.3 shows the relationship between user-centered GUI design (the shadowed rectangles) and system design. Linkages between system design and GUI design are shown

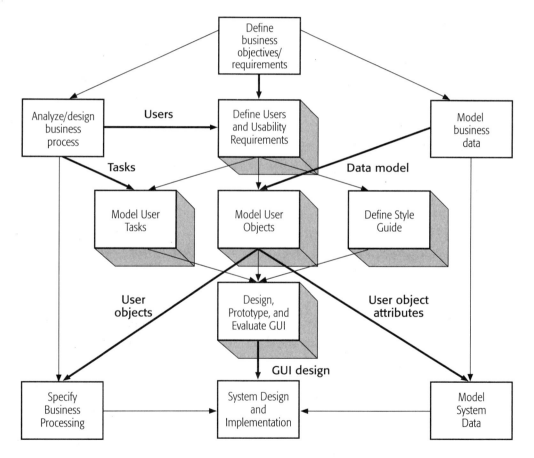

FIGURE 9.3 System and GUI analysis and design in GUIDE (adapted from Redmond-Pyle and Moore [1995, p. 45])

---

[9] For collectors of acronyms, LBMS stands for Learmonth and Burchett Management Systems.

with heavy arrows and are typical of the kinds of interactions that occur between user-centered and software design activities in many of the methods to be described.

GUIDE includes the following features, which we will come to recognize in this chapter as common to user-centered methods.

- Initial focus on user and task analysis
- Development of a user's conceptual model (partly derived from the business data model in GUIDE)
- Design of the user interface prior to system design

9.2.4.2 Logical User-Centered Interaction Design (LUCID)

The LUCID framework [Kreitzberg 1999] was developed at Cognetics Corporation from its approach to user interface design.[10] LUCID has enjoyed some exposure from the HCI community and appears in books and courses used in the teaching of user interface design (for example [Shneiderman 1998 pp. 104–107]). Its main phases are shown in Table 9.5 (from [Kreitzberg 1999]).

LUCID is also used as a basis for the Wisdom method described in Chapter 6.

9.2.4.3 Object, View, and Interaction Design (OVID)

OVID [Roberts et al. 1998] is one of the earliest user-centered design methods to adopt object-oriented modeling notations. However, rather than using a single domain model, the authors describe three design models based on Don Norman's notion of cognitive engineering [Norman 1986, pp. 45–48]. These models are worth describing in more detail as they are an important concept in user interface design. The relationship between the models is shown in Figure 9.4.

- *Designer's model.* The designer's model[11] expresses the intended user's conceptual model in terms of the objects and relationships that will be represented in the interface. Although the term "designer's model" is in keeping with Norman's original discussion, this is the model that most methods refer to as the user's conceptual model (or user model, or conceptual model).

---

[10] This approach was formerly called Quality Usability Engineering (QUE).

[11] The names of the models used here are those found in OVID and in Norman's writing. Chapter 10 discusses more recent terminology used in HCI. There an OVID designer's model is called a (narrow sense) conceptual model, an OVID programmer's model is called a development model, and an OVID user's conceptual model is called a mental model.

TABLE 9.5 Overview of LUCID Framework (used with permission of Cognetics Corporation)

Phase	Activity	Description
Concept	Envision	Develop a clear, shared, and communicable vision of the product. Decide on the usability goals for the interface design. Create a "user interface roadmap" to document the preliminary analysis and concepts developed during these activities.
Design	User and task analysis	Perform a comprehensive and systematic analysis of user and task requirements by studying users so as to understand their needs, expectations, tasks, and work processes; determine the implications of this information for the interface.
	Design and prototype	Create a design concept and create a key screen prototype to illustrate it.
	Evaluate and refine	Evaluate the prototype for usability and iteratively refine and expand the design.
Build	Complete detailed design and production	Complete the detailed screen design for the full program. Support late-stage changes.
	Evaluate and refine	Evaluate the complete prototype or early versions of the program for usability and iteratively refine the design.
Release	Release and follow up	Plan and implement the introduction of the product to users, including final usability evaluations to ensure that the product has met the goals established at the beginning of the process. Create and monitor feedback mechanisms to gather data for future releases.

- *Programmer's model.* The programmer's (or implementation) model is most commonly used in object-oriented development methods. It represents the implementation classes used to build the system.
- *User's conceptual model.* This model represents a user's understanding of a system and cannot be directly realized. Because it is not possible to design this model (it is dependent on an individual user's previous experience, for example), the term has come to be used for the *intended* user's conceptual model—that is, the designer's model in OVID. This rather confusing state of affairs is also described in Draper and Norman [1986, pp. 496–497].

OVID's authors make the point, as did Norman, that the user interface must accurately reflect the designer's model in order for users to acquire a suitable conceptual

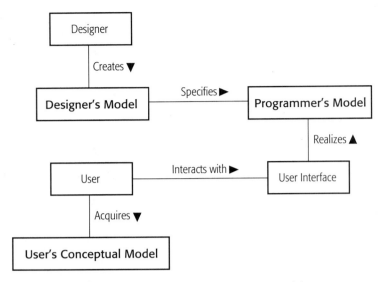

FIGURE 9.4 Relationship between OVID models

model. For this to happen, all aspects of the user interface must be determined by the designer's model, not the programmer's.[12]

The focus of the OVID method is in identifying objects of importance to users, grouping these objects into views that support users' tasks, and detailing the interactions between users and objects. Objects are initially identified through task analysis (although OVID does not prescribe a technique) and organized into a designer's object model, initially based on the user's model. If designed and implemented effectively, the users will understand the designer's model by interacting with the system. The various models are documented using appropriate object-oriented notation. The cycle of activities is shown in Figure 9.5.

Objects are users' conceptual models while *views* are collections of objects that are needed to support users' *tasks*. (OVID does not specify a particular type of task analysis, but use case and hierarchical task analyses are given as examples.) *Interactions* are the actions that are necessary in the interface in order to perform operations on objects.

Like most other user-centered design methods, OVID is iterative and relies on both low- and high-fidelity prototyping.

---

[12] Norman originally called the user interface the "system image" because it was intended to refer to all aspects of a system that users might experience (including documentation and training). He did not explicitly include the programmer's model.

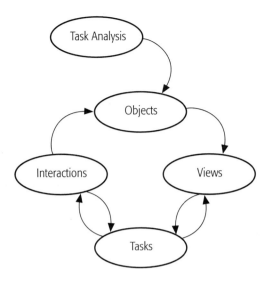

FIGURE 9.5 Cycle of activities in OVID (adapted from Berry et al. [1997]).

9.2.4.4 STructured User-Interface Design for Interaction Optimisation (STUDIO)

STUDIO [Browne 1993] is also based on its author's practical experience in GUI design at KPMG[13] Management Consultants in the early 1990s. Browne advocates using STUDIO for interface-intensive client applications while continuing the use of system-centered development for server-side applications. The main stages of the STUDIO development cycle are as follows.

- *Project planning and proposal.* Cost benefit analysis, quality planning
- *Usability requirements analysis.* Preparing the groundwork, evidence collection, task analysis, validation, reporting of findings
- *Task synthesis.* Task synthesis (convert analysis findings into a user interface design), style guide, design specification, user support documentation, formative evaluation
- *Usability engineering.* Planning, preparation of evaluation materials, prototype build and design audit (in parallel with other activities), prototype evaluation, impact analysis, update specification
- *User interface development.* Hand over specification, integration/interfacing, acceptance testing, termination reporting

---

[13] Another obscure acronym: Klynveld, Peat, Marwick, and Goerdeler.

STUDIO is very detailed in its description of each activity and its deliverables, but it provides noticeably less guidance on the actual interface design process compared with methods such as GUIDE and usage-centered design. However, in common with GUIDE and LUCID, STUDIO includes the development of a user interface style guide. This approach is not taken with the other methods, but it is useful in ensuring consistent user interface design, especially for large, multi-team projects.

9.2.4.5 Usage-Centered Design

According to Constantine, "usage-centered design focuses on the work that users are trying to accomplish and on what the software will need to supply through the user interface to help them accomplish it" [Constantine 1994, p. 23].[14] Constantine and Lockwood's method includes five key elements:

- Pragmatic design guidelines
- Model-driven design process
- Organized development activities
- Iterative improvement
- Measures of quality

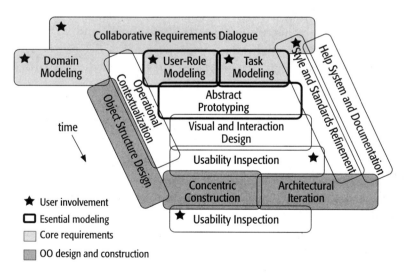

FIGURE 9.6 Usage-centered design activity model (adapted from Constantine and Lockwood [1999], used with permission)

---

[14] Don't confuse "*user*-centered design" and its acronym (user-centered design) with "*usage*-centered design." The latter is the name of Constantine and Lockwood's method.

These elements are common to many user-centered methods, although the extent to which they are found in individual methods varies. OVID, for example, does not provide pragmatic design guidelines for many of its suggested activities.

As part of the model-driven design process, three core models are used to identify users and their relationships to the system.

1. *Role model.* A collection of user roles and the needs, interests, behaviors, and responsibilities as they apply to each user role.
2. *Task model.* Essential use case model (a form of abstract use case, described in Chapter 7 and Section 9.4.4).
3. *Content model.* An abstract model of users' conceptual objects that is similar to the view model in OVID.

The first two of these models, shown near the top of Figure 9.6, are developed during the initial activities of the process. The content model is established during the abstract prototyping activity and contributes to visual and interaction design.

Other design activities are performed in parallel with the production of the core models. These activities are shown in a diagonal layout in Figure 9.6. Most are self-explanatory, with the exception of operational contextualization. In this activity, Constantine and Lockwood take the approach of adapting the design to the actual operating conditions and environment of the users. (Other methods prefer to resolve this at an earlier stage, although each has its benefits: an early and detailed understanding of context may reduce the design and contextualization effort, while contextualization in parallel with design may provide more realistic feedback.)

Concentric construction (in layers) and architectural iteration form the implementation phase of the process. Usability inspection (which includes a number of usability evaluation techniques) is performed during both design and implementation.

9.3 The Informal UML Method

UML is now published as an industry standard by the Object Management Group [OMG 1999]. It is also the subject of scores of books and papers. Of these, the first edition of Martin Fowler's *UML Distilled* [1997] is familiar to many object-oriented developers, because it was one of the first books to be published, and because it also presented UML in a very practical role as an informal method. This is shown in Figure 9.7, using a fairly self-explanatory workflow notation found in the Unified Software Development Process [Jacobson et al. 1999]. The method described here is based loosely on *UML Distilled* with the addition of the implementation and functional testing activities (which UML does not cover and Fowler mentions only briefly).

332 | **CHAPTER 9** Toward Unified Models in User-Centered and Object-Oriented Design

9.3.1 Perspectives

Fowler introduces the idea of perspectives based on the modeling approach of Cook and Daniels [1994].

- *Conceptual.* The conceptual perspective describes some real or imaginary situation without regard for any software that may be involved.[15] For example, a class diagram with a conceptual perspective is effectively a problem domain model. (If it were based on a user's understanding of the domain, it would be a user's conceptual model, but this issue was not raised by Cook and Daniels or by Fowler.)

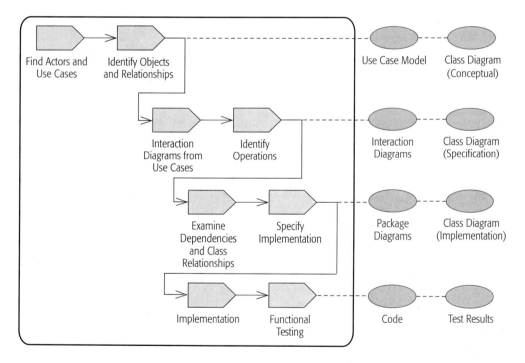

Note: Workflow diagrams do not usually show iteration. In common with most other object-oriented methods, the informal UML method *is* iterative, especially in the early activities.

FIGURE 9.7 Informal UML Method

---

[15] Cook and Daniels used the term "essential" in their original text [Cook and Daniels 1994, p. 12] and said that their use was different from that of some earlier authors. To prevent confusion, I will retain Fowler's substitution of "conceptual."

- *Specification.* Models produced from a specification perspective are more detailed than conceptual models and are somewhat closer to the solution domain.[16] Fowler describes this perspective as looking at the interface between objects,[17] not their implementation.
- *Implementation.* Full details of objects (classes), including their detailed behavior and internal representations of state and properties.

Armed with perspectives, Fowler's description of how the UML notation is applied, and my own practical experience in using and teaching UML, we can now consider the informal UML method in a little more detail, as shown in Table 9.6. Simply trying to slot

TABLE 9.6 Description of Informal UML Method by Activity

Activity	Description
Find actors and use cases	Actors and use cases are derived from informal scenarios obtained through discussions with users.
Identify objects and relationships	Objects and relationships are extracted from use cases. Unfortunately, no distinction is made between the domain and user models (i.e., a user's understanding of the domain). The result is a class diagram at the conceptual level, equivalent to a domain model.
Interaction diagrams from use cases	Interaction diagrams elaborate the use cases and aid in the identification of operations on objects (classes).
Identify operations	Each message in an interaction diagram must eventually have a corresponding operation.
Examine dependencies and class relationships	Generalizations (inheritance), aggregations, and associations are identified and refined.
Specify implementation	Iteration and refinement (in increasing detail) finally lead to an implementation-perspective class diagram. Other diagrams may also be used to illustrate object behavior.
Implementation	Coding and unit testing.
Functional testing	Tests that the implemented software performs according to its specification.

---

[16] It is helpful to view the entire process of software development as bridging a gulf between problem and solution domains.

[17] Classes define objects, but it is convenient to refer to both as objects in many discussions.

user interface design into this process is not very likely to succeed for the reasons that were mentioned in Section 9.1.3.

- Confusion over use cases.
- No separation of user and domain models.
- No deliberate user interface design.
- Lack of contextual information.
- No usability evaluation.

We need to consider these points in more detail.

9.3.2 Confusion over Use Cases

Ivar Jacobson is credited as the inventor of use cases, and his book *Object-Oriented Software Engineering* (OOSE) [Jacobson et al. 1992] is considered the authoritative source on the subject. However, in an earlier paper [Jacobson 1987] he described the importance of use cases in his object-oriented technique, Objectory.

Objectory was intended to allow a system to be built for its users. Jacobson made the point that in order to do this, the behavior of a proposed system must be described. Use cases are the means of achieving this. Figure 9.8 shows a sample use case diagram. The use cases themselves are usually narratives detailing interactions purely from an external perspective.

Even at an early stage, Jacobson was torn between two conflicting applications of use cases, which is a problem that recurs through many discussions up to the present day.

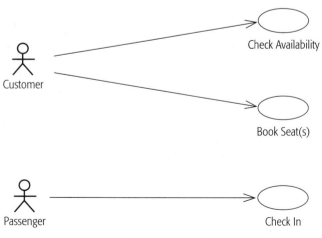

FIGURE 9.8 A use case diagram

First, use cases are a means of describing user interaction with a system from a user's perspective. Second, use cases are a means of describing system behavior from a designer's perspective. Superficially, these two applications may seem to be the same, but this apparent similarity depends on the correspondence of the user's and designer's perspectives.[18] Designers who take the user's perspective into account will write use cases that are much more likely to result in user-centered systems.

In contrast, however, consider this example from Jacobson's paper: "In a telephone exchange, the local calls and long distance calls constitute two different use cases. In both cases the user is an A-subscriber" [Jacobson 1987]. The concepts and terminology being used here are clearly those of a designer, not a user. Users do not consider local and long distance calls as two different tasks. Nor would they identify themselves as "subscribers." If the consequences of this example were to be implemented in a finished telephone system, we could expect a certain degree of user confusion and frustration.

This early description of use cases is very similar to the ones found in UML.

- Use cases constitute a "black box" description of behavior.
- Use cases include *roles* that interact with the systems.
- Roles are adopted by *users*.

Users later became *actors* in object-oriented software engineering (OOSE) and consequently the main focus of attention in use cases (the term "roles" became an abstract concept that did not appear in most use cases). This probably seemed to be an innocent generalization at the time. *Users* are human, but *actors* include any external entity that can adopt a role and interact with the system. In hindsight, this small change created the single most confusing aspect of use cases and certainly detracted from Jacobson's intended purpose of building systems for users. Use cases became, in effect, just another way of describing the dynamic behavior of a system without necessarily providing a clear user focus.

OOSE went on to describe how use cases and objects were different views of the same system [Jacobson et al. 1992, p. 175]. However, this approach failed to acknowledge that a user's view can be very different from a designer's. Object-oriented developers are left with the illusion that they are designing systems for users while the reality is that the application of use cases is no guarantee of success.

Following the publication of Jacobson's book, use cases were the subject of much debate and explanation. Jacobson published a series of articles in the *Report on Object-Oriented Analysis and Design* [Jacobson 1994a, 1994b, 1994c, 1994d, 1995b]. In these

---

[18] Don Norman discusses the relationship between designer and user models, which are closely related to these perspectives [Norman 1986].

articles, he expands on some of the concepts and practicalities of use cases that were not addressed in his book, such as the following.[19]

- *The definition of a good use case.* Jacobson notes that "a good use case when instantiated is a sequence of transactions performed by a system, which yields a measurable result of value for a particular actor" [Jacobson 1994a, p. 17].
- *How and why use cases are created.* Jacobson describes the observation of users in the workplace by interface designers as a key source of use scenarios. He also suggests that use-oriented design and usability testing are very important in understanding the envisioning of the user interface [Jacobson 1994a, p. 17]. Unfortunately, neither of these suggestions has made its way into the common object-oriented practice of generating use cases or into the description of use cases in UML.
- *The relationship between use cases and scenarios.* The term "scenario" is used by the object-oriented community to describe a particular instance of object interaction (given specific states and events): "a specific sequence of actions that illustrates behavior" [Booch et al. 1999, p. 466]. Jacobson observes that a use case class can be modeled as a state machine, with use case instances representing a particular series of states. He describes use scenarios (in the object-oriented sense) and use case instances as equivalent [Jacobson 1994a, p. 17].

Use cases influenced Grady Booch (although he adopted scenarios as an approximately equivalent technique [Booch 1994b, p. 3]). Use cases were incorporated into UML when the Booch, Objectory, and OMT methods were combined [Booch et al. 1999]. Regrettably, none of the standard UML references [OMG 1999, Booch et al. 1999, Rumbaugh et al. 1999] describes use cases in enough detail to allow consistent results, let alone provide guidance on user-centered design.

9.3.3 No Separation of User and Domain Models

The second problem I raised with respect to current object-oriented methods is the lack of separation of user and domain models. In HCI, a user's understanding of a system is called the "user's conceptual model" or sometimes just the "user model" or the "conceptual model." Object-oriented approaches tend to ignore the user model and instead concentrate on a domain model, which is intended to represent how the organization or

---

[19] Much of this material is also included in Jacobson [1995a].

system "really works."[20] Unfortunately, it is extremely rare for users to understand an organization or system in this way. Figure 9.9 shows a user's conceptual model of an elevator. In contrast, Figure 9.10 is a corresponding domain model (although a somewhat simplified one).

Because the user interface for an elevator is so simple, there is little chance that confusing or unnecessary concepts or terms can "leak" from the domain model into the user interface. However, this is a real problem for most software user interfaces.

Another substantial barrier to user-centered development from the domain model is that user interface objects tend to be ignored in the early phases of design. They get "discovered" in later, more detailed stages and a user interface materializes during implementation (see Section 9.3.4).

9.3.4 No Deliberate User Interface Design

The traditional software engineering view of user interface design is that it is an activity that falls outside of its scope. For example, only one of the three undergraduate software engineering textbooks on my shelf has as much as a single chapter devoted to user interface design [Sommerville 1995]. Of the other two, one [Pressman 1997, pp. 409–422] devotes only 24 of 885 pages to the subject, while the third, the most recent of the three [Pfleeger 1998], makes only a few passing references to it. Consequently, in many projects user interfaces evolve as developers discover the need for user interaction. Concepts

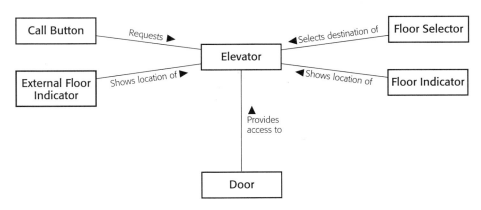

FIGURE 9.9 User's conceptual model of an elevator

---

[20] Editor's note: This use of "domain model" diverges strongly from the use promoted in Chapter 10 and other chapters, where the domain model is composed of users' referents (including, where required, business referents) and associations between these referents.

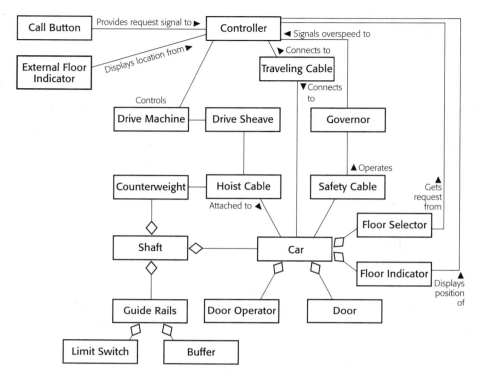

Note: Some of the objects (classes) shown in this diagram would be considered by many object-oriented designers to be implementation objects and not part of the domain model. I am not certain that you could get agreement as to which.

FIGURE 9.10 Simplified domain model of an elevator

and terminology in the user interface come straight from the underlying software. I have seen utterly unusable systems developed in this way.

9.3.5 Lack of Contextual Information

Whereas Fowler initially suggested, in his first edition, that use cases be based on interviews with users [Fowler 1997, p. 44], this particular recommendation mysteriously disappeared in the second edition [Fowler 2000]. This is a retrograde step for the development of user-centered systems. User-centered design means understanding the real circumstances or context of a system's use. Sitting in a development office talking to other developers certainly does not provide this. Talking to users is a step in the right direction, but watching and working with users is the best way. (This may not be necessary in all cases, but software development needs to move away from the situation in which developers have no idea what is happening in the real world.)

9.3.6 No Usability Evaluation

Software testing takes many forms and is a science in its own right. Unfortunately, usability evaluation is a completely separate science. Functional testing may prove that a piece of software meets its specifications, but that does not make it suitable for real users in the real world.

Informal usability testing is not difficult to conduct and requires no more than a handful of users [Nielsen 1993, Nielsen and Landauer 1993]. It needs to be an integral part of the design of any interactive system. Heuristic or expert evaluation of designs and prototypes can provide an effective alternative in some cases.

9.4 A Unified Approach to Use Cases and Scenarios

Most of the changes required to make the informal UML method user-centered are relatively straightforward. However, use cases are already part of UML and cannot be considered user-centered in their current form, thus requiring some modification. In contrast, most user-centered design processes are based on scenarios, which are one of the top ten user-centered techniques reported in the survey.

Since Jacobson's introduction of use cases, debates have raged over whether they are more appropriate for design than scenarios. Some authors have tried to avoid the issue by calling them broadly equivalent concepts. However, my own view is that it is preferable to separate the two concepts and to be clear about how they contribute to successful user-centered design. *Both* are required.

In this section we will explore the enigmatic nature of use cases and examine the need for them to be closely integrated with scenarios.

9.4.1 Goal-Based Use Cases

Use cases were not well understood by object-oriented developers in the early 1990s. Part of the confusion arose over Jacobson's lack of formality in defining them (a decision that he later defended as being necessary to their success [Cockburn and Fowler 1998]), but some confusion resulted from the tendency to adapt a good idea to the problem in hand. As a result, the terms "scenario" and "use case" are treated as approximately equivalent by many authors, while various sub-species of use cases have evolved.

In a two-part article, Alistair Cockburn [1997a, 1997b] described some of the variations he encountered in trying to adopt a coherent approach to use cases in object-oriented systems development. In the first part, he shows the variations occurring along the following four dimensions.

1. *Purpose.* Stories of use or requirements. This variation is a result of the confusion surrounding the concepts of use cases and scenarios, as well as the need to describe both existing and proposed systems. Scenarios are better suited to describing stories of use because they describe specific instances. Use cases describe classes of potential scenarios (use case instances) and so are more appropriate for requirements.
2. *Content.* Formal, consistent prose, or contradicting. Formal use cases are typically written in a form of structured English, while consistent prose is informal but self-consistent. Contradicting content is a likely consequence of describing stories of use.
3. *Multiplicity.* One or multiple scenarios per use case. Some use cases are really scenarios, because they describe only a specific use case instance.[21]
4. *Structure.* Unstructured, semiformal, or formal. This dimension may vary with purpose and content or may vary independently.

These dimensions are taken from 18 different types of use cases that Cockburn encountered. He identified <requirements, consistent prose, multiple scenarios, semiformal> as the most useful instance of these dimensions, as well as being the most consistent with Jacobson's original intentions [Jacobson et al. 1992]. Some of the dimensions occurred only in specific combinations. For example, contradicting content must be avoided when describing requirements, but it is inevitable in documenting stories of actual use.

In the second part of the article, Cockburn introduces three levels at which use cases can operate.

1. *Scope.* System or organization. Use cases can describe the behavior of a single system or of a system of systems (an organization). This is also discussed by Jacobson [1995b]. Organizational use cases are called business use cases in the Unified Software Development Process, which is the successor to Objectory [Jacobson et al. 1999].
2. *Goal specificity.* Summary goals, user goals, or sub-functions. User goals are relevant to system scope use cases. Summary goals can exist at either system or organization scope and are used to organize collections of user goals.
3. *Interaction detail.* Dialogue interface level or semantic interface level. The dialogue interface level describes the syntax interaction (in terms of button

---

[21] Cockburn uses the term "scenario" in its object-oriented sense.

presses, key clicks, and so on) and should be avoided during requirements gathering. The intent, but not the substance, of the interaction is provided by the semantic interface level.

Most of these dimensions have legitimate applications in system design, but they provide a confusing selection of possibilities for user interface design. Organization scope is useful for identifying actors and assigning roles, but if we assume that the business processes have already been decided, system scope should be our main focus of attention. The goal dimension provides similar choices. Summary goals allow a high-level view of system interaction but are not necessarily useful in designing a user interface. Interface design requires use cases to be presented at the user goal or, in moving further toward detailed design, the sub-function level. Finally, the interaction level determines the amount of detail provided in each use case. Cockburn makes the point that the dialogue level would be inappropriate for requirements analysis because it would commit designers to a specific interface implementation far too early in the process. (He uses "move to the next field" as an example of a dialogue interface description, whereas "enter address" represents a semantic description.)

The complete set of use case dimensions and the values of interest in user interface design are shown in Table 9.7. This combination of attributes gives us use cases that are focused on user goals, excludes unnecessary detail, and is suitable as a statement of requirements (rather than just a story of use). Because their interaction detail is semantic, this particular variety of use case can be described as abstract (as opposed to concrete).

TABLE 9.7 Use Case Dimensions and Values for User Interface Design

Dimension	Value
Purpose	Requirements
Content	Consistent prose
Multiplicity	Multiple scenarios per use case
Structure	Semiformal
Scope	System
Goal specificity	User goals
Interaction detail	Semantic interface level

9.4.2 Scenarios versus Use Cases

In user-centered design, scenarios usually describe a "rich picture"[22] of interaction—that is, they include not only the information passing through the interface but also a great deal about the context. Scenarios might typically include the following.

- The user's identity, background, experience, and working routine (this also might appear separately in a user profile rather than in the scenario itself)
- Why the user is performing the task at all and why it is being done at this particular time
- The situation or environment in which the interaction is taking place
- Copies of documents used in the interaction and photographs or videos of interactions, user artifacts, and equipment

Some of this might seem mildly absurd for the average office interaction, but it becomes very relevant in factories, warehouses, shop floors, farms, and so on. In fact, as computing becomes more pervasive, scenarios become more important.

Because scenarios are stories of use, what they give us that use cases do not is context—the "who, where, when, and why" of an interaction. As we extract[23] context and generalize the scenarios, we are in effect translating them into use cases, as shown in Figure 9.11.

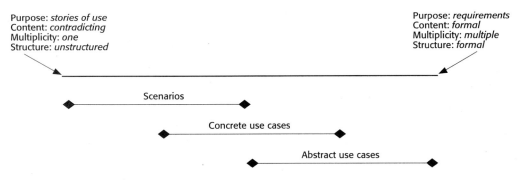

FIGURE 9.11 Relationship between scenarios and use cases

---

[22] I use the term "rich picture" to mean a broad, multi-faceted view. A rich picture is also a specific technique frequently used in conjunction with scenarios (see [Monk and Howard 1998]). Rich pictures in this latter sense originate from Soft Systems Methodology (SSM) described in [Checkland 1981] and [Checkland and Scholes 1990].

[23] Notice that I say "extract," not "discard." Context is retained as part of the non-functional requirements of design, as we will see in Section 9.4.5.

9.4.3 Context of Use

Entire books have been written about the importance of context in designing interactive systems (see [Beyer and Holtzblatt 1998]). For our purposes, the ISO standard *human-centered design processes for interactive systems* [ISO 1999] will suffice. It identifies the first step in human-centered design as understanding and specifying the context of use.[24] The attributes suggested are shown in Table 9.8 (they are not intended to be exhaustive).

It is useful to split the user context into two parts—user type and role—and then consider the relationships among all four contexts, as shown in Figure 9.12. This figure shows that every *task* is performed in a *role* taken by a *user* within an *environment*. Each of these contexts could have a significant impact on the design of an appropriate user interface. As a result, we are faced with a potentially large number of permutations. Even for a small system, there may be two environments (for example, an office and a customer site), three types of users (an administrative assistant, a sales expert, and manager), and six roles (telephone sales, external sales, and so on). Thus, there can be as many as 36 potential variations per task, although the set of realistic combinations is usually much smaller because not all tasks are performed by all roles taken by all users.

TABLE 9.8 Context of Use from the ISO Standard for Human-Centered Design

Context	Attributes
Tasks	Goals of use of the system, frequency and duration of performance, health and safety considerations, allocation of activities, and operational steps between human and technological resources. Tasks should *not* be described solely in terms of the functions or features provided by a product or system.
Users (for each different type or role)	Knowledge, skill, experience, education, training, physical attributes, habits, preferences, capabilities.
Environments	Social and cultural environment, ambient environment, legislative environment, technical environment, hardware, software, materials, physical and social environments, relevant standards.

FIGURE 9.12 Relationships among contexts

---

[24] See Chapter 8 for further discussion of the ISO standard.

9.4.4 Essential Use Cases

Clearly, tasks must be described individually, but a single description is unlikely to be appropriate for all permutations of context. One approach is to factor the user and environment contexts into the role description. This is the solution adopted by Constantine and Lockwood [1999] for their "essential" use cases. It involves providing a separate role for each significant permutation of role, user, and environment and then naming the resulting user role with a descriptive phrase rather than a simple noun. Compare, for example, the role "Customer" with the user roles "Casual Customer," "Web Customer," and "Telephone Customer." Constantine and Lockwood include details of the role itself plus details of its users (referred to as role incumbents) and the environment in each user role description.

The use cases described in UML (little changed from Jacobson's original) are not as straightforward in this respect [Jacobson et al. 1992, Booch et al. 1999]. An actor plays a set of roles, but the roles are not usually described and no mention is made of context or environment. However, this extremely vague state of affairs means that a more user-centered approach, along the lines of essential use cases, is certainly not precluded.

9.4.5 Use Cases as Requirements

It is always tempting to describe requirements analysis as the "what" of software development, with later technical design as the "how." But, as usual, such a simplistic view obscures some important complications. In this case, one complication is that it is almost impossible to say what a system must do without some indication of how it should do it [Davis 1991, Wirfs-Brock 1993]. In other words, we want to describe the proposed *behavior* of a system at a suitable level.[25] In fact, this was Jacobson's original intention for use cases [Jacobson 1987, p. 185].

For interactive systems, we want to arrive at this description of behavior in a way that takes account of its contexts of use. Object-oriented developers are already familiar with the process of starting with a scenario and discarding unnecessary information to arrive at a use case. In the process, however, they discard context. A user-centered approach to this problem is shown in Figure 9.13.

Details of context are extracted from the scenarios and documented separately (as required by the ISO standard [ISO 1999, Section 8.2.2]). The resulting analysis use cases

---

[25] Even in their most abstract form, use cases describe *behavior* and therefore include some element of implementation detail. The goal in applying use cases to requirements is to exclude inappropriate implementations while allowing designers suitable freedom to innovate.

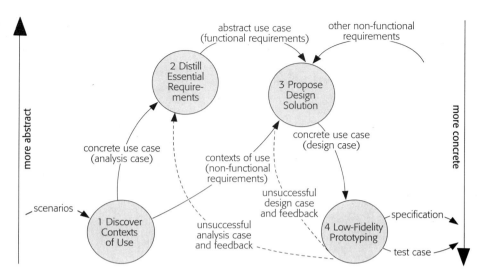

FIGURE 9.13 Relationships among scenarios, use cases, and contexts of use

(or "analysis cases," which is a lot easier to say) are generalized to produce abstract use cases. Being abstract, these use cases describe a whole universe of potential design solutions. Appropriate designs are then synthesized with the help of the contexts of use as well as other non-functional requirements (such as hardware and software platforms or networking constraints). The result is a more concrete version of the abstract use case, which is shown in Figure 9.13 as a design use case or, more simply, "design case." Design cases can be tested by considering specific scenarios, first just in concept, but later as low-fidelity prototypes tested with potential users.

Successful designs are specified in sufficient detail for implementation, with the design cases becoming yet more concrete in the form of test cases.[26] These provide the specific details necessary for functional testing once implementation and unit testing have taken place.

Notice that the approach shown in Figure 9.13 involves starting with concrete information in the form of scenarios, moving to a more general abstract form, and then returning to a concrete design that takes all of the required factors into consideration. This alternation between concrete and abstract is a standard approach to problem solving [Polya 1990] known as the generalize-specialize cycle (see Figure 9.14).

---

[26] It is not possible to test abstract use cases directly. The test cases take account of a specific design and provide the quality assurance team with the concrete information needed to conduct functional tests.

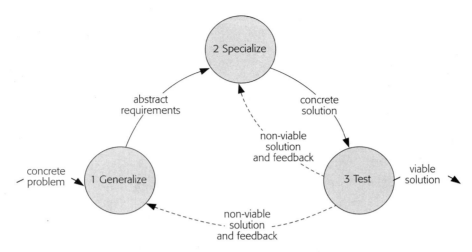

FIGURE 9.14 Generalize-specialize cycle in problem solving

9.5 A User-Centered UML Method

The ISO 13407 human-centered design standard (mentioned in Section 9.4.3) identifies four activities that should take place during system development:

1. Understand and specify the context of use.
2. Specify the user and organizational requirements.
3. Produce design solutions.
4. Evaluate designs against requirements.

So that we are not just arbitrarily adding user-centered techniques to UML, it is useful to make the resultant informal method comply with the ISO 13407 standard. In this section, we will incorporate the "top ten" user-centered methods (from Section 9.2.2) as required to meet the ISO 13407 standard, modify the informal UML method wherever needed (to meet the standard), and describe how the existing UML notation can be applied to user-centered design.

9.5.1 Incorporating the User-Centered Top Ten

Listed below are the ten most popular user-centered techniques from Section 9.2.2. Next to each technique I have indicated whether the technique is necessary in order to satisfy the ISO 13407 standard or to address other shortcomings of the current UML method.

1. *Informal usability testing.* Required in evaluating designs against user requirements.
2. *User analysis/profiling.* Required as part of understanding and specifying the contexts of use.
3. *Evaluate existing system.* Required as part of understanding and specifying the contexts of use.
4. *Low-fidelity prototyping.* Required in order to produce design solutions and to evaluate designs against requirements.
5. *Expert (heuristic) usability evaluation.* Not absolutely essential, but a cost-effective alternative to usability testing in some cases.
6. *Task identification.* Required as part of understanding and specifying the contexts of use.
7. *Navigation design.* Required in order to produce appropriate design solutions and as part of deliberate user interface design.
8. *Scenarios of use.* Required as part of understanding and specifying the contexts of use.
9. *Set usability requirements.* Required in evaluating designs against user requirements.
10. *Visual interface design.* Required in order to produce appropriate design solutions and as part of deliberate user interface design.

In my view, only expert usability evaluation is optional. However, I have still included it in the user-centered UML method because it is a very effective alternative to usability testing (although it cannot entirely replace it). The next step is to group the techniques into activities, as shown in Table 9.9.

These are also shown in **bold italics** as part of a user-centered UML method in Figure 9.15.

9.5.2 Modifying UML for User-Centered Design

Aside from the new activities previously described, the following changes in the informal UML method are needed for user-centered design.

- *Abstract use cases.* The design process needs to be based on abstract use cases as statements of requirements (see Section 9.4). They will be syntax-free, contain no premature design decisions, and be based entirely on a user's view of an interaction. Constantine and Lockwood's essential use cases meet these conditions and also have a structured format [Constantine and Lockwood 1999].

TABLE 9.9 Top Ten User-Centered Techniques Organized as Activities

Techniques	Activity	Description
Scenarios of use Evaluate existing system	Capture/develop scenarios	Observe and interview users in situ, document scenarios, and take photographs, videos, and copies of user artifacts.
		The scenarios artifact could be just narratives in the simplest case.
User analysis/profiling Task identification Set usability requirements	Contextual analysis	Identify and describe all aspects of context: tasks, users, and environments (see Section 9.4.3).
Navigation design Visual interface design Low-fidelity prototyping	Interface design	Define user's conceptual model; design visual appearance and navigation. Use low-fidelity prototyping to test designs with users.
		The interface design models artifact will consist of state charts (for navigation), low-fidelity prototypes, and other UML models for full description of user interaction (such as activity diagrams).
		In addition, as user interface design progresses, new classes will be identified so that the conceptual class diagram (domain model) is produced in parallel.
Expert usability evaluation Information usability testing	Usability evaluation	Evaluate usability before, during, and after implementation. Some usability testing must be done, but expert usability evaluation can be an effective adjunct.

- *User model.* A user's conceptual model is similar to a domain model, but entirely from a user's perspective (see Section 9.3.3). Identification of objects and relationships from the original UML method needs to produce a user model as its initial deliverable, with a conceptual class diagram being produced during user interface design. All concepts and terminology that will appear in the user interface must be consistent with the user model.

These modifications, in combination with the user-centered activities previously proposed, will shift the focus of UML-based software development from system-centered to user-centered.

9.5 A User-Centered UML Method | 349

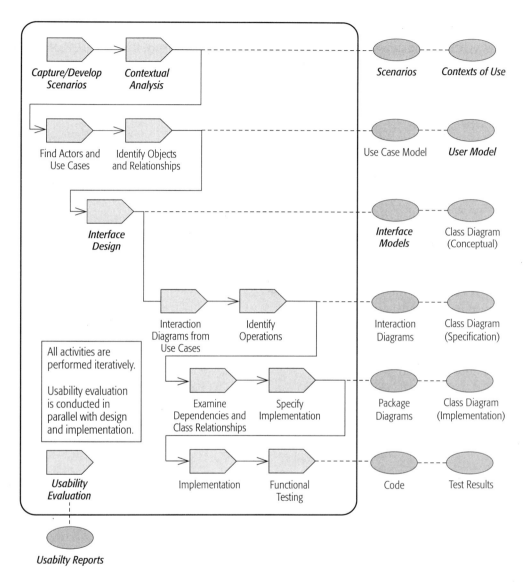

FIGURE 9.15 User-centered UML method

9.5.3 Applying UML Notation to User-Centered Design

The remainder of this section considers how existing UML notation can be used unchanged in user-centered design. One reason for this is that actors may appear where objects (classes) are shown. It is entirely a matter of preference whether actors are shown with the stick-figure representation or as rectangles.

9.5.3.1 Class and Domain Models

Class diagrams document the static relationships between all objects of their defining classes. Their most useful application in the early stages of user interface design is in the production of a user model (user's conceptual model). This is very similar to the domain model described by Fowler [2000], but it is produced entirely from a user's perspective. An example is shown in Figure 9.16.

The user model contains classes that are important from a user's perspective of a system. Some of these classes may not be realized in the detailed design of the system. For example, tickets and boarding cards are important from a user's perspective, but they are simply pieces of paper. They do not necessarily warrant their own classes when the software implementation is considered.

9.5.3.2 Sequence Diagrams

Sequence diagrams have a column showing a "lifeline" for each object involved in the interaction [Fowler 2000]. Early in the design process, the sequence diagrams would reflect the user model and abstract use cases, as shown in Figure 9.17.

9.5.3.3 Collaboration Diagrams

A collaboration diagram contains the same information as a sequence diagram, but it is presented so that the messages making up the interaction annotate the connecting lines (see Figure 9.18). The overall effect makes it more difficult to see the sequence of messages (which are now numbered) but shows the relationships between objects more clearly.

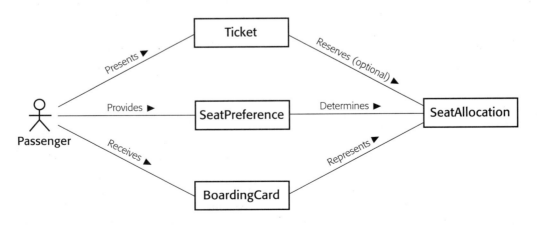

FIGURE 9.16 Simple domain model for passenger check-in (carry-on luggage only)

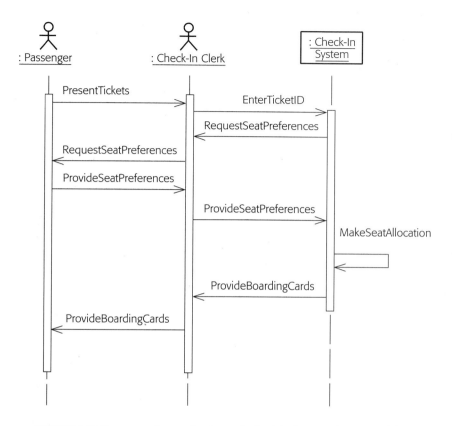

FIGURE 9.17 Sequence diagram for domestic check-in (carry-on luggage only)

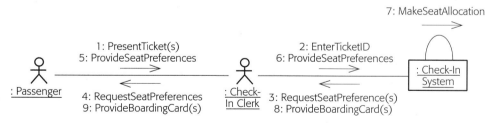

FIGURE 9.18 Collaboration diagram for domestic check-in (carry-on luggage only)

9.5.3.4 State Diagrams

UML's state diagrams are based on state charts used in real-time software engineering [Harel 1987]. Because a user interface can be viewed as a state machine, state diagrams are very appropriate for describing detailed interaction graphically. Perspective is still important, however, so that design decisions will not be taken prematurely. Figure 9.19 shows a simple

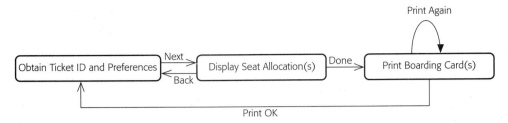

FIGURE 9.19 State diagram for Check-In System class (carry-on luggage only)

state diagram for the check-in example. This diagram has an essential perspective and includes only conceptual objects from the domain model shown in Figure 9.16. A specification perspective would include more detail and would be written with a specific interface design in mind. For example, a specification perspective diagram would show both provisional and final seat allocation activities nested within the appropriate states. While these are not important to the conceptual operation of the user interface, they are very important to its detailed operation. The implementation perspective would add detail relevant to the chosen interface platform (for example, Microsoft Windows, Java AWT, and so on).

9.5.3.5 Activity Diagrams

Activity diagrams combine the features of state charts, flowcharts, and dataflow diagrams (see Yourdon [1989] for descriptions of the latter two types of diagrams). They are activity based, and in their simplest form they resemble a state diagram. However, activity diagrams allow states to be associated with objects by placing states in appropriate columns (called "swimlanes"). Their resemblance to dataflow diagrams comes from the inclusion of an "object flow" notation that connects activities to the objects affected by them. A slightly contrived example is shown in Figure 9.20 (its use is not really warranted in such

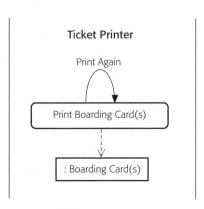

FIGURE 9.20 Simple activity diagram for the Print Boarding Card(s) activity

a simple case). In this example, the Print Boarding Card(s) activity is in the Ticket Printer "lane" and is therefore a state of a Ticket Printer object. The result of the activity is one or more objects of the Boarding Card class.

Because of their structure, activity diagrams are very suitable for modeling workflows.

9.6 Comparisons with Other Use Case-Driven Methods

Attentive readers will recall that use cases were introduced by Ivar Jacobson as part of his Objectory process [Jacobson 1987, Jacobson et al. 1992]. When Jacobson joined Rational Software, Objectory was developed into the Rational Objectory Process and then the Rational Unified Process (RUP).[27]

RUP [Kruchten, 1999] and usage-centered design [Constantine and Lockwood 1999] are software development approaches that describe themselves as use case-driven. Here we briefly compare them with user-centered modifications to the informal UML process, as described in this chapter (UCUML). UCUML is also use case-driven in that abstract use cases describe the desired behavior for the system under design.

9.6.1 Rational Unified Process

RUP is now a proprietary process framework sold by Rational as a Web-based CD-ROM. It is an extremely comprehensive process but does not claim to be user-centered. I have worked briefly with Rational to introduce user-centered design to RUP. Part of this effort was very educational for me, as I had not previously worked with such a large process. I discovered that it is *possible* to do user-centered design with RUP, but that developers would need quite a bit of guidance to be successful. Some of this guidance appears in the new user-centered design concepts document included as part of the most recent edition of the product, RUP 2000 [Rational 2000].

The following list shows some interesting parallels between RUP and UCUML.

- RUP has a deliberate user interface design activity. This is described by Kruchten in Chapter 5.
- User interface design in RUP starts with a "use case storyboard" that describes interactions at a high level (see "Guidelines: Use-Case Storyboard" in [Rational 2000]). These interactions are similar to abstract use cases.
- Primitive boundary classes represent users' conceptual objects as they appear in the user interface. While they are not organized into a single model, they

---

[27] For the history and general approach of this process including details of the Unified Software Development Process (also known as the Unified Process), see [Jacobson et al. 1999].

are the same objects that would appear in the user model suggested for UCUML.
- Contexts of use are established, but across a number of activities and artifacts, as shown in Table 9.10.

The differences between RUP and UCUML are as follows.

- RUP does not distinguish between domain and user models.
- Use cases in RUP are vaguely defined (except for the advice given as part of user interface design). Scenarios are viewed only as instances of use cases.

TABLE 9.10 Contexts of Use in RUP 2000 (from [Rational 2000], used with permission)

Context	RUP Artifact
Environments	High-level: - Business Vision [Section: Customer Environment] - Stakeholder Requests - Vision [Section: User Environment]
Users	High-level: - Business Vision [Section: Customer Profiles] - Stakeholder Requests - Vision [Section: User Profiles]
Roles	High-level: - Business Actor (external users) - Business Worker (internal users) Detailed: - Actor
Tasks	High-level: - Stakeholder Requests - Vision [Section: Product Features] Detailed: - Use-Case Storyboard - Use Case

- Usability evaluation is presented only as part of user interface prototyping. It is not considered to be part of overall system testing.
- RUP is an elaborate and very detailed process for software construction from beginning to end. By contrast, UCUML is a lightweight approach that gives only the general flavor of how *user-centered* software development should be done.

In reality, it is unlikely that an organization would be considering the extremes of a full-blown process such as RUP and a lightweight method such as UCUML. However, usage-centered design might provide a viable compromise for those in search of detailed guidance.

9.6.2 Usage-Centered Design

Usage-centered design [Constantine and Lockwood 1999] is described briefly in Section 9.2.4.5. Unlike RUP, usage-centered design *does* have a user-centered philosophy. Consequently, it has a number of points in common with the other user-centered processes considered in this chapter.

Features common to both usage-centered design and UCUML are as follows.

- *Abstract use cases.* Constantine and Lockwood refer to their particular form of abstract use cases as essential use cases (described in Section 9.4.4).
- *Deliberate user interface design.* Usage-centered design includes an interface content modeling activity that concerns itself with both navigation and content. The implementation modeling activity deals with visual design.
- *Usability evaluation.* Expert evaluations and usability testing are both included in usage-centered design.

The main differences in approach center around scenarios and contexts of use.

- *Scenarios.* Constantine and Lockwood do not value scenarios during analysis and design. They appear to be concerned that scenarios contain too much extraneous information [Constantine and Lockwood 1999, p. 106].
- *Contexts of use.* Usage-centered design does not directly address the issues of contexts of use as presented in the ISO 13407 standard (see Section 9.4.3). Confusingly, Constantine and Lockwood use the term "context" both in the sense that I have used it in this chapter and as the state that the user interface is in at a particular moment of interaction. Contextual inquiry [Beyer and Holtzblatt 1998] is mentioned but is not directly drawn into the method.

However, to be fair to usage-centered design, it is a complete method whereas UCUML is a skeletal approach. In addition, Constantine and Lockwood's description of their method [Constantine and Lockwood 1999] includes a large amount of information and advice on user interface and user-centered design. This provides developers with most of what is necessary to design user-centered systems, if only they can be persuaded to leave the mainstream approaches behind.

9.7 Conclusions

9.7.1 The Benefits

At the beginning of this chapter, I suggested that the benefits resulting from a convergence of UML and user-centered design would be similar to those derived from the widespread adoption of UML itself. Each of the following benefits applies to this convergence.

- *Increased awareness of user-centered issues among developers.* Developers do not set out to create unusable systems. It is naïveté rather than malice that leads to the usability problems with which we are all too familiar. Making user-centered design an integral part of the software development process is probably the most practical way of overcoming the current lack of awareness.
- *Better communication between designers and developers.* This benefit applies as much to user interface designers as it does to system designers. Conflicts frequently arise during development when there are differing goals. A common vision of how scenarios and use cases are captured and developed, a common notation in expressing a variety of design models, and a common understanding of usability evaluation would prevent some of these conflicts.
- *Skills are more readily transferred between projects.* If user-centered design became part of "mainstream" software development for interactive systems, there would be less difficulty in hiring and educating staff. Developers leaving one environment would not need to be retrained for another employer or project using alternative techniques or methods.
- *Improved development support from software tools.* User-centered methods currently have little support through software tools in comparison with UML. Adopting common notations (where possible) and incorporating user-centered techniques into UML would significantly improve this situation.

9.7.2 The Challenges

Still, combining user-centered design with UML raises a number of issues.

- *Lack of skills.* Although the transfer of skills between projects will eventually be an advantage to a unified approach, initially there will be a shortage. This will be particularly true for small projects in which developers will be expected to perform various roles, including those of a usability practitioner.
- *Lack of specialization.* Some members of the HCI community argue that usability and user interface design activities must be performed by specialists. While this is certainly true in complex cases, I have seen projects that would have benefited from *any* application of user-centered principles. In addition, greater awareness of user-centered design is likely to lead to greater involvement of usability practitioners in situations that require it, either in the direct performance of user-centered design activities or as facilitators, mentors, and educators.
- *False security.* Part of the argument over specialization is whether organizations would be deluding themselves that they were being user-centered when they were simply applying a few user-centered techniques badly. However, with disparate goals among members of the development team, pressing deadlines, and unenlightened management, we have pretty much the same result on many projects already. User interface designers fail to persuade developers to implement user-centered designs, contextual analysis is abandoned as having a detrimental effect on schedules, and usability tests are ignored for myriad reasons. Getting the entire development team pulling together in the same direction would reduce the acceptability of user-centered shortsightedness.
- *Lack of aptitude.* To make a long story short, the traditional wisdom is that user-centered design requires people skills, and software development requires engineering skills. We see developers who find it hard to accept that user-centered design is important, and we assume that this occurs because they do not have an aptitude for user-centered design. However, since most developers have not been taught user-centered design as an integral part of software engineering courses, it is hardly surprising that they view user-centered design activities as eccentric and not really relevant to them. Some developers may become very proficient at user-centered design, whereas others may not.
- *Lack of separation.* There is a view that in an ideal world, user-centered design would take place without the possibility of "contamination" from the software development process. Separate team members, tools, and notations would reduce the possibility of implementation concepts "leaking" into the user interface. At best, this argument is unrealistic in comparison with everyday practice.

In most cases, user-centered design is not being done at all, and the user interface concepts *are* the implementation concepts with a few alterations where sufficient complaints have been received from users.

- *Conflicts of interest.* Very few of us have the luxury of being single-minded in purpose. Deadlines, costs, resources, scheduling, and the status quo all conspire to make design decisions much more complex than we would like them to be. As both a developer and a user-centered designer, I frequently find myself having to weigh the usability of the design against the difficulty of its implementation. Is this a bad thing? I think not, for the following reasons:

  - It is a well-informed deliberation. I cannot hide from or overlook important issues in the hope of swaying the decision one way or another.
  - I own the problem. I cannot dismiss one side of the argument or the other just because it falls outside my area of concern.
  - I understand the impact of poor usability. Because I work with users, I empathize with their problems. Since I understand that software does not have to be inherently difficult to use, I have a low tolerance for design decisions that result in poor usability.

Am I uniquely gifted in being able to work both as a usability practitioner and as a developer? I seriously doubt it. All that it requires is an acceptance that users and user-centered design are important to the development of usable software.

9.7.3 The Future

This chapter has not been about introducing a new method for user-centered design that can be placed on the bookshelf and forgotten. I have proposed the convergence of user-centered design with UML—perhaps the most popular development technology ever known to the software industry. Just as UML has become the de facto standard for object-oriented development, UCUML needs to become the de facto standard for interactive systems. This might be achieved in part by the development of an extension of UML in the same way that real-time variations [Douglas 1999] and Web variations [Conallen 2000] of UML have arisen.

User-centered design needs to be adopted and taught as an integral part of interactive software development. It must not continue to be a specialized activity unknown to a large part of the software industry.

Finally, I encourage anyone working in a UML-based interactive development environment to try to incorporate some of the ideas presented here. This needs to be done not only by introducing user-centered techniques but also by trying to make the entire development philosophy user-centered. Please let me know of your successes or failures.

9.8 References

[Berry et al. 1997] D. Berry, S. Isensee, and D. Roberts. Designing for the User with OVID: Bridging User Interface Design and Software Engineering. Found at the IBM Corporation Web site, at *http://www.ibm.com/ibm/hci/guidelines/design/ovida.html.*

[Beyer and Holtzblatt 1998] H. Beyer and K. Holtzblatt. *Contextual Design: Defining Customer-Centered Systems.* San Francisco: Morgan Kaufmann, 1998.

[Booch 1994a] G. Booch. *Object-Oriented Analysis and Design with Applications.* Redwood City, CA: Benjamin/Cummings, 1994.

[Booch 1994b] G. Booch. The Booch Method: Scenarios. *Report on Object-Oriented Analysis and Design,* 1 (3), 1994, 3–6.

[Booch et al. 1999] G. Booch, J. Rumbaugh, and I. Jacobson. *The Unified Modeling Language User Guide.* Reading, MA: Addison-Wesley, 1999.

[Browne 1993] D. Browne. *STUDIO: STructured User-Interface Design for Interaction Optimisation.* New York: Prentice Hall, 1993.

[Carroll 1995] J. M. Carroll, ed. *Scenario-Based Design: Envisioning Work and Technology in System Development.* New York: John Wiley and Sons, 1995.

[Checkland 1981] P. Checkland. *Systems Thinking, Systems Practice.* Chichester: John Wiley and Sons, 1981.

[Checkland and Scholes 1990] P. Checkland and J. Scholes. *Soft Systems Methodology in Practice.* Chichester: John Wiley and Sons, 1990.

[Cockburn 1997a] A. Cockburn. Goals and Use Cases. *JOOP,* 10 (6), 1997, 35–40.

[Cockburn 1997b] A. Cockburn. Using Goal-Based Use Cases. *JOOP,* 10 (7), 1997, 56–62.

[Cockburn and Fowler 1998] A. Cockburn and M. Fowler. Question Time! About Use Cases, *Proceedings of the OOPSLA Conference.* New York: ACM, 1998, 226–243.

[Conallen 2000] J. Conallen. *Building Web Applications with UML.* Reading, MA: Addison-Wesley, 2000.

[Constantine 1994] L. L. Constantine. Essentially Speaking. *Software Development,* 2 (11), 1994, 95–96.

[Constantine 1995] L. L. Constantine. Essential Modeling. *Interactions,* 2 (2), 1995, 34–46.

[Constantine and Lockwood 1999] L. L. Constantine and L. A. D. Lockwood. *Software for Use: A Practical Guide to the Models and Methods of Usage-Centered Design.* New York: ACM Press, 1999.

[Cook and Daniels 1995] S. Cook and J. Daniels. *Designing Object Systems: Object-Oriented Modelling with Syntropy.* New York: Prentice Hall, 1994.

[Cooper 1999] A. Cooper. *The Inmates Are Running the Asylum.* Indianapolis: SAMS Publishing, 1999.

[Davis 1991] A. M. Davis. *Software Requirements Analysis and Specification.* Englewood Cliffs, NJ: Prentice Hall, 1991.

[Douglas 1999] B. P. Douglas. *Real-Time UML: Developing Efficient Objects for Embedded Systems,* 2nd Ed. Reading, MA: Addison-Wesley, 1999.

[Draper and Norman 1986] S. W. Draper and D. Norman, eds. *User Centered System Design.* Hillsdale, NJ: Lawrence Erlbaum Associates, 1986.

[Fleming 1998] J. Fleming. *Web Navigation: Designing the User Experience.* Sebastopol, CA: O'Reilly and Associates, 1998.

[Fowler 1997] M. Fowler. *UML Distilled: Applying the Standard Object Modeling Language.* Reading, MA: Addison-Wesley, 1997.

[Fowler 2000] M. Fowler. *UML Distilled: Applying the Standard Object Modeling Language.* 2nd Ed., Reading, MA: Addison-Wesley, 2000.

[Gould 1997] J. D. Gould. How to Design Usable Systems. In M. Helander, T. K. Landauer, and P. V. Prabhu, eds. *Handbook of Human-Computer Interaction.* 2nd ed., Amsterdam, Netherlands: Elsevier Science/North Holland, 1997.

[Graham 1997] I. Graham. Some Problems with Use Cases . . . and How to Avoid Them. In D. Patel, Y. Sun, and S. Patel, eds. *Oois '96: 1996 International Conference on Object Oriented Information Systems.* London: Springer, 1997, 18–27.

[Graham et al. 1997] I. Graham, B. Henderson-Sellers, and H. Younessi. *The OPEN Process Specification.* Harlow, England: Addison-Wesley, 1997.

[Hackos and Redish 1998] J. T. Hackos and J. C. Redish. *User and Task Analysis for Interface Design.* New York: Wiley and Sons, 1998.

[Harel 1987] D. Harel. Statecharts: A Visual Formalism for Complex Systems. *Science of Computer Programming,* 8 (3), 1987, 231–274.

[ISO 1999] International Standardization Organization. *ISO 13407. Human-Centred Design Processes for Interactive Systems.* Geneva, Switzerland: ISO, 1999.

[Jacobson 1987] I. Jacobson. Object Oriented Development in an Industrial Environment. In *Proceedings of the OOPSLA '87 Conference,* New York: ACM, 1987, 183–191.

[Jacobson 1994a] I. Jacobson. Basic Use-Case Modeling. *Report on Object-Oriented Analysis and Design,* 1 (2), 1994, 15–19.

[Jacobson 1994b] I. Jacobson. Basic Use-Case Modeling (Continued). *Report on Object-Oriented Analysis and Design,* 1 (3), 1994, 7–9.

[Jacobson 1994c] I. Jacobson. Toward Mature Object Technology. *Report on Object-Oriented Analysis and Design,* 1 (1), 1994, 36–39.

[Jacobson 1994d] I. Jacobson. Use Cases and Objects. *Report on Object-Oriented Analysis and Design,* 1 (4), 1994, 8–10.

[Jacobson 1995a] I. Jacobson. The Use-Case Construct in Object-Oriented Software Engineering. In J. M. Carroll, ed. *Scenario-Based Design.* New York: John Wiley and Sons, 1995, 309–336.

[Jacobson 1995b] I. Jacobson. Use Cases in Large-Scale Systems. *Report on Object-Oriented Analysis and Design,* 1 (6), 1995, 9–12.

[Jacobson et al. 1992] I. Jacobson, M. Christerson, P. Jonsson, and G. Övergaard. *Object-Oriented Software Engineering: A Use Case Driven Approach.* Reading, MA: ACM Press, 1992.

[Jacobson et al. 1999] I. Jacobson, G. Booch, and J. Rumbaugh. *The Unified Software Development Process.* Reading, MA: Addison-Wesley, 1999.

[Kreitzberg 1999] C. Kreitzberg. The LUCID Design Framework. Found at the Cognetics Corporation Web site, at *http://www.cognetics.com/lucid/lucid2aoverview.pdf.*

[Kruchten 1999] P. Kruchten. *The Rational Unified Process—An Introduction.* Reading, MA: Addison-Wesley, 1999.

[Mayhew 1992] D. J. Mayhew. *Principles and Guidelines in Software User Interface Design.* Englewood Cliffs, NJ: Prentice Hall, 1992.

[Mayhew 1999] D. J. Mayhew. *The Usability Engineering Lifecycle: A Practitioner's Handbook for User Interface Design.* San Francisco: Morgan Kaufmann, 1999.

[Monk and Howard 1998] A. Monk and S. Howard. Methods & Tools: The Rich Picture. *Interactions,* March and April, 1998, 21–30.

[Nielsen 1993] J. Nielsen. *Usability Engineering.* San Diego: Academic Press, 1993.

[Nielsen 1995] J. Nielsen. Scenarios in Discount Usability Engineering. In J. M. Carroll, ed. *Scenario-Based Design.* New York: John Wiley and Sons, 1995, 59–84.

[Nielsen and Landauer 1993] J. Nielsen and T. K. Landauer. A Mathematical Model of the Finding of Usability Problems. *Proceedings of ACM INTERCHI '93,* (Amsterdam, The Netherlands), New York: ACM, 1993, 206–213.

[Nielsen and Mack 1994] J. Nielsen and R. L. Mack. *Usability Inspection Methods.* New York: John Wiley and Sons, 1994.

[Norman 1986] D. Norman. Cognitive Engineering. In D. Norman and S. W. Draper, eds. *User Centered System Design.* Hillsdale, NJ: Lawrence Erlbaum Associates, 1986, 31–71.

[Olson and Moran 1995] J. Olson and T. Moran. Mapping the Method Muddle: Guidance in Using Methods for User Interface Design. In M. Rudisill, C. Lewis, P. Polson, and T. McKay, eds. *Human-Computer Interface Design: Success Cases, Emerging Methods and Real-World Context.* San Francisco: Morgan Kaufmann, 1995.

[OMG 1999] Object Management Group. *OMG Unified Modeling Language Specification.* Version 1.3, Needham, MA: OMG, 1999. Found at *http://www.omg.org*.

[Pfleeger 1998] S. L. Pfleeger. *Software Engineering: Theory and Practice.* Upper Saddle River, NJ: Prentice Hall, 1998.

[Polya 1990] G. Polya. *How to Solve It: A New Aspect of Mathematical Method.* 2nd Ed., London: Penguin Books, 1990.

[Pressman 1997] R. Pressman. *Software Engineering: A Practitioner's Approach.* 4th Ed., New York: McGraw-Hill, 1997.

[Rational 2000] Rational Software Corporation. *Rational Unified Process 2000.* Cupertino, CA: Rational Software Corporation, 2000.

[Redmond-Pyle and Moore 1995] D. Redmond-Pyle and A. Moore. *Graphical User Interface Design and Evaluation.* London: Prentice Hall, 1995.

[Roberts et al. 1998] D. Roberts, D. Berry, S. Isensee, and J. Mullaly. *Designing for the User with OVID: Bridging User Interface Design and Software Engineering.* Indianapolis: Macmillan Technical Publishing, 1998.

[Rouse 1991] W. B. Rouse. *Design for Success.* New York: John Wiley and Sons, 1991.

[Rumbaugh et al. 1991] J. Rumbaugh, M. Blaha, W. Premerlani, F. Eddy, and W. Lorensen. *Object-Oriented Modeling and Design.* Englewood Cliffs, NJ: Prentice Hall, 1991.

[Rumbaugh et al. 1999] J. Rumbaugh, I. Jacobson, and G. Booch. *The Unified Modeling Language Reference Manual.* Reading, MA: Addison-Wesley, 1999.

[Schneiderman 1998] B. Schneiderman. *Designing the User Interface,* 3rd Ed. Reading, MA: Addison-Wesley, 1998.

[Sommerville 1995] I. Sommerville. *Software Engineering,* 5th Ed. Harlow, England: Addison-Wesley, 1995.

[Tognazzini 1992] B. Tognazzini. *Tog on Interface.* Reading, MA: Addison-Wesley, 1992.

[Wieringa 1998] R. Wieringa. A Survey of Structured and Object-Oriented Software Specification Methods and Techniques. *ACM Computing Surveys,* 30 (4), 1998, 459–528.

[Wirfs-Brock 1993] R. Wirfs-Brock. Designing Scenarios: Making the Case for a Use Case Framework. *Smalltalk Report,* November–December, 1993, 9–20.

[Yourdon 1989] E. Yourdon. *Modern Structure Analysis.* Englewood Cliffs, NJ: Prentice Hall International, 1989.

PART V

Summary

CHAPTER 10

Interactive System Design Using Oo&hci Methods

Mark van Harmelen

Abstract

This chapter presents a characterization of methods that integrate human computer interaction (HCI) design with the earliest stages of the object-oriented software life cycle. This integration addresses a major cause of interactive system failure, namely the poor quality of user support that interactive systems often provide. Thus, the integration contributes to reliable and consistent design methods for effective and usable systems.

Because the integrated methods combine object-oriented modeling with human-computer interaction design, the resulting methods are dubbed oo&hci methods. This chapter contains a motivation for the oo&hci approach, background material on human-computer interaction for object practitioners, and a description of activities and artifacts that can be adopted in oo&hci methods. The latter material provides a unified framework within which to view existing oo&hci methods and to guide further work in the field.

10.1 Introduction

> "So all interactive system design is user interface design?"
> "Yes, but unfortunately it's currently a minority opinion."

The consistent and reliable delivery of usable interactive systems requires that designers address the needs of users at an early and formative stage in the software life cycle. This is more than a matter of good design of the surface features of the user interface after analysis. In order to support users adequately in their day-to-day activities, at least three things need to be designed in concert with each other: user work and activities, the inner or *core* facilities of the interactive system, and the user interface to those facilities. Moreover, because the design of computer systems is an engineering activity, these interrelated design artifacts must be formulated while undertaking any requisite technology and implementation platform motivated trade-offs.

This tripartite engineering view is that of user interface design in the human-computer interaction (HCI) field. The methods that are documented in this book adopt a similar approach as part of early design activities in object-oriented interactive system developments. The result brings users into central consideration for interactive system design, ideally[1] as active partners in the use of the new design methods.

Oo&hci is adopted as a term to describe the integrated approach and allied methods. The integration promoted here is based on commonalities between the fields. First, object models are used as structural descriptions by both software engineers and user interface designers. Second, there is a potentially exploitable commonality between use cases as used by object modelers and task-based descriptions of user behavior as used by user interface designers. These similarities allow for the integration of object modeling and user interface design at both notational and methodological levels.

The oo&hci methods described throughout this book vary considerably, but all of them can be accommodated in a framework that operates according to the following four principles:

1. The intervention of HCI design techniques in early analysis phases to allow up-front use of user-derived design information at the point in the development life cycle at which it has the best effect—that is, when the overall design of the system is being formed.
2. An emphasis on model building and user interface design as the means to establish interactive system scope, functionality, and a concrete user interface.[2]
3. Validation of the developing interactive system design by involving users in the evaluation of a range of prototypes throughout the design process.
4. Iterative redesign on the basis of prototype use and evaluation to converge on an interactive system design that specifies viable, efficient, and usable support for users' task-based behavior.

---

[1] This chapter serves the purpose of providing a framework in which to view the individual methods in this book. The framework also articulates directions for the developing field of integrated methods. Participatory design by users and developers is part of this framework, but is not a component of all methods in this book.

[2] The *concrete user interface* is the surface of the system as presented to the user for interactive purposes. For a GUI (as opposed to any other kind of interface, such as an auditory interface), the *concrete user interface design* includes the layout, the appearance of representations of the objects manipulated by the system, and the interactive behavior at the surface of the system. *Surface* is Norman's [1986] term. Here, "concrete" is used to differentiate the surface from the deeper internal contents of the system (the conceptual-core model in Sections 10.3.1, 10.3.4, and 10.3.5.3), and from abstract specifications of system interactivity (the interaction model in the same sections).

This framework is developed further in Section 10.3. The framework is strongly influenced by accumulated positive experience with HCI design that includes studies of users and their environments, user participation in the design and evaluation of interactive systems, and a view that identifies interactive system design as an integrated treatment of the design of work, core system functionality, interactive capability, and detailed (or *concrete*) design of the user interface of the system. In the HCI field, these four aspects of interactive system design are seen as being so closely interlinked that they cannot be designed effectively in isolation from each other. The same indivisibility permeates oo&hci methods.

The evidence in this book is that the adoption of an integrated oo&hci approach has an extremely positive effect on development projects. The benefits of this approach are that it (a) addresses the fundamental nature of interactive systems—that they are created for use by users; (b) enables specific support for the design of system use, scope, contents, capability, and user interface; and (c) significantly helps reduce the risk that a delivered system is inappropriate for its users.

10.1.1 Problems in Object-Oriented Practice

The motivation for an oo&hci approach is that traditional object-oriented methods have severe problems in properly addressing user concerns. These problems are centered on two issues: first, the suitability of conventional use case modeling as the primary vehicle for conveying user interface concerns, and second, the development of a user interface design during object-oriented design (OOD), separately from and after the performance of the object-oriented analysis (OOA).

Use cases are exceedingly useful for technical activities in the system development life cycle (see, for example, [Kruchten 1995; 1998, pp. 98–100] and [Jacobson et al. 1999, pp. 37–40] for a discussion of the unifying role that use cases can play in development projects). As such, use cases are central to and important in the development of object-oriented software systems. However, this importance should not be taken as evidence that use cases are, on their own, adequate for the design of the scope, the functionality, or the detailed user interface of an interactive system.

Use case modeling practice generally involves the construction of a use case model that, for different kinds of users, simultaneously describes user behavior and system functionality. Alternately, use cases are used as vehicles for requirements capture. There are, however, problems with the use of use cases:

- Modelers express concerns over use case granularity, the roles of primary and secondary actors, and the multiple ways in which they can express their use case models [Collins-Cope 1999].

- The semantics of use case models have not been well specified with regard to extending use cases, extension points, and the extends [OMG 1998] or extend [OMG 1999] stereotyped association.
- Use case models and simple textual use case descriptions are incapable of conveying most of the kinds of design data needed for reliable design of high-quality interactive systems.
- The design of use case models can easily be performed in isolation from users. This can lead to unfounded and inaccurate models, while erroneously giving the impression that user concerns have been adequately addressed.

These problems are compounded by the common sequence of analysis followed by a later and separate user interface design phase. The concomitant disadvantages are that this separation can lead to suboptimal user interfaces that are limited by analysis models, and that the later user interface design can be performed without users, thereby leaving the discovery of usability problems until after the system is delivered. Correcting these problems can be hard if, as often happens, changes need to be made deep inside the system to support modifications at the surface of the system.

This separation of interrelated design concerns (the design of the core of the system and its user interface) appears to be the legacy of systems analysis for batch systems, where the analysis did not need to be concerned with any user interface details. When interactive systems started to be designed, the existing internal analysis approach was retained, and user interface design was treated as a later post-analysis "add on" activity. Mainstream object-oriented analysis and design (OOAD) methods continue to treat interactive system design according to this inappropriate tradition.

10.1.2 Oo&hci Methods

Oo&hci methods all follow in the tradition of using analysis-level object models to specify core system functionality. Where they differ from conventional object-oriented approaches is that they incorporate design techniques[3] that help discover, articulate, and address users' needs. They integrate the use of these techniques with the development of object models and the design of a concrete user interface during analysis. As mentioned, at least three

---

[3] A *design technique* is a constituent part of a method. It consists of a process for design that results in the transformation of its inputs, which carry pertinent design information for use in the process to one or more outputs, which in turn carry further-refined design information. A *method* is similarly defined, except that its outputs are the end results of the entire design process. Something that is a design technique in the context of a larger method may be considered a method in its own right by a particular population of designers. Thus, for example, task modeling is a design technique in any full-fledged oo&hci method but is the method in itself for task analysts.

components are generally of central importance: a description of envisioned user behavior while using the system, a conceptual model of the system, and a concrete user interface description. Many methods use an enhanced use case-based approach or maintain compatibility with use cases, thereby enabling the important link to use case-based development activities in the remainder of the system development life cycle. Beyond these similarities, methods vary in the ways in which they adopt fuller user consideration and greater user involvement in the design process, and the ways in which models of interactive capability are employed in the development of the concrete user interface.

The remainder of this chapter includes a description of the oo&hci approach, including its HCI design antecedents, and the mechanisms for the integration of HCI and object modeling methods. To some extent, this represents my personal view of a state of a developing field and of its directions for growth. It is, however, also an integrative view across the field, and provides a framework in which to view the contributions in this book.

Section 10.2 provides an introduction to the HCI theory and practice that forms the basis for HCI components in current and future oo&hci methods. References to some pertinent parts of the HCI literature appear in this section, which is provided for those who are not familiar with HCI approaches. It discusses user-world phenomena and HCI approaches and methods that apply to interactive system design performed in an oo&hci style. HCI-familiar readers may want to skim or skip this section.

Section 10.3 contains further discussion of oo&hci methods: more about the principles behind the approach, identification of a range of individual design activities that can be combined in an oo&hci method, and the development of a UML model of users' and designers' worlds. This section provides a discussion of the design information, design processes, models, and artifacts[4] required to express user-world phenomena and interactive system designs. Readers who are unfamiliar with object modeling may want to skip over the detail of the object models in the UML diagrams that appear at the end of this section.

Section 10.4 considers some of the issues in the adoption of an oo&hci approach. This includes a discussion of the design and the adoption of custom methods that might be suited to particular design problems, projects, or organizations.

Section 10.5 summarizes and concludes the chapter.

10.2 An HCI View of the Design of Interactive Systems

This section provides HCI background that is relevant to oo&hci methods. The main focus here is on cognitive engineering approaches to modeling of users in terms of their

---

[4] An *artifact* is a product of work; here, it is the product of design. Interactive system design artifacts include different kinds of descriptions and models that are expressed in different notations, each at a particular level of abstraction with a particular degree of formality.

activities and knowledge, and on combining this approach with a broad, modern, user-centered design (user-centered design) approach. Readers who are interested in going beyond the material presented here will find that, besides the references in this section, there is an extensive HCI literature that discusses different approaches to design, different roles and degrees of integration of users throughout the design process, and different ways to evaluate systems from an HCI perspective. Dix et al. [1993], Preece et al. [1994], and Newman and Lamming [1995] provide textbook introductions. The *Handbook of Human-Computer Interaction* [Helander et al. 1997] contains a wealth of information organized by topic.

Much of the concern here is with the *usability* of interactive systems. We will have recourse to understand usability along the lines of the ISO 9241 definition: "Usability is the extent to which a product can be used by specified users to achieve specified goals with effectiveness, efficiency, and satisfaction in a specified context of use" [ISO 1998]. It is important to note that this definition includes high-level issues of system functionality and impact on work and user activities, and low-level issues that are concerned with the ease and efficiency with which users can invoke specific functionality and perform low-level tasks.

Two cautionary notes apply to the following HCI sections. First, readers should note that this treatment of HCI topics does not *concentrate* on attributions to authors who originated or were responsible for specific HCI topics, although there are plenty of first attributions sprinkled through the material. Readers who are interested in this kind of detail should look elsewhere, and I hope any of my HCI colleagues who are keen to see their first attributions will forgive me if I happen to have missed out a reference that is a first attribution in a particular field within HCI. Because of its centrality to this book, I have spent some time trying to record attributions for object-oriented conceptual modeling in Section 10.2.3.1. Second, I have taken a fairly broad view of HCI, and categorized as HCI topics various topics that can also be categorized elsewhere. This is purely a convenience in writing about topics that are important within the HCI field, and that relate to this work. Thus, for example, I have no intent to claim prototyping as an "HCI-only" technique, but I list it as an HCI technique because of its centrality and its applicability within HCI activities. The Dynamic System Development Method (DSDM) is certainly not an HCI method, but it is mentioned in an HCI section because it is, in part, founded on user participation in design, which is another HCI-central theme.

10.2.1 Cognitive Engineering

Cognitive engineering is the activity that considers mental models during interactive system design with the aim of designing systems that are suitable for an envisioned work or other system use situation. Although none of the chapters in this book stresses cognitive engineering as a theoretical framework, they generally incorporate a strong cognitive engineering approach.

Cognitive engineering, as formulated by Norman [1986], relies on cognitive psychology's understanding of human behavior. Cognitive engineering subscribes to the eminently believable notion that human beings use some form of mental model of reality and actions when acting in and negotiating the world. According to Norman, a *mental model* is "the model people have of themselves, others, the environment, and the things with which they interact. People form mental models through experience, training and instruction" [Norman 1988]. People use mental models to formulate goals, to plan tasks to realize goals, and to evaluate if goals have been met.

Since mental models are not directly observable, various forms of mental models have been proposed (for example, see [Schank and Abelson 1977] and contributions in [Gentner and Stevens 1983]). For cognitive engineering, the discovery of the exact form of representation of a mental model is unimportant. Rather, what is important (and possible) is to be able to describe users' mental models in terms of the constructs that the users use in conceptualizing and acting in the world while performing their work, leisure, and other activities. In particular, this can be done for domains involving the use of computer systems. The resultant *conceptual models* are created by designers to describe users' mental models in sufficient detail so as to serve as *adequate* and *useful* models for interactive system design purposes. Discovery of users' mental models at this conceptual model level and development of a system design to take account of existing mental models are clearly important for interactive system design if the user is to be able to easily exploit existing knowledge in the use of a new system, if new work or activities are to be designed, or if the system is to be introduced into the users' world with maximal benefit.

Because the introduction of a new interactive system into a user's world results in changes to that world, and because a mental model is a representation that enables a user to act in the world, changes initiated by system rollout and subsequent use of the system will initiate changes in that user's mental model. The terminology here is that *use of the new system engenders a new or changed mental model*. The goal of cognitive engineering is to design and engender appropriate mental models for work and activity with new systems.

Conceptual models can describe existing user models or anticipated (that is, envisioned) user models.[5] Here, the *existing conceptual model* is best constructed as an "idealization"

---

[5] This distinction between different kinds of conceptual models is not generally well treated in the literature. The naming of the distinction between existing and envisioned conceptual models is new. Some view conceptual models as mappings onto reality or as representations of ideal devices; these approaches do not seem to make useful distinctions between existing and envisioned models.

that ignores particular flawed views in individual mental models[6] while taking into account the way in which users "ideally" conceptualize about their domain. The existing model can be used in design activities, particular in forming an *envisioned conceptual model* for a new system. An envisioned conceptual model describes the mental model that the designers hope that users will acquire after the introduction of the new system, which will be designed according to the designer's ideas of the users' future, enhanced domain behavior with the system. In well-established domains the existing and envisioned models may be the same. The appropriateness of a new conceptual model can be discovered by the use of low-fidelity (low-fi) prototypes, and conceptual models can be iteratively redesigned until they are appropriate for the users' intended use.

Finally, by designing, producing, and delivering a system whose appearance and interactivity express an envisioned conceptual model, the designers hope to engender mental models that are similar to the system-articulated model. As a result, users' actions in the changed domain will be facilitated by their use of their enhanced mental models. However, prototype testing by users is the only way to test the suitability of the conceptual model and the system before implementation effort is expended.

Congruence between models is important; for a computer system user who has already, through experience, formed a mental model of some part of his or her work situation, a new interactive system should exhibit behavior that is congruent with that mental model. For a newcomer to the application area, the interactive system will help engender a mental model, which should itself reflect the world in which the user performs his or her activities. If the system presents itself in a way that is at odds with an existing mental model or engenders an incorrect mental model with respect to some part of the world, then operational difficulties will occur.

In summary, conceptual models, to different degrees, (a) model the reality of the domain as it appears to users in its most complete and cogent interpretation sufficient for their actions and (b) model how the future reality of the domain and/or system can be made to appear to users. When an operationally suitable conceptual model is articulated by the user interface to an interactive system, use of the system will engender a similar mental model in the user—a model that is suitable for effective use of the new system. In the latter aspect, conceptual modeling is cognitive engineering—the design and engendering of mental (cognitive) models.

---

[6] On an individual basis, mental models can be incomplete or incorrect with respect to the domain of endeavor. Cognitive engineering is easier under circumstances in which the user population has already acquired similar, sound mental models that are helpful in existing user activities.

10.2.1.1 Cognitive Engineering and Usability

Exploration of the approach inherent in cognitive engineering reveals some factors that are indicators of usability and that should be taken into account in interactive system design.

Goals are mental model constructs that represent desired or achieved changes in the state of the world. This definition includes goals that are as diverse as changes in human abilities (for example, a goal to learn to write in a way that minimizes the need for subsequent text editing activities) or changes in the physical world (for example, the goal of completing the writing of this chapter). *Interactive systems* are tools that help in the process of goal realization, and goals, therefore, should be important determinants in the design of those interactive systems. A goal may be realized by formulating a plan composed of tasks and then performing those tasks; a *task* is composed of some sequence of one or more subtasks and/or primitive actions that a user may perform in order to try to realize a goal. Sometimes task performance does not achieve a desired goal, and evaluation of the results of task performance against predicted goal states is critical in ensuring goal realization. Because there is often a recognizable isomorphism between goals and tasks, many HCI design methods (and many of the interactive system design methods here) concentrate on tasks rather than goals. For a fuller discussion of issues concerning goals and their realization, see [Card et al. 1983], [Norman 1986], and [Carroll 1991].

Given this framework, there is a cycle (adapted slightly from [Norman 1986]) involved in goal realization:

- Identifying or formulating a goal
- Forming the intention to realize the goal
- Planning what tasks and, ultimately, what actions to perform to try to realize the goal
- Performing those actions
- Perceiving and interpreting the effects of the actions on the world
- Evaluating if the goal has been realized

The individual elements of the cycle need not all be performed in a strict sequence; for example, there are many tasks that rely on continuous feedback between goal evaluation and continued task performance. Norman, and just about every author subsequently writing introductory HCI texts, discusses the implications of this goal realization cycle: users of a computer system need to establish goals, plan and formulate actions, perceive results, and determine if the goals have been realized. The amount of effort that this takes depends on how well the system matches the users' needs. Good matches between the system and the user's mental model, and between the task support offered by the system and the tasks that the user needs to perform in order to realize goals, helps minimize the effort involved in the use of the system. Good matches are direct indicators of system usability[7] and suitability for the user. Besides indicating user benefit, good matches are also indicators of a lack of need for post-implementation modification, cost-effectiveness in use, and marketability on the grounds of usability.

As well as looking for good matches, HCI practitioners often try to minimize the complexity of the task model so that goals can be realized via a minimum number of subgoals and tasks. It is also desirable to offer some degree of flexibility as to the way goals may be realized—for example, by adopting shortcuts for expert users, or by offering other convenient ways of reaching the intended goal states. As with many engineering concerns in HCI design, there may well be trade-off between flexibility and complexity. If a system can offer some flexibility without too much complexity, this is usually a good indicator of usability. [Dix et al. 1993] provides a fuller discussion of such principles of usability.

10.2.1.2 Conceptual Models and Terminology

For the purposes of design, the conceptual models discussed so far need to contain, as a minimum, representations of *referents* (objects referred to or manipulated by users while performing tasks), a structure of referents representing the relationship of referents to each other in the domain, and representations of tasks and the effects of task performance on the domain. Collectively, these items constitute a conceptual model.

However, when representing these concerns in practice, user interface designers often make a pragmatic separation and talk about two models. One is a representation of tasks, called a *task model*. The other is a representation of referents and their structure in the domain. Unfortunately, user interface designers often call the latter model a *conceptual model*. From this point on, as this chapter becomes more concerned with the pragmatics of HCI design, it increasingly uses the latter meaning of conceptual model—that is, as a model of referents and their relationships in the domain.

To differentiate between uses, "conceptual model" is sometimes referred to here as having a broad (the former) and a narrow (the latter) meaning. It is hoped that future treatments will adopt the broad definition of conceptual model. This treatment is made explicit toward the end of this chapter, in Figure 10.19.

---

[7] Usability results from a combination of matches as described above, together with low-level efficiency in the use of the system at a keystroke, layout, and menu-organization level. This interpretation of usability accords with the ISO definition proffered at the beginning of this section.

10.2.2 User-Centered Design and Human-Centered Design

User-centered design is defined by Norman [1986, p. 61] as follows:

- Design that starts "with the needs of the user"
- Design to build a system where "the purpose of the system is to serve the needs of the user"
- Design where the "needs of the user should dominate the needs of the interface, and the needs of the interface should dominate the rest of the system"

These characteristics define user-centered design as a broad and high-level user need based approach, rather than as a method that is composed of specific design techniques. This lack of explicitly mentioned components has led to user-centered design being characterized as "a concept that everyone subscribed to, but for which there seemed to be no definition" [Karat 1977a]. However, there is merit in Norman's definition in that user-centered design can develop over time. This is important (a) over the useful lifetime of the concept as new user-centered design techniques are developed and incorporated into the user-centered design approach, (b) over shorter periods covering the development of user-centered design practices in organizations, and (c) for designing custom user-centered design methods for individual projects, given their particular opportunities for (and constraints on) user-centered design.

In the latter half of the 1980s, many considered user-centered design to consist of the following three design principles proposed by Gould and Lewis [1985] in a paper on design for usability:[8]

- An early focus on users by "bringing the design team into direct contact with potential users," observing the use of similar systems, interviewing potential users, and looking at user work from a task perspective. Here, Gould and Lewis also recommended participatory design (discussed in Section 10.2.7.3) in which "potential users become part of the design team at the very outset when their perspectives can have the most influence" and in which they contribute directly to the design of the system itself.
- Empirical measurement: "actual behavioural measurements of learnability and usability" for a succession of prototypes, from initial low-fidelity prototypes onward. Low-fidelity prototypes are described by Gould and Lewis as "simulations."
- Iterative redesign on the basis of testing and measurement to converge on a usable design solution.

---

[8] A more modern, related reference is Gould [1997].

Unfortunately, in the late 1980s, some of the message was lost in practice, and it was only in the 1990s that the low-fidelity prototyping and participatory design approaches were integrated into mainstream user interface design. As Carroll [1996, pp. 285–286] points out, in North American HCI traditions (as opposed to European HCI traditions), participatory design is not viewed as an inherent part of user-centered design and is often adopted only as a technical solution to problems in HCI design that require participatory design in order to yield better results.

This chapter promotes the alternative view—that participatory design should be a *fundamental* component in a user-centered design approach for interactive system design. Dayton [2000] notes that the participation of users and technical staff tends to produce designs that are grounded in both parties' worlds: user participation brings user-world knowledge and experience to the design process, thereby complementing the tendencies of and needs for developers to perform system design in order to address their own technical concerns. A solution is cooperatively developed by both parties who contribute their own specialist knowledge to the process. The user participation and the consequent grounding in the users' world greatly increase the likelihood[9] of designing usable systems. Without participatory user involvement, there is a strong risk that the system will be grounded only in the world of technical developers, and usability will probably be severely compromised.

A recent user-centered design related definition, ISO Standard 13407, entitled *Human Centered Design Process for Interactive Systems* [ISO 1999], lists four design principles for *human-centered design*:

1. Appropriate allocation of functions between users and system
2. Active involvement of users
3. Iterations of design solutions
4. Interdisciplinary design teams

In this standard the recommended human-centered design cycle includes the following:

- Understanding and specifying the context of use
- Specifying organizational and user requirements
- Producing design prototypes
- Evaluating the design prototypes according to user and organizational requirements to determine how to iterate the design

---

[9] While users have the advantage of specialist user and domain knowledge, they can participate in creating a poor-quality design. Using formative evaluation makes the participatory design process much more likely to produce usable designs. Formative evaluation, discussed in Section 10.2.7.2, is evaluation that contributes information to redesign.

However, it is useful to continue to use the term "user-centered design," because of the openness, flexibility, and spirit of Norman's original definition. Without being overly prescriptive, today's user-centered design might involve a range of activities selected according to method use or project circumstances. These activities include an early focus on users and the satisfaction of user needs (including business needs, because users can operate in a business context), field and contextual studies (field studies may be conventional surveys and interviews or may be of the ethnographic tradition, including contextual investigation [Beyer and Holtzblatt 1998]), task analysis and modeling, conceptual modeling, appropriate allocation of functions to systems and to users (work design as much as interactive system design), users as participatory modelers and designers, scenario-based design, use of a range of prototypes across the design life cycle, cooperative evaluation (or, where appropriate, empirical measurement) of prototypes with usability goals defined by the users themselves [Dumas and Redish 1993], and, of course, iterative design to converge on a solution.

The word "centered" is worthy of comment. In the user-centered design approach as promoted here, the intent is not to make the development of the system a slave to user concerns so that real-world engineering constraints are ignored. In this vein, John Karat subscribes to user-centered design but uses caution with regard to the word "centered" and the amount to which users dominate the design process. He prefers to view design as an "engineering process that involves limited resources and trade-offs" [Karat 1977a, p. 38]. A modern user-centered design approach as defined here acknowledges this engineering nature of design while incorporating the users into the design process as formative, participatory partners to technical designers. This is in diametric opposition to approaches in which users passively supply information to a design team, and later sign off a user interface design that is formulated and presented to them by the team.

10.2.3 Model-Based User Interface Design

Model-based user interface design is a process in which abstract models are formed and then used to develop a concrete user interface design. In this process, the design of an interactive system is first expressed by using models to describe the users' task-based behavior and the proposed system's scope, content, and functionality without concern for user interface detail. The models are then used in the design of a concrete user interface, either in an informal process, or in a series of systematic steps that each add increasing amounts of concrete design information to the developing design. Eventually, the user interface places requirements on the operations to be supplied by the inner system core.

Model-based user interface design is important in the HCI field for three reasons: First, the abstract models can be used as conceptual models (in the broad sense, meaning models of system content and user behavior, see Section 10.2.1.2) in a cognitive engineering approach. Second, it is easy for early concrete user interface ideas to persist in a user interface design. Redesigning a concrete user interface from well-founded abstract models helps avoid the persistence of early suboptimal concrete design ideas. Third, but out of the scope of this book, model-based design is seen by some of the HCI community as a way to automate some of the more mundane aspects of the implementation of a concrete user interface design.

To reiterate, while making a few simplifications, one of the ways in which user interface designers strive to ensure that their systems will meet users' needs and expectations is by adopting a cognitive engineering approach: They design a conceptual model to model the users' understanding and use of the system being designed. Then they use the conceptual model as the basis for the detailed design of the user interface. By doing this, user interface designers attempt to maximize the ability of the delivered system to present a coherent model to the end users, such that this presented model is appropriate for the users' current and future mental models of the domain and their operation of systems within the domain.

Commonly, designers will utilize users' prior knowledge when developing a conceptual model for a new system. This involves understanding the users' knowledge and activities in relation to the things (referents, including existing systems in use) that are currently employed to carry out or support the tasks in question. To gain this understanding there is a requirement for user involvement in the requirements capture and design phases of the system life cycle. Thus, to a user interface designer, the formulation of conceptual models is not an isolated activity; user interface designers do not just sit down and sketch out a conceptual model independently of the world and the end users in the world. In order to ensure that a conceptual model is a suitable basis for the design of the interactive system, the designers must, in some way, involve the users of the system. The involvement of users can vary. At one extreme, they might be thought of as relatively passive information sources, as a resource to be queried by the designers. At another extreme, they may be brought into the development as active partners to help in modeling and design, providing expert knowledge of their activities to complement the technical skills of the designers (see Section 10.2.2 on user-centered design and Section 10.2.7.3 on participatory design). Yet another position, otherwise unexplored in this book, suggests that the users know only about some of their activities. Other activities will have been internalized, thus becoming part of the users' tacit knowledge, and this knowledge can only be revealed by observers who become immersed in the world and the everyday activities of the users.[10] Users are not the only source of conceptual model information. User interface designers also refer to others, for example, business analysts and domain

---

[10] This position is adopted by ethnomethodologists, for example, Suchman, [1987], Button and Dourish [1996], and ethnographers, for example Bowers [1996], working in system design.

experts. Occasionally, for new application domains, the user population will not have been formed at the time a system is designed, and in such a case the user interface designers will have to make do with surrogate users and other sources of conceptual model information.

The process of interactive system and user interface design is not simply a top-down process that proceeds from information that is used to form a conceptual model to a conceptual model, and thence to a concrete user interface design. In most design processes the design of the conceptual model will have been informed in part by concrete design artifacts such as sketches, storyboards, and prototypes, as well as by user reaction to these artifacts. The design process is generally one where concrete user interface design and prototype evaluation inform the design of the conceptual models. Later, when the conceptual model is treated as an analysis-level specification of the core of the interactive system, the user interface design places user interface support requirements on the core-conceptual model; core model objects need to offer operations that support the interaction model. The core-conceptual model and the interaction model are discussed later in Section 10.3; for now the curious might want to glance at Figure 10.3 at the beginning of that section.

Model based–user interface design is discussed in this book as follows: For conceptual models in the narrow sense, see Section 10.2.3.1. Here, object models are of central interest, and a brief history of object-oriented conceptual modeling is supplied. Section 10.2.3.2 provides a discussion on task models which are used to describe existing and envisioned user behavior. The transition from abstract to near-concrete models of interactive systems occupies much of this book; discussion of this topic appears in Section 10.3 and in other chapters. The activity of formulating the lowest-level concrete design decisions—for example, widget choice, layout, and so on—is generally omitted from this book because it is well described in many HCI textbooks. However, the detailed specification of concrete user interfaces is briefly discussed in Section 10.2.4.

10.2.3.1 Content Models: Object-Oriented Conceptual Models

Conceptual models that describe the content of interactive systems can be expressed in a variety of ways; for example, using frame-based models, entity-relationship models, or object models. Here we concentrate on object models. In these user referents are represented as objects, types, or classes and the relationships between and composition of referents are depicted by links or associations. Depending on the notational sophistication of the modeler, these *object-oriented conceptual models* might be represented in an informal object diagram, or in a more formally expressed object or class diagram that is constructed according to some language or set of conventions.

The objects depicted in a conceptual model of a computer system are limited to those referents that will be manipulated inside the system as a result of user interaction, independently of the user interface concerns. An object-oriented conceptual model of an interactive system can easily and usefully be thought of as an analysis-level depiction of the contents of the system, albeit a depiction that is composed of user-perceivable, task-relevant objects and their interrelationships.

Besides gaining an understanding of the users' world in the ways discussed in the preceding section, user interface designers can provide some of the contents of a conceptual model through the use of a user interface metaphor (see [Neale and Carroll 1997] and [Erikson 1990]). A *user interface metaphor* allows users to apply their existing knowledge of the world to the operation of a user interface. The adoption of an office metaphor by the designers of the Xerox Star [Smith et al. 1982] allowed users to apply their existing knowledge of offices to the operation of a computer desktop, including, for example, putting related documents into a single folder. Designers need to take into account the limitations of metaphors to avoid engendering expectations of undeliverable system capability; Norman [1986] discusses problems in the choice of appropriate metaphors.

An *object-oriented user interface* (OOUI) is one where a conceptual model is made explicit at the user interface. The term is *most often* applied to graphical user interfaces in which pictures represent parts of the conceptual model, users interact with the representations, and where a metaphor is likely to be employed to help users understand and interact with the system. In a book on the design of object-oriented user interfaces, Collins [1995] defines conceptual models (in the broad sense) as containing a content model, a task model, and a metaphor. The approach outlined here is different: A metaphor is not in itself a constituent of the broader conceptual model; the metaphor affects the choice of the objects and their relationships in a conceptual model.[11] The latter approach still allows for the design of object-oriented user interfaces as defined above. In another sense, an object-oriented user interface is simply a user interface that articulates an object-oriented content model, and in this latter sense all of this book is about the design of object-oriented user interfaces.

The use of object models to express conceptual models in the HCI field has a long but poorly documented history. Simula [Dahl and Nygaard 1966] was used to simulate physical systems; this might be claimed as the first use of an object-oriented conceptual model, but the claim is tenuous, because the simulation designers could not really be said to be acting in any strongly identifiable cognitive engineering sense. There was a stronger

---

[11] This may seem like splitting hairs, because the whole edifice of our endeavor is built on models that claim only adequacy and sufficiency for interactive system design (see Newell and Simon [1972, p. 13] for a short treatment of sufficiency). However, by excluding metaphors from the cognitive model, we simultaneously follow well-established paths in cognitive psychology and achieve adequacy and sufficiency while applying Occam's Razor to settle on a simple theory.

cognitive emphasis in early Smalltalk-based work at Xerox PARC; the designers focused on what was important to the users of those systems [Robson 2000].

The Smalltalk perspective was undoubtedly one of the influences on the method that was used to design the Xerox Star. The Star user interface design method was defined in *A Methodology for User Interface Design* [Irby et al. 1977]. Unfortunately, this report remains Xerox confidential, but it is clear that the report explicitly promoted the idea of an object-oriented conceptual model that was developed within a framework of task analysis. At that time, the model was referred to more as a mental model, but because it was a model formed by a designer, it is clearly a conceptual model.[12] Sources which throw light on the contents of the Star's design method and its object-oriented conceptual model are as follows.

- Part of the report is quoted in a paper [Smith et al. 1982] describing the design of the Star's user interface. Parts of that quote, with my added words in square brackets, are:

  > The descriptions of input and output [for tasks in a task model] should include an analysis of various objects, or individual type of information entity, employed by the user . . .
  > The purpose of task analysis is to simplify the remaining stages in user interface design. The current task description, with its breakdown of the information objects and methods presently employed, offers a starting point for the definition of a set of objects and methods to be provided by the computer system. The idea behind this phase of design is to build up a new task environment for the user, in which he can work to accomplish the same goals as before, surrounded now by a different set of objects, and employing new methods. [Irby et al. 1977] in [Smith et al. 1982]

- A paper on user testing in the Star project [Bewley et al. 1983] stresses that this design approach draws on cognitive psychology and includes the principle that "There should be an explicit users' model of the system and it should be familiar (drawing on objects and activities the user already works with) and consistent."
- William Newman [2000], one of the authors of the Star method, points to incorporation of some report material from page 445 onwards in Newman and

---

[12] In fact, the distinction between mental models (models in the users' heads) and conceptual models (designer-created models of mental models) only seems to become current in the HCI field later on, in the period 1983–1986.

Sproull's textbook, *Interactive System Design* [Newman and Sproull 1979].[13] As in the report, the discussion is phrased in terms of mental models,[14] but again the authors are writing about conceptual models. Objects are clearly identified as model constituents.

Besides being published in the Star user interface paper and in Newman and Sproull's book, the idea of an object-oriented conceptual model was spread in short courses. In the United Kingdom, for example, the government-sponsored Alvey Project (the U.K.'s fifth-generation project) spread the ideas by means of short courses from Computer Graphics Consultants [CGC 1982] and BetaChi (at that time, William Newman's consultancy).

Developments in the 1990s included short courses and pre-conference tutorials that promoted object-oriented conceptual models and allied modeling methods: [van Harmelen and Wills 1991] and [van Harmelen 1994b] were only two of these. Other courses and tutorial presenters included Larry Constantine and Lucy Lockwood, John Carroll and Mary Beth Rosson, Tom Dayton and colleagues, and Dave Roberts and colleagues.

Style guides that incorporated the notion of object models as conceptual models started to appear—notably, IBM's Common User Access (CUA) project [IBM 1991] and the later, multiorganization OpenDoc Project. CUA drew on diverse sources; the chain of derivation includes both Norman's [1986] work on models and the Macintosh user interface, which was itself derived from the Star design. CUA and Apple ideas (the latter via Dave Curbow) fed into Taligent, and then to OpenDoc. Members of the CUA team included Dave Roberts (the team leader) and Dick Berry, both of whom went on to develop OVID [Roberts et al. 1998] with others. Theo Mandel, the CUA evangelist, wrote a book on user interface design [Mandel 1997] that incorporated CUA conceptual model ideas. Dave Collins, who worked on a team allied with CUA, produced a book [Collins 1995] on the related topic of object-oriented user interfaces. In that book, Collins's notion of conceptual models included content, task, and metaphor components. John Artim, the author of Chapter 4 in this volume, was a CUA reviewer. CUA influenced OpenDoc and the later 1995 Windows Style Guide.

Methods that were developed and published in the 1990s included STUDIO [Browne 1993], Idiom [van Harmelen 1994a], Point-of-View Analysis, which was developed from ideas in [Robertson et al. 1994], GUIDE [Redmond-Pyle and Moore 1995], the LUCID Framework [Kreitzberg 1999], OVID [Roberts et al. 1998], The Bridge [Dayton et al.

---

[13] In this context, Newman writes "We didn't, for our sins, give credit to the Irby report because it wasn't publicly available" [Newman 2000].

[14] Newman and Sproull [1979] call mental models "users' models."

1998] and the Software for Use method [Constantine and Lockwood 1999]. Finally, there are the methods presented in this book.[15]

Early object-oriented conceptual models used ad hoc notations. In the late 1990s, the use of industry standard languages grew and conceptual models were expressed in commonly adopted modeling languages; for example, in OVID [Roberts et al. 1998], the conceptual model[16] was expressed in OMT [Rumbaugh et al. 1991]. Today, most methods (including OVID) use UML [OMG 1999], sometimes with extensions. Kovacevic [1999] discusses the use of UML in model-based interactive system design.

Four pre-conference workshops have helped gather the international community currently working in this area. The first and most influential of these [van Harmelen et al. 1997] was held before the ACM CHI Conference in 1977. The basic oo&hci framework, developed further in Section 10.3, was laid down during and after that workshop. The next two workshops, prior to the CHI98 and ECOOP'99 conferences, are respectively documented in [Artim et al. 1999] and [Nunes et al. 1999]. The most recent workshop, held in conjunction with the UML 2000 conference, is currently undocumented.

10.2.3.2 Task Models

The (narrow sense) conceptual model is complemented with a *task model*. In providing a task model, user interface designers are interested in specifying and understanding the relationships of tasks to each other when using the proposed system. Among other things, designers consider what tasks can be performed to realize the goals of larger tasks, the ordering of tasks, the centrality of tasks to the application area, the frequency of different tasks, and the referents used by the user while performing particular tasks. There is a broad variety of different types of task analysis; some methods concentrate largely on the tasks alone, while others incorporate cognitive aspects of the user. For overviews of task analysis, see [Daiper 1989, Johnson 1992, Hackos and Reddish 1998].

Task modeling generally has the following activities: observation and interview, analysis, and the actual construction of task models. To some extent, these activities may be interleaved. The tasks that are currently performed by users or domain workers are modeled in an *existing task model*. This is generally the basis from which future work activities and future interactive system use are designed. The resultant user tasks are expressed in an *envisioned task model*. Some of the challenge in producing a good user

---

[15] The references cited here are generally the first published references found, but obviously the development for all of these sources started earlier. For example, the first version of Idiom was developed in 1991 and 1992, but not published until 1994, and The Bridge was designed in early 1994 but was not published until 1998.

[16] Conceptual models are called "designers' models" in OVID.

interface is to support users in the performance of their current task set while providing new ways in which some of the current human workload can be off-loaded onto the computer system. In this way, user interface design is work and activity design.

Task models do have some problematic qualities. First, they can be very time-consuming to produce, especially if complex interactions with systems are developed in full detail. Furthermore, they take a restricted view of human-computer interaction that ignores the wider social setting in which computer use takes place. Ethnographic participant-observation field studies, such as [Heath and Luff 1991] and [Bowers et al. 1995], have consistently drawn attention to the fact that the wider social setting is a very important aspect of human-computer interaction. However, these factors do not discount the utility of task models; task modeling can form an important part of the analysis of work and subsequent work (re)design. In this, it remains useful to attempt to take a wider view of users within their work settings.

One or more tasks can be illustrated in a *scenario,* which is a description of task execution by particular users. Scenarios are discussed in the next section.

10.2.4 System Visualization and Design Using Scenarios

Scenarios are descriptions of actual or potential system use. They may be textual narratives, as in *user-interaction scenarios,* that describe the context of system use; users' motivations, goals, and actions, reasons for those actions, and system responses. More generally, scenarios may be expressed in forms other than narrative text, including structural text, pictorial storyboards, video mock-ups, and prototypes that are driven by a script describing a particular execution path. They may be expressed with varying amounts of detail. (These definitions echo Carroll's [1995, p. 3] definitions.)

Although scenarios might be thought of as illustrations of system use, as, for example, provided by use case instances, modern scenario-based design has other concerns, such as an exploration and development of the use and functionality of systems during the design process. Mack characterizes discussions of scenarios by various authors in [Carroll 1995][17] as having a "deeper and wide-ranging role, where scenarios become the functional specifications, and the driving force for design" [Mack 1995, p. 364]. In the

---

[17] The current emphasis on scenarios, see [Carroll 1995], is not itself an expression of a new phenomenon in user interface design. For example, a comprehensive survey of scenario technology was produced by MCC in the mid-eighties, and there have been many reports on the use of scenarios in the intervening years. As only one example, [van Harmelen, 1989] discussed scenarios, prototyping, and some limited participatory design in the context of exploratory user interface design. What is currently happening is that scenarios are being brought further into the mainstream of HCI design as formative influences on interactive system design (see [Carroll 2000]).

latter sense, part of the process of design with scenarios is an alternation between the development of the scenarios and reflection on the contents of the scenarios and the developing design as articulated by the scenarios [Carroll 1999].

There are problems to be solved regarding the use of scenarios. First, as noted by Nardi [1995], there may be problems with data quality. Here, Nardi notes that participatory approaches to scenario generation, in, for example, [Muller et al. 1995] and ethnographically generated contextual data in, for example, [Kyng 1995] are contenders for the solution to the data quality problem. Second, scenario coverage is also a problem. As yet, we do not have the experience or the means to be able to identify a set of scenarios for a "sufficiently full" exploration and articulation of system functionality, let alone methods for systematically producing such a set of scenarios. Third, scenario practice is intimately concerned with representations of concrete situations; unfortunately, this may lead to the problems that result from dealing with concrete designs too early in the life cycle, in that they may overly influence the final concrete design with inappropriate design features.[18]

However, these problems do not prevent the effective use of scenarios. If they are used with judgment and generated, critiqued, and improved with user participation, they are a valuable tool for the formative exploration of use and functionality. As such they are indispensable in interactive system design.

10.2.5 Describing Concrete User Interface Designs

A *concrete*[19] *user interface design* is a description or specification of the appearance and interactive behavior of the physical user interface as it is perceived and used by the system's users. For an interface that is to be implemented in a windowed GUI environment, the specification might include window types, contents and layouts, navigation between windows, the static and dynamic depiction of core application objects, menus and other means of command invocation, feedback during and after command invocation, and so on. Different kinds of user interface implementation technologies (for example, speech, GUI, and WAP technologies) will have different requirements for concrete user interface specification. The concrete user interface design should articulate the conceptual and task models in terms of the presentation and interactive behavior of the system. *Concrete user interface design* is the process of producing the concrete user interface.

---

[18] This problem, discussed elsewhere in this chapter, is endemic in user interface design. Inevitably, there is a tension between the needs of system visualization and the needs of unconstrained design solutions based on abstract models; progress is needed in finding systematic ways of resolving this conflict. For now, user evaluation of prototypes is the primary way of ensuring that early suboptimal concrete design solutions do not persist in the later concrete user interface design.

[19] "Concrete" as opposed to "abstract" (see Section 10.3 for the role of abstraction in oo&hci).

Concrete user interface designs can be specified using a range of media that includes textual descriptions, sketches, and prototypes. Sketches and prototypes form a continuum; a sketch can be used as a form of prototype as users and designers point at and pretend to use it, discussing the effects of the actions that they are acting out. Usefully, for an integrated approach involving prototyping, there is a fair amount of overlap between user interface design artifacts as specifications and as prototypes.

Some media are better at conveying different parts of the interface design than others. In particular, there are problems in the rendition of the dynamic aspects of a concrete user interface using nondynamic media and, for detailed concrete user interface design, in depicting a user interface using a prototyping medium that employs a different platform or a different look-and-feel to the final implementation platform. Generally, though, despite these problems, prototypes are useful as descriptions to be explored later by development staff who are designing and producing the implementation.

Most introductory books on HCI design contain information about the process of concrete user interface design and the aspects of the concrete user interface design that need to be specified. Consequently, this topic is often only dealt with in a cursory way in this book.

10.2.6 The Process of Interactive System Design

The process of user interface design can be characterized at both macro and micro levels. At the macro level, the process is one of iterative design, as shown in Figure 10.1. At the micro level, the process is characterized by multiple sources of design information,

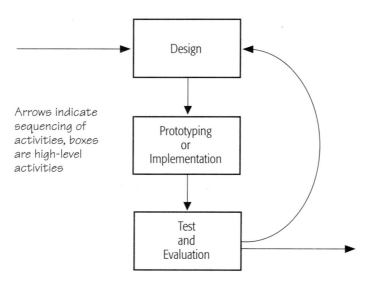

FIGURE 10.1 Interactive system design as an iterative process

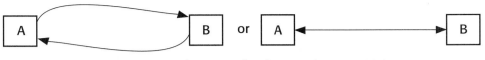

FIGURE 10.2 Information flows between mutually informing design processes

design activities that inform each other, and opportunistic design. *Informing* is the process in which the performance of one design activity creates design information that can be used in a second design activity. Frequently, design activities are *mutually informing* [Henderson 1991]. Figure 10.2 illustrates mutually informing activities A and B. Performance of A generates design information that is used in the subsequent performance of B, and performance of B generates design information that is used to further A. *Opportunistic design* occurs when a designer undertakes a design activity as soon as he or she perceives the opportunity to do so, often on the basis of newly acquired or generated design knowledge.

10.2.7 Ensuring Design Quality

Since the mid-1980s, HCI theorists and practitioners have seen user involvement in design projects as a primary determinant of successful systems that support their users' activities and work. Two kinds of user involvement are particularly important: (a) involvement in the use and evaluation of prototypes throughout the development of the design and (b) involvement in participatory design of the interactive system by users who apply their knowledge to the design problem together with the technical partners and other stakeholders. Here, evaluation prevents design errors from being transmitted to later design and implementation phases, and participatory design seeks to avoid potential errors in the first place by adding user knowledge and experience to the design process. Both of these topics are closely bound to the design and use of prototypes. Consequently all three topics are discussed in the next three sections.

10.2.7.1 Prototyping

The use and evaluation of prototypes by users are important ways in which user interface designers capture users' knowledge and gain users' reactions to the developing interactive system design, either at a high level in terms of gross functionality or in respect to the detail of the concrete user interface. Importantly, prototyping helps overcome a problem in the design of interactive systems: that there is no way in which designers can systematically predict the effects of the introduction of new systems or improved systems on users' work and/or activities [Button and Dourish 1996]. In this, prototyping helps as a way of imagining and evaluating the future. If users are asked to try to carry out their work using prototypes, it is possible to identify potential problems in future use, even at very early stages of design. These emergent problems can in turn direct further study and problem-solving work to feed into later design iterations. Prototyping, evaluation, study, and iterative design are all linked in a dynamic process.

Prototypes can be categorized along one or more of the following dimensions. On the basis of functional coverage, there are full, horizontal, and vertical prototypes [Floyd 1984] as well as scenario prototypes [van Harmelen 1989]. On the basis of the prototype development life cycle, there are throwaway, incremental, and evolutionary prototypes [Dix et al. 1993]. On the basis of the reproductive capability of the prototyping medium, there are low- and high-fidelity prototypes; see, for example, [Virzi et al. 1996]. See also sections 8.1.4, 8.2.2.1, and 8.2.31 for more categorizations of prototypes.

Fidelity, as discussed later in this section, determines what a prototype is used for and, frequently, when it is to be used. Malleability is another important property of prototypes. Malleability determines how easily and quickly a given prototype can be modified in response to detection of a problem. With a sufficiently malleable prototyping medium, low-cost prototypes can be constructed in the conceptual and task design phase, and prototype evaluation sessions can become participatory design sessions in which suggested improvements are tried out almost immediately.

A further categorization of prototypes is between abstract and concrete prototypes, although these are actually end-points on a continuum of prototypes that range from fully abstract to fully concrete. Abstract prototypes are used to evaluate the conceptual design of the system without consideration of the user interface. They consist of an envisioned task model and a (narrow sense) conceptual model. Prototype evaluation consists of exercising the task model against the conceptual model to ensure that the tasks and the system content are a suitable basis for further design. Part 2 of the Bridge [Dayton et al. 1998] includes evaluations of abstract prototypes. In the usage-centered design method, Constantine and Lockwood [1999] advocate a slightly less abstract kind of prototype (in that it includes consideration of interaction spaces for task execution), that they also call an abstract prototype. In this chapter, "abstract prototype" is used in the former general sense, rather than as a reference to the usage-centered designs abstract prototype. Concrete prototypes embody concrete design decisions; they may be used to test and evaluate both the (broad sense) conceptual model and whatever aspects of the concrete user interface design that are conveyed by the prototypes. Abstract prototypes can only be low-fidelity prototypes, but concrete prototypes can be positioned anywhere on a low- to high-fidelity continuum.

Low-fidelity or *low-fi prototypes,* some of which are *paper prototypes,* are constructed using low-technology materials such as pencils, marker pens, paper, cardboard, plastic, stickies, glue, and adhesive tape. "Low-fi prototyping" is a more encompassing term than "paper prototyping," because it implies a wider choice of materials. However, the lines of demarcation are often blurred. Low-fi prototypes are particularly well suited to low-cost rapid design and evaluation cycles. A desirable side effect of the use of low-technology materials is that they tend to focus the users' attention on the suitability of the prototype's content and functionality rather than its appearance or its look-and-feel. As such, low-fi prototypes are well suited to use during the early stages of system design, when it is more appropriate for the prototype to provide a test of the conceptual and task models independent of a particular concrete user interface design. The Web is a good source of instructional information about paper prototyping; a metasearch engine such as Google or Metacrawler helps in finding this information. Later, when the detailed concrete user interface design is being considered, it is more appropriate to use *high-fidelity* or *high-fi prototypes,* which display a greater fidelity to the end application and which are better suited to evaluation of presentational and interactional details. High-fi prototypes have been considered slow and expensive to create. With appropriate implementation technology, they can be created rapidly. However, their construction requires technical experience and technical skills, whereas paper prototypes can be created by users.[20]

As discussed in Section 10.2.5, sketches can be used as very simple prototypes. Sketches showing the effects of sequences of interactions can be combined in a *storyboard*. In a storyboard, the sequence of sketches helps bring the more static renditions of the individual sketches to life as kind of a scenario prototype.

10.2.7.2 Testing and Evaluation

Usability testing, typically performed when a sample of users try out a prototype, provides information on the suitability of the prototype for the sample population. The tests may be formal and quantitative tests, or less formal tests in which users contribute qualitative information about their experience with the prototype. Both of these kinds of usability tests can reveal errors in designers' assumptions about the users' world as well as design problems related to the scope, contents, functionality, and operation of the prototype. The general procedure is to test a prototype, evaluating its use in one way or another (this is where the greatest amount of divergence in the evaluation methods occurs), and then, if required, the designers redesign the system on the basis of the evaluation, repeating the

---

[20] As an example of the way in which technology has changed the use of high-fi prototypes, I have audited a DSDM project in which the JAD session participants (including users, technical staff, and a prototyper) successfully designed functional prototypes that were implemented in the JAD sessions by the prototyper using Borland's Delphi. (DSDM and JAD are discussed in Section 10.2.7.3.) However, despite such successes, there are dangers in substituting rapidly constructed high-fi prototypes for low-fi prototypes, such as loss of the low-fi emphasis on issues of content and functionality independent of particular user interface detail, and the loss of user ownership of and user ability to manipulate the prototyping technology by themselves.

cycle as often as necessary. Redesign on the basis of evaluation means that the evaluation is *formative* rather than *summative*. Summative evaluation takes place at the end of implementation—as in, for example, user acceptance testing. For a general guide to usability, testing, and evaluation techniques, see [Dumas and Redish 1993, Rubin 1994, Mayhew 1999].

Besides being able to detect design errors of a broad nature, testing and evaluation guard against a pervasive problem in user interface design—namely, the problem of user interface designers unknowingly introducing design errors into an interactive system by designing it according to their own preferences and biases. The resulting danger is the design of systems that are optimal for use by the designers but not by end users. This is not a motivation to dismiss user interface design but rather, at the very least, to use users as a quality assurance check on the developing design—otherwise, there is a severe danger that the delivered system will not satisfy its users' needs.

The way and extent to which users are involved in evaluating the developing design is very much an issue of when the evaluation is performed in the project life cycle and of the available resources and evaluation technologies. What is beyond doubt is the very definite need to test the developing design with a sample of the system's future users; in general, using any of the available usability techniques is deemed better than using none at all. It is wise to adopt the usability engineer's adage, "test early and often" [Dumas and Redish 1993]. This adage can be mutated a little to interpret "early" as meaning "during the development of the conceptual design and task models." Later, users can evaluate parts of the concrete user interface as they are designed.

10.2.7.3 Participatory Modeling and Participatory Design

Participatory design originated in Scandinavia in the 1970s in the tradition of trade unionism and workplace democracy (see [Clement and Besselaar 1993] for a historical review of this approach). Participatory design is now widely acknowledged and, at least to some extent, practiced throughout Europe and the United States [Schuler and Namioka 1993, Carroll 1996]. As a basic definition, *participatory design* represents an approach in which future users of a system are involved with the designers of that system during the design process. Users and designers both bring their knowledge to bear on the design problem so that the resulting design satisfies both parties. The kinds of concerns that users and developers might bring to participatory design meetings are illustrated by two examples: In the first example, users needed to undertake a particular task in a particular way: a global fleet-hire company acquired such large consignments of vehicles that it was economically infeasible for a user to repeatedly enter common details for each of the acquisitions, and a requirement emerged to be able to treat the identical information for similar vehicles in one transaction. In another example, developers had specific technical concerns: developers in an insurance company were insistent that, for update performance and overall transaction processing throughput reasons, information from different database tables in a legacy database should not be mixed in the same transaction windows in a new front-end. These are indicative of the concerns that stakeholders may bring to participatory design meetings, and that can be dealt with, after mutual learning, by the meetings' members.

Users can be involved in the design of a user interface in various ways, starting with the development of conceptual and task models and continuing with involvement in the detailed design of the concrete user interface and in decisions on how it is to be realized on a given implementation platform in terms of presentation, interaction, and system feedback in response to user interaction. Details of precisely how the user is involved in the design process vary according to different methods employed; see, for example, contributions in [Schuler and Namioka 1993]. However, most researchers argue for an integration of users throughout the entire design process—not only for participatory design purposes but also to the extent of focusing on the benefits of mutual learning between users and designers and on the possibilities of developing techniques and methods that support the participatory design process [Greenbaum and Kyng 1991]. Participatory ANalysis, Design, and Assessment (PANDA) methods involve users in the three important participatory activities that this acronym represents. Muller et al. [1997] list 61 different PANDA methods.

This chapter argues for the systematic integration of users throughout the design process using a participatory analysis, design, and assessment approach. Within this approach, the following aspects are currently emphasized: designing and building models of interactive systems, designing the presentational and interactive aspects of a system, and formatively evaluating prototypes (as discussed in Section 10.2.7.2). There is some overlap between these. In particular, formative evaluation is an essential component of successful participatory design.

Problems that can occur in participatory approaches are that users can be a scarce resource, and can become habituated to a particular design. Control must be dealt with carefully. High-level issues include how the session is run and facilitated; by whom and for what purposes. Pragmatic concerns include who is talking or has the ability to modify the design artifacts at a given point in time, and fairness in gathering input and design ideas from all participants. A perceptive, sympathetic, and agenda-free facilitator is a great help.

Participatory modeling can be thought of as the design process up until the stage in which existing and envisioned conceptual and task models are defined. The task of participatory modeling is based largely around users providing and structuring information about their current work or activities. Several methods are available for such purposes, including various field study techniques, workshops, and metaphor/card games; see [Muller et al. 1997]. The first step is to gain a detailed understanding of the present situation. Once this understanding has been achieved, or in parallel with this process, users can be involved in helping to design envisioned conceptual and task models, generally by analyzing models of current work and looking at how current practice may be supported, improved, and possibly automated. Inevitably, this involves teaching users some modeling techniques and notations that are accessible and usable without technical knowledge. Low-fi abstract prototypes can be used to test the models in an iterative design cycle.

Participatory user interface design is the process of transforming the envisioned models and user knowledge into a design for the concrete user interface to a new system. The process involves iterative prototyping and redesign to at least a final design, if not a final implementation.[21] At the beginning of the process, user interface requirements are identified. As a second activity, users can be involved in discussions of possible technological and implementational strategies with the developers. Because both the users and the usability of the system are affected by technology and implementation strategies, users need to have an active and contributory role in decisions about these matters [Kensing and Monk-Madsen 1993]. As a third activity, the user interface is designed, rapidly prototyped, tested, evaluated, and redesigned as needed, and the envisioned task and conceptual models may also be redesigned if needed with user participation in these activities. User involvement may continue into more detailed issues of design in which users are incorporated into the design team [Simonsen 1994] and become involved in prototyping and testing [Bødker and Gronbaek 1991].

The Bridge [Dayton et al. 1998] is an important participatory design method for interactive system design. The Bridge is for use in three- to five-day workshops by small, mixed groups of users and developers. It supplies a method that provides a foundation for design that is based in both the developers' and users' worlds, thus merging the specialist knowledge of both parties.[22] As such, the method provides a systematic way of eliciting and refining user needs and requirements that may not otherwise be apparent to developers. The Bridge can be situated within a larger method with more conventional requirements analysis and conventional back-end development activities. The Bridge consists of three stages, called Parts, involving cycles of refinement and usability testing.

Part 1 is aimed at eliciting and refining user tasks. As with most task modeling approaches, a set of existing tasks is identified and then, unusually, a "blue-sky" idealized set of tasks is developed. Finally, again in a conventional task modeling fashion, a set of envisioned tasks is identified for further development.

Part 2 consists of finding and refining a set of objects that are important for the execution of the individual tasks in the envisioned task set. The process of object identification

---

[21] This is one of the ways in which users can contribute to the project over the development life cycle. For other ways, see, for example, those in [DSDM 1995, Stapleton 1997].

[22] The Bridge is highly relevant to oo&hci methods. Besides finding the method [Dayton et al. 1998] in hard-copy versions of [Wood 1998], readers may find a soft copy of that book at http://www.itknowledge.com.

involves finding attributes and operations for each of the identified objects as well as information about containment in other objects. Information about operations on the objects is important because the operations become user commands during Part 3.

Together, Parts 1 and 2 comprise participatory modeling of the tasks and the core objects (inner application objects or entity objects) in the anticipated system. Interestingly, in its participatory modeling approach, The Bridge takes much of its user-centricity from an initial consideration of user tasks (as opposed to an initial consideration of important objects). This constrains the objects considered in Parts 2 and 3 to just those objects that are relevant to task execution. The usability tests in Part 2 are particularly important: "As of yet, any GUI is irrelevant. The team must do the usability test only at the rather abstract level of task flows and task objects. This *is* a usability test, but of the conceptual foundation, instead of the surface, of the GUI. Discovering usability problems at this early stage saves the resources you might otherwise have spent on designing the surface of the GUI incorrectly" [Dayton et al. 1998]. This is abstract prototyping (defined in Section 7.2.7.1).

Part 3 is concerned with the participatory design of aspects of the GUI itself. Certain details, such as the design of icons or detailed, platform-specific look-and-feel style issues, are left to specialists as an activity after participatory design. In itself, Part 3 concentrates on those activities that benefit most from participatory design and usability testing while designing a user interface for the objects and operations identified in Part 2.

Part 3 provides an example of participatory design of the surface of the interactive system, which is something quite different from the participatory design of the task and conceptual models in Parts 1 and 2, respectively.

The *Dynamic Systems Development Method* (DSDM) [DSDM 1995, Stapleton 1997], furthered by the DSDM Consortium, is a largely European user-focused method framework that provides a nonproprietary Rapid Application Development (RAD) method for system design and development. As framework aspects are not relevant here, I simply call DSDM a "method." The relevance of DSDM to this work is that it has participatory user involvement as a central element in the method. Users participate in teams that are empowered to make decisions about the software product, including its scope, functionality, appearance, and interactive behavior. This is merely part of an ongoing collaboration between a range of stakeholders that includes users and developers. Stakeholder teams include four user roles (executive sponsor, visionary, ambassador user, and advisor user) that are capable of dealing with a wide range of issues from the resolution of business issues to the detailed future day-to-day use of the proposed system. User roles are discussed most fully in the *DSDM Manual* [DSDM 1995, pp. 80–83]. Significantly, business needs, as defined by the user role stakeholders, are perceived as a major design determinant that must be satisfied during development (rather than merely satisfying developers' perceptions of business need). Testing and reversibility of all decisions allow stakeholders to focus on meeting both business and other user needs.

An important part of the DSDM method is functional model iteration, in which the earlier established business requirements are refined, where a functional model of the system to be built is developed, and where prototypes are developed and tested with users. Nonfunctional aspects of system design, such as response times, are left for later phases of the DSDM method. In DSDM, the requirements refinement and development of a functional model are performed by stakeholders in Joint Application Development (JAD) sessions. JAD sessions are described in [Martin 1991, August 1991, Wood and Silver 1995, McConnell 1996].

There are other centrally important aspects of DSDM, such as functional prioritization and time-boxed development, which are not relevant here.

10.2.8 HCI Summary

The HCI approaches outlined in this chapter cover system visualization, cognitive engineering, mental and conceptual models, task models, model-based design, user-centered design, scenarios, concrete user interface design, prototypes, testing and evaluation, and participatory design. The design of interactive software is seen as the design of more than just the presentational and interactive aspects of an interactive system and also includes the scope, contents, and deep functionality of the system. Importantly, interactive system design encompasses a range of design activities from work and leisure design, through conceptual model and high-level system-functionality design, to the detailed design of the user interface. During these design activities, users are seen as indispensable contributors to the improvement of the developing design.

10.3 Creating an Integrated Oo&hci Approach

The creation of an integrated oo&hci approach builds on the foundations for integration discussed in Section 10.3.1, and expands them in light of the foregoing HCI material. Models of activities, artifacts, and actors in the process are developed. As an illustration of various, but not all, oo&hci themes, there are cross references to oo&hci methods in this volume and elsewhere.

10.3.1 The Foundations of an Integrated Approach

Three similarities between design artifacts used by object modelers and human-computer interaction designers enable the development of oo&hci methods:

- Object-oriented conceptual models are very similar to analysis-level object models, without the OOA concern for the internal functionality of ook models.

Both use the same concepts to determine system contents. An object-oriented conceptual model is shown as a *conceptual-core model* in Figure 10.3. This model is not only a conceptual model as discussed in Section 10.2.3.1, but, independently of user interface details, also determines the core around which the interactive system will be built.

- Scenarios closely resemble use case instances. Both describe system use, allowing visualization and extraction of abstract renditions of user behavior and referents.
- Task models provide abstractions of existing and envisioned user behavior. Besides their other uses, use case models can provide more limited abstractions of envisioned user behavior. User behavior can and should determine system functionality; use cases provide a growth path for more useful descriptions of user behavior via task models or enriched use case models.

One opportunity for further useful modeling presents itself:

- Object modeling and allied notations can effectively specify interactive capability: object models can specify what facilities the user has when interacting with the core of a system, and allied notations can specify related behavioral aspects.

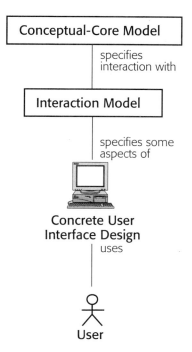

FIGURE 10.3 The role played by the interaction model

These models appear as an aggregate *interaction model* in Figure 10.3 and in subsequent figures. The interaction model may contain models of interaction and interactive capability that are rendered at different levels of abstraction. Such models are the products of design and make the transition from the abstract interactive system (as rendered in the conceptual-core model) to a near concrete user interface design.

All of the bulleted items above are concerned with representations. The first three bullets describe the commonality between user interface design and object-development artifacts so that design techniques in HCI may be used with object-oriented representations, and object-oriented modeling techniques may be used with HCI representations. The fourth bullet represents an extension of object-modeling usage to describe the *what* (not the OOD *how*) of interactive system appearance and behavior.

Consequently it is relatively easy to co-opt and develop user interface design techniques and to integrate them with object modeling techniques. Much of the key to this is to choose HCI techniques that provide useful design information that is structured in a way that is accessible for the construction of object models. In turn, the object and related models should be carefully developed to contain information that is of real use to interactive system designers. In the latter, there may be problems. Nontechnical participatory designers will need to be shielded from all obtuse notations, and, depending on design team composition, HCI designers may need to learn parts of an object-oriented language such as UML.

Adopting an object modeling approach raises the possibility of the wider use of two modeling techniques:

- Abstract operations have long been described in terms of pre- and post-conditions on system state. Use case descriptions sometimes employ this technique. As examples, the Unified Process, also known as the Unified Software Development Process (USDP), includes pre- and post-conditions in use case descriptions [Jacobson et al. 1999, p. 157], and Schneider and Winters include pre- and post-conditions in their use case template [Schneider and Winters 1998, p. 174]. In the same way, user interactions can be described in conditions over the state of the conceptual-core model and/or the interaction model.
- Similarly, invariants over a model's state can be applied to both the conceptual-core model and the interaction model. This may be useful in expressing domain and interaction design constraints.

If pre- and post-conditions and invariants are used for interactive system design purposes, expressing them in natural language rather than in a formal language such as OCL [Walmer and Kleppe 1999] will enable much wider authorship, understandability, and use.

10.3.2 Characteristics of an Oo&hci Approach

Four major principles underpinning an oo&hci approach were listed in Section 10.1. Refining these, often in light of the HCI approaches discussed in Section 10.2, yields the following principles for oo&hci approaches:

- Express contact between designers and users.
- Adoption of a user-centered design approach.
- Design of an appropriate division of work and functionality between users and interactive systems.
- Use of HCI design techniques in the early analysis phases allow up-front application of user-derived design information at the point in the development life cycle where it has the best effect—that is, when the overall design of the system is being formed.
- Performance of field studies of users in their environments to yield design information about user behavior, user needs, and the context for interactive system use.
- Use of descriptions of user behavior, often task models, based on real-world observations.
  - For pragmatic technical system design reasons, if object development methods are used later, descriptions should be transformable to use case notation (if the descriptions do not already employ use case notation).
- Formation of the conceptual models according to (designer perceptions of) users' mental models and domain knowledge.
- Adoption of a very strong emphasis on model building and user interface design as the means of establishing the scope, functionality, and user interface of the interactive system.
- Use of an object-oriented conceptual model and some form of description of envisioned user behavior as central constituents that systematically shape the interactive system design, including the design of the user interface.
- Design of abstract interactive capabilities and concrete interaction may inform the design of the domain, conceptual, and task models.
  - Particularly, the interactive facilities determine operations in the conceptual model when it is treated as a specification of the core of the system.
- Avoidance of prematurely constraining concrete design decisions early in the design process in favor of emphasis on abstract expressions of user interaction and interactive system behavior.
  - However, early visualization before abstraction is likely to be performed in concrete design terms.

- Development and validation of the interactive system design by involving users in testing and evaluation of a range of prototypes.
- Iterative redesign to coverage on viable, efficient, and usable support of users' task-based behavior.
- Adoption of an engineering approach that acknowledges and caters to real-world technological constraints while, wherever possible, trying to make suitable design trade-offs that preserve the user's conceptual model and the usability of the delivered system.
- Treatment of users as equal partners in design, conveying their knowledge of their needs and their work and leisure contexts and processes to the design team.

As a minimum, user contact and a user-centered and model-based design approach are prerequisites for any oo&hci method, but the more principles that are adopted, the better. Evangelically, all of the above *should* be adopted, but some may find that participatory design is contentious or hard to implement, particularly if there is lack of management support and accompanying user resource. It is worth noting that, as the oo&hci field is in development, the list above is open to refinement in the light of accumulating experience, and that the methods in this book are characterized by these principles in different degrees.

10.3.3 Activities in the Oo&hci Process

Figure 10.4 shows major divisions of oo&hci activities. The shaded area represents the oo&hci concerns of this chapter, and further development activities that follow interactive system design are shown at the right. In Figure 10.5, the abstract modeling and user interface design activity of Figure 10.4 is decomposed into three further activities. Arrows in both of these diagrams show the most important ways in which these activities inform (or supply design information to) each other.

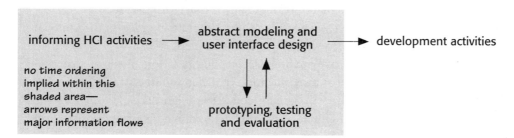

FIGURE 10.4 Interactive system design (shaded) as a front end for interactive system development

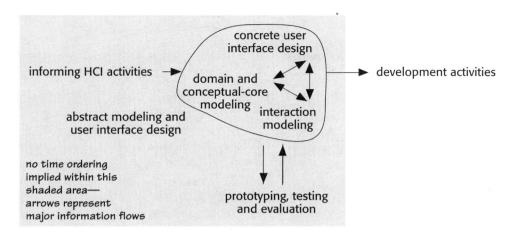

FIGURE 10.5 Abstract modeling and user interface design decomposed into three further activities

A further decomposition of design activities is useful. Ten fine-grained interactive system design activities are represented as a cluster of small ovals in Figure 10.6. The ovals overlap each other to some extent[23] showing chains of informing activities. The chains do not represent any temporal ordering of activities except for a completion ordering. Two larger shapes represent traditions of field work and participatory design, which, besides representing schools of practice in which the ten activities may be performed, are also activities in their own right. Diagrammatically, if an activity can be performed in a particular school of practice, that activity is (at least partially) superimposed on the corresponding larger shape. There is no strict compunction to perform the activity in the school of practice that it overlaps. Thus, for example, low-fi prototyping and evaluation might be performed with or without participatory design practices and may or may not be performed in the field. However, since user contact is mandatory, some kind of field work is required at some stage.

Figure 10.7 simultaneously shows how the ten activities from the cluster in Figure 10.6 can be partitioned among the five design activities in Figure 10.5 and shows the schools of practice within which individual activities might be performed. A darkly rendered cluster activity is one that is being performed, and a lightly rendered cluster activity is one that is being performed as a side effect of a darkly rendered one (in one place only). A darkly shaded school or tradition is one that *must* be adopted (in one place only), and a lightly shaded school or tradition is one that *may* be adopted.

---

[23] Mutual informing is difficult to show in a diagram, as is the richness of informing between activities.

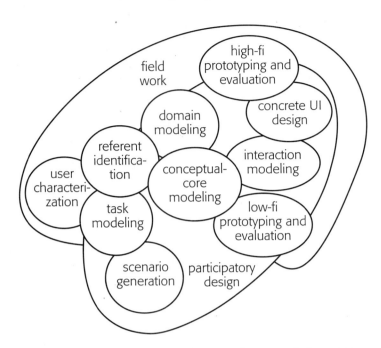

FIGURE 10.6 Finer-grained oo&hci interactive system design activities

The flow of design information among activities is shown in Figure 10.7 in an under-specified manner. Arrows indicate major flows of informing design information among the larger activities. Fine-grained activities touching or near shaded fine-grained activities may, at a first approximation, be taken as either informants or mutual informants for the shaded activities. Thus, for example, interaction modeling and high-fi prototyping and evaluation are mutual informants for concrete user interface design.

10.3.4 Activities and Examples

Individual activities and approaches from Figures 10.3 and 10.4 are briefly discussed here. Information supplementing the HCI material in section 10.2 has been added where necessary.

Field work: There are several approaches to field work, all involving designer-user contact, ranging from simple survey and questionnaire administration to observation-based approaches. In this book, there is only one discussion (in Chapter 8) of immersive field work techniques, which put the design team in the users' environment. However, the general HCI themes of meeting, understanding, questioning, and observing users

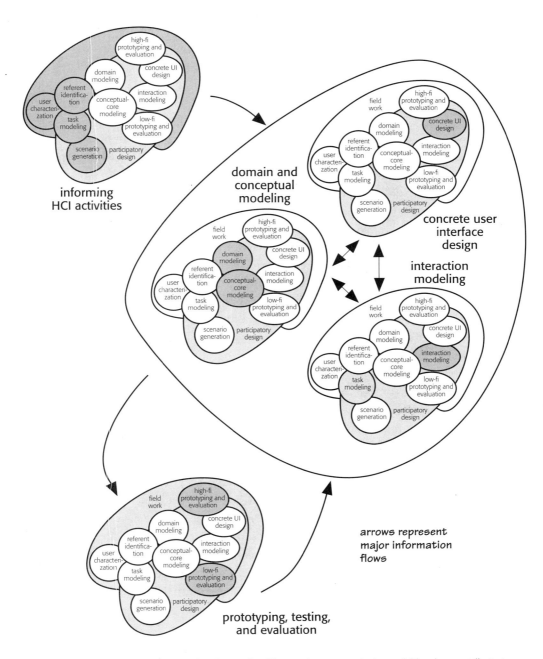

FIGURE 10.7 An approximate model of fine-grained interactive system design activities that contribute to various parts of the oo&hci approach

underpin all of the contributions here. For example, Rosson and Carroll (Chapter 2) mention meeting users as part of the background for scenario-based design activities. Elsewhere, Viller and Sommerville [1999] describe how ethnographic analyses can affect models of interactive systems and provide an example of how the UML can be used to express ethnographically derived design information. This latter approach is longer term research.

Participatory design: Three chapters in this volume discuss or touch on participatory design. McGinnes and Amos (Chapter 1) discuss experiments and experience with the ABC method and its tools for participatory modeling. ABC uses symbols to represent objects or classes while avoiding the need for users to know UML: symbols are used to represent objects. Natural language sentences are generated by a tool to explain the developing model and enable users to check their modeling activities. A prototype generator can construct initial prototype user interfaces from the finished model. Rosson and Carroll (Chapter 2) mention that their scenario-based design approach is partially situated in the context of participatory design. Nunes and Cunha (Chapter 6) use a variant on Part 1 of The Bridge [Dayton et al. 1998] to perform domain and business analysis, user profiling, and/or requirements discovery within Wisdom. Wisdom also allows for Parts 2 and 3 of The Bridge to be used later in the generation of object-oriented user interface designs.[24]

User categorization: Known as "user profiling" in sources in the HCI field, is an activity that forms part of all methods in this book. Categorizing user roles and, as part of this, describing the people who play out those roles are fundamental to all HCI and oo&hci methods. Gathering the data for user categorization is always a field work activity. This is expressed by shading both user categorization and field work in the top left of Figure 10.7.

Scenario generation: As this activity is very much a system visualization exercise, similar visualization activities, such as storyboarding and use case instance construction, can be included in this activity. Rosson and Carroll (Chapter 2) use narrative scenarios at three different levels of detail, partially as a means of constructing an object model and partially as a means of designing aspects of a concrete user interface in a model-based design process. Object models and user interface designs are generated from scenarios, and claims analysis is used to evaluate the positive and negative consequences of various scenario-inspired design choices.

---

[24] As discussed in Section 10.2.3.1, an object oriented user interface design (OOUID) is a design in which conceptual-level objects are exposed to the user at the surface (that is, the concrete user interface) of the system. In the extreme, an OOUID is a direct manipulation environment, but even a form-based interface can be an OOUID if the interface articulates and engenders notions of an underlying object-oriented conceptual model. Collins [1995] discusses the design of OOUIDs.

In Idiom, van Harmelen (Chapter 3) augmented an earlier specification-concerned design method with narrative scenario-based design in order to assist designers in the early stages of system visualization and formulation. In Idiom, scenarios inform task modeling and referent identification activities.

For ETP (Chapter 4) Artim uses scenarios which are more structured than narrative scenarios; ordered steps of enacted tasks illustrate enacted task performance.

In all three methods, scenarios are written in user language, which allows for the possibility of participatory design and evaluation of the scenario sets.

Task Modeling (including, here, **use case modeling**): The oo&hci approach requires some kind of behavioral description of envisioned user activities; candidates include task models and augmented use case models. One convenient way of viewing behavioral models is to assume that task models fulfill this role and that use case models are a kind of task model. This allows common task modeling information, such as task frequency, to augment the use case models (see Chapter 4) and allows use case models to be generated from a simple textual task model (see Chapter 3). Constantine and Lockwood (Chapter 7) provide a discussion of different kinds of use case models.

Although use cases are discussed with tasks here, in later figures (10.11, 10.12, 10.15, and 10.16) use cases are shown separately from tasks. This slight shift is made intentionally, to emphasize the centrality and importance of use cases within the subsequent OOA and OOD development process.

Essential use cases [Constantine and Lockwood 1999] (and see Chapter 7) are developments and refinements of general use cases that serve as, and are equivalent to, a simple and effective task model. An essential use case is an abstract description of user and computer interaction that is free of user interface and technology details. Subsequent design from essential use cases allows for wide consideration of different design solutions, unhindered by prior and possibly constraining design decisions at a less abstract and more concrete level.

Nunes and Cunha (Chapter 6) employ use cases as the top-level structure in their description of user behavior and document task detail within the use cases. Here, the use cases are top-level tasks.

In the Rational Unified Process (RUP), Kruchten et al. (Chapter 5) retains a purer use case approach, but use cases are accompanied by use case storyboards that include task information and basic data to enable usability-motivated interactive system design choices.

Gulliksen et al. (Chapter 8) mention the use of User Interface Modeling (UIM) [Lif 1999], which is a method for gathering user requirements in conjunction with use cases, to provide information that is directly applicable to the design of user interfaces. Using observation, UIM can be used to discover tacit information that has been internalized by the users for use in their everyday activities.

Referent identification is performed prior to or during object modeling activities. All the methods in this book involve this activity in some way. Referent identification from scenarios is discussed by Rosson and Carroll (Chapter 2). This has advantages when designing a system because it encourages designers to think anthromorphically about objects in the proposed system and to imagine and add new object behaviors to the developing object model, in turn affecting the overall system functionality. In Idiom (Chapter 3), referent identification happens at about the same time that tasks are described.

Frequently, referent identification is scoped by the tasks that the user undertakes; see [Dayton et al. 1998] and, for example, Chapters 3, 4, 6, and 8. This scoping is very important in limiting the domain and conceptual-core models to domain- and system-relevant referents. Referent identification can be participatory; see [Dayton et al. 1998] and see Chapters 1 and 6. Referent identification can and should also be based on field work that examines referents and their use in the users' work or leisure context. [Beyer and Holtzblatt 1998] provides a good example of how this may be undertaken as a field activity.

Domain modeling has its conventional meaning in software engineering: it models relevant objects in the application domain. In the oo&hci approach, relevance limits the domain model to objects of interest and utility to users—namely, referents (including, where required, users). The end result of domain modeling is an object model that is likely to emphasize the structural aspects of the domain rather than its dynamic behavior. Many types (classes) in the model will be found by referent identification activities. Other important types may come from domain experts or business descriptions, activities, and models. These types will probably be eventually annotated with operations (methods) that are important to users and that correspond to high-level tasks in the envisioned task model. Domain models may encompass more than the scope of a single system and may include referents that are not intended for representation or implementation in any computer system in the domain. An interactive system design is based on a derivation or selection of part of the domain model called the conceptual-core model. Consequently, it is important that the domain model be an articulation of users' perceptions of the domain. Participatory modeling activities by users can help ensure this, as in the approaches taken by McGinnes and Amos (Chapter 1), Nunes and Cunha (Chapter 6), and Dayton et al. [1998].

Although interactive system design is *not* concerned with the internal dynamics of domain and conceptual-core model behavior (see Chapter 7 for a discussion of this in relation to essential use case design), good practice would suggest that the computational soundness of any nontrivial domain or conceptual-core model be checked by developing internal interactions for envisioned tasks or use cases during development of the model. Because the domain model is a depiction of the users' understanding of the real world sufficient to consider the design of interactive systems for users, any domain model improvements suggested by designers must be consistent with the existing user understanding of the world.

In general, domain models are useful in the oo&hci approach (a) to situate interactive system design amid important domain objects, (b) to approach the division of functionality between user and system, (c) to provide a framework in which to view the scopes of related systems, and (d) to provide the basis for further interactive system design under conditions of system maintenance and extension or during the subsequent design of related systems.

Many of the methods in this volume do not include domain modeling. Those that do include a domain model are ABC (Chapter 1), Idiom (Chapter 3), Wisdom (Chapter 6), and the Software for Use method (Chapter 7). Wisdom allows a business model to serve as a domain model; this is catered to in the models depicted later in Figures 10.16 and 10.18.

While the approach recommended in this chapter limits domain model types to referent types and their generalizations, in Hudson's approach (Chapter 9) domain models can include objects that are other than referents.

Conceptual-core modeling: As explained in Section 10.2, conceptual modeling is fundamental to interactive system design. The activity of conceptual modeling establishes the deep content and structure of the system from a user's point of view, and a system that makes this model explicit at the concrete user interface engenders a compatible mental model. A conceptual model specifies the domain objects that are to be represented or implemented within the core of the interactive system, independent of the user interface. For this reason, the model might be called "conceptual model," "core model," or "conceptual-core model." The term favored here is "conceptual-core model," but sometimes the other terms are used to emphasize different properties of the model.

All the methods in this volume use some form of object model as a conceptual-core model. UML models are used throughout the book except in Chapter 1, where the model is rendered in symbols and words, and in Chapter 2, in which a textual Point-of-View model is used.

Interaction modeling:[25] With the introduction of a new interactive system into their world, users will acquire additional mental model constructs that represent interactive aspects of the system, such as physical realizations of computer-based contexts in which to perform tasks, tool palettes, and (dynamic) feedback that indicates the system state. Strictly speaking, when cognitive representations of interactive features are engendered and incorporated into users' mental models, the corresponding conceptual models should be changed.[26] However, to facilitate a division of concerns, the conceptual-core model is just a representation of referents that are part of the domain and that are represented in the computer system so that the user can use these objects. The *interaction*

---

[25] Interaction modeling also has a meaning in UML: the generation of sequence or collaboration diagrams.

[26] For convenience, we ignore the fact that users often change the use of systems after the systems are introduced into their world. In this way, users are capable of changing, for example, the envisioned task model.

model is the model that is used to depict aspects of user interaction with the core objects in the system. The interaction model might contain various kinds of views of core objects, representations of task flows, selection facilities, and so on. As such, the interaction model contains aspects of both abstract and concrete interaction with the system. If, for example, a partial redesign were to be performed, only part of the interaction model might change. In a radical redesign with different implementation technologies and different interaction modalities, such as the use of a speech-driven auditory interface as opposed to a GUI, the entire interaction model may change. In that core operations are determined by the interaction model, some core operations may also be required to change.

The interaction model might be expressed in a variety of ways that center on an object modeling approach. There may be a structural model of objects and associations, with objects representing interactive components in the system, such as windows, tool palettes, menus, selection capability, and representations of core objects that are rendered at the interface. Parts of this model may be concerned with the specification of views of the core objects that are realized, for example, in windows, so that the user may interact in order to perform tasks. As with the conceptual-core model, the emphasis in the interaction model is entirely one of specification—*what* the interactive behavior of the system is rather than *how* it is to be implemented.

An important construct that is expressed in several methods' interaction models is the notion of a task-execution or interaction space that contains all the information and all the command invocation mechanisms needed to support one or more tasks performed by a particular kind of user, preferably without the need to navigate between different spaces. In Idiom (Chapter 3) these are called task execution spaces; in ETP (Chapter 4) they are represented by presenters; in Wisdom (Chapter 6) they are called interaction spaces; in the Software for Use Method (partially discussed in Chapter 7) they are called interaction contexts; and in the User Interface Modeling method (Chapter 8) they are called workspaces.

Interaction models can also contain specifications of system behavior. Here, a variety of notations can be used. For example, Nunes and Cunha (Chapter 6) adopt a UML of ConcurTaskTrees [Paternò 1999] to document presentation flow.

Low-fi and high-fi prototyping and evaluation: The contributions here do not concentrate on prototyping and evaluation issues. As with user profiling, these are often taken as a given. The potential advantages of formative evaluation before programming investment indicates that low-fi prototyping is a very important activity. However, there are also aspects of designs that can only be tested by using high-fi prototypes.

Prototyping is specifically mentioned in some chapters: For example, McGinness and Amos (Chapter 1) automatically generate initial computer-based prototypes from user-created models, Artim (Chapter 4) discusses dealing with prototyping in the context of design projects, Nunes and Cunha (Chapter 6) use an evolutionary prototyping approach, and Hudson (Chapter 9) includes prototype testing in a wider survey and recommendation of effective usability techniques. Nunes and Cunha (Chapter 6) and Gulliksen et al. (Chapter 8) recommend a short prototype-evaluation cycle.

10.3.5 An Oo&hci Domain Model

In examining, understanding, comparing, categorizing, and designing oo&hci methods it is useful to have models that describe the methods. The model in Figure 10.7 is one such model; it describes activities that might be performed during the use of a method. Here, a second model is developed; a UML model that describes those parts of the users' and the designers' worlds (including people, referents, and design artifacts) that are relevant to oo&hci methods. This model is a domain model for oo&hci methods; it is composed of things that are of interest during interactive system design. Figures 10.8 to 10.17 are concerned with the development of the domain model, which is depicted in Figure 10.18. Figure 10.19 illustrates the most important components of an interactive system design and Figure 10.20 is an extraction of design artifacts from the domain model.[27]

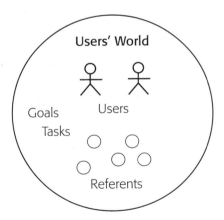

FIGURE 10.8 A users' world

---

[27] All the models in this section are copies or derivations of models that appear in [van Harmelen et al. 1997]. The models in that paper were developed by this author from discussions in the CHI97 Workshop and an initial model of four types (User, Designer, Referent, and Description) drawn by Dave Roberts during the workshop. John Artim provided significant help in critiquing and improving the 1997 model.

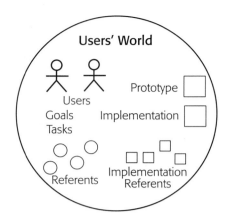

FIGURE 10.9 Users' world with added implementation referents

In the following subsections, the design of an interactive system is assumed to include both the conceptual design and a concrete user interface design specifying presentation and interaction. Such a design is a specification of *what* the system does rather than *how* it is to be implemented. The latter can be performed using conventional OOD activities. However, apart from user interface implementation technology's influence on the concrete user interface design, the oo&hci approach is independent of implementation design methods and implementation technology, and can be coupled with any suitable method. For example, Wisdom (Chapter 6) has been successfully used for the design of 4GL-implemented systems.

In formulating the following UML models, my intent is to inform the development of oo&hci methods, rather than to be pedantically correct. As always happens with models, these UML models are approximations of reality that pick up on certain details, ignore others, and make simplifying assumptions, particularly with respect to the boundaries of the categories that describe certain design artifacts and descriptions. Thus, for example, I ignore the facts that abstract and concrete prototypes form a continuum, that there are strong similarities between task and use case models, and that there are strong similarities between scenarios and use case instances. Apart from this, the UML models that follow have survived several critiques, and, for the current purposes in hand, are a reasonable and adequate representation of the world.

10.3.5.1 The Users' World

In building models of design artifacts, we start by examining what we are designing for—namely, users using interactive systems to help them perform tasks and realize goals within some users' world. Formally, a *users' world* is simply a system that is of interest to a population of users and, for a lesser period of time, to interactive system designers. In such a world, users realize their goals by performing tasks that change the state of the world. *Referents* are entities in the users' world that have meaning to users and that are used in the process of task execution. Referents may be other people, physical objects, tasks, events, and computer-based artifacts. A users' world is shown in Figure 10.8.

Computer-based artifacts, *implementation referents,* will be introduced into the users' world by the use of prototypes and interactive systems. They include the following:

- The interactive system itself
- Referents representing existing or future physical world objects: Jane, the architectural plan
- Referents representing time and transient or instantaneous events: anticipated collision time, meeting on 23-3-2001
- Referents that are documents or forms that do not have a physical realization: input form
- Referents that are other kinds of electronic domain objects: hyperlink
- Controls and feedback that become referents through the use of the interactive system: file menu, selection feedback
- Referents representing tasks in, for example, some Electronic Performance Support Systems.

A UML model of the use of an interactive system in the context of a users' world is shown in Figure 10.10. In this model, implementation referents, computational objects,

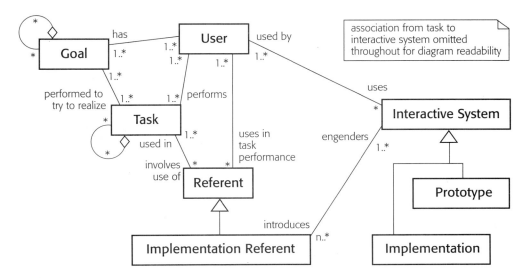

FIGURE 10.10 A UML model of the users' world

and mechanisms made physical by the user interface are considered to be as real and as functional as non-implementation referents such as paper forms or hammers. Arguably, as far as users are concerned, the interactive system is composed only of implementation referents. However, this, and the allied argument that the interactive system is an implementation referent composed of implementation referents, are largely ignored here.

10.3.5.2 The Designers' World

Given the structure of the users' world, interactive systems designers, some of whom may be users themselves, are properly concerned with the design of system purpose, functionality, and impact on users' activities and the users' world. In part, they do this by forming descriptions of various current aspects of the users' world (users, tasks, referents), and descriptions of important additions in the future (the computer system being designed and the ways in which the users will use that system). A model of how the designers' world intersects with the users' world appears in Figure 10.11. This basic model serves as a rough depiction of the users, the designers, and the things that they work with, including referents, descriptions, prototypes, and implementations. This model provides the basis for the development of UML models of aspects of the users' and designers' worlds in Figures 10.12 through 10.20. To allow for participatory design, the users in Figures 10.11, 10.12, and 10.18 may also be designers.

Incomplete, contradictory, or competing descriptions are common during design; a complete set of descriptions can never fully describe the richness of the users' world, just as a designer can never hope to fully understand the totality of the users' world.

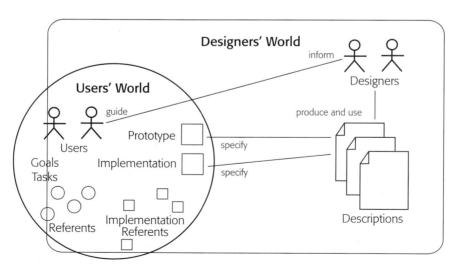

FIGURE 10.11 The users' and designers' worlds

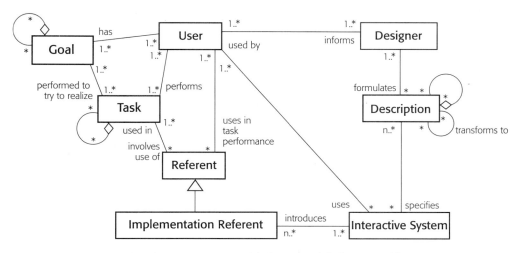

FIGURE 10.12 A UML model of users' and designers' worlds

Nonetheless, one view of interactive system design is that it is a process of resolution of incompleteness and inconsistency in descriptions while satisfying real-world needs and constraints in order to try to provide an optimal solution to a design problem for the users and other stakeholders. While this is an important view of design, for simplicity the models presented in Figures 10.11 to 10.20 do not articulate the inevitable incompleteness of, inconsistency of, and competition among different design descriptions during this process. Nor do the models approach the fact that, for the overall design of systems with different kinds of users (different actors modeled here with different user profiles), the domain and conceptual-core models must each be the union of several different models, one for each kind of user. Alternately, each kind of user must have a different, possibly overlapping aspect of the domain and core model. See discussions in Chapter 3 and [Collins 1995].

For interactive system design, it is important to use descriptions that capture the domain and application at different levels of abstraction on a continuum from abstract to concrete descriptions:

- *Abstract descriptions* are determinants or "placeholders" that can usefully represent, for the early stages of design, a variety of different concrete design solutions. Use of abstract descriptions frees designers from committing themselves to concrete design choices before the conceptual and high-level task design is decided on. Using an abstract or essential approach enables a subsequent broad exploration of the concrete design space, free of earlier constraints on solutions in that space. An *essential* description is an important kind of abstract description that is *entirely* free of implementational and technological constraints [Constantine and Lockwood 1999] (and see Chapter 7).

- *Concrete descriptions* specify the appearance and behavior of interactive systems in detail.

To reiterate, both abstract and concrete descriptions specify *what* is to be implemented; they never specify *how* it is to be implemented—not even in object model descriptions that reflect some of the concrete organization of the user interface. Conceptual-core models are at an abstract level, whereas interaction and the interactive part of the system can (and should) be described by models at different levels of abstraction.

Besides varying according to their level of abstraction, descriptions may vary according to the subject matter. Descriptions are recorded using a notation and a medium. The notations used to record descriptions may vary according to semantics, syntax, their use of text and graphics, and their level of formality. The medium used to record the description may be static or dynamic. Prototypes (except for sketches and storyboards as prototypes) are a special case of description: they use dynamic media to convey a simulation that approximates the behavior of a future system.

Figure 10.12 shows the union of the users' and designers' worlds in UML. As yet, there is no refinement of descriptions. In this model, designers are merely assumed to formulate and work with descriptions of parts of the world and of the interactive system being designed. Types which are shaded in later diagrams are subtypes of Description, as illustrated in Figure 10.13.

Figures 10.12 and 10.13 show two reflexive associations. Descriptions may be composed of other descriptions (for example, task models contain tasks, tasks are composed of subtasks; use case models contain use cases which may use and may be extended by other use cases). Interactive system design is composed of activities, many of which use descriptions in the generation of further descriptions: a description may be used by a designer to create a further description, or a description may be used as input to a program that generates a new description. The role name transforms to indicate both of these possibilities.

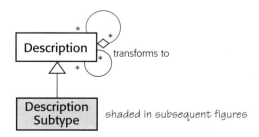

FIGURE 10.13 Relation of descriptions to other descriptions

We still need to clarify the relationships between different kinds of descriptions and various items in the users' world—namely, users, tasks, and referents. Figure 10.14 explores these relationships. *Referents* are described by *referent descriptions*. These descriptions comprise text and/or images that describe the referents; abstraction based on type is shown later. *Users* are categorized, and the categories are described, in *user profiles,* one for each kind of user. In HCI approaches, users are commonly described in terms of their (organizational) role, computer skills and experience, ability to acquire new skills, level of domain and application knowledge, motivation, sex, age, and any special needs they have. We assume that these descriptions contain or are given actor names to make the important link to use case actors so that readers and developers of the use cases can refer easily to user profiles. *Tasks* are described in *task descriptions,* with the somewhat clumsy name distinction being used to avoid ambiguity in the model. In practice, designers generally refer to "tasks" and use the context of the discussion to work out if a task or a task description is being referred to. Some tasks correspond to specific *use cases* that specify user interaction with the system at some level of detail. A use case is a description of a task to be performed by a user. Here, because of the user-centered design approach inherent in oo&hci methods, the more normal system-centric meaning of use case as an interaction that produces an observable result is ignored; tasks are far more relevant to interactive system *design* than to interaction that produces an observable result. However, the system-centric meaning of use cases becomes important

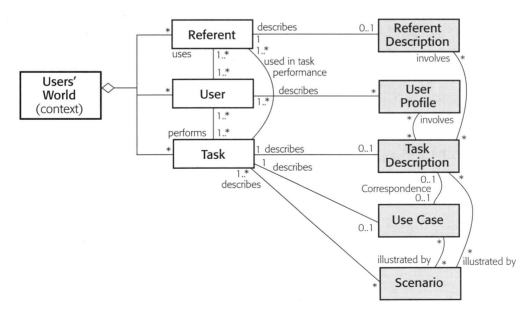

FIGURE 10.14 A UML model of user-world phenomena and designer world artifacts

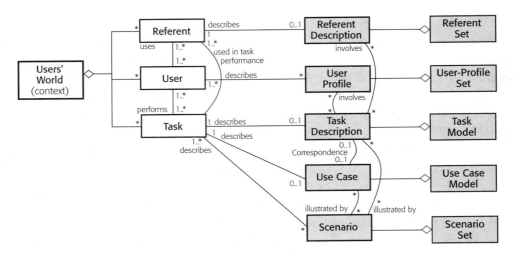

FIGURE 10.15 A UML model of parts of users' and designers' worlds

later in development. *Scenarios* are concrete illustrations of one or more tasks, task descriptions, or use cases that involve particular users and particular referents. They are plausible depictions of system use that are most often written as narratives but also usefully include storyboard techniques. To reduce the complexity of the subsequent models, scenarios are taken to include use case instances. Strictly, a scenario depicts application of one or more tasks by one or more users; a *use case instance* depicts the application of a single use case by one or more actors.

For each kind of description, there is a corresponding model consisting of descriptions that are, in some way, structured or related together. These models appear at the right in Figure 10.14. Each model is a description in its own right, because it is an aggregation of finer-grained descriptions.

10.3.5.3 Models of Interactive Systems

Sections 10.3.5.1 and 10.3.5.2 respectively introduced models that depict users' and designers' world phenomena as part of the HCI strand in the oo&hci approach. The object modeling strand is considered in this section. The two strands are merged in section 10.3.5.4.

Object modeling is discussed here as a way of recording a developing interactive system design for further design purposes and as a way of later conveying the interactive system design to analysts and developers as a basis for the remaining OOA, all OOD, and all implementation purposes. These topics are both reflected in Figure 10.16, in which the inheritance hierarchy on the right depicts a range of object models that are significant in the oo&hci approach. The *domain model* contains referents that are important to users

10.3 Creating an Integrated Oo&hci Approach | 415

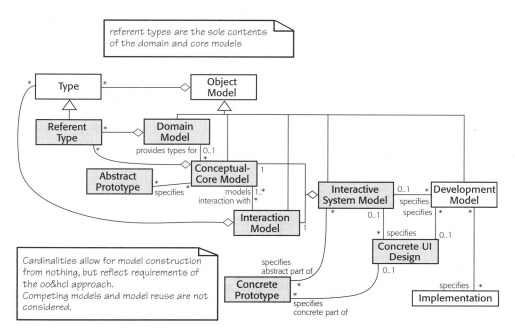

FIGURE 10.16 A UML model of models, prototypes, and implementations that are design artifacts

in their activities in the application domain. The *conceptual-core model* contains the domain referents to be represented in and manipulated by use of the interactive facilities of the system. As distinct from the situation that often exists with conventional OOAD methods, the domain and conceptual-core model design is very much informed by and founded on user-derived design information. The conceptual-core model can be thought of as an essential OOA-level model that is free of objects that do not represent referents and free of consideration of the user interface, apart from eventually being populated by operations that support the interaction model. The *interaction model* provides object-oriented specifications of the design of a particular user interface to the core model objects. It is interaction-specific; different interaction models could exist for implementations on different platforms or for different interaction styles. The interaction model may be composed of a variety of models, each of which may describe different aspects of interaction, probably at different levels of abstraction. In combination, a conceptual-core model and an interaction model form an object-oriented specification of an interactive system called an *interactive system model*.

For completeness, a further object model, the *development model,* is shown in Figures 10.16 and 10.18. The development model represents any extra OOA models and all OOD models that are needed for implementation purposes. The association of the interactive system model to the development model alludes to the process of use of the interactive system model by the analysts and developers. The choice of an object model is only illustrative; development could proceed using other paradigms.

Some aspects of interactivity cannot be depicted using object models. Notably these include detailed user interface appearance and behavior as well as some intermediate design descriptions. Suitable renditions of these aspects of interactivity are varied. One description, which groups together non-object-oriented descriptions of the concrete user interface design, is illustrated in Figure 10.17.

10.3.5.4 A Unified Domain Model

Figure 10.18 unifies the model fragments presented in Figures 10.12 to 10.17, and provides a model that relates users, designers, phenomena from the users' world, and design artifacts in a domain model for oo&hci methods. The oo&hci process[28] results in the creation of a set or subset of the shaded descriptions in Figure 10.18, and the end result of the process is an interactive system design, as modeled in Figure 10.19. To emphasize the design artifacts specifying the end product, Figure 10.20 shows important descriptions in isolation from the rest of the model.

10.4 Adopting an Oo&hci Approach

The oo&hci methods area has been moving fast since the first workshop on integration in the area at CHI in 1997 [van Harmelen et al. 1997]. In 1998 and 1999, while this book was being written, several of the methods that appear here evolved in significant incremental steps. It is worth asking if there is benefit in adopting methods from a rapidly moving field. Certainly, as argued in this chapter, and as demonstrated elsewhere in this book, there is a real usability benefit to be gained from utilizing an integrated approach. However, questions remain. For example, what is the best method to adopt, should a team create a custom method, and what are the staffing requirements for an oo&hci project?

FIGURE 10.17 An encompassing type for non-object-oriented descriptions of the concrete user interface design

---

[28] Depicted as an informal model in Figure 10.7.

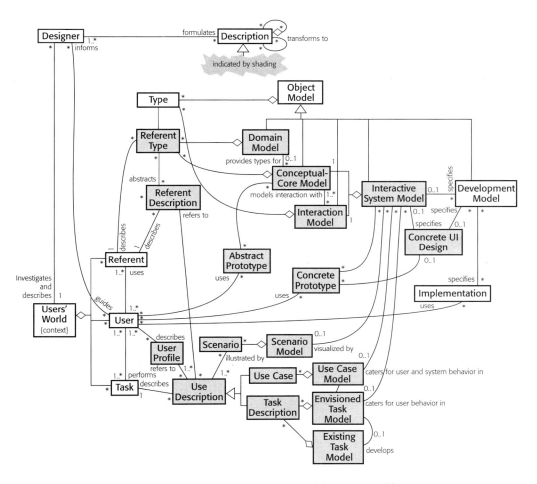

FIGURE 10.18 Intersecting users' and designers' worlds

Which interactive system design method should one use in a forthcoming project? The choice of method depends partially on the problem domain and the design problem within the domain, on the currently adopted work methods and existing designer skill sets, on resources (including participatory users), and on the extent of management support.

If none of the methods described in this book fits your particular environment and project, you can design your own method. This is not as fearsome as it might seem: computer professionals frequently design the ways in which they work in order to fit particular circumstances. If you understand the framework formulated in this chapter and have

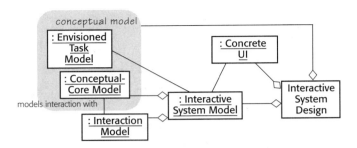

FIGURE 10.19 An interactive system design

read elsewhere in this book, it should be feasible for you to design a method that provides the framework for a project team to do the following:

- Gather user input in some well-founded way
- Involve users in modeling and user interface design
- Adopt an abstract or essential approach
- Build models of the core and interactive parts of the system and design concrete user interfaces
- Iteratively design the interactive system, producing prototypes, testing them with users, and using the test results in the process of any necessary redesign of the users' envisioned tasks, the conceptual basis (the content and the functionality) of the interactive system, and the user interface

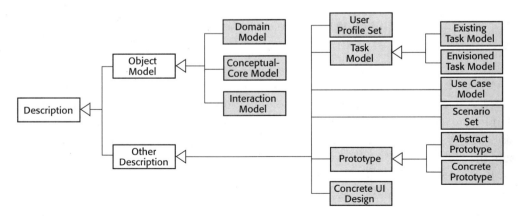

FIGURE 10.20 A UML model of useful design artifacts

In this, individual design techniques within the method need to employ notations that economically and tractably convey results from the application of the technique. Notations can often be valuable in themselves: "Different notations enhance and enrich the design process by bringing different kinds of knowledge about the [users and] the system to the fore" [unknown, possibly George Casaday in a workshop position paper 1991]. Design techniques should inform each other, and there should be a clear route (or better yet, a set of routes) from the user inputs to the interactive system model and thence onto the concrete user interface design. The use of any method should be subject to a previous process documentation step so that the designers of the method understand how their method will work, and so that users of the method—the interactive system designers—are clearly guided as to the use of the method. This documentation subsequently provides the basis for process improvement together with assessments and/or reflexive monitoring of the performance and efficacy of the method.

Although there is skill involved, designing your own method is not that difficult. Many authors claim that, as standard practice, user interface design methods should be varied to fit the different design circumstances of different projects. See, for example, Section 4.2.

On the other hand, working with per-project custom methods is undesirable in terms of load on the design staff in dealing with different methods in different projects. In line with this perspective, Gulliksen et al. (Chapter 8) describe the development of a method for use as a standard practice within the Swedish Tax Board, taking into account that organization's particular requirements and existing work practice. This is method customization on a per-organization basis.

Method development for a particular type of organization is illustrated by Wisdom (Chapter 6). Wisdom provides a method suitable for small-to-medium-sized enterprises that produce software and that do not have or are only beginning to embark on a process of method improvement [SPC 1996, Caputo 1998].

Staffing of an oo&hci project requires designers who understand both object-oriented and human-computer interaction based approaches. Currently, it is rare to find individuals who combine skills in both of these areas. Often professionals skilled in one area do not have the skill sets to perform tasks in the other area; Gulliksen et al. (Chapter 8) mention this in the context of software engineers performing HCI design tasks and recommends that there be a specialist usability expert-cum-champion on the design team. It is quite possible to combine open-minded object-oriented and HCI professionals on the same design team and for these staff members to work cooperatively and productively alongside each other.

Incorporation of users into the design team for the purpose of grounding the interactive system design in the users' world, and for other participatory design purposes is important and should be done whenever possible. Sometimes this is seen as expensive in terms of both time and money. Nardi [1996], writing about user participation in the context of developing scenarios, states that the "need to reduce time-to-market is one of those brutal competitive realities that will not go away." Nardi goes on to state that "if we can adhere to short product development cycles *and* infuse designs with rich insightful material from carefully conducted user studies, so much the better." I claim that participatory design is one way of achieving (some of) this infusion.

The participatory techniques promoted in this chapter need not be expensive in terms of development time and resources. In fact, one technique discussed here—The Bridge [Dayton et al. 1998]—is remarkable; it involves a three- to five-day user and developer workshop to lay out the fundamental design of the contents of the contents, functionality, and user interface to an interactive system. For larger systems (the Bridge has been used for the design of systems with up to thirty distinct user populations), multiple content-synchronized workshops are used.

Considering user participation in terms of usability, cost-benefit analysis will undoubtedly throw up motivating statistics. With respect to other techniques for improving usability, Claire-Marie Karat [1997b] mentions returns on usability work that are as high as ten times the cost of the work, as well as pointing to other significant benefits of usability work. In her Figure 1 [Karat 1997b, p. 770], she lists the benefits of usability engineering as improved user productivity, improved product definition, improved product design, increased product performance, increased user satisfaction, reduced development time, reduced development costs, increased sales and revenue, reduced training and help-desk costs, reduced maintenance costs, and reduced personnel costs. I suggest that many of these benefits may also be achieved through participatory design.

10.5 Conclusion

There is a very simple motivation for the changes suggested in this book: interactive systems succeed only when they adequately support the activities of their end users. Object-oriented development methods do not currently address this concern, but they can be augmented to provide support for designers intent on designing usable interactive systems. The resultant oo&hci methods integrate suitable HCI design techniques with object modeling at the beginning of the development life cycle so as to formulate a high-level design for an interactive system together with a design for a concrete user interface. This serves as a primary input, together with nonfunctional requirements, for the remainder of the OOA and all of the OOD activities in the project life cycle.

HCI constituents advocated for oo&hci approaches include the following: *Descriptions of use* via scenarios, tasks, and use cases; *Abstract* and *essential approaches* as a way of deferring concrete user interface design choices until the conceptual and task basis of the interactive system is established; an *active and equal participatory design partnership* between designers and users. Design activities in which such a partnership is possible include participatory modeling and participatory concrete user interface design. To some, participatory design will perhaps have been the most radical suggestion in this chapter. However, for many in the HCI field, such activities form the core of their user interface and interactive system design practice. *Field study techniques,* in which designers meet and observe users in their environments, allow designers to understand users and the context of user activities. Social science-based approaches remain to be integrated into the framework discussed here; in general, this remains a research topic. *Testing, evaluation, and validation* techniques include low-fi and high-fi prototyping, and evaluation of prototypes with users to formatively influence iterative design.

Oo&hci methods can be extended in many directions; research topics abound. Areas for fruitful development[29] include increasing participatory practice and greater method guidance regarding the capturing of context and its exploitation for design purposes.

Tool support is generally lacking and is an area for further work. However, simple tools often can be used with remarkable effect. Examples include pieces of paper for envisioning with sketches and for performing participatory design, and word processors for textual task modeling. Some specialized tools exist for particular kinds of design activities, but there is no integrated set of tools to support both HCI and object modeling activities.

Finally, the content of this chapter is merely a summary and an extension of a gathering change in the ways in which we design interactive systems. Pragmatism and a focus on product improvement demand that we move interactive system design toward meeting and supporting user need and requirements as an integral part of interactive system design. The next step in this is to *widely* adopt, use, and extend HCI techniques within the framework of an oo&hci methods, thus effectively integrating object modeling and user interface design practice.

---

[29] In the development of methods and notations for interactive system design, I would like to make a plea for usability. All too often, methods are developed without consideration of usability for the end users of the method. Much of this chapter and this book is, in one way or another, about usability and ways of trying to increase the usability of interactive systems. Many of the techniques that are applicable to interactive system design are also applicable to method design. These techniques include field study, prototyping methods, user involvement in method design, and observation of method application. This process is to some extent taking place; for example, in this book. McGinnes and Amos (Chapter 1) performed empirical experiments to compare the efficacies of modeling methods, and Gulliksen et al. (Chapter 8) involved users (software professionals) in the design of a method for their use within the Swedish National Tax Board. The general notion of software process improvement is well known, and the techniques mentioned earlier in this section are tools for that purpose.

10.6 Acknowledgments

This chapter could not have been written without input from colleagues in various workshops, particularly the CHI97 [van Harmelen et al. 1997] and CHI98 [Artim et al. 1998] workshops. Dave Martin helped with some of the references for Section 10.2. William Hudson supplied some of the references to early oo&hci methods. Dave Martin, John Artim, John Carroll, and Tom Dayton commented on Section 10.2, and Nuno Nunes and Srdjan Kovecevic commented on Figures 10.12 to 10.20. Tom Dayton was particularly helpful and supportive via e-mail, despite my never having met him. He, as well as John Artim and Nuno Nunes, must be thanked for general encouragement while I was writing this chapter. My thanks are also extended to various colleagues who, sometimes without knowing me, corresponded with me regarding technical and/or historical matters. Some of these kind individuals are mentioned in the references, while others will, I hope, accept my thanks without explicit mention. Mistakes and inaccuracies, of course, remain my responsibility.

10.7 References

[Artim et al. 1998] J. Artim, M. van Harmelen, K. Butler, J. Gulliksen, A. Henderson, S. Kovacevic, S. Lu, S. Overmyer, R. Reaux, D. Roberts, J.-C. Tarby, and K. Vander Linden. Incorporating Work, Process and Task Analysis into Industrial and Commercial Object-Oriented Systems. *SIGCHI Bulletin*, 30(4) October 1998.

[August 1991] J. August. *Joint Application Design*. Englewood Cliffs, NJ: Yourdon Press, 1991.

[Beyer and Holtzblatt 1998] H. Beyer and K. Holtzblatt. *Contextual Design: Defining Customer-Centered Systems*. San Francisco: Morgan Kaufmann, 1998.

[Bødker and Gronbaek 1991] S. Bødker and K. Gronbaek. Co-operative Prototyping Studies. In J. Bowers and S. Benford, eds. *Studies in CSCW*. Amsterdam, Netherlands: North Holland Elsevier, 1991.

[Bowers 1996] J. Bowers. Hanging Around and Making Something of It: Ethnography. In J. Haworth, ed. *Psychological Research: Innovative Methods and Strategies*. New York: Routledge, 1996.

[Bowers et al. 1995] J. Bowers, G. Button, and W. Sharrock. Workflow from Within and Without: Technology and Cooperative Work on the Print Industry Shopfloor. *Proceedings of the Fourth European Conference on Computer-Supported Cooperative Work*, Dordrecht, Netherlands: Kluwer Academic Publishers, 1995.

[Browne 1993] D. Browne. *STUDIO: STructured User-Interface Design for Interaction Optimisation*. Englewood, Cliffs, NJ: Prentice Hall, 1993.

[Button and Dourish 1996] G. Button and P. Dourish. Technomethodology: Paradoxes and Possibilities, in *Proceedings of ACM CHI '96 Conference on Human Factors in Computing Systems*. 1996.

[Caputo 1998] K. Caputo. *CMM Implementation Guide.* Reading, MA: Addison-Wesley, 1998.

[Card et al. 1983] S. Card, T. Moran, and A. Newell. *The Psychology of Human-Computer Interaction.* Hillsdale, NJ: Lawrence Erlbaum Associates, 1983.

[Carroll 1991] J. M. Carroll, ed. *Designing Interaction: Psychology at the Human Computer Interface.* Cambridge: Cambridge University Press, 1991.

[Carroll 1995] J. M. Carroll, ed. *Scenario-Based Design: Envisioning Work and Technology in System Development.* New York: John Wiley and Sons, 1995.

[Carroll 1996] J. M. Carroll. Encountering Others: Reciprocal Openings in Participatory Design and Use-Centered Design, in *Human-Computer Interaction,* Vol. 11. 1996.

[Carroll 1999] J. M. Carroll. Five Reasons for Scenario-Based Design, in *Proceedings of the 32nd Hawaii International Conference on System Sciences.* IEEE, 1999.

[Carroll et al. 1997] J. Carroll, R. Mack, and W. Kellog. Interface Metaphors and User Interface Design. In M. Helander, T. K. Landauer, and P. V. Prabhu, eds. *Handbook of Human-Computer Interaction.* Amsterdam, Netherlands: Elsevier Science/North Holland, 1997.

[CGC 1982] Computer Graphics Consultants, Inc. *Workstation User Interface Design,* Short course, 1982.

[Clement and Besselaar 1993] A. Clement and P. Besselaar. A Retrospective Look at PD Projects. *CACM,* 36 (4), 1993.

[Collins 1995] D. Collins. *Designing Object-Oriented User Interfaces.* Menlo Park, CA: Benjamin/Cummings, 1995.

[Collins-Cope 1999] M. Collins-Cope. Unpublished manuscript, 1999.

[Constantine and Lockwood 1999] L. L. Constantine and L. A. D. Lockwood. *Software for Use: A Practical Guide to the Models and Methods of Usage-Centered Design.* Reading, MA: Addison-Wesley, 1999.

[Dahl and Nygaard 1966] O. J. Dahl and K. Nygaard. SIMULA in An ALGOL-Based Simulation Language. Communications of the ACM, September 1966.

[Daiper 1989] D. Daiper, ed. *Task Analysis for Human-Computer Interaction.* Hemel Hempstead, UK: Ellis Horwood, 1989.

[Dayton 2000] T. Dayton. E-mail correspondence with the author, 2000.

[Dayton et al. 1998] T. Dayton, A. McFarland, and J. Kramer. Bridging User Needs to Object Oriented GUI Prototype via Task Object Design. In L. Wood, ed. *User Interface Design.* Boca Raton, FL: CRC Press, 1998.

[Dix et al. 1993] A. Dix, F. Finlay, G. Abwood, and R. Beale. *Human-Computer Interaction.* Englewood Cliffs, NJ: Prentice Hall, 1993.

[DSDM 1995] The DSDM Consortium. *Dynamic System Development Method.* Consortium Members' Handbook, Version 2, Surrey, UK: Tesseract Publishing (for the DSDM Consortium), 1995.

[Dumas and Redish 1993] J. S. Dumas and J. C. Redish. *A Practical Guide to Usability Testing.* Norwood, NJ: Ablex, 1993.

[Erikson 1990] T. Erikson. Working with Interface Metaphors. In B. Laurel, ed. *The Art of Human-Computer Interface Design.* Reading, MA: Addison-Wesley, 1990.

[Floyd 1984] C. Floyd. A Systematic Look at Prototyping, in Approaches to Prototyping. *Proc. Namur,* I, 1983.

[Gentner and Stevens 1983] D. Gentner and A. L. Stevens. *Mental Models.* Hillsdale, NJ: Lawrence Erlbaum Associates, 1983.

[Gould 1997] J. D. Gould. How to Design Usable Systems. In M. Helander, T. K. Landauer, and P. V. Prabhu, eds. *Handbook of Human-Computer Interaction.* Amsterdam, Netherlands: Elsevier Science/North Holland, 1997.

[Gould and Lewis 1985] J. D. Gould and C. Lewis. Designing for Usability: Key Principles and What Designers Think. *Comm. ACM,* 28 (3), 1985.

[Greenbaum and Kyng 1991] J. Greenbaum and M. Kyng, eds. *Design at Work: Cooperative Design of Computer Systems.* Hillsdale, NJ: Lawrence Erlbaum Associates, 1991.

[Hackos and Reddish 1998] J. T. Hackos and J. C. Reddish. *User and Task Analysis for User Interface Design.* New York: John Wiley and Sons, 1998.

[Heath and Luff 1991] C. Heath and P. Luff. Collaborative Activity and Technological Design: Task Coordination in London Underground Control Rooms. In L. Bannon, M. Robinson, and K. Schmidt, eds. In *Proceedings of the Second European Conference on Computer Supported Cooperative Work.* Dordretch Netherlands: Kluwer Academic, 1991.

[Helander et al. 1997] M. Helander, T. K. Landauer, and P. V. Prabhu, eds. *Handbook of Human-Computer Interaction.* Amsterdam, Netherlands: Elsevier Science/North Holland, 1997.

[Henderson 1991] A. Henderson. A Development Perspective on Interface Design and Theory. In J. M. Carroll, ed. *Designing Interaction: Psychology at the Human-Computer Interface.* Cambridge: Cambridge University Press, 1991, 254.

[Henderson 2000] A. Henderson. E-mail correspondence with the author, 2000.

[IBM 1991] IBM Corporation CUA Team. *Common User Access Guide to User Interface Design.* Systems Application Architecture, SC34-4289-00. 1991.

[ISO 1998] International Standardization Organization. *ISO9241. Ergonomic Requirements for Office Work with Visual Display Terminals (VDTs),* Part 11, *Guidance on Usability.* ISO, 1998.

[ISO 1999] International Standardization Organization. *ISO13407. Human Centred Design Process for Interactive Systems.* ISO, 1999.

[Jacobson et al. 1999] I. Jacobson, G. Booch, and J. Rumbaugh. *The Unified Software Development Process.* Reading, MA: Addison-Wesley, 1999.

[Johnson 1992] P. Johnson. *Human-Computer Interaction: Psychology Task Analysis and Software Engineering.* New York: McGraw-Hill, 1992.

[Karat 1997a] J. Karat. *Evolving the Scope of User-Centered Design.* Comm. ACM, **40**(7), 1977.

[Karat 1997b] C.-M. Karat. Cost-Justifying Usability Engineering in the Software Life Cycle. In M. Helander, T. K. Landauer, and P. V. Prabhu, eds. *Handbook of Human-Computer Interaction.* Amsterdam, Netherlands: Elsevier Science/North Holland, 1997.

[Kensing and Monk-Madsen 1993] F. Kensing and A. Monk-Madsen. Participatory Design: Structure in the Toolbox. *CACM,* 36 (4), 1993.

[Kreitzberg 1999] C. Kreitzberg. The LUCID Design Framework. Available at *http://www.cognetics.com/lucid/lucid2a-overview.pdf*. Cognetics Corporation, 1999.

[Kruchten 1995] P. Kruchten. The 4+1 View Model of Architecture. *IEEE Software,* 12 (6), 1995. Also available at *http://www.rational.com*.

[Kruchten 1998] P. Kruchten. *The Rational Unified Process.* Reading, MA: Addison-Wesley, 1998.

[Kyng 1995] M. Kyng. Creating Contexts for Design. In J. M. Carroll, ed. *Scenario-Based Design: Envisioning Work and Technology in System Development.* New York: John Wiley and Sons, 1995.

[Kyng et al. 1997] M. Kyng, L. Mathiassen, and K. Braa. *Computers and Design in Context.* Cambridge, MA: MIT Press, 1997.

[Liddle 2000] D. Liddle. E-mail correspondence with the author, 2000.

[Lif 1999] M. Lif. User Interface Modelling—Adding Usability to Use Cases. *International Journal of Human-Computer Studies,* 3, 1999.

[Mack 1995] R. L. Mack. Discussion: Scenarios as Engines of Design. In J. M. Carroll, ed. *Scenario-Based Design: Envisioning Work and Technology in System Development.* New York: John Wiley and Sons, 1995.

[Mandel 1997] T. Mandel. *The Elements of User Interface Design.* New York: John Wiley and Sons, 1997.

[Martin 1991] J. Martin. *Rapid Application Development.* New York: Macmillan, 1991.

[Mayhew 1999] D. J. Mayhew. *The Usability Engineering Lifecycle: A Practitioner's Handbook for User Interface Design.* San Francisco, CA: Morgan Kaufman Publishers, 1999.

[McConnell 1996] S. McConnell. *Code Complete.* Seattle, WA: Microsoft Press, 1996.

[Muller 1991] M. J. Muller. PICTIVE—An Exploration in Participative Design, in *Proceedings of CHI '97.* 1991.

[Muller et al. 1995] M. J. Muller, L. G. Tudor, D. M. Wildman, E. A. White, R. W. Root, T. Dayton, R. Carr, B. Diekmann, and E. Dykstra-Erickson. Bifocal Tools for Scenarios and Representations in Participatory Activities with Users. In J. M. Carroll, ed. *Scenario-Based Design: Envisioning Work and Technology in System Development.* New York: John Wiley and Sons, 1995.

[Muller et al. 1997] M. J. Muller, J. H. Hallewell, and T. Dayton. Participatory Practices in the Software Lifecycle. In M. Helander, T. K. Landauer, and P. V. Prabhu, eds. *Handbook of Human-Computer Interaction.* Amsterdam, Netherlands: Elsevier Science/North Holland, 1997.

[Nardi 1995] B. Nardi. Some Reflections on Scenarios. In J. M. Carroll, ed. *Scenario-Based Design: Envisioning Work and Technology in System Development.* New York: John Wiley and Sons, 1995.

[Neale and Carroll 1997] D. C. Neale and J. M. Carroll. The Role of Metaphors in User Interface Design. M. Helander, T. K. Landauer, and P. V. Prabhu, eds. In *Handbook of Human-Computer Interaction.* Amsterdam, Netherlands: Elsevier Science/North Holland, 1997.

[Newell and Simon 1972] A. Newell and H. A. Simon. *Human Problem Solving.* Englewood Cliffs, NJ: Prentice Hall, 1972.

[Newman 2000] W. M. Newman. E-mail correspondence with the author, 2000.

[Newman and Lamming 1995] W. M. Newman and M. G. Lamming. *Interactive System Design.* Reading, MA: Addison-Wesley, 1995.

[Newman and Sproull 1979] W. M. Newman and R. F. Sproull. *Principles of Interactive Computer Graphics.* New York: McGraw-Hill, 1979.

[Norman 1986] D. A. Norman. Cognitive Engineering. In D. A. Norman and S. W. Draper, eds. *User Centered System Design.* Hillsdale, NJ: Lawrence Erlbaum Associates, 1986.

[Norman 1988] D. A. Norman. *The Psychology of Everyday Things.* New York: Basic Books, 1988.

[Nunes et al. 1999] N. Nunes, M. Toranzo, J. Cunha, J. Castro, S. Kovacevic, D. Roberts, J.-C. Tarby, J. M. Collins-Cope, M. van Harmelen. Interactive System Design with Object Models. In A. Moreira and S. Demeyer, eds. ECOOP'99 Workshop Reader. *Lecture Notes in Computer Science,* Number 1743, Berlin: Springer-Verlag, 1999.

[OMG 1998] Object Management Group. *OMG Unified Modeling Language Specification.* Version 1.2, 1998.

[OMG 1999] Object Management Group. *OMG Unified Modeling Language Specification.* Version 1.3 R9, 1999.

[Paternò 1999] F. Paternò. *Model-Based Design and Evaluation of Interactive Applications.* Heidelberg, Germany: Springer, 1999.

[Preece et al. 1994] J. Preece, Y. Rogers, H. Sharp, D. Benyon, S. Holland, and T. Carey. *Human-Computer Interaction.* Reading, MA: Addison-Wesley, 1994.

[Redmond-Pyle and Moore 1995] D. Redmond-Pyle and A. Moore. *Graphical User Interface Design and Evaluation.* London: Prentice Hall, 1995.

[Roberts et al. 1998] D. Roberts, D. Berry, S. Isensee, and J. Mullaly. *Designing for the User with OVID: Bridging User Interface Design and Software Engineering.* Hemel Hempstead, UK: Macmillan Technical Publishing, 1998.

[Robertson et al. 1994] S. R. Robertson, J. M. Carroll, R. L. Mack, M. B. Rosson, S. R. Alpert, and J. Koenemann-Belliveau. ODE: A Self-Guided, Scenario-Based Learning Environment for Object-Oriented Design Principles, *Proceedings of OOPSLA '94,* Indianapolis, IN: ACM, 1994.

[Robson 2000] D. Robson. E-mail correspondence with the author, 2000.

[Rogers et al. 1992] Y. Rogers, A. Rutherford, and P. Bibby, eds. *Models in the Mind: Theory, Perspective and Application.* Orlando, FL: Academic Press, 1992.

[Rubin 1994] J. Rubin. *Handbook of Usability Testing.* New York: John Wiley and Sons, 1994.

[Rumbaugh et al. 1991] J. Rumbaugh, W. Premerlani, F. Eddy, and W. Lorensen. *Object-Oriented Modeling and Design.* Englewood Cliffs, NJ: Prentice Hall International, 1991.

[Schank and Abelson 1977] R. Schank and R. Abelson. *Scripts, Plans, Goals and Understanding.* Hillsdale, NJ: Lawrence Erlbaum Associates, 1977.

[Schneider and Winters 1998] G. Schneider and J. P. Winters. *Applying Use Cases: A Practical Guide.* Reading, MA: Addison-Wesley, 1998.

[Schuler and Namioka 1993] D. Schuler and A. Namioka, eds. *Participatory Design: Principles and Practices.* Hillsdale, NJ: Lawrence Erlbaum Associates, 1993.

[Smith et al. 1982] D. C. Smith, C. Irby, R. Kimball, B. Verplank, and E. Harslem. Designing the Star User Interface. *Byte,* 7 (4), 1982.

[SPC 1996] Software Productivity Consortium. *Improving the Software Process Through Process Definition and Modeling.* International Thomson Computer Press, 1996.

[Stapleton 1997] J. Stapleton. *Dynamic Systems Development Method: The Method in Practice.* Reading, MA: Addison-Wesley, 1997.

[Suchman 1987] L. Suchman. *Plans and Situated Action: The Problem of Human-Machine Communication.* Cambridge: Cambridge University Press, 1987.

[van Harmelen 1989] M. van Harmelen. Exploratory User Interface Design Using Scenarios and Prototypes. *People and Computers V,* Proceedings of BCS HCI '89, Cambridge: Cambridge University Press, 1989.

[van Harmelen 1994a] M. van Harmelen. Object Oriented Modelling and Specification for User Interface Design. *Interactive Systems: Design, Specification and Verification,* Proceedings of First Eurographics ISDV Workshop (ISDV '94), 1994, Berlin, Germany: Springer, 1995.

[van Harmelen 1994b] M. van Harmelen. *Object Oriented Modelling for User Interface Design.* Slides and notes for a tutorial at HCI '94, August 1994.

[van Harmelen 1996] M. van Harmelen. Melding Object Modeling and User Interface Design. *Object Expert,* Nov./Dec. 1996.

[van Harmelen 1997] M. van Harmelen. Combining Object-Oriented Modeling with User Interface Design Techniques. Proceedings of *Object-Expo Europe,* Sigs Publications, 1997.

[van Harmelen and Wills 1991] M. van Harmelen and A. C. Wills. *Object Oriented User Interface Design.* Slides and notes for a tutorial at HCI '91, August 1991.

[van Harmelen et al. 1997] M. van Harmelen, J. Artim, K. Butler, A. Henderson, D. Roberts, M. B. Rosson, J.-C. Tarby, and S. Wilson. Object-Oriented Models in User Interface Design: A CHI '97 Workshop. *SIGCHI Bulletin,* October 1997.

[Viller and Sommerville 1997] S. Viller and I. Sommerville. Coherence: An Approach to Representing Ethnographic Analyses in Systems Design, in Cooperative Systems Engineering Group Technical Report CSEG/7/1997. Available at *http://www.comp.lancs.ac.uk/computing/research/cseq/97_rep.html.* Submitted to Special Issue of *Human-Computer Interaction (HCI)* journal on Representations in Interactive Systems Development.

[Walmer and Kleppe 1999] J. Walmer and A. Kleppe. *The Object Constraint Language: Precise Modeling with UML.* Reading, MA: Addison-Wesley, 1999.

[Wood 1998] L. Wood, ed. *User Interface Design.* Boca Raton, FL: CRC Press, 1998.

[Wood and Silver 1995] J. Wood and D. Silver. *Joint Application Development.* 2nd Ed., New York: John Wiley and Sons, 1995.

About the Authors

Stefan Ahlqvist

Stefan Ahlqvist works as a Senior Usability Designer for Jaczone. He has a Master of Science degree in Computer Science and Engineering, and has worked in the user interface field since 1987. Prior to his employment at Jaczone, Stefan worked for Rational for five years, one of which was spent on the research for the user interface parts of Rational Unified Process. Stefan has also worked for TeleLogic/TeleSoft and was one of the key people behind TeleUSE—a commercial GUI builder for Motif—that reached a large international market. Stefan has been a presenter at various conferences, including OOPSLA, Object Computing and Norska Datafåreningen.

E-mail: stefan.ahlqvist@jaczone.com
http://www.jackzone.com
Kronborgsgränd 7
SE-164 46 Kista
Sweden

Johnny Amos

Johnny Amos is an independent consultant. Previously, he was a senior consultant with Coras Information Consulting Ltd., of Dublin, Ireland. He has 30 years' experience in programming, design, consulting, teaching, and project management. Johnny has been specializing in RAD/JAD approaches to systems development and has ten years' practical experience in making these approaches work in complex object-oriented developments.

E-mail: johnny.amos@oceanfree.net
1 Del Val Avenue
Sutton
Dublin 13
Republic of Ireland

John M. Artim
John M. Artim is a user interface architect and development process methodologist at Zoho, a business-to-business start-up company serving the hospitality industry. John has 12 years of industry experience including work at another start-up company, Savi Technology, at a container shipping company, Orient Overseas Container Lines, and at IBM. John's work has included user analysis, user interface design, use of style guides in coordinating large projects, look-and-feel specification, object-oriented analysis and design, user interface development, and framework design and development in support of user interface. He holds a masters degree in Experimental Psychology. John was a co-organizer of the CHI98 workshop, "Incorporating Work, Process, and Task Analysis into Commercial and Industrial Object-Oriented Systems Development."

E-mail: jartim@acm.org
John M. Artim
Zoho Corporation
470 Potrero Avenue
Sunnyvale, CA 94085

Stefan Bylund
Stefan Bylund currently works as a Senior Process Architect for Jaczone, where he contributes to product development and works as a consultant with issues related to software development processes for e-businesses. Prior to this, Stefan worked for Rational Software Corporation and for Objectory AB. During his time with Rational, Stefan primarily contributed to the development of several successive versions of the Rational Unified Process (previously called Rational Objectory Process and before that Objectory). This work included the creation of "product state" material for external release, and included the creation of internal research reports, articles in journals (JOOP), and reviews, together with some process-related teaching, consulting, and sales presentation.

E-mail: stefan.bylund@jaczone.com
http://www.jackzone.com
Kronborgsgränd 7
SE-164 46 Kista
Sweden

John M. Carroll

John M. Carroll is Professor of Computer Science, Education, and Psychology, and Director of the Center for Human-Computer Interaction, all at Virginia Tech. His research interests include methods and theory in human-computer interaction, particularly as applied to networking tools for collaborative learning activities. He has written more than 250 technical papers, more than 20 conference plenary addresses, and 12 books, including *Scenario-based Design: Envisioning Work and Technology in System Development* (Wiley, 1995), *Design Rationale: Concepts, Methods and Techniques* (Erlbaum, 1996, with T. P. Moran), *Minimalism Beyond "The Nurnberg Funnel"* (MIT Press, 1998), and *Making Use: Scenario-based Design of Human-Computer Interactions* (MIT Press, 2000). He serves on nine editorial boards for journals and handbooks, and, in 1999, served on six conference program committees. In 1994, he won the Rigo Career Achievement Award, from ACM (SIGDOC) for contributions to research in documentation, and in 1998 he received the Silver Core Award from IFIP. He manages a research project on networking tools for collaborative learning activities supported by the U.S. National Science Foundation, the U.S. Office of Naval Research, and the Hitachi Foundation.

Center for Human-Computer Interaction and
Computer Science Department
660 McBryde Hall, Virginia Tech
Blacksburg, VA 24061-0106

Larry L. Constantine

Larry L. Constantine, a pioneer of modern software engineering practice, is highly regarded as an authority on the human side of software development. A leading international lecturer, author, editor, and consultant, he has ten books and more than 120 published papers to his credit.

E-mail: larry@foruse.com
http://www.foruse.com
Constantine & Lockwood, Inc.

João F. Falcão e Cunha

João F. Cunha lectures at the University of Porto, in Portugal, on information systems and databases. He holds a Ph.D. in Computing Science from Imperial College (1989), a M.Sc. in Operational Research from Cranfield University (1984), and a first degree from the University of Porto. He is a member of ACM and the IEEE Computer Society, and is currently the Chair of the IEEE Portugal section. He has been involved with theoretical and experimental work in software engineering for the past 15 years. His research interests include object-oriented modeling, decision support systems, graphical user interfaces, and electronic commerce.

E-mail: jfcunha@fe.up.pt
Faculdade de Engenharia da Universidade do Porto
Rua Dr. Roberto Frias
4200-465 Porto
Portugal

Bengt Göransson
Bengt Göransson is a Usability Designer at Enea Redina AB. He has a background in computer science with a special interest in and knowledge of human-computer interaction. Bengt has been working on the topics of user-centered design, usability, and interaction design for over ten years. He currently holds a position as Usability Designer and mentor in usability issues at Enea Redina, Sweden. He has been responsible for the usability of numerous systems in several client projects. He is also at the Department of Human-Computer Interaction at Uppsala University, Sweden, as a Ph.D. student. Bengt has contributed to several scientific articles and papers.

E-mail: bengt.goransson@enea.se
Usability Designer
Enea Redina AB
Smedsgränd 9
SE-753 20, Uppsala
Sweden

Jan Gulliksen, Ph.D., M.Sc.
Jan Gulliksen is an associate professor in Human-Computer Interaction at the Department of Information Technology at Uppsala University, Sweden, where he is in charge of a research group on user-centered design. Jan is also a guest researcher at the Centre for user-oriented IT-design (CID) at the Royal Institute of Technology in Stockholm. Jan is chair of the Swedish HCI Interest group, STIMDI, and as such he was the general chair of NordiCHI 2000, held in Stockholm in October 2000. He is also chair of the International Federation for Information Processing (IFIP) working group 13.2 on Methodologies for User-centered Systems Design. Jan is an expert member in working groups on software ergonomics and human-centered design in the International Organization for Standardization (ISO). Jan's research deals with practical methods for user-centered design throughout the entire system development process and the research is performed in cooperation with the industry.

E-mail: jan.gulliksen@hci.uu.se
Department for Human-Computer Interaction
Uppsala University
PO Box 337
SE-75105 Uppsala, Sweden

William Hudson

William Hudson is a software and user interface design specialist with 30 years' experience in development, consulting, and teaching. He has been involved in human-computer interaction and object-oriented design since the early 1990s. William is founder of Syntagm Ltd., an Oxford-based consultancy specializing in user-centered design and development. He has written articles on user interface and web design for the ACM's interactions magazine and the SIGCHI Bulletin.

E-mail: whudson@syntagm.co.uk
Syntagm Ltd.
10 Oxford Road
Abingdon
Oxon OX14 2DS
United Kingdom

Philippe Kruchten

Philippe Kruchten is the lead architect of the Rational Unified Process product. He has more than 25 years' experience in the development of large, software-intensive systems in the areas of telecommunication, defense, aerospace, transportation, and software development tools. He holds a degree in mechanical engineering from the Ecole Centrale de Lyon and a doctorate in computer science from the French Institute of Telecommunications.

E-mail: pbk@rational.com

Magnus Lif

Dr. Magnus Lif is the Chief HCI Officer at Icon Medialab London (IML). He has seven years' experience in user-centered design of graphical user interfaces and has been with Icon Medialab, an e-business consultancy, for two years. At IML he has worked as a human-computer interaction (HCI) consultant in several large e-commerce projects, and has also been involved in developing strategies for user-centered design and in integrating methods for analysis, design, and evaluation into Icon Medialab's development model. Before starting at IML he finished a Ph.D. in HCI at Uppsala University in Sweden. He has published several articles and book chapters focusing on the integration of HCI methods into the software development process.

E-mail: magnus.lif@iconmedialab.co.uk
Icon Medialab London
Classic House
180 Old Street
London EC1V 9BP
United Kingdom

Lucy A. D. Lockwood
Lucy A. D. Lockwood has more than a dozen years' experience in programming and project management. An international consultant, teacher, and writer, she chairs the User Interface Design Track of the Software Development Conference.

E-mail: lucy@foruse.com
http://www.foruse.com
Constantine & Lockwood, Inc.

Simon McGinnes
Simon McGinnes is a software consultant and lecturer in computer science at Trinity College, Dublin. He has worked in the IT industry in Ireland, the United Kingdom, and Australia for many commercial, government, and academic organizations, in software project management, systems analysts and design, and systems development. As a practitioner and researcher, his interests lie in the automation of software design and the encapsulation of expert design principles into automated design processes. In 1995 Simon McGinnes founded CORAS Information Consulting Ltd. Simon McGinnes holds a Ph.D. from the University of London in the psychological aspects of software requirements analysis, modeling, and system design.

E-mail: simon.mcginnes@tcd.ie
Dept. of Computer Science
O'Reilly Institute, Trinity College
Dublin 2
Republic of Ireland

Nuno Jardim Nunes
Nuno Jardim Nunes is a teaching assistant and researcher in the Computer Science Unit of the University of Madeira, Portugal, where he is currently finishing his Ph.D. in object modeling and user-interface design. He holds a degree in informatics (1994) from IST-University of Lisbon and a M.Phil. degree (1997) in software engineering from the

University of Madeira. Nuno is the leading author of the Wisdom OO method and works actively with small software companies introducing object technology. Currently his research interests include user-interface design, object orientation and lightweight software engineering. Nuno was the main organizer of two workshops on object modeling and user-interface design at ECOOP '99 and UML 2000. He is a member of ACM, SIGCHI, and IEEE Computer Society.

E-mail: njn@uma.pt
Dep. de Matemática
Universidade Madeira
Campus Universitário da Penteada-Piso 2
9000-390 Funchal, Portugal

Mary Beth Rosson
Mary Beth Rosson is Associate Professor of Computer Science at Virginia Tech. Her research interests include scenario-based methods for the design and evaluation of interactive systems, the use of network technology to support collaboration, especially in learning contexts, and psychological issues in the learning and use of the object-oriented design paradigm. She is the author of *Instructor's Guide to Object-Oriented Analysis and Design with Applications* (Benjamin Cummings, 1994), along with numerous articles, book chapters, and tutorials. Dr. Rosson is active in both ACM SIGCHI and ACM SIGPLAN, serving in numerous Technical Program roles for the CHI and OOPSLA annual conferences. She served as General Chair for OOPSLA 2000.

Department of Computer Science
660 McBryde, Virginia Tech University
Blacksburg, VA 24061

About the Editor

Mark van Harmelen is an independent consultant and researcher who has worked in both object-oriented and human-computer interaction areas since 1985. Educated in Psychology and Computer Science at the University of Cape Town in South Africa, he later gained a Ph.D. in Computer Science from the University of Manchester in the United Kingdom. Mark has worked as a consultant for most of the past thirteen years. For part of that time he has also held a series of Honorary Research Fellowships in the Department of Computer Science at the University of Manchester in the United Kingdom, and a position as a Senior Visiting Researcher at Matsushita Electric Industrial's (Panasonic's) Tokyo Research Laboratory. Previously he was employed as a tenured member of the academic staff at the University of Manchester, and in various positions in industry.

Recently, Mark has concentrated on the oo&hci area, and was responsible for initiating international cooperation in this area in 1997. He continues to encourage cooperation between interested parties working in the area.

Mark is one of the authors in this volume who provide consultancy and training. Some of the areas in which he works include project review and audit, software engineering methods, object-oriented technologies, human-computer interaction, and, of course, the adoption and use of oo&hci methods. Besides being open to offers of consultancy work, he is also open to offers of longer-term employment.

E-mail: mark@oohci.com, mark@oohci.org, mark@cutsys.com, mark@cs.man.ac.uk
http://www.oohci.com
Cutting Edge Systems Ltd.

Index

The number in parentheses preceding the page number(s) is the chapter number.

80/20 rule, (1) 17–18

A
ABC modeling
80/20 rule, (1) 17–18
automating design, (1) 16–17
conceptual meaning, developing, (1) 15–16
CORAS™ Concept tool, (1) 14–15
current practices, (1) 13–14
database structures, creating from models, (1) 16–17
definition, (1) 3–4
evaluating requirements, (1) 13
generic functionality, (1) 19
"good enough" designs, (1) 17–18
integrating user interface design, (1) 14–17
model construction, (1) 15
modeling, combined with construction, (1) 14
philosophy, (1) 13–14
prototypes, creating from models, (1) 16–17
prototyping, current practices, (1) 13
reducing design choices, (1) 17–20, (1) 33–35
software designers, role of, (1) 18–20
stereotypical solutions, (1) 18
task analysis, (1) 19
thinking-out-loud technique, (1) 13
ABC modeling, *vs.* object modeling
correctness, (1) 26–27
designer experience levels
causes of results, (1) 33
design strategies, (1) 27
future research on, (1) 31–32
Hawthorne Effect, (1) 33
live workshops, (1) 33
model correctness, (1) 26–27
productivity, (1) 27
prototyping, (1) 23–25
unbiased model correction, (1) 33
designer learning curve, (1) 31–32
facilitated workshops, (1) 20–21
future research
designer domain knowledge, (1) 30
designer training and experience, (1) 31–32
model states, (1) 29
sample size, (1) 29–30
variation in domain difficulty, (1) 30–31
modeling patterns, (1) 27–28
productivity, (1) 26–27
prototyping
design clichés, (1) 24–25
experience level of designers, (1) 23–25
migrating data between prototypes, (1) 24
re-keying test data, (1) 24
role playing, (1) 21–22

437

438 | INDEX

ABC modeling (cont.)
　qualitative results, (1) 23–25
　quantitative results, (1) 25–27
　role-playing, (1) 21–22
　test methodology, (1) 22–23
Abstract prototypes, (7) 251–252
Abstract use cases, (9) 347
Accelerated Business Concept modeling
　See ABC modeling
Actions
　See Tasks
Activities, (5) 162, (5) 163
　See also Tasks
Activity diagrams, UML, (9) 352–353
Advisor users, (8) 297–298
Ahlqvist, Stefan, xxi,
　biography, (ATA) 429
Ambassador users, (8) 297–298
Amos, Johnny
　biography, (ATA) 429
　participatory design, xix–xx
Analysis architectural model, (6) 212
Analysis model, (5) 167
Analysis workflow
　creating, (6) 229–233
　notation, (6) 217–219
Arch architectural model, (6) 209–210
Architecture
　interaction, (6) 214–216
　system, (4) 120–121, (6) 231–233
　user interface
　　See also ETP classification
　　analysis model, (6) 212
　　Arch model, (6) 209–210
　　business model, (6) 211–212
　　definition, (6) 208
　　design model, (6) 213, (6) 220–222
　　dialogue model, (6) 213, (6) 220–222
　　domain model, (6) 211–212

ETP, (4) 121–123
　interaction model, (6) 212–213
　presentation model, (6) 213, (6) 220–222
　Seeheim model, (6) 209–210
　use case model, (6) 212
　Wisdom model, (6) 210–214
Artifacts
　oo&hci, (10) 369
　RUP, (5) 162, (5) 163–164
Artim, John M.
　acknowledgments, xxv, (3) 111, (6) 240, (10) 422
　biography, (ATA) 430
　oo&hci, (10) 382
　task-based design, xxi
Asynchronous use case extensions, (7) 271–272
Attitude questionnaires, usage survey, (9) 324
Attribute values, average, (5) 189
Automating design, (1) 16–17
Autonomy, and scenario development, (2) 62–64
Averages
　action usage, (5) 189–190
　attribute values, (5) 189
　time devoted to interface design, (6) 202, (8) 285
　user interface code, (6) 202, (8) 285
　volume of objects, (5) 189

B
Basic user interaction scenarios
　definition, (2) 43
　example, (2) 45–49
Berry, Dick, (10) 382
Bitmaps, as prototyping tools, (5) 182–183
Booch, Grady, (9) 336
Boundary class diagrams, storyboarding, (5) 191
Boundary object interaction diagrams,

storyboarding, (5) 191–193
Brainstorming, (6) 226
Bridge method, (6) 206–208, (6) 236
Bridgeford, Charlie, (4) 156
Brittle analyses, (4) 133
Business architectural model, (6) 211–212
Business modeling
　See ABC modeling
Business rules, in use cases, (7) 275–276
Bylund, Stephan, xxi
　biography, (ATA) 430

C
Carroll, John M.
　acknowledgments, (10) 422
　biography, (ATA) 431
　oo&hci, (10) 382
　task-based design, xx
Case analysis, usage survey, (9) 323
Castro, Jaelson, (6) 240
CHI97 workshop, (4) 117–118, (6) 238–239
Christman, Lillian, (4) 156
Claims analysis, (2) 44, (2) 59–60
Class models, UML, (9) 350
Class Responsibility Collaborators, (2) 49–52
Coarse-grained task modeling, (3) 80–81
Cockburn, Alistair, (9) 339–341
Cognitive engineering, (8) 286, (10) 370–374
Collaboration
　among objects
　　See Object interaction and scenario development, (2) 62–64
Collaboration diagrams, UML, (9) 350–351
Collins, Dave, (10) 382
Comparison of tools, techniques and methods
　See Survey of tools, techniques, methods
Concept labels, (4) 132–133

Conceptual-core modeling, (2) 43, (10) 405
Conceptual models
  oo&hci
    definition, (10) 374
    envisioned, (10) 372
    existing, (10) 371–372
    object-oriented, (10) 379–383
    terminology of, (10) 373
    vs. mental models, (10) 381
  SBD, (2) 44
  scenario development, (2) 44
  usage survey, (9) 323
  vs. mental models, (2) 55
Concrete use cases, (7) 248–249
Concrete user interaction scenarios
  See also SBD
  See also Scenarios
  definition, (2) 44
  example, (2) 57
Concrete user interface design
  Idiom, (3) 102–107
  oo&hci, (10) 365, (10) 385–386
Conditional interaction, (7) 269
Constantine, Larry L.
  acknowledgments, (3) 111
  biography, (ATA) 431
  oo&hci, (10) 382
  use case based design, xxii
Content models, (10) 379–383
Contextual analysis, usage survey, (9) 323
CORAS™ Concept tool, (1) 14–15
Core models, (3) 89–92
Core system models, (3) 75
Cost of user interface design, (4) 147, (8) 284, (8) 285
Craft approach, (8) 286
CRC, (2) 49–52
CUA Object-View paradigm, (4) 151–152

Cunha, João F.
  biography, (ATA) 431–432
  use case-based design, xxii
Curbow, Dave, (10) 382

D
Database structures, creating from models, (1) 16–17
Dayton, Tom
  acknowledgments, xxv, (6) 240, (10) 422
  oo&hci, (10) 382
Delegation, and scenario development, (2) 62–64
Design, definition, xv
Design architectural model, (6) 213, (6) 220–222
Design workflow
  creating, (6) 233–238
  notation, (6) 220–222
Designers
  See Software designers
  See User interface designers
Designers models
  See Conceptual models
Development methods, software
  See Software development methods
Development methods, system
  See System development methods
Development models, Idiom, (3) 76
Dialogue architectural model, (6) 213, (6) 220–222
Domain analysis
  brevity, (4) 134–135
  brittle analyses, (4) 133
  categorizations, (4) 133
  concept labels, (4) 132–133
  domain concepts, (4) 132
  encyclopedias, as verification tools, (4) 133
  initial interface segmentation, (4) 135–139
  object-view paradigm, (4) 139
  operational definitions, (4) 132

  preferred terms, (4) 132
  primary views, (4) 138
  secondary views, (4) 138
  state behavior, (4) 142–144
  statechart, (4) 142–144
  tasks, in terms of user questions, (4) 139
  user navigation, (4) 139–142
Domain concepts, (4) 132
Domain difficulty, effects of, (1) 30–31
Domain knowledge, and software designers, (1) 30
Domain modeling
  Idiom, (3) 75, (3) 86–87
  separating from user models, (9) 336–337
  UML, (9) 336–337, (9) 350
  usage-centered design, (7) 251
  user analysis, (3) 86–87
  user interface architecture, (6) 211–212
  Wisdom, (6) 211–212
Drawings, as prototyping tools, (5) 182–183
DSDM
  advisor users, (8) 297–298
  ambassador users, (8) 297–298
  definition, (1) 8–9
  frequency of product delivery, (1) 9–10
  high-level baselines, (1) 11
  iterative and incremental development, (1) 10
  and oo&hci, (10) 393–394
  principles of, (1) 9–11, (8) 295
  product fitness for purpose, (1) 10
  prototyping, (8) 295–297
  reversing changes, (1) 10
  stakeholder cooperation, (1) 11
  team empowerment, (1) 9
  testing, (1) 11
  usability designers, (8) 300–301
  user-centered design, (8) 294–298

DSDM (*cont.*)
  user involvement, (8) 297–298
  visionary users, (8) 297–298
Dynamic System Development Method
  See DSDM
Dynamic view model, (3) 97

E
80/20 rule, (1) 17–18
Encapsulation, and scenario development, (2) 62–64
Encyclopedias, as verification tools, (4) 133
Enhanced software engineering approach, (8) 286
Entities, (4) 122
Entity, Task, and Presenter classification
  See ETP classification
Envisioned task models, (10) 383–384
Escoto, Debbie, (4) 156
Essential use cases
  definition, (7) 249
  Identification section, (7) 265–266
  Process section, (7) 267–268
  Relationships section, (7) 266–267
  SBD, example, (2) 48–49
  structure of, (7) 264–268
  UML, (9) 344
  usage survey, (9) 323
  vs. scenarios, (2) 48–49
ETP classification
  architecture
    definition, (4) 120
    system, (4) 120–121
    user interface, (4) 121–123
  categorizations in design phase, (4) 154–155
  CHI97 workshop, (4) 117–118
  domain analysis
    brevity, (4) 134–135
    brittle analyses, (4) 133
    categorizations, (4) 133

concept labels, (4) 132–133
domain concepts, (4) 132
encyclopedias, as verification tools, (4) 133
initial interface segmentation, (4) 135–139
object-view paradigm, (4) 139
operational definitions, (4) 132
preferred terms, (4) 132
primary views, (4) 138
secondary views, (4) 138
state behavior, (4) 142–144
statechart, (4) 142–144
tasks, in terms of user questions, (4) 139
user navigation, (4) 139–142
entities, (4) 122
introduction, (4) 116
language changes, effects of, (4) 155–156
ontological drift, (4) 155–156
presenters, (4) 122
problem specification, (4) 118–119
solution specification, (4) 119–120
stability in design, (4) 123
storyboarding, (4) 149–150
system design and implementation
  change, analyzing effects of, (4) 153
  ETP categorizations in design phase, (4) 154–155
  impact analysis, (4) 153
task analysis
  definition, (4) 124
  discrete task goals, (4) 131
  individual tasks, (4) 125
  rich picture technique, (4) 127
  scenarios, (4) 127–130
  stereotyping, (4) 129–130

task decomposition, chunking, (4) 135–139
task decomposition, creating, (4) 130–131
task overviews, (4) 125–127
use case diagrams, (4) 125–127
user profiles, (4) 124–125
user questions, identifying, (4) 131
user questions, purpose of, (4) 139, (4) 140
user questions, tasks from, (4) 139
user work context, (4) 124–125
tasks, (4) 122
usability testing, (4) 152
user interface design
  cost of, (4) 147
  increasing awareness of, (4) 148
  look-and-feel, (4) 147
  patterns, compound, (4) 148
  patterns, definition, (4) 144–145
  problem-space representation, (4) 146–148
  prototyping, (4) 149–150
  screen real estate, (4) 152
  storyboarding, (4) 149–150
  transactions, (4) 150–151
  units of work, (4) 150–151
  user interface layout, (4) 145–146
  user navigation, (4) 151–152
  view behavior, (4) 151–152
  visual formalism, (4) 146–148
  visual language, (4) 146–148

Index

windowing techniques, (4) 151–152
user navigation, (4) 139–142, (4) 151–152
user profiling, (4) 124–125
Evaluating existing system, usage survey, (9) 323
Evolutionary prototyping, (6) 205–206
Executables, as prototyping tools, (5) 182–183
Existing task models, (10) 383–384
Extensions, use case, (7) 270–272

F
Facilitated workshops, (1) 20–21
Field work, (10) 400–402
Fine-grained task modeling, (3) 92
Fixed navigation, (4) 140
Flexible navigation, (4) 140–142
Flow of events, storyboarding, (5) 186–187
Flow of events-storyboards *See* Use cases, storyboarding
Fulcher, Richard, (4) 156

G
Goal-based use cases, (9) 339–341
Goals, (10) 373–374
"Good enough" designs, (1) 17–18
Göranson, Bengt
 biography, (ATA) 432
 user-centered design, xxii–xxiv
Graphical User Interface Design and Evaluation, (9) 325–326
GUIDE, (9) 325–326
Gulliksen, Jan
 biography, (ATA) 432–433
 user-centered design, xxii–xxiv

H
Hawthorne Effect, (1) 33
HCI activities
 increasing awareness of, (4) 148
 and object-oriented design *See* Oo&hci method
 organizing *See* ABC modeling *See* ETP classification
Help, storyboarding, (5) 187–189
High-level task model *See* Coarse-grained task modeling
Hudson, William
 acknowledgments, (10) 422
 biography, (ATA) 433
 user-centered design, xxii–xxiv
Human-centered design, (10) 375–377
Human-Centered Design Process for Interactive Systems, (8) 290–291
Human-computer interaction *See* HCI
Human factors engineering *See* HCI
Hurwood, Barbara, acknowledgments, xxv

I
Idiom
 concrete user interface design, (3) 102–107
 core models, (3) 89–92
 core system models, (3) 75
 definition, (3) 71
 design activities, (3) 73–77
 development models, (3) 76
 domain models, (3) 75, (3) 86–87
 field evaluation of, (3) 108–111
 history of, (3) 71–73
 inappropriate assumptions, (3) 88–89
 informing activities, (3) 73
 interaction sequences, (3) 87–89, (3) 103–104
 interaction specifications, (3) 76
 interaction techniques, (3) 75
 interactive system models, (3) 76
 iterative design, (3) 73
 mutually informing activities, (3) 73
 object types, (3) 73
 opportunistic design, (3) 73
 prototyping, (3) 104–107
 referent types, (3) 86–87
 referents, (3) 84–85
 scenario development, (3) 79
 sketching, (3) 87–89
 storyboards, (3) 87–89
 sub-optimal design choices, (3) 89
 system descriptions
  core models, (3) 89–92
  fine-grained task modeling, (3) 92
  view models, (3) 92–102
 task descriptions, (3) 85–86
 tasks, mapping to views, (3) 94–96
 task modeling, coarse-grained, (3) 80–81
 task modeling, fine-grained, (3) 92
 UML sequence diagrams, (3) 82–84
 usability of, (3) 111
 use cases, generating, (3) 107
 user input methods, (3) 75
 user interface design, (3) 77–78
 view models
  definition, (3) 76
  dynamic view model, (3) 97
  example, (3) 93
  static view models, (3) 92, (3) 97–100
  top-level views, (3) 94–95
  transactions (modeling constructs), (3) 100–102
  view behavior, (3) 97
  view structure, (3) 97–100
  view transition machine, (3) 97
Idiom94, (3) 71–73

Implementation referents, (10) 409
Implementation workflow, (6) 222–223
Included use cases, (7) 269
Informing, (10) 387
Informing activities, (3) 73
Inheritance, and scenario development, (2) 62–64
Interaction architectural model, (6) 212–213
Interaction contexts, (7) 251–252
Interaction modeling, (10) 405–406
Interaction sequences, (3) 87–89, (3) 103–104
Interaction specifications, (3) 76
Interaction techniques, (3) 75
Interactions, OVID, (9) 328
Interactive system design
 See Oo&hci
 See Wisdom
Interactive system models, (3) 76
Interactive systems
 definition, (10) 373
 domain modeling, (10) 414–416
 Human-Centered Design Process for Interactive Systems, (8) 290–291
 ISO 9241, (10) 370
 ISO 13407, (8) 290–291
Interface architecture design, (6) 231–233
Interiorizing the project, (6) 226
Internal system analysis, (6) 229–232
Internal system design, (6) 233, (6) 235
ISO 9241, (10) 370
ISO 13407
 context of use, (9) 343
 human-centered design cycle, (10) 376
 principles of human-centered software, (8) 290–291
 system development activities, (9) 346

ISO standard for human-centered design
 See ISO 13407
Iterative design
 DSDM, (1) 10
 Idiom, (3) 73
 user-centered design process, (8) 289

J
Jacobs, Jan, (4) 156
Jacobsen, Ivar, (9) 334–336
JAD workshops, (8) 297–298
Joint Application Development workshops, (8) 297–298

K
Karat, Claire-Marie, (10) 420
Karat, John, (10) 377
Kawakami, Katsura, Dr., xxv–xxvi, (3) 111
Kruchten, Phillippe
 biography, (ATA) 433
 use case-based design, xxi

L
Language changes, effects of, (4) 155–156
Leung, Tony, (4) 156
Lif, Magnus
 biography, (ATA) 433–434
 user-centered design, xxii–xxiv
Lightweight software engineering
 See Wisdom
Lockwood, Lucy A. D.
 biography, (ATA) 434
 oo&hci, (10) 382
 use case-based design, xxii
Logical User-Centered Interaction Design, (9) 326
Look-and-feel, (4) 147
Low-fidelity prototyping, usage survey, (9) 323
LUCID, (9) 326

M
Main primary window, prototyping, (5) 178–179

Mandel, Theo, (10) 382
Martin, Dave, (10) 422
McGinnes, Simon
 acknowledgments, (4) 156
 biography, (ATA) 434
 participatory design, xix–xx
MDI, (4) 152
Mental models
 brain mechanisms and, (1) 5
 conceptual meaning, developing, (1) 15–16
 conceptual schemata, (1) 4
 definition, (1) 4
 emergent concepts, (1) 6
 oo&hci, (10) 370–374
 recognizable analogues, (1) 4
 structure mapping, (1) 5
 vs. conceptual models, (2) 55
Methods, comparison of
 See Survey of tools, techniques, methods
Microsoft Multiple Document Interface, (4) 152
Model-based user interface design, (10) 377–384
Model-first design, (2) 61–62
Modeling
 See also ABC modeling
 See also Conceptual models
 See also Domain modeling
 See also ETP classification
 See also Mental models
 See also Task modeling
 See also View models
 See also Wisdom
 combining with construction, (1) 14
 patterns of, (1) 27–28
 use cases
  oo&hci, (10) 403
  RUP, (5) 171–176
Multiple Document Interface, (4) 152
Mutual informing, (10) 387
Mutually informing activities, (3) 73
"My baby" syndrome, (8) 288

Index | **443**

N
Narrative style, use cases
abstraction, (7) 260–262
continuous narrative, (7) 257
elements of style, (7) 268–272
importance of, (7) 256
interaction diagrams, (7) 260
numbered sequences, (7) 258
partitioned narratives, (7) 259–260
pre- and post-conditions, (7) 260–262
pseudo-code, (7) 260
suitable vagueness, (7) 262
Navigation, user
See User navigation
Navigation design, usage survey, (9) 324
Nike approach to software development, (6) 201–202
Norman, Donald
mental models, (10) 371–372
user-centered design, xxii–xxiv, (10) 375
Notations
UML
activity diagrams, (9) 352–353
class models, (9) 350
collaboration diagrams, (9) 350–351
domain models, (9) 350
sequence diagrams, (9) 350
state diagrams, (9) 351–352
use cases, (7) 249–250
Wisdom
analysis workflow, (6) 217–219
definition, (6) 217
design workflow, (6) 220–222
implementation workflow, (6) 222–223
requirements workflow, (6) 217
Nunes, Nuno
biography, (ATA) 434–435

acknowledgments, xxv, (3) 111, (4) 156, (10) 422
use case-based design, xxi
user-centered design, xxii

O
Object, View, and Interaction Design, (9) 326–329
Object collaboration
See Object interaction
Object interactions
definition, (2) 40
and scenario development, (2) 44
Object metaphor, and scenario development, (2) 62–64
Object modeling
See ABC modeling
See Idiom
Object models, and scenario development, (2) 43–44
Object-oriented design
See also DSDM
See also Oo&hci
See also RUP
See also UML
See also User-centered design
definition, (2) 40
learning, (8) 287–288
POV scenarios, (2) 49–52
problem analysis, (2) 40–41
responsibility-driven design, (2) 41–42
Object-oriented user interface, (10) 380
Object-oriented user interface design, (2) 44
Object types, (3) 73
Objects
OVID, (9) 328
storyboarding average volume of, (5) 189
use cases, (7) 268–269
Online help, storyboarding, (5) 187–189
Ontological drift, (4) 155–156
Oo&hci method
abstract descriptions, (10) 411–412

adopting, (10) 416–420
artifacts, (10) 369
characteristics of, xvii–xix
cognitive engineering, (10) 370–374
conceptual models
core, (10) 415
definition, (10) 374
envisioned, (10) 372
existing, (10) 371–372
object-oriented, (10) 379–383
terminology of, (10) 373
vs. mental models, (10) 381
concrete descriptions, (10) 412
concrete user interfaces, (10) 365, (10) 385–386
content models, (10) 379–383
designer's world, (10) 410–414
development models (10) 415
DSDM, (10) 393–394
goals, (10) 373–374
human-centered design, (10) 375–377
implementation referents, (10) 409
informing, (10) 387
interaction models, (10) 415
interactive systems, (10) 414–416
introduction, (10) 365–367
mental models, (10) 370–374
model-based user interface design, (10) 377–384
mutual informing, (10) 387
need for, (10) 367–368
opportunistic design, (10) 387
participatory design, (10) 390–394
prototyping, (10) 387–389
purpose of, (10) 404–405
quality assurance, (10) 387–394
referents, (10) 374, (10) 409, (10) 413

Oo&hci method (*cont.*)
 scenarios, (10) 384–385, (10) 414
 task models, (10) 374, (10) 383–384
 tasks, (10) 373, (10) 413
 unified domain models, (10) 416
 usability testing, (10) 389–390
 user-centered design, (10) 375–377
 user interface metaphors, (10) 380
 user profiles, (10) 413
 users' world, (10) 408–410
Oo&hci method, integrated approach
 activities of, (10) 398–400
 characteristics of, (10) 397–398
 conceptual-core modeling, (10) 405
 domain modeling, (10) 404–405
 domain models
  abstract descriptions, (10) 411–412
  conceptual-core models, (10) 415
  concrete descriptions, (10) 412
  designer's world, (10) 410–414
  development models, (10) 415
  implementation referents, (10) 409
  interaction models, (10) 415
  referents, (10) 409, (10) 413
  scenarios, (10) 414
  tasks, (10) 413
  unified domain models, (10) 416
  user profiles, (10) 413
  users' world, (10) 408–410
 field work, (10) 400–402
 foundations of, (10) 394–395
 interaction modeling, (10) 405–406
 participatory design, (10) 402
 prototyping, (10) 406–407
 referent identification, (10) 404
 scenario generation, (10) 402–403
 task modeling, (10) 403
 use case modeling, (10) 403
 user profiling, (10) 402
OOUI, (10) 380
OOUID, (2) 44
Operational definitions, (4) 132
Operational models, (7) 251
Opportunistic design, (3) 73, (10) 387
OVID, (9) 326–329

P
PANDA, (10) 391
Paper prototyping, usage survey, (9) 323
Partial ordering, use cases, (7) 269–270
Participatory ANalysis, Design, and Assessment, (10) 391
Participatory design
 See also ABC modeling
 definition, xix–xx
 oo&hci, (10) 390–394, (10) 402
Patterns
 of modeling strategies, (1) 27–28
 of user interfaces, (4) 144–145, (4) 148
Personas, usage survey, (9) 323
Point-of-view scenarios, (2) 44, (2) 49–52
Polymorphism, and scenario development, (2) 62–64
POV scenarios, (2) 44, (2) 49–52
Preferred terms, (4) 132
Presentation architectural model, (6) 213, (6) 220–222
Presenters, (4) 122
Primary views, (4) 138
Primary windows, prototyping
 designing, (5) 181–182
 identifying, (5) 178–179
 operations of, (5) 180
 visualizing, (5) 179–180
Problem-space representation, (4) 146–148
Productivity, ABC modeling *vs.* object modeling, (1) 26–27
Prototypes
 abstract, (7) 251–252
 creating from models, (1) 16–17
 design clichés, (1) 24–25
 high-fidelity, (10) 389, (10) 406–407
 low-fidelity, (9) 323, (10) 388–389, (10) 406–407
 oo&hci, (10) 387–389, (10) 406–407
 paper
  oo&hci, (10) 388–389, (10) 406–407
  RUP, (5) 182–183
  UML, (9) 323
 storyboarding, (5) 195
 usability testing, (5) 184–185
Prototyping
 See also ABC modeling
 See also RUP
 See also User interface modeling
 with bitmaps, (5) 182–183
 current practices in, (1) 13
 definition (RUP), (5) 176–177
 and designer experience levels, (1) 23–25
 with drawings, (5) 182–183
 DSDM, (8) 295–297
 ETP, (4) 149–150
 evolutionary, (6) 205–206
 with executables, (5) 182–183
 experience level of designers, (1) 23–25
 feedback from, (5) 183–185
 Idiom, (3) 104–107
 implementation forms, (5) 182–183

main primary window, (5) 178–179
migrating data between prototypes, (1) 24
oo&hci, (10) 387–389, (10) 406–407
primary windows
  designing, (5) 181–182
  identifying, (5) 178–179
  operations of, (5) 180
  visualizing, (5) 179–180
purpose, (5) 177
re-keying test data, (1) 24
role playing, (1) 21–22
RUP, (8) 293
task analysis, (4) 149–150
UCEP, (6) 197–198
usage survey, (9) 323
use tests, (5) 184–185
user-centered design, (8) 289
vs. real product, (5) 183
walkthroughs, (5) 184
Wisdom, (6) 205–206

Q
Quality assurance, (10) 387–394

R
Rational Unified Process
  See RUP
Reducing design choices, (1) 17–20, (1) 33–35
Referent types, (3) 86–87
Referents
  identifying, (10) 404
  Idiom, (3) 84–87
  implementation, (10) 409
  oo&hci, (10) 374, (10) 404, (10) 409, (10) 413
  types of, (3) 86–87
  in user analysis, (3) 84–85
Requirements
  See System requirements
  See Usability requirements
Requirements discovery, (6) 227
Requirements workflow
  creating, (6) 226–229
  notation, (6) 217
Responsibility-driven design, (2) 41–42

Rich picture technique, (4) 127, (9) 342
Roberts, Dave, (6) 240, (10) 382
Role-playing, (1) 21–22
Rosson, Mary Beth
  acknowledgments, (3) 111, (4) 156
  biography, (ATA) 435
  oo&hci, (10) 382
  task-based design, xx
RUP
  activities, (5) 162, (5) 163
  analysis model, (5) 167
  artifacts, (5) 162, (5) 163–164
  definition, (5) 161–162
  field evaluations of, (8) 293–294
  guidelines, (5) 165
  prototyping, (8) 291–294
  steps, (5) 163
  stereotyping, (5) 167
  storyboards, use case
    average action usage, (5) 189–190
    average attribute values, (5) 189
    average volume of objects, (5) 189
    boundary class diagrams, (5) 191
    boundary object interaction diagrams, (5) 191–193
    creating, (5) 172–176
    description, (5) 169–171, (5) 185–186
    flow of events, (5) 186–187
    maintaining, (5) 195
    online help, identifying need for, (5) 187–189
    task frequency, (5) 189–190
    usability aspects, example, (5) 190–191
    usability requirements, capturing, (5) 193–195
    user interface modeling, (5) 171–176
    and the user interface prototype, (5) 195
  units of work

    See Activities
  usability designers, (8) 300
  use case model, (5) 171–176
  user-centered design, (8) 291–294
  user interface modeling, (5) 171–176
  user interface prototype
    bitmaps, (5) 182–183
    definition, (5) 176–177
    drawings, (5) 182–183
    executables, (5) 182–183
    feedback from, (5) 183–185
    implementation forms, (5) 182–183
    main primary window, (5) 178–179
    primary windows, designing, (5) 181–182
    primary windows, identifying, (5) 178–179
    primary windows, operations of, (5) 180
    primary windows, visualizing, (5) 179–180
    purpose, (5) 177
    use tests, (5) 184–185
    vs. real product, (5) 183
    walkthroughs, (5) 184
  vs. UML, (9) 353–355
  workers
    definition, (5) 162, (5) 163
    user interface designer, (5) 168–169
  workflow
    definition, (5) 164
    and user interface design, (5) 167–168

S
SBD
  See also Scenarios
  See also Task analysis
  See also Use cases
  analyzing with claims analysis, (2) 44
  basic user interaction scenarios, (2) 43

SBD (cont.)
  conceptual-core models, (2) 43
  conceptual models, (2) 44
  concrete user interaction scenarios
    definition, (2) 44
    example, (2) 57
  example
    autonomy, (2) 62–64
    basic user interaction scenarios, (2) 45–49
    claims analysis, (2) 59–60
    collaboration, (2) 62–64
    CRC, (2) 49–52
    delegation, (2) 62–64
    encapsulation, (2) 62–64
    essential use cases, (2) 48–49
    inheritance, (2) 62–64
    mental models vs. conceptual models, (2) 55
    model-first design, (2) 61–62
    object metaphor, (2) 62–64
    object-oriented design, (2) 49–52
    polymorphism, (2) 62–64
    POV scenarios, (2) 49–52
    Scenario Browser, (2) 64–65
    scenario generation heuristic, (2) 47–48
    system-responsibility descriptions, (2) 48–49
    thumbnail scenarios, (2) 46–47
    tools for, (2) 64–65
    trade-off analysis, (2) 52–55, (2) 59–61
    typology of user concerns, (2) 47–48
    unit tasks, (2) 49
    usability studies, (2) 60–61
    user-intention descriptions, (2) 48–49
  user interactions, (2) 55–58
  what-if scenarios, (2) 54–55
  object interactions, (2) 44
  object models, (2) 43–44
  object-oriented design, (2) 40–42
  OOUID, (2) 44
  POV scenarios, (2) 44
  task-object interactions, (2) 42–45
  use cases, (2) 42
  user consequence analysis, (2) 44
  user interaction scenarios, (2) 42
Scenario-based design
  See also ETP classification
  See also Idiom
  See also SBD
  definition, xx
Scenario Browser, (2) 64–65
Scenarios
  See also Idiom
  See also SBD
  See also Task analysis
  See also Use cases
  generation heuristic, (2) 47–48
  Idiom, (3) 79
  oo&hci, (10) 384–385, (10) 402–403
  in task analysis, (4) 127–130
  usage-centered design, (7) 253–255
  usage survey, (9) 323
  vs. use cases, (9) 336, (9) 342
Schrier, Jaclyn, (4) 156
Screen real estate, (4) 152
Secondary views, (4) 138
Seeheim architectural model, (6) 209–210
Sequence diagrams, UML, (9) 350
Sketching, (3) 87–89
Software designers
  ABC modeling vs. object modeling
    causes of results, (1) 33
    design strategies, (1) 27
    domain knowledge, (1) 30
    future research on, (1) 31–32
    Hawthorne Effect, (1) 33
    learning curve, (1) 31–32
    live workshops, (1) 33
    model correctness, (1) 26–27
    productivity, (1) 27
    prototyping, (1) 23–25
    unbiased model correction, (1) 33
  role of, (1) 18–20
Software development companies, and user interface design
  See Wisdom
Software development methods
  See also ABC modeling
  See also DSDM
  See also Idiom
  See also Wisdom
  barriers, (1) 7–8
  Bridge method, (6) 206–208, (6) 236
  comparison of
    See Survey of tools, techniques, methods
  deliberate simplicity, (1) 8
  enablers, (1) 7–8
  facilitated workshops, (1) 11–12
  facilitators, (1) 12
  GUIDE, (9) 325–326
  iterative evolution, (6) 205–208
  JAD, (1) 11–12
  LUCID, (9) 326
  Nike "just do it," (6) 201–202
  OVID, (9) 326–329
  rate of project failure, (8) 284
  self-correction, (1) 8
  SSDs, (6) 201–202
  STUDIO, (9) 329–330
  Trojan horse, (6) 206
  usage-centered design, (7) 252
  user involvement, importance of, (8) 284

whitewater evolution, (6) 205
Wisdom process, (6) 203–208
SSDs, and user interface design
See Wisdom
Stakeholder meetings, usage survey, (9) 322
State behavior, (4) 142–144
State diagrams, UML, (9) 351–352
Statechart, (4) 142–144
Static view models, (3) 92, (3) 97–100
Steps, (5) 163
Stereotyping
  RUP, (5) 167
  in task analysis, (4) 129–130
  Wisdom, (6) 215–217, (6) 219
Storyboarding
  ETP, (4) 149–150
  Idiom, (3) 87–89
  RUP
    average action usage, (5) 189–190
    average attribute values, (5) 189
    average volume of objects, (5) 189
    boundary class diagrams, (5) 191
    boundary object interaction diagrams, (5) 191–193
    creating, (5) 172–176
    description, (5) 169–171, (5) 185–186
    flow of events, (5) 186–187
    maintaining, (5) 195
    online help, identifying need for, (5) 187–189
    task frequency, (5) 189–190
    usability aspects, example, (5) 190–191
    usability requirements, capturing, (5) 193–195
    user interface modeling, (5) 171–176

and the user interface prototype, (5) 195
use cases
  See Use cases, storyboarding
STructured User-Interface Design for Interaction Optimisation, (9) 329–330
STUDIO, (9) 329–330
Style guides, usage survey, (9) 324
Survey of tools, techniques, methods
  frequency of use, (9) 320
  methods
    GUIDE, (9) 325–326
    included in survey, (9) 318
    LUCID, (9) 326
    OVID, (9) 326–329
    STUDIO, (9) 329–330
    usage-centered design, (9) 330–331
  respondent breakdown, (9) 319
  survey methodology, (9) 317–320
  techniques
    attitude questionnaires, (9) 324
    case analysis, (9) 323
    contextual analysis, (9) 323
    essential use cases, (9) 323
    evaluating existing system, (9) 323
    included in survey, (9) 318
    low-fidelity prototyping, (9) 323
    navigation design, (9) 324
    paper prototyping, (9) 323
    personas, (9) 323
    scenarios, (9) 323
    stakeholder meetings, (9) 322
    style guides, (9) 324
    task analysis, (9) 323
    task identification, (9) 323

usability checklists, (9) 324
usability evaluations, (9) 324
usability goals, quantifying, (9) 323
usability requirements, setting, (9) 323
usability surveys, (9) 324
usability testing, (9) 324
user analysis, (9) 323
user conceptual models, (9) 323
user profiling, (9) 323
visual interface design, (9) 324
ten most popular, (9) 321–322, (9) 346–347, (9) 348
tools included in survey, (9) 318
Swedish National Tax Board, (8) 304–309
Synchronous use case extensions, (7) 271
System architecture
  See Architecture, system
System context, understanding, (6) 226–227
System design and implementation
  change, analyzing effects of, (4) 153
  ETP categorizations in design phase, (4) 154–155
  impact analysis, (4) 153
System development methods
  DSDM, (8) 294–298
  ISO 13407, (8) 290–291
  JAD workshops, (8) 297–298
  RUP, (8) 291–294
System requirements
  evaluating, (1) 13
  from use cases, (9) 344–345
System-responsibility descriptions, (2) 48–49

T

Task analysis
  See also SBD
  See also Scenarios
  See also Task modeling
  See also Use cases
  alternatives to, (1) 19
  definition, (4) 124
  discrete task goals, (4) 131
  individual tasks, (4) 125
  mapping tasks to views, (3) 94–96
  rich picture technique, (4) 127
  scenarios, (4) 127–130
  stereotyping, (4) 129–130
  task descriptions, (3) 85–86
  task overviews, (4) 125–127
  usage survey, (9) 323
  use case diagrams, (4) 125–127
  user profiles, (4) 124–125
  user questions
    identifying, (4) 131
    purpose of, (4) 139, (4) 140
    tasks from, (4) 139
  user work context, (4) 124–125
Task-based design, xx
  See also ETP classification
  See also Idiom
  See also SBD
Task decomposition
  chunking, (4) 135–139
  creating, (4) 130–131
Task flows, (6) 206–208
Task modeling
  See also Idiom
  See also Task analysis
  coarse-grained, (3) 80–81
  fine-grained, (3) 92
  oo&hci, (10) 374, (10) 383–384, (10) 403
  usage-centered design, (7) 251, (7) 253–255
Task-object interactions, and scenario development, (2) 42–45
Task overviews, (4) 125–127
Tasks
  derived from user questions, (4) 139
  ETP definition of, (4) 122
  frequency, storyboarding, (5) 189–190
  goals, in use cases, (7) 263–264
  oo&hci, (10) 373
  OVID, (9) 328
Techniques, comparison of
  See Survey of tools, techniques, methods
Technologist approach, (8) 286–287
Thinking-out-loud technique, (1) 13
Thumbnail scenarios, (2) 46–47
Tools
  comparison of
    See Survey of tools, techniques, methods
  Scenario Browser, (2) 64–65
  for scenario development, (2) 64–65
  user-centered design process, (8) 285–287
  user interface design
    See ABC modeling
    See DSDM
    See Idiom
    See RUP
    See UML
    See Wisdom
Top-level views, (3) 94–95
Trade-off analysis, (2) 52–55, (2) 59–61
Transactions, (4) 150–151
Transactions (modeling constructs), (3) 100–102
Typology of user concerns, (2) 47–48

U

UCEP, (6) 197–198
UIM, (8) 302–304
UML
  benefits of, (9) 356
  compared to
    RUP, (9) 353–355
    usage-centered design, (9) 355–356
  future of, (9) 358
  notation
    activity diagrams, (9) 352–353
    class models, (9) 350
    collaboration diagrams, (9) 350–351
    domain models, (9) 350
    sequence diagrams, (9) 350
    state diagrams, (9) 351–352
  use cases
    abstract, (9) 347
    context of use, (9) 343
    drawbacks, (9) 316–317, (9) 332–334
    essential, (9) 344
    goal-based, (9) 339–341
    as requirements, (9) 344–345
    vs. scenarios, (9) 336, (9) 342
  user-centered design
    barriers to, (9) 334–339, (9) 357–358
    contextual information, (9) 338
    deliberate user interface design, (9) 337–338
    incorporating, (9) 316–317
    ISO 13407, (9) 343, (9) 346
    modifications for, (9) 347–349
    need for, (9) 313–315
    perspectives, (9) 332–334
    rich picture technique, (9) 342
    separation of user and domain models, (9) 336–337
    top ten techniques, (9) 346–347, (9) 348
    usability evaluation, (9) 339
    user models, (9) 348
UML sequence diagrams, (3) 82–84
Unified Modeling Language
  See UML
Unified Process *vs.* Wisdom, (6) 227
Unit tasks, (2) 49

Units of work, (4) 150–151
  See also Activities
  See also Tasks
UP *vs.* Wisdom, (6) 227
Usability
  definition, (8) 284
  failure
    consequences of, xv
    example, xvi–xvii
  goals, quantifying, (9) 323
  of Idiom, (3) 111
  storyboarding, example, (5) 190–191
Usability checklists, usage survey, (9) 324
Usability designers
  See User interface designers
Usability evaluations
  See Usability studies
  See Usability testing
Usability requirements
  setting, (9) 323
  storyboarding, (5) 193–195
Usability studies, (2) 60–61
Usability surveys, usage survey, (9) 324
Usability testing
  ETP, (4) 152
  oo&hci, (10) 389–390
  on prototypes, (5) 184–185
  UML, (9) 339
  usage survey, (9) 324
Usage-centered design
  See also Use cases
  See also User-centered design
  abstract prototypes, (7) 251–252
  definition, (7) 250
  domain models, (7) 251
  interaction contexts, (7) 251–252
  operational models, (7) 251
  scenarios, (7) 253–255
  and software development processes, (7) 252
  task modeling, (7) 253–255
  task models, (7) 251
  usage survey, (9) 330–331
  use case decomposition, (7) 255
  use case maps, (7) 251
  use cases, (7) 253–255
  user role maps, (7) 251

user role models, (7) 251
  vs. UML, (9) 355–356
  vs. user-centered design, (9) 330–331
Use case architectural model, (6) 212
Use case-based design
  See also RUP
  See also Wisdom
  definition, xxi
Use case diagrams, (4) 125–127
Use case maps
  definition, (7) 251
  representing relationships, (7) 273–275
  representing use cases, (7) 273
  usage-centered design, (7) 251
Use case modeling
  oo&hci, (10) 403
  RUP, (5) 171–176
Use cases
  See also RUP
  See also Scenarios
  See also Task analysis
  See also UML
  See also Usage-centered design
  abstract, (9) 347
  asynchronous extensions, (7) 271–272
  business rules, (7) 275–276
  concrete, (7) 248–249
  conditional interaction, (7) 269
  context of use, (9) 343
  decomposition, (7) 255
  definition, (7) 246–248, (9) 336
  drawbacks, (9) 316–317, (9) 332–334
  essential
    definition, (7) 249
    Identification section, (7) 265–266
    Process section, (7) 267–268
    Relationships section, (7) 266–267
    structure of, (7) 264–268
    UML, (9) 344
  extensions, (7) 270–272

  generating in Idiom, (3) 107
  goal-based, (9) 339–341
  included, (7) 269
  narrative style
    abstraction, (7) 260–262
    continuous narrative, (7) 257
    elements of style, (7) 268–272
    importance of, (7) 256
    interaction diagrams, (7) 260
    numbered sequences, (7) 258
    partitioned narratives, (7) 259–260
    pre- and post-conditions, (7) 260–262
    pseudo-code, (7) 260
    suitable vagueness, (7) 262
  notation, (7) 249–250
  objects, (7) 268–269
  partial ordering, (7) 269–270
  as requirements, (9) 344–345
  storyboarding
    average action usage, (5) 189–190
    average attribute values, (5) 189
    average volume of objects, (5) 189
    boundary class diagrams, (5) 191
    boundary object interaction diagrams, (5) 191–193
    creating, (5) 172–176
    description, (5) 169–171, (5) 185–186
    flow of events, (5) 186–187
    maintaining, (5) 195
    online help, identifying need for, (5) 187–189
    task frequency, (5) 189–190
    usability aspects, example, (5) 190–191
    usability requirements, capturing, (5) 193–195

Use cases (*cont.*)
   user interface modeling, (5) 171–176
   and the user interface prototype, (5) 195
   synchronous extensions, (7) 271
   task goals, (7) 263–264
   usage-centered design, (7) 253–255
   user intentions, (7) 263–264
   vs. scenarios, (9) 336, (9) 342
   vs. user interaction scenarios, (2) 42
   Wisdom, (6) 206–208
User analysis
   See also Scenarios
   See also Task analysis
   See also Use cases
   domain model, (3) 86–87
   inappropriate assumptions, (3) 88–89
   interaction sequences, (3) 87–89, (3) 103–104
   referent types, (3) 86–87
   referents, (3) 84–85
   scenario development, (3) 79
   sketching, (3) 87–89
   storyboards, (3) 87–89
   sub-optimal design choices, (3) 89
   task descriptions, (3) 85–86
   task modeling
      coarse-grained, (3) 80–81
      fine-grained, (3) 92
   UML sequence diagrams, (3) 82–84
   usage survey, (9) 323
User-centered design
   See also Oo&hci
   See also RUP
   See also Usage-centered design
   See also User interface design
   cognitive engineering approach, (8) 286
   craft approach, (8) 286
   definition, xxii–xxiv
   enhanced software engineering approach, (8) 286
   field experiment with, (8) 304–309
   GUIDE, (9) 325–326
   introducing to the development process, (8) 306–308
   iterative design, (8) 289
   LUCID, (9) 326
   methods, (8) 285–287
   "my baby" syndrome, (8) 288
   object-oriented design, (8) 287–288
   obstacles to, (8) 308–309
   oo&hci, (10) 375–377
   OVID, (9) 326–329
   prototyping, (8) 289
   STUDIO, (9) 329–330
   system development processes
      DSDM, (8) 294–298
      ISO 13407, (8) 290–291
      JAD, (8) 297–298
      RUP, (8) 291–294
   technologist approach, (8) 286–287
   tools, (8) 285–287
   with UML
      barriers to, (9) 334–339, (9) 357–358
      contextual information, (9) 338
      deliberate user interface design, (9) 337–338
      incorporating, (9) 316–317
      ISO 13407, (9) 343, (9) 346
      modifications for, (9) 347–349
      need for, (9) 313–315
      perspectives, (9) 332–334
      rich picture technique, (9) 342
      separation of user and domain models, (9) 336–337
      top ten techniques, (9) 346–347, (9) 348
      usability evaluation, (9) 339
   user models, (9) 348
   usability, definition, (8) 284
   usability designers, (8) 298–301
   user interface modeling, (8) 301–304
   user involvement, importance of, (8) 284
   vs. usage-centered design, (9) 330–331
User-Centered Evolutionary Prototyping, (6) 197–198
User-centered techniques and methods, comparison of
   See Survey of tools, techniques, methods
User conceptual models, usage survey, (9) 323
User-intention descriptions, (2) 48–49
User interaction scenarios *vs.* use cases, (2) 42
User interface architecture
   See Architecture, user interface
User interface design
   See also ABC modeling
   See also DSDM
   See also ETP classification
   See also Idiom
   See also Oo&hci
   See also RUP
   See also Scenarios
   See also Task analysis
   See also UML
   See also Usage-centered design
   See also Use cases
   See also User-centered design
   See also Wisdom
   average time devoted to, (6) 202, (8) 285
   cost of, (4) 147, (8) 284, (8) 285
   increasing awareness of, (4) 148
   initial interface segmentation, (4) 135–139
   integrating in the development process, (1) 14–17

Index

look-and-feel, (4) 147
patterns
  compound, (4) 148
  definition, (4) 144–145
  percentage of code involved, (6) 202, (8) 285
  problem-space representation, (4) 146–148
  screen real estate, (4) 152
  transactions, (4) 150–151
  units of work, (4) 150–151
  user interface layout, (4) 145–146
  user navigation, (4) 151–152
  view behavior, (4) 151–152
  visual formalism, (4) 146–148
  visual language, (4) 146–148
  windowing techniques, (4) 151–152
User interface designers
  See also HCI
  DSDM, (8) 300–301
  RUP, (5) 168–169, (8) 300
  user-centered design process, (8) 298–301
User interface layout, (4) 145–146
User interface metaphors, (10) 380
User interface modeling
  See also Prototyping
  See also Storyboarding
  RUP, (5) 171–176
  user-centered design process, (8) 301–304
User interface prototypes
  See Prototypes
User involvement
  See also ABC modeling
  See also Participatory design
  DSDM, (8) 297–298
  importance of, (8) 284
User models, UML, (9) 348
User navigation
  See also View behavior
  ETP, (4) 139–142, (4) 151–152

object-view paradigm, (4) 139
  windowing techniques, (4) 151–152
User profiling
  See also SBD
  See also Scenarios
  See also Task analysis
  See also Task modeling
  See also Use cases
  ETP, (4) 124–125
  oo&hci, (10) 402
  usage survey, (9) 323
  Wisdom, (6) 227
User questions
  identifying, (4) 131
  purpose of, (4) 139, (4) 140
  tasks from, (4) 139
User role maps, (7) 251
User role models, (7) 251
User scenarios
  See SBD
User work context, (4) 124–125
User-world objects
  See Referents
Users
  alienating, (1) 6
  concerns, typology of, (2) 47–48
  consequence analysis, (2) 44
  input methods, (3) 75
  intentions, use cases, (7) 263–264
  interactions, and scenario development, (2) 55–58
Users models
  See Mental models

V

Van Harmelen, Mark
  acknowledgments, (4) 156, (6) 240
  biography, (ATA) 435–436
View behavior, (3) 97, (4) 151–152
  See also User navigation
View models
  definition, (3) 76
  dynamic view model, (3) 97
  example, (3) 93

Idiom, (3) 92–102
OVID, (9) 328
static view models, (3) 92, (3) 97–100
top-level views, (3) 94–95
transactions (modeling constructs), (3) 100–102
view behavior, (3) 97
view structure, (3) 97–100
view transition machine, (3) 97
View structure, (3) 97–100
View transition machine, (3) 97
Virtual science fair example
  See SBD, example
Visionary users, (8) 297–298
Visual formalism, (4) 146–148
Visual interface design, usage survey, (9) 324
Visual language, (4) 146–148

W

Walkthroughs, (5) 184
What-if scenarios, (2) 54–55
Whitewater Interactive System Development with Object Models
  See Wisdom
Wills, Alan, (3) 111
Wilson, Stephanie, (3) 111
Windowing techniques, (4) 151–152
  See also Primary windows, prototyping
navigation
  See View behavior
Wisdom
  analysis workflow creating, (6) 229–233
  notation, (6) 217–219
  architecture, interaction, (6) 214–216
  architecture, user interface analysis model, (6) 212
  Arch model, (6) 209–210
  business model, (6) 211–212
  definition, (6) 208
  design model, (6) 213, (6) 220–222

Wisdom (*cont.*)
    dialogue model, (6) 213, (6) 220–222
    domain model, (6) 211–212
    interaction model, (6) 212–213
    presentation model, (6) 213, (6) 220–222
    Seeheim model, (6) 209–210
    use case model, (6) 212
    Wisdom model, (6) 210–214
  brainstorming, (6) 226
  CHI97 metamodel, (6) 238–239
  design workflow
    creating, (6) 233–238
    notation, (6) 220–222
  evolutionary prototyping, (6) 205–206
  history of, (6) 197–201
  implementation workflow notation, (6) 222–223
  interface architecture design, (6) 231–233
  interiorizing the project, (6) 226
  internal system analysis, (6) 229–232
  internal system design, (6) 233, (6) 235
  Nike approach to software development, (6) 201–202
  notation
    analysis workflow, (6) 217–219
    definition, (6) 217
    design workflow, (6) 220–222
    implementation workflow, (6) 222–223
    requirements workflow, (6) 217
  requirements discovery, (6) 227
  requirements workflow
    creating, (6) 226–229
    notation, (6) 217
  software development approaches
    Bridge method, (6) 206–208, (6) 236
    iterative evolution, (6) 205–208
    Nike "just do it," (6) 201–202
    SSDs, (6) 201–202
    Trojan horse, (6) 206
    whitewater evolution, (6) 205
  Wisdom process, (6) 203–208
  stereotypes, (6) 215–217, (6) 219
  task flows, (6) 206–208
  understanding system context, (6) 226–227
  use cases, (6) 206–208
  user interface design, (6) 235–238
  user profiling, (6) 227
  vs. UP, (6) 227
Workers
  definition, (5) 162, (5) 163
  user interface designer, (5) 168–169
Workflow
  definition, (5) 164
  and user interface design, (5) 167–168

X
Xerox Star, (10) 380–381

Y
Yeh, Wenchi, (4) 156